# Time Out

# Cape Town

**timeout.com/capetown**

**Published by Time Out Guides Ltd,** a wholly owned subsidiary of Time Out Group Ltd.
Time Out and the Time Out logo are trademarks of Time Out Group Ltd.

**© Time Out Group Ltd 2007**
Previous edition 2004.

10 9 8 7 6 5 4 3 2 1

**This edition first published in Great Britain in 2007 by Ebury Publishing**
A Random House Group Company
20 Vauxhall Bridge Road, London SW1V 2SA

**Random House Australia Pty Limited** 20 Alfred Street, Milsons Point, Sydney, New South Wales 2061, Australia
**Random House New Zealand Limited** 18 Poland Road, Glenfield, Auckland 10, New Zealand
**Random House South Africa (Pty) Limited** Isle of Houghton, Corner Boundary
Road & Carse O'Gowrie, Houghton 2198, South Africa

Random House UK Limited Reg. No. 954009

**For details of distribution in the Americas, see www.timeout.com**

ISBN 10: 1-904978-55-X
ISBN 13: 978-1-90497855-8

A CIP catalogue record for this book is available from the British Library

Printed and bound by Firmengruppe APPL, aprinta druck, Wemding, Germany

The Random House Group Limited makes every effort to ensure that the papers used in our books are made from
trees that have been legally sourced from well-managed and credibly certified forests. Our paper procurement policy
can be found on www.randomhouse.co.uk.

**Time Out Guides Limited**
**Universal House**
**251 Tottenham Court Road**
**London W1T 7AB**
Tel + 44 (0)20 7813 3000
Fax + 44 (0)20 7813 6001
Email guides@timeout.com
www.timeout.com

### Editorial

**Editor (Cape Town)** Lisa van Aswegen
**Editor (London)** Dominic Earle
**Editorial Assistant** Annette Klinger
**Copy Editor** Albert Buhr
**Listings Editors** Annette Klinger, Pieter Tredoux
**Proofreader** Patrick Mulkern
**Indexer** Jackie Brind

**Managing Director** Peter Fiennes
**Financial Director** Gareth Garner
**Editorial Director** Ruth Jarvis
**Deputy Series Editor** Dominic Earle
**Editorial Manager** Holly Pick

### Design

**Art Director** Scott Moore
**Art Editor** Pinelope Kourmouzoglou
**Senior Designer** Josephine Spencer
**Graphic Designer** Henry Elphick
**Junior Graphic Designer** Kei Ishimaru
**Digital Imaging** Simon Foster
**Ad Make-up** Jenni Prichard

### Picture Desk

**Picture Editor** Jael Marschner
**Deputy Picture Editor** Tracey Kerrigan
**Picture Researcher** Helen McFarland

### Advertising

**Sales Director** Mark Phillips
**International Sales Manager** Fred Durman
**International Sales Consultant** Ross Canadé
**International Sales Executive** Simon Davies
**Advertising Sales (Cape Town)** New Media Publishing
**Advertising Assistant** Kate Staddon

### Marketing

**Group Marketing Director** John Luck
**Marketing Manager** Yvonne Poon
**Sales and Marketing Director North America** Lisa Levinson

### Production

**Group Production Director** Mark Lamond
**Production Manager** Brendan McKeown
**Production Coordinator** Caroline Bradford

### Time Out Group

**Chairman** Tony Elliott
**Financial Director** Richard Waterlow
**Time Out Magazine Ltd MD** David Pepper
**Group General Manager/Director** Nichola Coulthard
**Time Out Communications Ltd MD** David Pepper
**Time Out International MD** Cathy Runciman
**Group Art Director** John Oakey
**Group IT Director** Simon Chappell

### Contributors

**Introduction** Lisa van Aswegen. **History** Max Du Preez, Mark van Dijk. **Cape Town Today** Mark van Dijk. **Rising Stars** Vicki Sleet (*Reality bites* Karen Rutter). **Where to Stay** Vicki Sleet (*The best hotels* Lisa van Aswegen; *The best hotel bars* Casey O'Neil). **Sightseeing** Karen Robertson (*The best sights* Lisa van Aswegen; *Cape Town for free* Anelde Greeff; *Table Mountain uncovered* Annette Klinger, Albert Buhr; *It's all kicking off, March of the penguins* Mark van Dijk; *Boat trips, Secret beaches, Take a hike* Karen Robertson; *Top ten South African tipples* Cathy Marston; *Just when you thought it was unsafe...* Karen Rutter). **Restaurants & Cafés** Lisa van Aswegen, Vicki Sleet. **Pubs & Bars** Casey O'Neil (*The best places* Lisa van Aswegen; *My kind of town* Annette Klinger). **Shops & Services** Vicki Sleet (*Music to your ears, Tribal trends* Albert Buhr). **Festivals & Events** Annette Klinger, Robert Whitaker. **Children** Mark van Dijk. **Comedy** Mark van Dijk (*My kind of town* Annette Klinger). **Film** Mark van Dijk. **Galleries** Karen Rutter. **Gay & Lesbian** Ernst Swart (*My kind of town* Annette Klinger). **Music** Albert Buhr (*My kind of town* Annette Klinger). **Nightlife** Casey O'Neil. **Sport & Fitness** Dan Nicholl, Dominique le Roux. **Theatre & Dance** Karen Rutter, Mark van Dijk. **Winelands** Mark van Dijk. **Whale Route** Adele Horler. **Garden Route** Vicki Sleet, Chantal Taylor. **West Coast** Karena du Plessis. **Directory** Annette Klinger (*Time for a detour* Karen Robertson).

**Maps** JS Graphics (john@jsgraphics.co.uk). Maps are based on material supplied by New Holland Publishing (Cape Town).

**Photography** Jurie Senekal, except: pages 13, 19 Reuters; pages 16, 17 Corbis; pages 20, 21 Stephen Francis and Rico/Rapid Phase; pages 32 Mikhael Subotzky; page 84 Albert Buhr; page 92 Cape Town Routes Unlimited; page 155 Sarah Struys; page 156 Sacha Park; page 157 Fireworks for Africa; page 163 (bottom left) M-net; page 163 (top right) Dave Bloomer; page 166 Courtesy Ster-Kinekor Distributions; pages 171, 172 Michael Stevenson Contemporary; page 180 Tim Henry; page 185 Sony BMG; pages 193, 199, 202 www.downhilladventures.com; page 196 Touchline Photo; pages 208, 209 Garth Stead; page 210 OBZ Café Archives; pages 223, 231 4Corners; pages 224, 236, 241 Images of Africa; pages 226, 228, 232, 239 Alamy; page 227 Travel Library; page 235 Photolibrary; page 240 Getty; page 242 Robert Harding.
The following images were provided by the featured establishments/artists: pages 37, 39, 43, 46, 47, 50, 144, 164, 177, 182, 186, 206

*Time Out Cape Town* is based on the 2007 *Cape Town Visitors' Guide* produced by New Media Publishing (www.newmediapub.co.za).

# Contents

# Introduction

Where else in the world can you start off your morning being woken by the call to prayer from the muezzin in the Bo-Kaap, then have a chat in French with a Congolese car guard, enjoy a perfect Arabica coffee in the funkiest of spots, gaze at a colossal table-shaped mountain and walk next to the roaring ocean all before 9am?

In the Mother City, Cape Town, of course. With its spectacular setting, cosmopolitan vibe and African roots, this place has a certain special something for even the most blasé traveller.

The undeniably striking natural beauty of Cape Town is truly staggering to behold: with the Atlantic on its doorstep, Table Mountain overseeing goings-on in the City Bowl, and the majestic (and intoxicating) Winelands, there is enough to occupy any visitor – whether their idea of a perfect day is shark cage diving or a leisurely amble through a vineyard and a bit of pinotage tasting on a terrace with a view over the Stellenbosch mountains.

There's no doubt, however, that this is still a city in Africa, and poverty is apparent from the word go: you will drive past endless shantytowns lining the highway from the airport to the city, and see street children begging at traffic lights.

Yet there is optimism in the air, an undeniable feeling that Cape Town is on the right track. The date on everyone's lips at the moment is 2010, when the football World Cup kicks off in South Africa, and every year sees more and more local and international visitors streaming in to enjoy this wonderfully compact city.

And Cape Town does indeed feel very compact. Here six degrees of separation become about two, and more often than not a stroll down Long Street means bumping into friends and acquaintances. But don't worry: the compact nature of the City Bowl means that you can meander from the V&A Waterfront to the upper end of Company Gardens, at the foot of Table Mountain, in a little over an hour – if you don't make any stops along the way.

But there's a catch. Of course you'll stop along the way. Taking part in café society is a must, and it is the perfect way to experience laid-back city life. While our up-country brothers from Gauteng may view Capetonians as too relaxed for their own good, locals refute this claim and merely blame it on all the wonderful views there are to enjoy.

Cape Town, along with the Winelands, can also boast most of the top restaurants in the country. But whether it's fine dining, a spicy Cape Malay *bredie* (stew), dim sum or tapas you're after, you're sure to find something to appeal (all accompanied by some of the excellent local wines).

Cape Town feels at once like a European city with its café terraces; an African city with its boisterous street traders; and a South African city with its laid-back, tongue-in-cheek locals. And it is this ability to combine First World flair with a palpable Third World energy that keeps the locals here, and the visitors coming back again and again.

## ABOUT TIME OUT CITY GUIDES

This is the second edition of *Time Out Cape Town*, one of an expanding series of Time Out guides produced by the people behind the successful listings magazines in London, New York and Chicago. Our guides are all written by resident experts who have striven to provide you with all the most up-to-date information you'll need to explore the city or read up on its background, whether you're a local or a first-time visitor.

## THE LIE OF THE LAND

For convenience, we've divided Cape Town into manageable areas (such as City Bowl, Atlantic Seaboard). We've used these areas throughout the guide, either to divide a chapter or in the address itself. Where relevant, we have indicated a cross street as not all venues have street numbers. There is limited public transport in the city, so we have not given it in the listings.

## ESSENTIAL INFORMATION

For all the practical information you might need for visiting the area – including visa and customs information, details of local transport, a listing of emergency numbers, information on local weather and a selection of useful websites – turn to the **Directory** chapter at the back of this guide. It begins on page 246.

## THE LOWDOWN ON THE LISTINGS

Above all, we've tried to make this book as useful as possible. Opening times, admission prices, websites and credit card details are all included in our listings. And, as far as possible, we've given details of facilities, services and events, all checked and correct at the time we went to press. However, owners and managers can change their arrangements at any time. Before you go out of your way, we'd strongly advise you to telephone and check opening times and other particulars. While every effort has been made to ensure the accuracy of the information in this guide, the publishers cannot accept responsibility for any errors that it may contain.

## PRICES AND PAYMENT

We have indicated whether venues such as shops, hotels and restaurants accept credit cards but have only listed the major international cards, such as American Express (**AmEx**), Diners Club (**DC**), MasterCard (**MC**) and Visa (**V**). Few shops, restaurants and attractions will accept travellers' cheques; it's advised that you change your money before heading out for the day.

## Advertisers

We would like to stress that no establishment has been included in this guide because it has advertised in any of our publications and no payment of any kind has influenced any review. The opinions given in this book are those of Time Out writers and entirely independent.

The prices we've listed in this guide should be treated as guidelines, not gospel. If prices vary wildly from those we've quoted, ask whether there's a good reason. If not, go elsewhere. Then please let us know. We aim to give the best and most up-to-date advice, so we want to know if you've been badly treated or overcharged.

## TELEPHONE NUMBERS

The area code for Cape Town is 021. Even though we have included this code in the guide entries, there is no need to use it within the city, unless you're calling from a mobile. The country code for South Africa is 27. For more on telephones and codes, *see p255.*

## MAPS

The map section at the back of this book includes an overview map of the city and detailed street maps. The maps start on page 268 and now pinpoint the specific locations of hotels (**❶**), restaurants and cafés (**❶**), and pubs and bars (**❶**). There is also a map of the Western Cape on page 268, and a street map of Stellenbosch on page 272.

## LET US KNOW WHAT YOU THINK

We hope you enjoy the *Time Out Cape Town Guide*, and we'd like to know what you think of it. We welcome tips for places that you consider we should include in future editions and take note of your criticism of our choices. You can email us at guides@timeout.com.

There is an online version of this book, along with guides to over 100 international cities, at **www.timeout.com**.

# TOKARA

## HOME TO VINEYARDS AND OLIVE TREES

The location of the TOKARA winery, on the crest of the Helshoogte Pass outside Stellenbosch, is a picturesque combination of vineyards and olive groves. Situated on the southern slope of the Simonsberg Mountain, the farm offers exceptional views over rolling hills towards Table Mountain and False Bay.

This picture perfect destination is home to elegant wines and olive oils, an award-winning potstill brandy, a gallery of fine art and a restaurant run by iconic chef Etienne Bonthuys.

The winemaking team at TOKARA consists of winemaker Miles Mossop and viticulturist Aidan Morton. Their goal is to produce elegant, complex wines which age well and show a sense of place.

Wines were initially bottled under the ZONDERNAAM label, with the first TOKARA branded wines released in September 2005. The four premium wines are the flagship Bordeaux-style TOKARA Red, the TOKARA

Stellenbosch Chardonnay (barrel fermented), the TOKARA White (barrel fermented Sauvignon blanc) and the TOKARA Walker Bay Sauvignon blanc (tank-fermented). TOKARA continues to produce under the well established ZONDERNAAM label and the growing collection of gold medals from respected wine competitions, confirms the quality of these wines.

The winery has also released a TOKARA Five year old Potstill Brandy, which is bottled in 750 ml bottles and sells for R300 ex-cellar.

Anne-Marie Ferreira's love for cooking inspired the planting of the olive trees which grace the three TOKARA farms, runs The Olive Shed - a boutique-style olive oil production plant on the Stellenbosch property.

A blended olive oil as well as single varietal Mission, Frantoio and Leccino olive oils are bottled under The Olive Shed at TOKARA label. There is also a premium TOKARA-branded olive oil which is a multi-varietal blend.

TOKARA restaurant serves fine food in a comfortable contemporary space overlooking vineyards and olive groves. The winery is also a venue for young aspiring and established South African artists to exhibit their work, and it hosts an annual Wine Made Art event in which artists take new and creative approaches to incorporating wine experience in art.

TOKARA Winery is open for tasting between 9am and 5pm weekdays and from 10am to 3pm on Saturdays and Sundays.

**For more details:**
visit www.tokara.com
or email wine@tokara.com
or phone +27 21 808 5900.

# In Context

**Table Mountain Cableway**. *See p70.*

# A MULTI-FACETED EXPERIENCE

Jewel Africa is one of Cape Town's best-kept secrets.
Specialising in both ready-made and custom designed jewellery, our pieces range from the conventional to the avant-garde.

For an unforgettable time, visit Jewel Africa.

To arrange an appointment, call us on:
+27(0)21 424 5141 • A/h: +27(0)82 658 8712

Open: Mon - Fri 09h00 - 19h30, Sat & public holidays 09h00 - 17h30, Sun 16h00 - 19h00

www.jewelafrica.com

*Free shuttle service available.*

Parliament.

# History

The Mother City has come a long way in the last 500 years, from colonial outpost to continental leader.

South Africa is an ancient land. Its rocks and plains date from the time Africa was still part of Gondwanaland, a composite continent made up of South America, Africa, Antarctica, India and Australia that existed until more than 100 million years ago. Human beings walked these plains and rocks hundreds of thousands of years ago, when the species developed along the east side of Africa. Some of the oldest fossilised remains of our pre-human ancestors were found in South Africa, in places such as the Cradle of Humankind outside Johannesburg.

The area around present-day Cape Town and along the coastlines to the west and east was inhabited by homo sapiens long before other continents were discovered. The human remains excavated in caves at Klasies River Mouth on the southern Cape coast were between 75,000 and 120,000 years old – the oldest examples of homo sapiens to date. In 1993 it was proved that the people who occupied the Blombos Cave in the same area, at least 77,000 years ago, had a well-developed culture.

It was around this time that some parties started to leave Africa, gradually moving through the Middle East, southern Europe and southern and southeast Asia. Climate, culture, diet and genetic isolation meant that those living in Europe, Asia and the Americas developed different physical features over time. Only 500 years ago did those pale-skinned humans return to 'discover' the southern part of the continent of their origin.

## REAL PEOPLE

At the time of colonisation, the indigenous people of the area were known collectively as the Khoikhoi ('men among men', or 'real people', as khoi means 'person'). The first Europeans to meet them named them the Hottentots, apparently after a word used in the Khoikhoi welcoming dance. Historians now believe the Khoikhoi derived from aboriginal hunters who lived in northern Botswana, and that they moved down the Atlantic Coast to the western Cape about 2,000 years ago, after they had switched from hunting to herding. At first they only kept fat-tailed sheep, but by the time the Europeans encountered them, they had acquired cattle, most likely from the Bantu-speaking farmers in the eastern Cape.

The Khoikhoi were closely related to a hunter-gatherer people whose ancestors probably never left the subcontinent. The first Dutch settlers called these hunters Bosjesmannen (men of the bush, later Boesmans or Bushmen) and the Khoikhoi called them Sonqua or San. They spoke a variety of languages characterised by the use of clicks or implosive consonants, very similar to the sounds of the Khoikhoi.

## 'In 1499 Vasco Da Gama planted a cross on the Mossel Bay dunes.'

While the San lived mainly in caves and overhangs in small, mobile groups with a weak hierarchical system, the Khoikhoi lived in round reed huts in larger settlements. Each clan had a headman, a hereditary position, and the villages of a particular tribe fell under a chief. The chief ruled by the consent of a council of elders. They acted as a court to settle disputes and hear criminal cases. The Khoikhoi had a complex system of customs such as initiation rituals, weddings and funerals, and livestock were central to much of their culture. Biogeneticists recently found that the San and Khoikhoi have genetic threads linking them to the first ever human beings.

### EARLY STRUGGLES

In February 1488 the Portuguese seafarer Bartholomeu Dias rounded the Cape and landed at Mossel Bay, east of Cape Town. He was met by the Khoikhoi, and when they tried to defend their precious watering hole, Dias's men killed one of their group with a crossbow. This incident could be regarded as the first act of resistance by the indigenous people of southern Africa against European colonialism, and the beginning of the struggle for land. Others point to an incident 11 years later when Dias's colleague, Vasco Da Gama, planted a cross and a *padrao* (commemorative pillar) on the Mossel Bay dunes. As they sailed away, they saw the Khoi men defiantly push the cross and the *padrao* over.

If Dias and Da Gama had travelled a little further along the east coast, they would have come across another group of indigenous people, the amaXhosa. They were part of a large family of farmers, together called the Bantu-speakers, who had migrated in stages from Africa's Great Lakes District to the south around 2,000 years ago.

The early European settlers, and to some extent even the Bantu-speakers, regarded the San hunter-gatherers as primitive beings not worth much more than animals. Many were killed in unequal battles with settlers. Only small groups of San survive today in Namibia and Botswana, but their ancestors left an astonishing legacy in the form of rock paintings and engravings all over southern Africa, the oldest surviving examples being 20,000 years old. The paintings reflect a very complex spiritual relationship with the environment. Thousands of examples have, remarkably, survived across South Africa. Many San were assimilated into Bantu-speaking societies – the clicks in the Xhosa language are a result of this.

### CAPE COLONY

After Bartholomew Dias's 1488 visit, many European ships on their way to the East stopped at the Cape to replenish water and food supplies. Without exception, the seafarers' diaries reflect the astonishment they experienced when Table Mountain, the peaks of the Peninsula and the bay came into view. Dias himself named it Cabo de Boa Esperanca, Cape of Good Hope, although neither he nor Da Gama actually went into Table Bay. Antonio de Saldanha was probably the first European to land there in 1503. He climbed the mountain and named it 'The Table of the Cape of Good Hope'.

It was not before 1652 that Europeans settled at the Cape. The Dutch East India Company, or VOC, had decided that the mortality rate among sailors of their fleet trading with the East was too high, especially due to scurvy, and ordered Jan Van Riebeeck to establish a halfway refreshment station with vegetable gardens and a hospital at the Cape. On 6 April 1652 Van Riebeeck arrived with three ships in Table Bay. He was met by Autshomato, also called Herrie die Strandloper, a Khoikhoi chief who had spent a year with the English on a trip to the East between 1631 and 1632. Fluent in English, he was enlisted as Van Riebeeck's interpreter. Later he fell out of favour and was jailed at first in Van Riebeeck's fort and then on Robben Island (*see p22* **The long walk to freedom**), from where he escaped in a leaky boat.

Initially the VOC had no intention of creating a colony on the Cape. But within five years it allowed a number of its employees to set up private farms around Cape Town. The presence of 'free burghers' increased quickly over the next few decades.

The new colony needed more people, and before the end of the 17th century groups of French Huguenots (1688) and German immigrants joined the Dutch settlers at the Cape. Most of them were Calvinist Protestants.

The descendants of these settlers would later call themselves the Afrikaners. Most of the Huguenots were given farms in the Franschhoek ('French corner') and Paarl areas and contributed greatly to South Africa's wine-making culture. Almost from the beginning the free burghers were in conflict with the authorities, and distrusted the government. Their sense of vulnerability as frontiers people would inform their behaviour for three centuries.

The development of commercial agriculture soon threatened the Khoikhoi's way of life. As early as 1659 a group of Khoikhoi attacked the settler farms, driving off much of the livestock. Van Riebeeck tried to keep settlers and Khoikhoi apart by planting a hedge of bitter-almond on the outskirts of Cape Town. The Khoikhoi society quickly disintegrated under settler pressure. Many resorted to lives as labourers on settler farms, others moved inland, only to be displaced later by settler farmers. Many Khoikhoi died during the smallpox epidemic of 1713.

**SLAVE TRADE**
The VOC did not want to encourage more European labourers to come to the Cape, because they proved to be troublesome. Still, they did need more workers on the farms, so in 1658 the first ships carrying slaves arrived at the Cape. The slaves came from Dahomey, Angola and Mozambique in Africa and from India, the East Indies and Madagascar. Between the arrival of the first slave ships and the end of the slave trade in 1807 about 60,000 slaves had been brought to the Cape.

Slavery changed the basic political and social character of the Cape of Good Hope. By 1795 two-thirds of the burghers around Cape Town and three-quarters of the farmers in the districts of Stellenbosch and Drakenstein owned slaves. The burghers' European tradition dictated that the sanctity of property rights was central to their own freedom. Slave owners included their slaves on inventories of property together with their cattle and sheep. All slaves were black, and this instilled a distorted image of black people in many white minds. Add to this the perpetual fear of slave uprisings on isolated farms and it becomes easier to understand white attitudes in the following centuries, which ultimately resulted in formalised apartheid.

**APARTHEID RULES**
Apartheid, the ideology of racial separation formally adopted by the National Party government in 1948, theoretically presupposed that pure races existed in South Africa. Yet there had been thousands of 'mixed' marriages during the first century of colonialism on the

Cape, the majority between settler men and slave women. Virtually all old Afrikaner families can trace a slave mother somewhere in their past.

A slave woman who married a white man was integrated into white society, together with her children. It was a female slave's easiest way to get her freedom. There were more white men than women in the colony and almost twice as many male slaves as females. On the farms outside Cape Town, the best chance male slaves had to find a wife was among the Khoikhoi. A child between a slave and a Khoikhoi would be born free, but forced to work on the farm for a period. These offspring were later called Baster Hottentotte, and they occupied a very low position on the social ladder. Descendants of white and Khoikhoi relationships outside of marriage and without formal acceptance by the church were called Basters, and they enjoyed much more freedom than the Baster Hottentotte. The Basters later formed the nucleus of the Reheboth Basters of Namibia and the Griqua, mostly of the northern Cape.

Between the two main cultural-economic groups, those being the Christian European group and the Muslim or 'Cape Malay' group, another group existed at the Cape – some were slaves, some were freed slaves, some were Baster Hottentotte, some were the offspring of white and black liaisons but were not claimed by their white fathers. This group was later called the Cape Coloureds.

> **'By the end of the slave trade in 1807, about 60,000 slaves had been brought to the Cape.'**

The VOC had discouraged the use of French and German among the first settlers, with Dutch being the dominant language. But the slaves, the Basters, the Cape Malays and the Baster Hottentotte who worked on the farms and in the kitchens developed a creolised version of Dutch to communicate with their masters and one another. This developed into a fully fledged indigenous language later called Afrikaans – the language white Afrikaner nationalism later claimed as its own property and tribal symbol.

In 1795 Britain conquered the Cape, then returned the colony to the Dutch eight years later – only to reclaim it in 1806. It would remain a British colony for more than a century.

Under pressure from British missionaries working in the Cape and humanitarians in Britain, the British government scrapped the regulations limiting the rights of the Khoisan and freed slaves in 1828. In 1834 all slaves were

liberated, although they had to serve four years of 'apprenticeship' before they were completely free. By this time, the settler farmers had expanded their operations in the interior and along the coast to what became known as the Eastern Cape, where they started to compete with another indigenous group, the amaXhosa. This conflict had the same root as the conflict with the Khoikhoi: land.

### SOCIAL UPHEAVAL

Around 3,000 years ago black farming peoples who lived in the region of the Great Lakes of Africa developed a common language that was later called Bantu. During the next 1,000 years many of them migrated south. These farmers kept cattle, sheep and goats and grew sorghum and millet. They had an advanced social culture and mostly lived in large permanent settlements. A thousand years ago one of the main centres of power of the Bantu-speakers of southern Africa was at Mapungubwe Hill on the border between South Africa and Zimbabwe, now best known for the finely crafted gold artefacts which were found there.

The migrators split into four language groups as they moved into South Africa: the Nguni-speakers moved down the east coast,

the Venda and Tsonga stayed in the north, and the Sotho-Tswana-speakers migrated down the centre. The Xhosa were the Nguni-speakers who moved all the way down to the Eastern Cape, while those who spoke the Zulu dialect of Nguni settled in present-day KwaZulu-Natal.

At the end of the 18th century these black farmers (the term 'Bantu' that was used to depict them became a derogatory word during the apartheid years) were living in a number of small chiefdoms. The early years of the 19th century brought a great social upheaval. It was a period of serious suffering, but also nation-building. By the end of it Shaka had forged the Zulu nation from several chiefdoms and Mzilikazi established the Ndebele and Matabele under his leadership. Moshoeshoe, an extraordinary diplomat and statesman for his time, had collected a number of chiefdoms and thousands of refugees – Nguni-speakers as well as Sotho-Setswana-speakers – at his mountain stronghold in Lesotho and formed the Basotho. The Tsonga and Venda remained in their mountainous territory in the north; Sekwati built up the Pedi; Sobhuza the Swazi. In the Eastern Cape, the Xhosa developed a form of unity with smaller groups such as the Thembu, the Mfengu and the Mpondo.

Robben Island. *See p22.*

A small community, the Lemba, whose individuals have great artistic skill, believe that they are descendants of black Jews from the Middle East, and they still live among the Venda. Their claim was recently proved to be correct after extensive DNA testing. Many Lemba still live strictly as orthodox Jews.

## WAR TORN

The trekboers, as the burghers who had moved well away from the Cape were called, waged war against the Xhosa, but while the trekboers had firearms, the Xhosa had greater numbers. When the British Army was deployed against the Xhosa after 1811, the balance of power was tipped. During the brutal war of 1834-35 the Xhosa king, Hintsa, was decapitated. The Eighth Frontier War of 1850-52 was the most savage war against the Xhosa. Some 16,000 Xhosa were killed, and large numbers of settlements burned and cattle captured.

A great tragedy that befell the Xhosa can partly be explained by the trauma of these wars. In 1856 a young woman called Nongqawuse had a vision in which two men who were long dead told her that a great resurrection of her people was about to occur. To ensure that it happened, the people had to kill all their cattle and not plant any more crops. She convinced her uncle, a well-known seer named Mhalakaza, of the authenticity of the vision and he convinced paramount chief Sarili. The killing took place over the next year. By the end of December 1857 tens of thousands, perhaps as many as 50,000, Xhosa had died of starvation. More than 25,000 left for the Cape Colony to seek work.

## BRITISH RULE

In 1820 the British settled some 4,000 British subjects, mostly farmers and tradesmen, in the eastern Cape. The colonial government started promoting the use of English at the expense of Dutch-Afrikaans and elevated the new British settlers into public positions. This caused deep bitterness among the Cape burghers.

Around the middle of the 19th century developments in South Africa started to move away from the Mother City. But events in the central and northern interior would have a direct and lasting impact on Cape life.

After the 1835 war against the Xhosa, the Afrikaner trekboers in the Eastern Cape started to plan to move north into the interior of South Africa. They were unhappy about Britain's abolition of slavery, felt insecure so close to the frontier with the Xhosa, and needed more land for their cattle. Between 1835 and 1845 15,000 Afrikaners, accompanied by 5,000 servants, had left the colony in convoys of oxwagons and on horseback. They were called Voortrekkers.

Their migration, which was later known as the Great Trek, would change South Africa fundamentally and ultimately lead to the formation of a formal nation-state. The Voortrekkers took with them the European convictions and traditions of white dominance and used these in structuring their relations with the black peoples of the interior.

The Voortrekkers staked out farms in what are today the provinces of KwaZulu-Natal, Gauteng, the Free State and Mpumalanga. The black societies in most of these regions were still suffering the after-effects of the great upheavals of the beginning of the century. Some of these areas were therefore not actively occupied at the time of the Voortrekker settlement, but others were and this led to violent clashes with the black tribes.

## 'Virtually overnight a city sprang up, named Johannesburg.'

The Voortrekkers declared the Republic of Natalia in Natal, but Britain annexed it as a colony in 1843. Most of the Voortrekkers trekked further west and declared the South African Republic with Pretoria as its capital in 1843 and the Republic of the Orange Free State with Bloemfontein as its capital in 1854. With the Cape and Natal under British colonial rule, the whole country was now occupied by whites.

From 1860 onwards another population group was added to South Africa's ethnic diversity. Shiploads of indentured labourers from India were taken to Natal to work in the new sugar plantations. Later, Indian traders came to South Africa under their own initiative, mainly to set up shops in the towns of Natal, the Free State and the Transvaal. In 1893 an Indian lawyer arrived on a legal assignment to Indian traders in Pretoria. He decided to stay on when he suffered racial discrimination by whites and realised that Indians' rights were threatened. His name was Mohandas Ghandi, and he later became one of the most powerful moral influences in the world.

### DIAMOND DISCOVERY

Britain's two South African colonies were not regarded as prize possessions back in London, but this changed dramatically when diamonds were discovered near the confluence of the Gariep and Vaal Rivers in 1867 and gold outside

Pretoria in 1886. But the Boers of the Free State, as well as the Griqua of Griqualand, claimed ownership of the diamond area and the gold reef fell inside the South African Republic. The diamond fields were extraordinarily rich and attracted fortune-seekers from all over the world. The town of Kimberley developed rapidly amid the abundant diamond pipes. The British declared that the Orange Free State border ran about a mile east of the richest mines, and annexed the area into the Cape Colony, together with the whole of Griqualand West.

In 1889 Cecil John Rhodes, an entrepreneur and ardent believer in British imperialism, acquired the monopoly over the four Kimberley diamond pipes. His company was called De Beers Consolidated Mines. Rhodes later became the prime minister of the Cape Colony. Tens of thousands of black people from all over South Africa rushed to Kimberley in the hope of finding jobs. It was De Beers who first started the practice of employing rural black men and putting them up in closed barracks. Thus a system which lasted in some form to the end of the 20th century was established. Men from the rural areas were employed in the cities and put up in single-sex accommodation, only seeing their families once or twice a year. It was called the migrant labour system.

In 1886 a reef of gold, the richest deposit in the world, was discovered in the South African Republic. Once more there was a rush of fortune-seekers, but again big mining houses stepped in and within a few years eight conglomerates controlled all the mining on what became known as the Witwatersrand. Virtually overnight a city sprang up, named Johannesburg. Black workers from across the subcontinent rushed to the mines and were employed under similar conditions to those at the diamond mines.

### SCORCHED EARTH

The discovery of diamonds and gold gave a new urgency to British plans for a confederation of the four political units in South Africa. It put such pressure on the South African Republic that its president, Paul Kruger, declared war with Britain in 1899. The Republic was joined by the Republic of the Orange Free State.

It was the fiercest war ever fought on the African subcontinent. More than 300,000 British soldiers took on the two republics with a total white population of around 300,000 and fewer than 70,000 soldiers. It was an uneven war, but the Boer commandos were highly mobile, sometimes using tactics that would later be called guerrilla warfare. By 1902 most Boer women and children were in diseased concentration camps and the captured men and boys in prisoner-of-war camps in Ceylon, St Helena and

Prison to parliament: **Nelson Mandela** spent 27 years in jail before his release in 1990.

South African daily life laid bare: the long-running **Madam and Eve** cartoon strip features

Burma. These practices did much to destroy the Boers' spirit, as did the British 'scorched earth' policy toward the end of the war, burning farmsteads and crops and killing cattle. In May 1902 the two republics surrendered and signed the Peace of Vereeniging.

The war, which was for a long time called the Anglo-Boer War but is now called the South African War, did not only affect the Boers and the British soldiers. Thousands of black and Coloured South Africans fought on both sides, although most fought with the British. Tens of thousands of blacks, mostly farm workers, were also put in concentration camps and 30,000 died there. Some 110,000 white women and children were put in concentration camps; 27,000 of them died. And 30,000 farms were destroyed. The war created deep bitterness and anti-British sentiment among Afrikaners for generations.

**WHITE DOMINATION**
In May 1908 delegates from the Cape, Natal and the two former republics met at a National Convention to negotiate the establishment of a united South African state. Only white delegates were invited. Despite the fact that there were four times as many black people as whites in the four regions, black people were only given a very limited franchise in the Cape alone. The South Africa Act was approved by the British Parliament. On 31 May 1910 the Union of South Africa with four provinces came into being. Parliament was to be seated in Cape Town. The exclusion of the majority black population from political power in South Africa was now formalised.

Black intellectuals and community leaders protested against the new constitution, but when their protest fell on deaf ears in Cape Town and London, they formed the South African Native National Congress in January 1912. It was the first national body of indigenous people in South Africa and the first coordinated movement to resist white domination. The

executive of 11 were all highly educated, five of them having studied in the US or Britain. The movement later changed its name to the African National Congress. The ANC stepped up their protest in 1913, after the Native Land Act was adopted, limiting black land ownership to about eight per cent of the land surface. A figure that was then increased to 13 per cent in 1936.

Two years after the ANC's birth, white Afrikaners also formed their first national political party, the National Party. In 1918 a secret males-only body, the Afrikaner Broederbond, was formed to further the cause of Afrikaner nationalism in business, education and culture. It became very powerful in later years. In 1938 Afrikaner nationalism experienced a massive upsurge with a national re-enactment of the Great Trek a century earlier. Ten years later the National Party defeated the United Party of General Jan Smuts in the general election. The party ruled South Africa until 1994.

**SEPARATE DEVELOPMENT**
Racial separation and a denial of black South Africans' political and human rights began in 1652 and continued under British rule until 1948. But the National Party turned these practices and attitudes into a formal ideology they called apartheid, literally meaning 'separateness'. The new government spent considerable energy during its first years in power to write numerous apartheid laws. The population was classified according to race; sex between mixed couples and marriages across the colour bar were criminalised; separate residential areas and public amenities were enforced; separate education was instituted; and the movement of black South Africans was regulated by the carrying of pass books.

The National Party later called their policies 'separate development', protesting that they did not discriminate, but that for the sake of peace and fairness black Africans should exercise their political rights in ten tribal states or

Gwen Anderson (Madam) and Eve Sisulu, her 'domestic maintenance assistant'.

homelands. The theory was that South Africa proper was white man's land where blacks would enjoy limited rights, but that their homelands would eventually become independent, sovereign states where they would enjoy full rights. Some of those Bantustans, like Transkei, Ciskei and Bophuthatswana, did later become 'independent', but South Africa was the only country that recognised them.

The man who championed the homelands policy and under whose leadership South Africa left the Commonwealth and became a republic in 1961 was Dr Hendrik Verwoerd, the National Party's third prime minister who came to South Africa from the Netherlands as a child.

The ANC slowly grew as a movement and organised a successful 'Defiance Campaign' in 1952 to protest against unjust laws. In 1955 delegates from all over the country gathered in Kliptown outside Johannesburg to adopt the Freedom Charter. This document, which was headed 'The people shall govern!', remained the ANC's ideological compass for four decades. But a group of Africanists in the ANC did not like the fact that the Charter acknowledged whites as full citizens with equal rights, and in 1957 they broke away to form the Pan Africanist Congress (PAC) with Robert Sobukwe as their first leader.

In 1960 the PAC organised protests against the pass laws, forming large demonstrations. It was at one of these demonstrations, in Sharpeville south of Johannesburg, that police panicked and killed 69 people.

Later the same day a crowd of 6,000 from Langa and Nyanga just outside Cape Town marched to the city, led by a young PAC activist, Philip Kgosana. The police opened fire and killed three and injured 47.

These two events were turning points in South African history. The government banned the ANC and PAC, and both organisations went underground and formed military wings, the ANC formed Umkhonto we Sizwe (Spear of the Nation) and the PAC formed Poqo (Pure). Most of the first Umkhonto we Sizwe leaders, including the young lawyer Nelson Mandela, were arrested in 1963 and jailed on Robben Island. Some ANC leaders went into exile.

It was also during this time that many African colonies gained their independence. In March 1960 Verwoerd declared: 'A psychotic preoccupation with the rights, the liberties and the privileges of non-white peoples is sweeping the world – at the expense of due consideration of the rights and merits of white people. The fundamental reality being disregarded is that without white civilisation, non-whites may never have known the meaning of idealism or ambition, liberty or opportunity.'

Verwoerd was stabbed to death in his seat in Parliament, Cape Town, in September 1966. A court declared that his killer, a parliamentary messenger named Demitrio Tsafendas, was mentally disturbed.

## CAPE CLEARANCES

One of the cruellest aspects of apartheid was that over three million blacks were forcibly removed over four decades because the areas where they lived were declared 'white'. In Cape Town, this was a particularly painful experience.

District Six was a vibrant, colourful suburb situated right next to the Cape Town City Centre at the foot of Devil's Peak. The majority of the residents were Coloured – their ancestors had been living there since the emancipation of the slaves in the 1830s – but whites, blacks, Indians and Chinese also lived in the area. Between 1965 and 1967 it was declared a 'white' area under the Group Areas Act. The same fate befell Coloured residents living in Kalk Bay and Simonstown.

The residents were moved to new Coloured townships miles away on the Cape Flats and Mitchell's Plain behind Strandfontein. District Six was then razed to the ground, saving only the churches and mosques. The new townships

# The long walk to freedom

Robben Island is rather innocently called Seal Island ('rob' is the Dutch word for seal), but the story of this place is mostly a sad, and often brutal, one.

The island was known for thousands of years to the indigenous San and Khoikhoi people, but it is unlikely that they ever went there before the first European ships arrived in the 15th century. And when they did go to the island, it was more often than not as prisoners. During the 16th and early 17th century many Khoikhoi who displeased the Dutch, English or Portuguese seafarers were left on the island as punishment. But it was also used as a post office during this period,

because many of the seafarers were afraid of the Khoikhoi on the mainland and preferred to pick up their post, fresh water and seal or penguin meat here.

In 1610 ten English criminals who had escaped the gallows and been taken to work in the Cape instead, fled from the mainland and lived on the island for more than a year. The 'Newgate Men' as they were called, were eventually taken back to England and hanged.

After Jan van Riebeeck of the Dutch East India Company established a permanent refreshment station at Cape Town, many 'troublesome' Khoikhoi were banished to Robben Island, the first being a man called

# Cape Town Today

AIDS, crime and poverty cast a shadow, but it's still one of the most magical cities in the world.

Cape Town's city centre – charmingly called the City Bowl, as it rests between the mountain and the bay – can easily be crossed on foot within half an hour. In summertime rush hour, it's often quicker to walk from a restaurant in the V&A Waterfront to a cocktail bar on the lower slopes of Table Mountain than it is to navigate the one-way streets and gridlocked intersections.

And as you stroll across the city centre, you'll find yourself wondering whether you've stepped into a curiously Afrocentric European city, or a curiously Eurocentric African city. Cape Town, Kaapstad, iKapa, the Mother City. Far as it is from both the Old World and Darkest Africa, the city is a cultural crossroads. Hundreds of tiny stalls litter the pavements outside the Shell and LG skyscrapers, the Renault dealerships and the Apple stores, as African immigrants from the Congo, Zimbabwe, Burundi and beyond (some legal, some not) briefly rub shoulders with investors from Europe, the United States and the Far or Middle East.

Contrast is a recurring theme in Cape Town. In the seaside suburb of Hout Bay, for example, a sprawling shantytown lies across the valley from some of the most expensive real estate on the continent. Yet it's that same sense of disparate unity that allows a minibus taxi and a new Mercedes to meet at a set of traffic lights; that allows a German tourist and a Rwandan refugee to share the same patch of shade in Company Gardens; that allows a well-heeled company CEO and a toothless car guard to queue for the same morning newspaper.

## COLOUR CODED

Under the former government's racially divisive apartheid system, and especially under the infamous Group Areas Act of 1950 (repealed in 1991), people of different ethnicities and race groups were shunted and shifted into colour-specific neighbourhoods.

Many of those divides still exist. Leafy suburbia remains mostly a 'white' area, while the less affluent neighbourhoods and

# Mind your motor

We may misplace your baggage at the airport, and we may give you five days of rain in the middle of summer. But when you visit Cape Town there's one thing we can guarantee: we'll take good care of your car.

It's nigh-on impossible to park your car in Cape Town without somebody volunteering to help you do it. The city's battalion of car guards are divided into three main groups: official, formal and informal.

The official ones are the City-approved parking attendants who walk the streets in brightly coloured bibs, checking parking meters and selling metered parking time.

The formal ones are employed by parking lot owners to ensure the safety of patrons' vehicles. These ones usually have their own business card (no, really), and they may or may not choose to greet you. If they don't greet you, it's possibly because they don't speak your language. Many of them – like Manuel (he doesn't give a last name) from Rwanda – are out-of-work immigrants from elsewhere in Africa. Manuel doesn't say much, but he's clearly no one's fool. Many of his peers – countrymen or neighbours who fled the wars of central Africa – arrived in South Africa as dentists, doctors, vets and teachers only to end up working 12-hour shifts in the car park of the upmarket Constantia Village shopping mall.

The third group are the informals: they're completely unofficial and completely informal, and they're all over the City Bowl.

The short stretch of street between Greenmarket Square and the Cape Town Tourism Centre is 'guarded' (and we use the term loosely) by a grey-bearded, dentally challenged informal car guard named Freddy.

'That's my street name,' he says when pressed for a last name. 'Look here, I'm legal. Here, here's my book of life.' He retrieves a dirty, dog-eared green ID book from his pocket. The document reveals his real name (Cecil Christy) and his date of birth (he turned 45 last September).

Freddy's been working on this street for the past five or six years. Watching him work is like watching a car crash about to happen. He dances across the road, waving his arms like an inebriated conductor, orchestrating cars into and out of bays... and, with unnerving regularity, almost into each other.

There's really no need for him to be here. This section of Burg Street is already serviced by two official parking attendants, and Freddy's efforts – for which he's occasionally paid a rand or two by charitable motorists – cause more traffic jams than anything else.

But Freddy has a vested interest in keeping the traffic here in order. Freddy is unemployed and homeless. He sleeps on this street.

communities remain mostly 'coloured' (mixed race) – with many of the poorer 'coloured' areas, especially those on the Cape Flats, haunted by American-style street gangs who push drugs like the very popular, very dangerous methamphetamine called *tik*.

And the ramshackle, crime-riddled shantytowns – the 'locations' or 'townships' – are still populated almost exclusively by people who simply can't afford to leave the neighbourhood. These townships aren't the run-down ghettos of Harlem or South Central Los Angeles: many of the houses here are made of corrugated iron or repurposed shipping crates, and water, electricity and basic sanitation are by no means guaranteed.

### FORWARD THINKING
As recently as 2005, Capetonians were still talking about the ten-year anniversary of the birth of South Africa's post-apartheid democracy. Much had changed – socially and economically – since the country's law-makers inked South Africa's first democratic Constitution, and there was plenty to talk about.

> **'In 2003, 21.5 per cent of the adult population was estimated to be HIV-positive.'**

But then South Africa was awarded the right to host the 2010 FIFA World Cup, and suddenly the focus shifted. Instead of looking back at the relics of apartheid and marvelling at 'how far we've come', South Africans and Capetonians were suddenly looking forward, away from the gloomy past and into the hopeful future, marvelling instead at 'how far we can still go'.

### LAW AND DISORDER
One constant across all of Cape Town's neighbourhoods – from the inner-city 'coloured' suburb of the Bo-Kaap to the houses high on the hills of Hout Bay – is crime. A chilling Interpol report published in 2002 ranked South Africa as the country with the world's highest murder rate (114.8 murders per 100,000 inhabitants – five times the second-ranked country, Brazil).

Thankfully, violent crimes have decreased in recent years – due in part to the government's gun amnesty programme – but rape, hijackings and cash heists remain as common as ever.

Despite its efforts, the government has been criticised for not doing enough to combat crime and minister of safety and security Charles Nqakula didn't help the cause in June 2006 when he reportedly told an opposition MP that people who complain about the crime rate should stop whining and leave the country.

Many have. Since 1995 South Africa's white population – traditionally the more affluent, better-educated and more skilled group – has fallen by some 841,000 as thousands of disillusioned locals have emigrated to Australia, New Zealand and the UK.

### BURNING ISSUE
Another problem that's been casting a long, dark shadow over Cape Town's sunny present is the issue of HIV and AIDS. South Africa's first recorded AIDS-related death occurred in 1982; within a decade the number of recorded AIDS cases had risen to more than a thousand, and by the mid-1990s it was over 10,000.

South Africa's HIV/AIDS statistics make for grim reading: in 2003, 21.5 per cent of the country's adult population was estimated to be HIV-positive; and in 2005 global AIDS charity AVERT ranked South Africa as the country with the world's highest total number of orphans due to AIDS (an estimated 1.2 million).

Again, matters weren't helped when, in October 2002, President Thabo Mbeki stated that AIDS drugs were dangerously toxic, and questioned if HIV is the true cause of AIDS.

It's not all bad news, though. Most of Cape Town's tourist areas are as safe as anywhere else in the world and, for the most part, crime is restricted to the 'wrong side' of town.

Heart of the city: **Adderley Street**.

**Company Gardens** – a favourite lunch spot for oxygen-starved office workers.

Pickpockets and beggars are the major threats you're likely to face as you walk through the red-bricked pedestrian walkways of the central city. You'll have to walk or drive yourself, though – Cape Town's public transport system is still a mess of overcrowded minibus taxis, sporadically reliable train lines and overpriced sedan cabs.

### SPORT FOR ALL

One thing Capetonians do well – and if not well, then at least enthusiastically – is sport. Every March the city comes to a standstill for the annual Pick 'n' Pay Cape Argus Cycle Tour. Now in its third decade, the event attracts as many as 35,000 entries from across the globe.

Then, over the Easter weekend, the roads are closed again as the Old Mutual Two Oceans Marathon is run along the Cape Peninsula.

> **'The city is strewn with cranes and half-completed hotels and offices.'**

Table Bay isn't without its sporting traffic, either: it's one of the stops on the prestigious Volvo Ocean Race. Elsewhere, the waves at Dungeons near Hout Bay host the annual Big Wave Africa surfing contest.

Ball sports are also popular. Cricket, football and rugby union are the main spectator sports of choice, with seats at the world-class cricket and rugby venues in Newlands always selling well for international Test matches. Football is usually played at Athlone Stadium, but that's set to change once the Green Point Stadium is upgraded for the 2010 World Cup (*see p73* **It's all kicking off**).

### IN THE PINK

Cape Town enjoys its 'Pink City' status and boasts a vibrant gay scene. While there's a cluster of gay bars and clubs in the De Waterkant area around the Waterfront, almost all of Cape Town's many and varied nightspots offer spaces where gay and straight clientele can enjoy each other's company.

The annual Mother City Queer Project is Cape Town's biggest party of the year. And in typically come-one-come-all Cape Town style, you're likely to find equal numbers of straight and gay people – and all of them will be dressed up fabulously in the MCQP's annual theme.

### UNDER CONSTRUCTION

It used to be that Table Mountain was the only noticeable feature of Cape Town's horizon. These days, though, the city's skyline is strewn with cranes and half-completed hotels, offices and apartment blocks. Cape Town is boom town. Walking through the city centre, it's almost impossible not to lift your head instinctively upwards to admire the various building works in progress.

If you're coming to Cape Town and you're not coming as a traveller, you'll probably be one of the thousands of delegates who file into the city's state-of-the-art International Convention Centre. The CTICC, as it's known locally, is located at the city's north-eastern entrance, and is within walking distance of the V&A Waterfront and the city centre. Mind you, everything's within walking distance of everything else in central Cape Town.

And that's just as well – the city plans to host several thousand visitors in the build-up to 2010. See? There we go, talking about the future again…

Bin Collective.

# Rising Stars

Places to go, people to see.

A mark of any city on the up is a strong creative force and though South Africa certainly doesn't lack a wealth of older talent (including world-renowned artists, Oscar-winning actors and Nobel prize-winning authors), it is the palpable energy of an increasing band of twenty- and thirty-somethings who are making their mark in the Mother City. From writers and designers to curators and musicians, a brigade of talented rising stars are standing up to be counted.

## VISUAL ARTS

One of the most noticeable signs of Cape Town's ever increasing contemporary arts culture is the plethora of edgy galleries that can be found dotted in and around the city. At **What if the World Gallery** (11 Hope Street, City Bowl, 021 461 2573, www.whatif theworld.com, open 10am-6pm Mon-Fri, 10am-2pm Sat; **photo** *p33*), curators Justin Rhodes

and Cameron Munro actively seek out alternative ways to help Capetonian artists express themselves. From T-shirt exhibitions to night markets where artists and manufacturers can sell their wares, exhibitions are always innovative and the pair are tireless in their enthusiasm for local creativity. With headquarters at their Hope Street space and a new satellite gallery at the Old Biscuit Mill (021 448 1438, open 10am-4pm Tue-Fri, 9am-2pm Sat; *see also p132* **Love thy neighbour**) in Woodstock, it's clear that they are fulfilling a need for affordable, original art.

Meanwhile at the **Bin Collective** (105 Harrington Street, City Bowl, 021 465 8314, www.thebin.co.za, open 10am-4pm Mon-Fri, 10.30am-2.30pm Sat), the brainchild of Blaise Janichon, Pierre Coetzee, Warren Lewis and Cecil Wehmeyer, unknown artists are given a forum in which to express themselves in a supportive environment. Mixed media works

# Reality bites

It can't be easy to earn 100 per cent for your final year mark at one of the best universities in the country, but young photographer **Mikhael Subotzky** did just that.

As the top student in 2004 at the Michaelis School of Fine Arts, University of Cape Town, he cracked the perfect score with his controversial and critically acclaimed body of work *Die Vier Hoeke* (The Four Corners). Shot over a period of several months in Pollsmoor Prison, Cape Town, it details the living conditions of male prisoners in a series of compelling and unsentimental frames.

Hailed as much for its social commentary as for its 'challenging new vision of the photographic subject through portraiture', *Die Vier Hoeke* opened both local and international doors for Subotzky. He was invited to Art Basel 2005, the Turin Triennial and the Rencontres Photographiques de Bamako 2005, and released a follow-up series called *Umjiegwana* (The Outside; *pictured*), which looks at ex-prisoners and the hardships they face once they leave jail.

Although Subotzky chose a serious and, some might say, shocking subject to launch his name, he is not about sensationalism. His talent is clear, and he is also well aware of the political and social contradictions that can happen behind the camera.

'I'm influenced by a long tradition of documentary photography that is socially committed but, in itself, is not without its problems as a medium,' he says.

Subotzky has set a benchmark against which not only his own endeavours will be measured, but also those with a much longer photographic pedigree. Definitely someone to be watched.

are encouraged and range from graffiti expression to digital art, while related items such as books and one-off clothing designs are also on sale.

More into flying under the radar and pottering around in her city studio is **Frauke Stegmann**. Having trained as a graphic designer in both Germany and London, Frauke brought her impressive talents back to the Mother City, harnessing them through her label 'I need time to think about wildlife'. Kept busy with conceptual work and private commissions (ranging from ceramic artworks to a range of gold-embossed, wildlife-emblazoned CD covers), Frauke has still found time to develop the visual thread at her family's quirky Birds Boutique Café (*see p103*), where some of her work is also available to buy.

Ceramics is **Andile Dyalvane**'s passion and his exquisite vessels are rapidly becoming objects of desire for design cognoscenti all over the world. Andile manages to marry his own cultural context into contemporary creations, with many of his exquisite works including decorative references to traditional Xhosa scarification. Andile's new studio at the Old Biscuit Mill (073 505 7147; *see p31*) in Woodstock is open to the public.

Delving into the creative wealth of the city sparks up something of a paper trail. If you happen to be browsing at local lifestyle shop Story (*see p149*), keep an eye out for **Sarah Wright**'s delicate animal paper chains. Laser-cut paper animals are painstakingly stitched together to form decorative streamers to pretty up any space. Another paper whizz is **Heather Moore**. This multi-talented comic book writer, illustrator and artist loves nothing more than creating cut-out artworks where layer upon layer of pieces of paper or adhesive vinyl are cut away to reveal graphic scenes and shapes. Her label SkinnylaMinx (www. skinnylaminxblog.blogspot.com) showcases her work.

Quirky stationery is on the radar of many a design aficionado and with the creations of local paper doll **Daley Muller**, there's plenty to smile about. Wrapping paper, cards, stationery packs and gift boxes are all emblazoned with this graphic designer's Afro-Zen creatures, from plump elephants to puppy dogs and cheerful little girls. Available at Wallflower (*see p149*).

## FASHION

On the fashion scene, the array of gifted talent is always on the increase. Whether designing virtual one-offs with an undeniable urban edge, like **Doreen Southwood** at MeMeMe or **Saskia Köner** at Misfit (for both, *see p139*), or building a boutique filled with their own brand of glam items for the glossy posse, Cape Town's fashion pack are proving a force to be reckoned with. At Wembley Square, an urban oasis of restaurants and cutting-edge stores, two girls whose stars are shining bright are **Benita Allen** of Chica Loca (www.chicaloca.co.za) and **Mandy Gilder**, owner of Mandy G (021 461 5485, www.mandyg.co.za), an affordable local jewellery brand. Allen's fantastic space is her first retail venture and is filled with an assorted array of sexy yet sophisticated frocks, as well as an ever-changing array of pretty but practical leisurewear. Gilder's slice of a shop features a glittering selection of eye-catching girly pieces that reiterate her philosophy: 'Why fake it?'

Local designer **Suzannah Garland** (www.petticoat.co.za) is also creating a stir with her fabulously flirty clothes, most of which are one-off seasonal designs. Having started off with making pumps in a kaleidoscope of pretty fabrics for her label Petticoat, Garland has since broadened her horizons to everything from the perfect vest to 1950s-inspired swimwear, must-have frocks and pretty petticoats designed to peep out from under skirts.

The Crayon girls **Janet Kinghorn** and **Tamsyn Rogers** (021 424 5993, www.ilovecrayon.com) are no strangers to fashion-aware Capetonians and every season sees their collections of stylish shoes (ranging from ballet slipper pumps in every colour under the sun to go-with-everything killer heels) increase in quality and cutting-edge style. Another local shoe star is **Cara Elizabeth**. Her eponymous range of stylish and surprisingly affordable own-design footwear is a hit with those in the know and can be found in some of the most stylish boutiques in town, including Cigar Fashion & Contemporary Art (Shop B14, Cape Quarter, 72 Waterkant Street, Atlantic Seaboard, 021 683 3582).

For accessories, all eyes are currently on **Chloe Townsend** (021 422 2609; *see also p143* **Bright young things**). The talented twentysomething keeps a low profile in her city studio, preferring to toil away at her trademark laser cut leather designs, which are turned into bags and belts of an exceptional standard.

One talent who makes the crossover from fashion to art seem effortless is **Sam Bulgin**. A name to note as a fashion designer for the past few years, her move to translating her work into one-dimensional framed form has been a successful one, with annual exhibitions of doodle-like line drawings and screen printing proving to be sell-outs. Her work is available at What if the World (*see p31*).

## MUSIC

One of the best places to pick up on the local music scene is at **Mercury Live** (*see p184*). This intimate space is situated on the fringes of the city and plays host to an ever changing roster of local musical talent. From the likes of **Bed on Bricks** and their infectious live music acts to the electro strings and African voice offerings of **Coda**, this legendary venue offers excellent insight into what makes locals tick. Other names to note include **Three Bored White Guys**, who have garnered a loyal following for their toe-tapping countrybilly tunes, and the hard-hitting alt indie-rock style of the **Dirty Skirts**.

**What if the World Gallery**. *See p31.*

# Where to Stay

**Where to Stay** 37

## Features

**Daddy Long Legs**. *See p40.*

# CITY CENTRE LUXURY

Situated in Heritage Square in the heart of Cape Town, the Cape Heritage is a four star boutique hotel that is:-

• Historic with contemporary touches • Intimate and fun • Stylish and cosy

Built in 1771, the hotel has 15 individually decorated bedrooms, that not only retain the charm of its past but are also equipped with an array of modern comforts.

Meanwhile, meals can be enjoyed al fresco in the intimate courtyard, from one of Heritage Square's six well renowned restaurants.

CAPE HERITAGE HOTEL

# Where to Stay

Take your pick – from Cape colonial to boutique chic.

Colonial comfort at the **Mount Nelson**.

Seen one hotel, you've seen them all. Right? Wrong. Cape Town's accommodation options reflect the city's diversity – and your room for the night could be anything from a bog-standard chain hotel to an individually decorated explosion of colour, comfort and convenience.

Diversity is one thing; quality and comfort is something else. And here Cape Town's hotels show a similar diversity. Some are dodgy fleapits, some are decent but horrendously overpriced, and others combine comfort and service with good value for money. The ones listed here represent a cross-section of the best.

But first a word on local hospitality. A decade on from the start of Cape Town's post-apartheid tourism boom, the city now does its

> **❶** Green numbers in the chapter correspond to the location of each hotel as marked on the street maps. *See pp273-277.*

best to welcome visitors with open arms. Most of the old hotels have been restored and renovated – the ones that haven't have fallen quickly and mercilessly by the wayside.

But the boom also produced a cottage industry of large residential houses being converted into overnight B&Bs, and the city now probably has more hotels than it needs. This is good news for visitors, who now have more choice than ever.

But that doesn't mean you won't battle to find a room in high season. All the hotels fill up pretty quickly around the Christmas summer holidays. If you have left it a bit late in the day, don't despair – **www.mtbeds.co.za** and **www.lastminute.co.za** offer good deals.

All rates listed below are per double room, unless otherwise stated. Rates are subject to change and can vary dramatically from season to season.

## City Bowl

### Deluxe

### Mount Nelson Hotel
*76 Orange Street (021 483 1000/www.mount nelson.co.za).* **Rates** (incl breakfast) R3,855-R6,340. **Credit** AmEx, DC, MC, V. **Map** p274 G5 **❶**
This Cape Town landmark is famed for its trade-mark pink buildings, its nine acres of lush gardens and its famous visitors. An established colonial hotel, the 'Nellie' draws on several years of tradition

# Hotels

### For spa indulgence
**Twelve Apostles Hotel & Spa** (*see p45*); **Angsana Spa at the Vineyard Hotel** (*see p47*); **Arabella Sheraton** (*see p38*).

### For sexy surroundings
**The Metropole** (*see p40*); **Daddy Long Legs** (*see p41*); **Sugar Hotel** (*see p43*).

### For colonial splendour
**Mount Nelson Hotel** (*see p37*); **Cape Cadogan** (*see p39*); **Cape Heritage Hotel** (*see p40*).

as one of the city's finest establishments. If you can't afford to stay, at least enjoy high tea in the lounge or lush gardens – it's a Cape Town institution. *See also p49* **Hotel bars. Photo** *p37.*
*Bar. Business centre. Concierge. Disabled-adapted rooms. Gym. Internet (high-speed/wireless in public areas/dataport in room). No-smoking rooms. Valet parking (free). Pools (2 outdoor). Restaurants (2). Room service. Spa. TV.*

## Expensive

### Alta Bay Guest House
*12 Invermark Crescent (021 487 8800/www.alta bay.com).* **Rates** from R1,500. **Credit** AmEx, MC, V.

Five-star luxury is alive and well and tucked away in this sophisticated city escape. Alta Bay is set high above the city in the suburb of Higgovale. Whether you choose to drink in the surroundings from your private terrace or mix with fellow guests at the pool, your impression of Mother City hospitality will be long-lasting at this restful luxury retreat.
*Bar. Internet (wireless). No-smoking rooms. Parking (free). Pool (outdoor). Room service. Spa. TV.*

### Arabella Sheraton
*Convention Square, 1 Lower Long Street (021 412 9999/www.sheraton.com/capetown).* **Rates** (incl breakfast) R3,510-R3,720. **Credit** AmEx, DC, MC, V. **Map** p275 H3 ➋

# Cape Town DIY

If wake-up calls, check-out times and having to put on a happy face when bumping into fellow guests are not your cup of tea, then perhaps it's best to book yourself into a self-catering establishment.

Whether you choose to indulge in midnight feasts or an all-day breakfast, it's all up to you – use the opportunity to visit the local harbour to pick up a fish to *braai* (barbecue) or stock up on local cheeses and wines to enjoy at your leisure in the comfort of your temporary home. Thankfully, the city is home to a plethora of self-catering apartments and homes – from slick city escapes to rustic retreats.

Thanks to the increase in urban living, there are plenty of stylish city pieds-à-terre on the holiday rentals market. **De Waterkant Village** (021 409 2500, www.dewaterkant.com) is a company that specialises in supplying self-catering boltholes for visitors wanting to immerse themselves in the friendly, laid-back atmosphere of this charming sector of the city, while those who'd like to be close to the CBD are likely to feel right at home at the **Côte Sud** apartments and private villa (021 422 5124, www.cotesud.co.za).

The Atlantic Seaboard is thick with rental apartments, ranging from the simplest studios to the swankiest penthouses with uninterrupted views of the ocean. The website **www.capestay.co.za** is an excellent source of self-catering accommodation – from a two-person studio in Mouille Point to five-star style in the famous Lido apartment block in Sea Point.

Villa rental is becoming very big business in Cape Town, and in Camps Bay this is especially true. Contact the people at

**www.rentalsincapetown.com** and they will happily match your holiday and rental requirements in this sun-splashed suburb by the sea – the villas on their books ensure stress-free holidays in the lap of luxury.

At **www.capetownvillas.net**, properties like the pretty Shell Cottage in Camps Bay are available for would-be renters to view. This charming seaside escape is a four-bedroom cottage and comes complete with a garden, restful interior and secluded position.

Further afield, on the other side of the mountain in Kalk Bay, the beautiful **Bishop's View** (021 701 5140, www.capevillarentals. co.za) is situated in the heart of this quaint harbourside village. A minimalist interior includes modern collectibles, while the space is self-catering, a housekeeper is also on hand to make your stay more comfortable. Arrangements can also be made for meal delivery from any one of the fantastic nearby eateries.

Meanwhile, at **South Winds Guest House** (021 701 5140, www.capevillarentals. co.za) near Simonstown, seclusion comes in the form of your own marine and nature reserve literally on your doorstep. This Cape Cod-style cottage is blessed with uninterrupted views of the ocean and also includes access to turquoise rock pools on the property.

The seductive and very stylish surroundings of **Lighthouse Point** (021 788 1739, www.lighthousepoint.co.za) in nearby Simonstown are perfect for an uninterrupted seaside break – it sleeps six and is a mere 50m from the sea. Just a few days here and you'll wonder how you ever managed to survive not living on African Time.

On the up: the high-tech, high-rise **Arabella Sheraton**. *See p38*.

This towering, glass-fronted hotel is perched next to the Cape Town International Convention Centre. The high-tech Arabella Sheraton provides what you'd expect from a hotel of its calibre: comfortable rooms and excellent service.
*Bars (2). Business centre. Concierge. Disabled-adapted rooms. Gym. Internet (wireless). No-smoking rooms. Parking (free). Pool (indoor). Restaurants (2). Room service. Spa. TV.*

### Cape Cadogan

*5 Upper Union Street (021 480 8080/www.cape cadogan.com)*. **Rates** (incl breakfast) R1,200-R1,940. **Credit** AmEx, DC, MC, V. **Map** p274 F5 ③
Just off the buzz of Kloof Street, the Cape Cadogan offers extreme elegance in opulent surroundings – a Georgian-era national monument no less. With only 12 bedrooms, this boutique hotel is discreet and the rooms are light and airy. The lounges are perfect for relaxing in front of the fire. **Photo** *p43*.
*Concierge. Internet (ADSL). No-smoking floors. Parking (free). Pool (outdoor). TV.*

### Protea Hotel Victoria Junction

*Corner Somerset & Ebenezer Roads (021 418 1234/ www.proteahotels.com/victoriajunction)*. **Rates** R904-R1,850. **Credit** AmEx, DC, MC, V. **Map** p274 G2 ④
This modern hotel's double-storey loft apartments offer floor-to-ceiling windows with views of Table Mountain above and the buzz of Green Point's Somerset Road below. Extra touches in the rooms include exercise bikes and telescopes.

*Bar. Business centre. Concierge. Disabled-adapted rooms. Internet (wireless). No-smoking rooms. Parking (R30 per night). Pool (outdoor). Restaurants (2). Room service. TV.*

### Southern Sun Waterfront Cape Town

*1 Lower Buitengracht Street (021 409 4000/ www.southernsun.com)*. **Rates** from R1,640. **Credit** AmEx, DC, MC, V. **Map** p275 H3 ⑤
The former Holiday Inn at the Waterfront has been renamed, and its new persona and contemporary interior make visitors feel right at home. There are over 500 rooms, but details like a 24-hour concierge and hands-on service help to make guests feel welcome. The advantages are the hotel's proximity to the V&A Waterfront and many of the city's other attractions, as well as all the conveniences of an international chain – from the fitness centre to the outside pool and high-tech business facilities.
*Bar. Business centres (2). Concierge. Disabled-adapted rooms. Gym. Internet (high-speed). No-smoking rooms. Parking. Pool (outdoor). Restaurant. Room service. TV.*

## Moderate

### Cape Diamond Hotel

*Corner Parliament & Longmarket Streets (021 461 2519/www.capediamondhotel.co.za)*. **Rates** from R490. **Credit** AmEx, DC, MC, V. **Map** p274 H4 ⑥

**Daddy Long Legs.**

The Cape Diamond is situated slap-bang in the centre of downtown, and the happening nightlife, shops and entertainment facilities are literally on your doorstep. The renovated art deco building hosts 60 rooms furnished in tasteful earthy tones, and with its reasonable rates it's no surprise that it's such a popular choice for visiting business travellers and tourists. The on-site Patat restaurant is situated at street level and affords diners a good view of Cape Town life.
*Bar. Business centre. Concierge. Disabled-adapted room. Internet (wireless). No-smoking rooms. Parking (R50/day). Restaurant. Room service. TV.*

### Cape Heritage Hotel
*90 Bree Street (021 424 4646/www.capeheritage. co.za).* **Rates** (incl breakfast) R510-R1,150. **Credit** AmEx, DC, MC, V. **Map** p274 G3 ❼
Set on the restored complex of Heritage Square, this boutique hotel shares a courtyard with some of the best restaurants in the area. Rooms are individually decorated (we recommend the room with the four-poster bed) and have Cape yellow wood floorboards.
*Business centre. Concierge. Gym. Internet (wireless). No-smoking floors. Parking (R25/day). Room service. TV.*

### Extreme Hotel, Protea Fire & Ice
*98 Bree Street (021 488 2555/www.extreme-hotels.com).* **Rates** R600-R1,200. **Credit** AmEx, DC, MC, V. **Map** p274 G4 ❽
This hotel in a word? Unexpected. Decor includes streamlined, high-tech lazy chairs with built-in TVs and quirky crystal chandeliers suspended by climbing rope. The mood is urban and edgy, and the bar and lounge area has become a popular hangout for the young and gorgeous. Enjoy a 'Wake and Bake'

breakfast at the gourmet burger restaurant, while ogling the early-morning swimmers through the floor-to-ceiling glass wall that divides the dining room from the pool. The 130 rooms are minimally furnished in comparison with the rest of the hotel, but stocked with all the essentials. **Photo** *p47.*
*Bar. Business centre. Concierge. Disabled-adapted rooms. Internet (broadband/wireless). No-smoking rooms. Parking. Pool (outdoor). Restaurant. Room service. TV.*

### iKhaya Lodge
*Dunkley Square, Wandel Street (021 461 8880/ www.ikhayalodge.co.za).* **Rates** R730-R1,300. **Credit** AmEx, DC, MC, V. **Map** p274 G5 ❾
iKhaya means 'home' in Xhosa, and this African-themed lodge on trendy Dunkley Square offers just the right blend of rural 'African-ness' and urban comfort. The rooms are comfortably furnished with natural materials and are equipped with an enclosed balcony and wonderful views of Table Mountain.
*Bar. Business centre. Disabled-adapted rooms. Internet (wireless). No-smoking floors. Parking (free). Restaurant. TV.*

### The Metropole
*38 Long Street (021 424 7247/www.metropole hotel.co.za).* **Rates** (incl breakfast) R1,190-R2,800. **Credit** AmEx, DC, MC, V. **Map** p275 H3 ❿
Hidden behind a Victorian façade is this modern, luxury boutique hotel. The Metropole boasts 29 rooms with all the e-necessities and the softest French linen bedding. Have a drink at the very red M-Bar or try some delicious food at the Veranda restaurant. The Long Street setting is ideal for exploring the city centre on foot. *See also p49* **Hotel bars.**

*Bar. Concierge. Internet (wireless). No-smoking rooms. Parking (R50/day). Restaurants (2). Room service. TV.*

## Budget

### Ashanti Lodge

*11 Hof Street (021 423 8721).* **Rates** from R55. **Credit** MC, V. **Map** p274 G5 ⑩
Regularly voted one of Africa's best backpackers', Ashanti is perfectly situated just minutes from the CBD. Based in a huge, old Victorian mansion, it boasts everything from camping facilities to dormitories and single and double rooms. For those wanting a little more luxury, the Ashanti Guesthouses (there are two) based in the same road are more sophisticated options and feature ensuite rooms in quieter surrounds. Renowned for their excellent (read rowdy) social activities, it's no surprise that Ashanti is a must-stop for any backpacker or gap year traveller. The lodge also has a pool, garden and internet facilities.
*Bar. Internet (pay terminal). No-smoking rooms. Pool (outdoor). Restaurant. TV room.*

### Castle Street Backpackers

*57 Castle Street (021 424 7524/www.castlestreet. co.za).* **Rates** R220 private room. **No credit cards**. **Map** p275 H3 ⑫
Located just a block away from Berg Street's Tourist Information Centre, this small, clean hostel is within walking distance of just about everything in the City Bowl, with St George's Mall just around the corner and Cape Town Station just down the street.
*Bar. Internet (ADSL). No-smoking floors. Room service. TV.*

### Daddy Long Legs

*134 & 263 Long Street (021 422 3074/086 121 3141/www.daddylonglegs.co.za).* **Rates** R450-R695. **Credit** AmEx, DC, MC, V. **Map** p274 G4 ⑬
Just when you think every hotel room looks the same, along crawls this unique, arty, boutique backpacker hotel. It's hard to describe, and harder still to take in: each of the 13 rooms has been individually decorated by a Cape Town artist – and the results range from the sublime (Room 11, Antony Smyth's *The Photobooth*) to the mind-bending (Room 12, Daya Heller's *Open*).
*Bar. Concierge. Internet (free terminal/wireless R25 per day). No-smoking floors. Parking (free). Room service. TV.*

### Long Street Backpackers

*209 Long Street (021 423 0615/www.longstreet backpackers.co.za).* **Rates** from R90. **No credit cards**. **Map** p274 G4 ⑭
Long Street's original backpacker hostel has a hard-earned reputation for comfort, convenience and hospitality. The on-site security is reassuringly tight too – this is the only hostel in Cape Town that has a 24-hour police camera set up right outside the door.
*Bar. No-smoking floors. Parking. TV room.*

## Atlantic Seaboard

### Deluxe

### Cape Grace

*West Quay Road, V&A Waterfront (021 410 7100/www.capegrace.com).* **Rates** (incl breakfast) R3,690-R4,565. **Credit** AmEx, DC, MC, V. **Map** p275 H2 ⑮
Elegant, discreet and understated, the Cape Grace occupies its own quay at the V&A Waterfront, boasting the majestic backdrop of Table Mountain. Combining the intimacy of a small hotel with the standards of a big hotel, it also harbours the outstanding one.waterfront restaurant and the Bascule whisky bar (which stocks a selection of more than 400 whiskies). The hotel spa is exclusive to guests and is inspired by the people and cultures of southern Africa and traditional African remedies. *See also p49 Hotel bars.*
*Bar. Business centre. Concierge. Disabled-adapted rooms. Internet (high-speed/wireless). Parking (free). Pool (outdoor). Restaurant. Room service. Spa. TV.*

### Expensive

### Bay Hotel Camps Bay

*69 Victoria Road, Camps Bay (021 430 4444/www. thebay.co.za).* **Rates** (incl breakfast) R1,470-R4,030. **Credit** AmEx, DC, MC, V. **Map** p277 A8 ⑯
Looking out on to the fashionable Camps Bay strip, this chic, elegant hotel offers five-star treatment and amenities without losing its intimacy.

# EXPERIENCE A FEW OF THE WONDERS OF SPIER.

**THE SPIER HOTEL** A refuge for those who need to escape, either for a relaxing holiday or while attending a business function. 155 fully-serviced luxury rooms in traditional Cape-style buildings, with 6 private courtyards and swimming pools.
*reservations@spier.co.za*          *Bookings (021) 809 1100*

**THE SPIER RESTAURANT** Open seven days a week for breakfast and dinner, The Spier Restaurant is a favourite with those seeking superb cuisine and service. Enjoy breathtaking views across lush lawns to the Helderberg Mountain.
*Bookings (021) 809 1914*

**THE CHEETAHS & EAGLES** Experience a personal encounter with a hand-raised cheetah. Entrance donations help fund the Cheetah Outreach Programme. Fascinating flying demonstrations are held daily at the Raptor Rehabilitation Centre.
*Bookings: Eagles (021) 842 3684, Cheetahs (021) 809 1188*

**THE SPIER DELI** Set alongside a peaceful lake, the deck of the Spier Deli offers breathtaking views of the Helderberg Mountains. Enjoy a relaxed meal as indigenous ducks glide passed in the water. For lakeside picnics, choose something from our delicious selection of specialities.     *Bookings (021) 809 1983*

**THE AWARD-WINNING WINES AT SPIER** We invite you to consult with our wine education team for tastings that are incomparable and exciting, tailormade to your needs.
*Bookings (021) 809 1984*

**JONKERSHUIS RESTAURANT** Indulge yourself with an extensive a la carte menu. A full Cape style buffet is available by arrangement for a minimum of 40 guests. Jonkershuis offers alfresco dining adjacent the Eerste River as well as an inside setting in a traditional Cape Dutch style. Open seven days a week for breakfast and dinner. Wedding and function enquiries are welcome.
*rouvlin@kristensen.co.za*          *Bookings (021) 809 1172*

redwooddesign.co.za SPIER71/E

*Tel: +27 21 809 1100*
*www.spier.co.za*

Immerse yourself in the Georgian opulence of the **Cape Cadogan**. *See p39.*

*Bar. Business centre. Concierge. Disabled-adapted rooms. Internet (high-speed). No-smoking rooms. Parking (free). Pools (4 outdoor). Restaurants (3). Room service. Spa. TV.*

## Peninsula All Suite Hotel

*313 Beach Road, Sea Point (021 430 7777/ www.peninsula.co.za).* **Rates** R1,370-R1,880. **Credit** AmEx, DC, MC, V. **Map** p273 A3 ⑰

Situated on the city's Platinum Mile, the Peninsula All Suite Hotel offers 110 large, luxurious, sea-facing rooms. The hotel also offers wedding and conference facilities.

*Bar. Concierge. Disabled-adapted rooms. Gym. Internet (wireless). No-smoking rooms. Parking (R40/day). Pools (2 outdoor). Restaurants (2). Room service. TV.*

## Radisson SAS Hotel Waterfront

*Beach Road, Granger Bay (021 441 3000/www. capetown.radissonsas.com).* **Rates** (incl breakfast) R3,850-R6,350. **Credit** AmEx, DC, MC, V.

Perched on the water's edge at Granger Bay, gazing out over Table Bay and the V&A Waterfront, the Radisson has one of the best sundecks in the city.

The rooms are modern and comfortable, and the hotel is within walking distance of the Waterfront. *See also p49* **Hotel bars**.

*Bar. Business centre. Concierge. Disabled-adapted rooms. Internet (wireless). No-smoking floors. Parking (free). Pool (outdoor). Restaurant. Room service. Spa. TV.*

## Sugar Hotel

*1 Main Road, Green Point (021 430 3780/www. sugarhotel.co.za).* **Rates** R1,650. **Credit** AmEx, DC, MC, V. **Map** p274 G2 ⑱

The epitome of smart city chic, this Green Point hotel is much loved by well-clad urbanites – who are drawn to it by the excellent business facilities and proximity to the city's hotspots. The rooms are an exercise in contemporary style and boast everything from flat-screen TVs and DVD machines to a filtered drinking tap. With just seven rooms, staff are primed to fulfil your every whim. A spa, restaurant and buzzing bar make this a very attractive deal for city slickers.

*Bar. Concierge. Internet (wireless/ADSL). No-smoking rooms. Parking (free). Pool (outdoor). Restaurant. Room service. Spa. TV.*

## Twelve Apostles Hotel & Spa
*Victoria Road, Camps Bay (021 437 9000/www.
12apostleshotel.com).* **Rates** (incl breakfast)
R4,500-R18,500. **Credit** AmEx, DC, MC, V.
Named as one of the Top 100 hotels in the world by
*Condé Nast Traveler* magazine in 2005, the Twelve
Apostles boasts a gorgeous setting on the open
coastal road between Camps Bay and Hout Bay. The
excellent Azure restaurant, private cinema, luxurious spa and intimate service just about justify the
price tag (fairly high by local standards). Luckily,
if you're flexible, they also have some excellent
winter specials which merely bruise the bank. *See
also p49* **Hotel bars. Photo** *p50.*
*Bar. Business centre. Concierge. Disabled-adapted
rooms. Gym. Internet. No-smoking rooms. Parking
(free). Pools (2 outdoor). Restaurants (3). Room
service. Spa. TV.*

## Moderate

### Breakwater Lodge
*Portswood Road, V&A Waterfront (021 406 1911/
www.breakwaterlodge.co.za).* **Rates** R746-R786.
**Credit** AmEx, DC, MC, V. **Map** p274 G2 ⑲
This former prison on the V&A Waterfront is one
of Cape Town's best-value hotels. The rooms are
functional, practical and fairly basic, and the hotel
has two restaurants: self-service Stonebreakers and
à la carte Treadmill.

*Bar. Business centre. Disabled-adapted rooms.
Internet (wireless/pay terminal). No-smoking floors.
Parking (free). Restaurants (2). TV.*

### Romney Park Luxury Suites & Wellness Centre
*Corner Hill & Romney Roads, Green Point (021
439 4555/www.romneypark.co.za).* **Rates** from
R900 per apartment. **Credit** AmEx, DC, MC, V.
**Map** p274 E2 ⑳
If R&R translates as 'spa' to you, then Romney
Park is your kind of getaway. This award-winning
all-suite hotel is home to a host of fully serviced luxury suites and penthouses that come complete with
their own kitchens for in-room dining. Perfect for
business visitors, it's also a popular choice for guests
who can't face eating out every night of their stay
(they even have a service that fills your fridge). One
of the major draw cards here is, of course, the excellent Wellness Centre. Book a few treatments or take
advantage of their special packages.
*Business centre. Internet (wireless). Parking
(R45/day). Pool (outdoor). Restaurant. Room
service. Spa. TV.*

## Budget

### House on the Hill
*25 Leinster Road, Green Point (021 439 3902/www.
houseonthehillct.co.za).* **Rates** from R265. **No credit
cards. Map** p274 F2 ㉑

# Small and secluded

If you want to stay close to the action but
far enough away not to hear the madding
crowds, check into **Rosedene Lodge
Guest House** (021 424 3290, www.
rosedenelodge.co.za, R690-R1,100 incl
breakfast). Nestled below Table Mountain
in Tamboerskloof, this contemporary space
is home to 11 ensuite bedrooms decorated
in eclectic Balinese chic.

At **Les Cascades de Bantry Bay** (021
434 5209, www.lescascades.co.za,
R1,150-R2,650) your enviable perch on the
mountainside is enhanced by the incredible
views of the ocean. With choices of rooms
in the main lodge or the smaller villa, and
no fewer than three pools, you might just
never want to leave.

Further along the coastline and closer to
the action at Camps Bay lies **Camps Bay
Retreat** (021 438 3972, www.campsbay
retreat.com, R1,470-R3,500). This enormous
estate and private nature reserve plays host
to the gracious Earl's Dyke Manor House, as
well as the more contemporary Deck House

and the Private Villa. Facilities include a skin
and body treatment centre, private tennis
court and swimming pool.

Over the mountain and in the heart of
the leafy Southern Suburbs lies the
wonderful **Villa Coloniale** (021 794 2052,
www.villacoloniale.com, R800-R1,400 incl
breakfast), a peaceful retreat complete with
lush garden and trickling stream in the heart
of Constantia, just a stone's throw from its
historic winelands.

Further south again lies the splendour
of **Colona Castle** (021 788 8235, www.
colonacastle.co.za, R1,300-R3,900) where
sweeping views across False Bay and the
peninsula are the perfect backdrop to an
idyllic and luxurious experience.

If you feel you need a spot of spa
treatment, then book yourself into
**Stillness Manor & Spa** (021 713 8800,
www.stillnessmanor.com, R1,390-R2,970),
which provides utter seclusion in suites
overlooking lush gardens, endless mountain
views and a fab spa to unwind in.

A cross between grungy backpacker joint and B&B, this reasonably priced spot is well loved by travellers and boasts a number of ensuite rooms. Owner-run, it is the ideal place to meet fellow adventurers and share stories and travelling tips within comfortable Afro-chic surroundings. The team offer a wealth of information and will gladly assist with tour bookings.
*Internet. Parking (free). TV.*

## Southern Suburbs

### Deluxe

#### The Constantia
*Spaanschemat River Road, Constantia (021 794 6561/www.theconstantia.com).* **Rates** from R2,950. **Credit** AmEx, DC, MC, V.
This small, luxury guesthouse in the Southern Suburbs boasts just six suites and is the ideal home-from-home for Cape Town visitors. Perfectly placed away from the hustle and bustle of the city but close to many attractions, top-notch restaurants and some of the country's oldest wine estates, it is an ideal haven for visitors seeking R&R in private surroundings. Large and elegant suites include all the luxury details one might expect from a first-class hotel, while services like an on-site chef (for private dinners) will seduce those who like the idea of living it up in the lap of luxury.
*Bar. Internet (ADSL). No-smoking rooms. Parking (free). Pool (outdoor). Restaurant. TV.*

## Expensive

### The Bishopscourt
*18 Hillwood Avenue, Bishopscourt (021 797 6710/ www.thebishopscourt.com).* **Rates** from R1,700. **Credit** AmEx, DC, MC, V.
Bishopscourt is regarded as one of the best and most affluent suburbs in the city, and properties here boast acres of space and uninterrupted views of the mountain. The Bishopscourt is no exception. Once a gracious home, it has now been converted into a luxury guesthouse-cum-boutique hotel. Facilities include a tennis court, a large pool and a chef who's on hand to prepare your latest culinary craving. Just a few minutes from the Kirstenbosch Botanical Gardens, this is an idyllic retreat.
*Bar. Internet (ADSL). No-smoking rooms. Parking (free). Pool (outdoor). Restaurant. TV.*

### Greenways
*1 Torquay Avenue, Upper Claremont (021 761 1792/www.greenways.co.za).* **Rates** (incl breakfast) R1,560-R1,952. **Credit** AmEx, DC, MC, V.
This five-star boutique hotel is set in a historic homestead with six acres of landscaped gardens and woodlands. Completely refurbished, Greenways now offers a combination of luxury accommodation and cordon bleu cuisine at Ashton's restaurant.
*Business centre. Concierge. Disabled-adapted rooms. Internet (wireless/shared terminal). No-smoking rooms. Parking (free). Pool (outdoor). Restaurant. Room service. TV.*

Suburban splendour: landscaped gardens and luxury living at the **Vineyard**. *See p47.*

### Steenberg

*10802 Steenberg Estate, Tokai Road, Constantia (021 713 2222/www.steenberghotel.com).* **Rates** (incl breakfast) R2,595-R4,265. **Credit** AmEx, DC, MC, V.
Located in the Constantia winelands, this historic estate dates back to 1682. The serene, five-star boutique hotel offers 30 elegant rooms in the original manor house and restored barn. The estate also includes an 18-hole championship golf course and a wine farm.
*Bar. Internet (wireless). No-smoking throughout. Parking (free). Pools (2 outdoor). Restaurant. Room service. Spa. TV.*

### Vineyard Hotel

*Colinton Road, Newlands (021 657 4500/www. vineyard.co.za).* **Rates** R1,465-R3,395. **Credit** AmEx, DC, MC, V.
This historic 73-room hotel (originally a private residence for Lady Anne Barnard in 1799) has all the comforts and luxuries of a four-star deluxe property. It's set in six acres of landscaped parkland, in the leafy suburb of Newlands on the banks of the Liesbeeck River, and it boasts three outstanding restaurants, a state-of-the-art fitness centre and the Angsana Spa. **Photo** *p46.*
*Bar. Business centre. Concierge. Disabled-adapted rooms. Gym. Internet (dataport). No-smoking rooms. Parking (free). Pools (1 indoor, 1 outdoor). Restaurants (3). Room service. Spa. TV.*

## Moderate

### Banksia Boutique Hotel

*14 Banksia Road, Rosebank (021 689 2992).* **Rates** from R550. **Credit** AmEx, DC, MC, V.
This generously sized and renovated grand Victorian home is based in an unlikely city suburb but is surprisingly close (just 15 minutes' drive) to the malls, beaches, city centre or airport. Sophisticated decor reigns supreme, with plenty of plush details in the eight rooms – from deep-buttoned headboards to the softest bed throws. Stylish and tasty breakfasts, pretty views of the garden or the mountain and luxurious lounge facilities ensure that many guests are loyal returnees.
*Business centre. Internet (wireless/ADSL). No-smoking rooms. Parking (free). Pool (indoor). Restaurant (breakfast only). TV.*

## Budget

### Green Elephant Backpackers

*57 Milton Road, Observatory (021 448 6359/ www.hostels.co.za).* **Rates** R95-R350. **Credit** AmEx, DC, MC, V.
Set in the Bohemian student suburb of Obs, the Green Elephant has a laid-back atmosphere to go with its solar-heated swimming pool, internet access, hot jacuzzi and four-poster beds.
*Bar. Internet (wireless/pay terminal). No-smoking rooms. Parking (free). Pool (outdoor). TV room.*

**Extreme Hotel, Protea Fire & Ice.** *See p40.*

## Southern Peninsula

## Moderate

### Chapmans Peak Hotel

*Main Road, Hout Bay (021 790 1036).* **Rates** (incl breakfast) R600-R800. **Credit** AmEx, DC, MC, V.
Set at the foot of the famous Chapmans Peak Drive, the Chapmans Peak Hotel has ten light and airy rooms – six of which have sea views across Hout Bay Harbour. The hotel's popular restaurant serves a variety of seafood dishes.
*Bar. Business centre. No-smoking rooms. Parking (free). Restaurant. TV.*

### House at Pooh Corner Guest Cottages

*Corner Village Lane & Main Road, Noordhoek (021 789 1440/www.poohcorner.co.za).* **Rates** from R550 (2 adults & 2 children). **Credit** AmEx, DC, MC, V.
Though it may not be situated in the hundred-acre wood, the woodland surrounds of these cosy guest cottages are picture-book pretty. A variety of cottages on the property range from basic to more luxurious. Guests can choose bed and breakfast or self-catering options, and nearby Noordhoek Farm Village plays host to two excellent restaurants and a pub. Beautiful Noordhoek beach is a few minutes away by car.
*No-smoking rooms. Parking (free). Room service. TV.*

# Hotel bars

### Bascule Whisky Bar & Wine Cellar
*Cape Grace Hotel, West Quay Road, V&A Waterfront, Atlantic Seaboard (021 410 7100/www.capegrace.com).* **Open** 11am-late daily. **Credit** AmEx, DC, MC, V. *See also p41.*
Situated on its own private jetty with stunning views, this is simply one of the best locations in central Cape Town to enjoy a summer evening. It's in a five-star hotel so it ain't cheap, but the 460 different whiskies make it worth extending the mortgage for.

### Leopard Lounge
*Twelve Apostles Hotel, Victoria Road, Camps Bay, Atlantic Seaboard (021 437 9000/www.12apostleshotel.co.za).* **Open** 11am-midnight daily. **Credit** AmEx, DC, MC, V. *See also p45.*
Pleasant place to visit in a Sunday drive kind of way. The view's great but the faux Africana decor is a bit much and the location at a five-star hotel in the middle of nowhere means that it scores very low on the atmosphere barometer. But like we said, the view is great.

### M-Bar & Lounge
*1st Floor, Metropole, 38 Long Street, City Bowl (021 424 7247/www.metropole hotel.co.za).* **Open** 10am-late daily. **Credit** AmEx, DC, MC, V. *See also p40.*

This little Versace-inspired gem is hidden in the back of one of Cape Town's funkiest boutique hotels. With manga in the oh-so-opulent lounge and fish tanks in the loos, you know you are in for a divine experience.

### Planet Champagne & Cocktail Bar
*Mount Nelson Hotel, 76 Orange Street, City Bowl (021 483 1000/www.mountnelson.co.za).* **Open** 5pm-late daily. **Credit** AmEx, DC, MC, V.
The old pink lady has had a major makeover of late. The fact that it plays host to super-celebs Robbie Williams, Ralph Fiennes and Colin Farrell might have something to do with its sudden stratospheric rise in the cool stakes. Whatever the reason, this swanky five-star cocktail bar is one of the most happening spots in town.

### Tobago's Pub & Restaurant
*Radisson SAS Waterfront, Beach Road, Granger Bay, V&A Waterfront, Atlantic Seaboard (021 441 3414/www.radisson.com).* **Open** 6.30am-10.30pm daily. **Credit** AmEx, DC, MC, V. *See also p43.*
The perfect spot for a lazy sundowner on a warm Friday afternoon. Sit with the beautiful people and watch yachts sailing by while sipping on a decadent cocktail. Although the service may be a bit hit and miss, the setting is perfect – and so are the bar snacks.

### Simonstown Quayside Hotel & Conference Centre
*Jubilee Square, Simonstown (021 786 3838).* **Rates** from R575. **Credit** AmEx, DC, MC, V.
This intimate four-star hotel is perfectly situated right on the water's edge. Magnificent views are standard here, with the hotel boasting both mountain- and sea-facing rooms. Proximity to the cobbled streets of Simonstown ensures a real taste of this pretty seaside enclave. A number of quality eateries on the main street ensure you don't have to stray too far to stay well watered and fed.
*Business centre. Internet (wireless). Restaurant. Room service. TV.*

## Budget

### Boulders Beach Lodge
*4 Boulders Place, Boulders Beach, Simonstown (021 786 1758/www.bouldersbeach.co.za).* **Rates** (incl breakfast) R790. **Credit** AmEx, DC, MC, V.

Ideally situated right on the beach at Boulders, with penguins on your doorstep, the rooms are clean and comfy, and the complimentary sherry goes down very well. Self-catering cottages are also available. The adjoining restaurant has great views for serious whale-spotting in season.
*Internet (wireless). No-smoking throughout. Parking (free). Restaurant. Room service.*

### Southern Right Hotel
*12-14 Glen Road, Glencairn (021 782 0314/www.southernright.info).* **Rates** from R295. **Credit** AmEx, DC, MC, V.
The further south you travel down the peninsula, the fewer hotels there are, so the Southern Right is a welcome addition to the accommodation scene. Situated in the old Glencairn Hotel, it has undergone sensitive restoration and is now a charming place that hints at its historic past – down to the stripped Oregon floors and roll-top baths. A beautiful view of the sea, on-site restaurant and quirky Africana touches set the scene for a charming seaside escape.

**Twelve Apostles Hotel & Spa** – if you can afford it, this is as good as it gets. *See p45.*

*Bar. Internet (wireless). No-smoking rooms. Parking (free). Restaurant. Room service. TV room.*

## Northern Suburbs

### Expensive

#### Lodge at Atlantic Beach

*100 Fairway Drive, Atlantic Beach Golf Course, Melkbosstrand (021 553 4653/www.thelodge atatlanticbeach.co.za).* **Rates** (incl breakfast) R875-R1,200. **Credit** AmEx, DC, MC, V.
Set on an 18-hole links-style golf course, the Lodge features a clubhouse restaurant, leisure centre, fitness centre and health spa. There are 12 deluxe rooms, four luxury rooms and four premier rooms.
*Bar. Business centre. Concierge. Disabled-adapted rooms. Gym. Internet (wireless). No-smoking rooms. Parking (free). Pool (outdoor). Restaurant. Spa. TV.*

### Moderate

#### Lagoon Beach Hotel

*Lagoon Beach Road, Milnerton (021 528 2000/ www.lagoonbeachhotel.co.za).* **Rates** from R960. **Credit** AmEx, DC, MC, V.

A stylish escape on the other side of Table Bay, this luxury hotel is blessed with magnificent views of the mountain, ocean and Robben Island, as well as facilities that include a spa, 'ice' bar and sprawling ocean-side pool deck. Popular with business travellers, the property also has a number of semi self-catering apartments available for longer stays that include access to all the hotel facilities. The on-site Abalone restaurant provides a taste of the Cape in elegant surroundings.
*Bar. Business centre. Concierge. Disabled-adapted rooms. Gym. Internet (wireless/ADSL). No-smoking rooms. Parking (free). Pool (outdoor). Restaurant. Room service. Spa. TV.*

### Budget

#### D'Aria Guest Cottages

*Tygerberg Road, M13, Durbanville (021 975 5802/ www.daria.co.za).* **Rates** R500-R700. **Credit** AmEx, DC, MC, V.
Set in the D'Aria Vineyards outside Durbanville, these 12 four-star cottages are fully serviced and include 24 rooms. Also on site is the award-winning Poplars restaurant.
*Bar. Disabled-adapted rooms. Internet (dataport). No-smoking rooms. Parking (free). Restaurant. Room service. TV.*

# Sightseeing

**Castle of Good Hope**. *See p58.*

# Inverdoorn Game Reserve

## the luxury of contrast

- 10 000 ha of pure bliss in the Great Karoo, at only two hours from Cape Town.
- 7 Bungalows - air conditioning with exclusive furniture.
  2 Guest Houses - personalised and luxurious comfort for families or groups.
- 2 1/2 Hour Safari trips to bring you close and personal with Lions Buffalos, Oryx, Giraffes, Cheetas, Lechwe, Rhinos, Nyialas, Elands and much more...
- Exclusive French cuisine combined with a South African touch reserves for an extra delectable taste.
- 4 Star accommodations, modern designed pool, enjoying a cocktail terrace, cactus garden, golf range, quad bike, conference facilities.

*"Evolving with Africa into the 21st century"*
**Inverdoorn team**

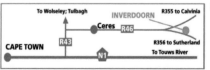

**ENQUIRIES AND RESERVATIONS**

tel : +27 (0)23 316 12 64
fax : +27 (0)23 312 21 87
**WWW.INVERDOORN.COM**
info@inverdoorn.com

# Introduction

The most laid-back city in South Africa.

It won't take long for Cape Town to bowl you over. Ocean, mountains, vineyards, beaches and culture – everything a traveller could desire is combined in a naturally beautiful and accessible setting. Ask the millions of tourists swarming the seaside city each year (many of them back for their second, third or fourth fix), as well as the locals who wouldn't want to live anywhere else in the world – the classic surf 'n' turf combo of sea and mountain works a treat.

## THE LIE OF THE LAND

Thankfully the city of Cape Town is well planned, so it's fairly easy to wend your way around its gems. Table Mountain keeps her beady eye on the goings-on beneath her rumpled skirt, thoughtfully providing both the backdrop to your holiday snaps and a handy beacon to guide you – it's even lit up at night during summer.

Surrounded by Table Bay, Table Mountain, Lion's Head and Devil's Peak, the Mother City is a bundle of energy just begging to be explored. Put on your walking shoes, tuck a map in your back pocket and take to the streets. It's here, among the art deco buildings, the hustle of the open-air markets and the sidewalk

cafés, that you'll find your bearings and experience at first hand the variety of people and cultures Cape Town has to offer.

The picturesque area of **Bo-Kaap** is criss-crossed by cobbled streets and lined with crayon-coloured houses and mosques. Originally inhabited by slaves from India, Madagascar and Sri Lanka, the area retains a distinct flavour. Wander the streets (leave time to pop in at the Bo-Kaap Museum) or join a walking tour guided by residents.

Cast your eyes towards Table Bay and chances are you'll glimpse a giant funnel from one of the cruise liners docked in Cape Town harbour just a few minutes away. Here at the **V&A Waterfront**, the working harbour combines with a tastefully designed shopping centre to create an attraction that should satisfy even the pickiest of travellers' tastes. Take in an arthouse film, face off with a shark at the aquarium (the feeding frenzy begins at 3.30pm), buy your souvenirs or gorge on local seafood, all to the symphony of barking seals and honking tug boats. Here, near the old Clock Tower, you'll also find the embarkation point for trips to **Robben Island**. This former maximum-security prison, where veterans of

# Sights

## For nature lovers

Cape of Good Hope Nature Reserve (*see p84*); **Company Gardens** (*see p64*); **Kirstenbosch National Botanical Gardens** (*see p76*); **Table Mountain** (*see p70*).

## For political awareness

**Bo-Kaap Museum** (*see p70*); **District Six Museum** (*see p59*); **Robben Island** (*see p71*); **Slave Lodge Museum** (*see p69*).

## For sea views

**Boulders African Penguin Colony** (*see p87*); **Two Oceans Aquarium** (*see p72*).

## For street life

**Church Street** (*see p59*); **Long Street** (*see p61*); **Sea Point Promenade** (*see p75*).

## For sunsets

**Blouberg Beach** (*see p90*); **Camps Bay** (*see p73*); **Chapman's Peak** (*see p86*).

the anti-apartheid struggle were incarcerated, offers tours led by former inmates who give visitors accounts of their time on the island.

If people-watching is more your bag, a stroll along Sea Point Promenade on the **Atlantic Seaboard** will allow you to ogle an eclectic bunch of blue-rinse grannies and their pooches, or svelte model types putting in some serious jogging time. Head beyond Sea Point and you're among the most beautiful beaches in the world. Take your pick, from the creamy sands of **Clifton** all the way to **Llandudno**. And you'd be silly to miss an opportunity to sip cocktails as the sun sets over the palm tree-lined strip of **Camps Bay**. Designer shades are de rigueur here.

On the Southern Peninsula, a drive along **Chapman's Peak** is eye-popping, not just for the winding roads and dizzy heights but also for the sheer feat of engineering that it represents. The road was carved from the mountainside by Italian prisoners during World War II. On through the pastures and protected milkwood trees of **Noordhoek**, the surfer's hotspot of **Kommetjie** and sleepy **Scarborough**, and you arrive at **Cape Point Nature Reserve** – home to inquisitive baboons, stately zebra and, in September, a stunning array of spring flowers.

Back towards the city centre, you'll pass through the once-British naval base of **Simonstown**. Stuck in time, it looks like it could be scooped up, Lord Nelson Inn and all, and transplanted to the south coast of England without anyone batting an eyelid. Take your time to stroll through the fishing village of **Kalk Bay** a little further on. You can haggle over freshly caught fish or trawl through the tumbling antiques stores. Further on, **Muizenberg** beckons, especially if you like to surf or you're up for trying.

A short stint on the highway and you're in the 'burbs. The upper-class residential area of **Constantia** is also home to Groot Constantia, the oldest grape-growing estate in South Africa. **Newlands** is a residential neighbourhood too, but its visitors come not to peer over garden fences, but to enjoy the **Kirstenbosch Botanical Gardens.** A haven for beady-eyed botanists the world over, the spectacular gardens display over 22,000 indigenous plants. If you've brought your hiking boots, walk up **Table Mountain** (along routes of varying difficulty). Make sure you go with an experienced local hiker, though, and take plenty of water along. When you reach the giddy top, you'll realise that the mountain really is slap-bang in the middle of the city. With 360º views of the Cape coast, you'll be able to retrace your steps, regain a steady breathing flow and eyeball a lizard or two. And if the thought of the mountain descent fills you with awe, there's a cable car to deposit you neatly at the bottom.

### RESOURCES

The **Cape Town Tourism Visitor Centre** (Corner Castle & Burg Streets, 021 426 4260, www.tourismcapetown.co.za) is on hand to give you advice and help you plan your visit.

## 48hrs in Cape Town

So much to see, so little time. Here's our must-do itinerary if you only have a weekend to spare in the Mother City.

### Day 1

**7AM**

Land at **Cape Town International Airport** (*see p246*), grab your bags and hop into your rental car. Take the N2 highway north to Cape Town, and wonder what the rush was all about as you sit in the morning traffic. Follow Eastern Boulevard into the City Bowl, turn left at the Cape Town International Convention Centre, and then right into Long Street. A few blocks up the road is **Daddy Long Legs** (*see p41*), your base for the next 48 hours.

### 8.20AM
Check into Daddy Long Legs. When they called this boutique backpackers' place an art hotel, they weren't joking – each of the 13 rooms has been decorated by a different local artist. Room 2, called Travel Dog, is one of the more quietly decorated rooms. Open (Room 12) and Bert Pepler's Emergency Room (Room 4) are more likely to keep you up at night. Once you've checked in, freshened up and admired the decor, hop in the car and head down to the **V&A Waterfront** complex (*see p71*).

### 9AM
Have breakfast at **Societi Bistro** (*see p112*). Their anchovy toast (with spread made from lashings of butter and fresh anchovies) always works, but the eggs Benedict is the real breakfast of champions. Work them off by strolling around the Waterfront complex, browsing the shops and exploring the Red and Blue Shed craft markets.

### 10.30AM
Head across the complex to the **Two Oceans Aquarium** (*see p72*), where you'll find more than 3,000 marine creatures. Sprint past the swaying seaweed of the kelp forest and head straight to the shark tank.

### 11.55AM
Catch the noon ferry to **Robben Island** (*see p71*) at the Clocktower Precinct's Nelson Mandela Gateway. Over the years Robben Island has served as a leper colony and an apartheid-era maximum security prison, which housed the likes of Walter Sisulu and Nelson Mandela. These days it's a UN World Heritage Site. The standard tour of the island is three-and-a-half hours long.

### 3.30PM
On your return from Robben Island, pick up your car and drive straight on up Kloof Nek Road to **Table Mountain**'s Lower Cable Station (*see p70*). Cable car rides from the Lower Cable Station to the top of Table Mountain leave every 10-15 minutes (depending on the weather conditions). The view from the Upper Cable Station is amazing, and the terrain up top is fairly flat, so do some walking and exploring while you're up there. Maclear's Beacon, Table Mountain's highest point (1,086m/3,563ft), is an easy 20-minute hike from the Upper Cable Station.

### 6.30PM
Take the cable car back down again, then find your table at **Fork** (*see p98*) and end your first day in Cape Town with a fabulous array of tapas and some local wine to wash it down. The pasta roulade with aubergine, tomato and rocket is sublime.

### 9.30PM
The night is young, and Daddy Long Legs is just down the road, so there's no excuse for turning in early. Plus, Long Street's bars and pubs probably won't let you get much sleep anyway. Start out by taking on the pool sharks

**Clifton**. *See p74.*

at **Stones** (166 Long Street), then boogie at **Jo'burg** (see *p122*) all night long. Fill up with an emergency midnight snack at **Fontana Famous Roastery** (166 Long Street, downstairs from Stones, 021 423 6057). Their spicy chicken prego rolls are the perfect pick-me-up. Then, after challenging that Stones pool shark to a rematch, stagger down to Daddy Long Legs for a pre-dawn power nap.

## Day 2

### 7AM
Stumble out of bed and drive out on to De Waal Drive heading out of Cape Town. Just past the University of Cape Town on the M3 follow the signs to **Rhodes Memorial** (see *p82*).

### 7.20AM
First stop Rhodes Memorial, which was built in honour of British Imperial poster boy Cecil John Rhodes. Enjoy the sunrise and the view over Cape Town's southern suburbs from the monument's steps. After Rhodes Memorial, continue along the M3 highway, and turn right at the Newlands Avenue crossroads, following the signposts to Kirstenbosch. Arrive at **Kirstenbosch National Botanical Gardens** (see *p76*) just as the gates are opening at 8am. Enjoy breakfast at the coffee shop and take a stroll through the lush gardens.

### 10AM
After that big, green blast of fresh air, go back to the M3 highway and follow it over Wynberg Hill towards Constantia. Take the turn-off on the M41, and follow this road all the way until you arrive at the historical **Groot Constantia** wine estate (see *p79*). Enjoy a spot of wine tasting at South Africa's oldest estate, which was founded in 1685.

### NOON
Follow the M41 through Constantia, up to Constantia Nek and into Hout Bay. Turn right at the second traffic circle, and follow Princess Road to Hout Bay Harbour. Arrive at **Mariner's Wharf** (see *p116*), and fill up on takeaway fish and chips. Watch the waves break on Hout Bay beach, and buy a shark's tooth from the souvenir shop.

### 1.30PM
Leave Mariner's Wharf, drive back down Princess Road and turn left towards Chapman's Peak. Follow the **Chapman's Peak Drive** (see *p86*) toll road as it winds its way along the Atlantic coastline, and continue all the way south through Noordhoek. Turn right on to Kommetjie Road, then left on to Slangkop Road, and follow your nose towards Cape Point.

### 2.30PM
Arrive at the **Cape of Good Hope Nature Reserve** (see *p84*), park your car – if the baboons let you – and admire the view from the lighthouse at the end of Cape Point. Although the waters around you are, strictly speaking, all Atlantic Ocean, the fact that the water is cool on the west side and warm on the east side is enough to convince us that the catchy slogan is correct: this is the place where two oceans meet.

### 4.30PM
Leave Cape Point and follow the M4 on the False Bay side to Simonstown. Stop at Jubilee Square and enjoy a quick cup of coffee across the road at **Two & Sixpence** (88 St George's Street, 021 786 1371). Before you leave, pay your respects to Cape Town's meanest junkyard dawg at the statue of Able Seaman Just Nuisance (see *p88*).

### 5.30PM
Backtrack slightly on the M4 and stop in at **Boulders Beach** (see *p87*). Here you'll be able to watch the braying jackass penguins as they slide out of the surf and doddle up the sand to their nests on the beach. You'll understand where their name comes from once you hear them. As the sun sets and the wind starts blowing, follow the M4 back through Simonstown, and through Fish Hoek to the picture-perfect town of Kalk Bay.

### 7PM
Stop for dinner at the **Harbour House** (see *p116*) in Kalk Bay harbour. Phone ahead and reserve a table by the window. The menu is all seafood and if tuna is the catch of the day, dig in. While you enjoy your meal, expect a few waves to crash suddenly against the glass to remind you exactly where you are. After dinner, drive north on the M4 and join up with the M3 highway at Steenberg. Follow the famous 'Blue Route' all the way back to Cape Town.

### 9.45PM
Go to town with a drink or two (or three) and a plate of nibbles at **Rick's Café Américain** (see *p106*). Then head back to the hotel for an early start tomorrow. Resist the urge to go back to Stones for another pool match.

## Day 3

### 5AM
Check out of Daddy Long Legs, load up the car and return to Cape Town International Airport in time to return your rental car and catch your flight out.

# City Bowl

The beating heart of the Mother City.

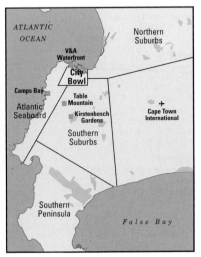

Public transport being what it is in Cape Town, it's handy that the city centre is compact enough to explore on foot. Many of the most interesting spots sit conveniently next to one another along Museum Mile and, with Company Gardens thoughtfully plonked nearby, you can prevent museum burn-out by lazing on the grass under the oaks and feeding a friendly squirrel or two (bags of nuts are sold for that very purpose).

If you want to get a feel for that authentic 'Cape colour' you'll have seen advertised in every brochure in town, the city centre is where it's at. Does anyone actually work in this place? You'll certainly wonder as you watch the locals coming and going while sipping an espresso in a sidewalk café on bustling Long Street.

Here you'll get a good feel for the laid-back attitude Capetonians are well known for and you'll also find truth in that other cliché you've heard bandied about: 'melting pot'. Where else can you walk past a mosque, a bottle store, a sex shop and a church all on the same street? And a wander among the buildings in the City Bowl area, with influences as diverse as British colonial, Victorian, Gothic and Cape Dutch, shows that, in fact, it's been this way all along.

## City centre

### Cape Town Holocaust Centre & the Great Synagogue

*88 Hatfield Street (021 462 5553/www.ctholocaust. co.za).* **Open** 10am-5pm Sun-Thur; 10am-1pm Fri. **Admission** free. **Map** p274 G5.

The links between the South African Nationalist Party's policy of racial discrimination and religious intolerance and the racist ideology of the Nazi regime provides a springboard for this powerful tribute to the persecuted Jewish community of Europe. The use of original artefacts such as a prison jacket worn by a member of the Dachau concentration camp, Hitler Youth film-strips encouraging anti-Semitism and a battered copy of *Mein Kampf* offer a poignant warning to future generations. It's free, so there are no excuses not to see this superbly constructed exhibit. The Great Synagogue, strikingly designed in the style of central European baroque churches with a big dome and two towers on either side, is also right next door.

### Cape Town International Convention Centre

*Convention Square, 1 Lower Long Street (021 410 5000/www.capetownconvention.com).* **Open** 8am-late daily. **Admission** free. **Map** p275 H3.

Designed by the famous local architect Revel Fox, this impressive complex was completed in 2003 in response to the growing demand for a versatile space to house international conventions, consumer exhibitions and trade shows. And versatile it certainly is, having hosted everything from home exhibitions to jazz concerts. It is also has been used as the venue for the popular annual Mother City Queer Project's fancy dress party (*see p156*).

### Castle of Good Hope

*Corner Buitenkant & Darling Streets (021 787 1249/www.iziko.org.za/castle).* **Open** 9am-4pm daily. **Admission** R20; R10-R15 concessions; half-price Sun. **No credit cards**. **Map** p275 I4.

This is the oldest building in South Africa (although curators at Het Posthuys in Muizenberg would beg to differ). Building of the castle was begun for fear of a British attack on the Cape. Stop-start construction continued over a period of 13 years (it was completed in 1679), with the building works revved up a notch whenever the threat of an attack loomed. The castle's military history is somewhat patchy, however, with it having seen a lot more ballrooms than bullets (two bullets to be precise). Form following function, it's not particularly inviting from the outside, but do venture within the castle's walls

City Hall. *See p60.*

because here you'll find the torture chamber (every well-to-do castle at the time had one) – note the creepy century-old scratchings on the walls – as well as the reconstructed forge and bakery, and the William Fehr Collection of 17th, 18th and 19th-century art, furniture and ceramics. Ghostbusters will thrill at the news of the three resident ghosts – there's the legless soldier, demonic black hound or Lady Anne Barnard, take your pick.

## Church Street

**Map** p274 G3.
The street is filled with antiques dealers, art galleries and coffee shops, and the small pedestrianised section bulges with an antiques market. This is a great spot to pick up quirky souvenirs.

## De Waterkant

**Map** p274 G3.
This quaint, cobbled area, west of the foreshore and north of Bo-Kaap, is the self-proclaimed 'gay village' of Cape Town. Restored, brightly painted 18th-century houses (originally built by ex-slaves) with their cheerful hanging flower baskets create a cottagey, neighbourhood feel. It's a lively, cosmopolitan spot, bustling with boutiques, side-street cafes, home stores and trendy clubs, and has become one of the hippest areas in Cape Town. The Cape

Quarter in the area is worth a visit – shops, restaurants, delis and wine bars all in one spot makes this the perfect place to get your evening started, and if you move on to one of the clubs nearby (dress to impress), it won't end until the following day.

## District Six Museum

*25A Buitenkant Street (021 466 7200/www.district six.co.za).* **Open** 9am-3pm Mon; 9am-4pm Tue-Sat; by appointment Sun. **Admission** R15; R5 concessions. **Credit** AmEx, DC, MC, V. **Map** p275 H4.
Musty, snore-inducing museum this ain't. It's a vibrant testament to the 60,000 people uprooted when the area of District Six was declared 'white' in 1965. Neighbours forced apart, homes bulldozed to the ground in front of their residents' eyes – the tales are tragic but the people are far from it. The vibrancy of the area lives on, from the calico sheet embroidered with the names of ex-residents, to the floor mosaics scribbled with children's vivid removal-day memories. Climb the stairs plated with the original street names and you'll be greeted at the top with the voices of ex-residents wafting gently from the ceiling. Give yourself at least an hour to absorb the photographs, video interviews, artworks, newspaper clippings and household bits and bobs. You'll leave feeling privileged to have been immersed in an extraordinary family album.

From boutique hotels to backpacker bars, **Long Street** is 20 blocks of fun. *See p61.*

### Gold of Africa Museum

*Martin Melck House, 96 Strand Street (021 405 1540/www.goldofafrica.com).* **Open** 9.30am-5pm Mon-Sat. **Admission** R20; R10-R16 concessions. **Credit** AmEx, DC, MC, V. **Map** p275 H3.

Treasure, and lots of it, is what you'll find at this museum housed in the 18th-century Martin Melck House. Dedicated to 19th- and 20th-century gold artefacts from those African countries lucky to be blessed with about a third of the world's gold, the impressive collection was acquired from Geneva's Barbier-Mueller Museum. Marvel at the cheerful-looking gold lion, gold crown, tribal masks and even golden sandals from Mali, Senegal, the Ivory Coast, Ghana and Zimbabwe. There's a wine cellar for those who fancy a tipple, and a goldsmith's shop where you can watch the artists at work.

### Grand Parade & City Hall

*Corner Buitengracht & Darling Streets.* **Map** p275 H4.

Despite the imposing façade of City Hall (a library and concert space) overlooking the parade, this cultural meeting spot has lost most of its charm. You probably won't want to linger too long here unless it's to pick up some local blooms from the flower-sellers in the area. With an uninspiring flea market on Wednesdays and Saturdays, it's a handy parking lot for city folk the rest of the time. This is the spot where, on 11 February 1990, 100,000 South Africans gathered beneath the balcony of City Hall to hear Nelson Mandela give his first speech after his release from prison. The development potential for the spot is huge and plans are thankfully afoot to rejuvenate this important site. **Photo** *p59.*

### Heritage Square

*Corner Bree & Shortmarket Streets (www.heritage.org.za).* **Map** p274 G3.

Saved from parking-lot purgatory by the Cape Town Heritage Trust, this group of 18th-century townhouses has been lovingly restored and now houses a boutique hotel, shops, trendy bars, restaurants and a working blacksmith. The restoration project was the biggest of its kind in the country and uncovered an original 18th-century door with lock and handles intact, as well as the oldest vine in the country, thought to have been planted back in the 1770s. Head here before you hit the heaving Long Street clubs. **Photo** *p61.*

### Jo'burg Bar & Gallery

*218-222 Long Street (021 422 0142).* **Open** 5pm-4am Mon-Fri; 2pm-4am Sat; 7pm-late Sun. **Credit** AmEx, DC, MC, V. **Map** p274 G4.

This hardly qualifies as an art gallery, but there is an eclectic display of good stuff by the likes of Brett Murray, Ed Young and others on the walls of this popular Long Street pub. Owner Bruce Gordon was once sold as an artwork himself (you can ask him about it when you're there), and his partner Sue Williamson is one of South Africa's top visual artists, so the place has become something of a hangout for artists, art collectors and piss artists in general. Live music and lively arguments complement the cold beers.

## Koopmans-De Wet House

*35 Strand Street (021 481 3935/www.iziko.org.za/ koopmans)*. **Open** 9.30am-4pm Tue-Thur. **Admission** R5; R2 concessions; free under-6s. **No credit cards**. **Map** p275 H3.

With its sash windows and large entrance doors this beautiful building offers a solid example of Cape Dutch architecture from the 18th century. The former residence of Maria Koopmans-De Wet, prominent in the Cape social and political scene, this was the first private townhouse to be opened to the public as a museum (in 1914). It's furnished as a lived-in home with a superb collection of antique Cape furniture, Chinese and Japanese ceramics and Dutch Delft.

## Long Street

*www.longstreet.co.za*. **Map** p275 H3.

Running poker-straight from the foreshore up towards the mountain, Long Street is one of Cape Town's oldest, covering 20 blocks of the CBD. You'll want to leave a day to explore the eclectic strip lined with Victorian-era buildings restored to house restaurants, bars, pubs, backpacker's lodges, boutique hotels, antique shops, second-hand book stores and vintage clothing stores frequented by every magazine stylist in town. It may look a bit shabby but that's part of the appeal. And when the lights go down, the Cape Town party people come out to play (most of the fun bits are up towards the mountain end of the street). With everything from pubs to lounge bars and clubs straining at the seams, there's little chance of you leaving before the early hours of the morning. **Photo** *p60*.

## Long Street Baths

*Corner Long & Orange Streets (021 400 3302)*. **Open** *Ladies* 9am-6pm Mon, Thur, Sat; 9am-1pm Tue. *Gents* 1-7pm Tue; 8am-7pm Wed, Fri; 8am-noon Sun. **Admission** *Turkish baths* R52; R73 with a massage (women only). *Pool* R9; R6 concessions. **No credit cards**. **Map** p274 G4.

The Long Street Baths at the top of Long Street have been around for almost 100 years (they were built in 1908), so don't expect a contemporary candle-lit spa experience. This is a traditional Turkish bath house where you can steam away city stress without paying through your teeth. Be warned, though, some seedier elements have been known to hang out here too. There are separate days for men and women and massages are also available. They also have a large indoor swimming pool.

## Metropolitan Methodist Church

*Greenmarket Square (021 422 2744)*. **Open** 10am-2pm Mon-Sat. *Services* 10am Sun; 1.10pm Tue. **Admission** free. **Map** p275 H4.

**Heritage Square**. *See p60*.

Once regarded as the finest place of worship in the country, it would be easy to miss this Gothic church, hunched as it now is next to heaving Greenmarket Square and dwarfed by the surrounding buildings. Do linger, though, to take a look at the inspiring architecture of pointed arches and flying buttresses. Keep your wits about you: chances are you'll be targeted by street kids and beggars in this area, so keep your wallet tucked away and have a response at the ready.

## Old Town House

*Longmarket Street, Greenmarket Square (021 481 3932/www.iziko.org.za/michaelis)*. **Open** 10am-5pm Mon-Fri; 10am-4pm Sat. **Admission** free (donation appreciated). **Map** p275 H4.

The Michealis Collection of old Dutch and Flemish masters is housed in the stately former City Hall built in the Cape Rococo style of 1755 bang on Greenmarket Square – by day it's a world-renowned collection of art from 17th-century artists including Anthony van Dyck, Frans Hals and Rembrandt, by night it's a popular venue for chamber music concerts and lectures. Inside you'll find the exact centre of Cape Town (marked by a circle on the floor), which is the point from which all measurements are taken. Outside, a courtyard provides a tranquil respite from the clamour of the square, making this gallery worth a visit even if it's just to put your feet up for a while.

# one Point, a million points of view

## Discover!

From its rugged, rocky cliffs to the fynbos covered plains, Cape Point holds much in store for visitors to these shores. A day of discovery will reward you with spectacular views, fine food, remarkable encounters with nature and history… and memories to treasure forever.

## Fine wining and dining!

From the Two Oceans Restaurant, you'll take in sweeping views of False Bay, way below. The restaurant offers an extensive menu - from breakfasts and light lunches to seafood feasts and hearty South African grills. Alternatively, pick up a bite at the Two Oceans Food Shop @ Cape Point.

## Reach new heights!

An exhilarating ride in the Flying Dutchman funicular lifts you 238 m above the ocean, to where the old lighthouse keeps watch over the seas. What had originally been a diesel bus, named after the "Flying Dutchman" ghost ship, has given way to an environmentally friendly funicular – the only one of its kind in the world.

Cape Point is a beautiful place where mystique and myth are shrouded in seashore mist: is this indeed where the two oceans meet? Come and discover for yourself!

What better way to remember your visit than with a keepsake from one of Cape Point's three ultimate souvenir shops?

**Two Oceans Restaurant bookings**
Tel +27 (0)21 780 9200
Fax: +27 (0)21 780 9060
E-mail: info@two-oceans.co.za
www.destinationrestaurants.co.za

**OPEN TIMES**
**Table Mountain National Park**
Summer (Sept – April): 07:00 – 18:00
Winter (May – Aug): 07:00 – 17:00

**Cape Point Funicular**
Summer: 09:00 – 18:00
Winter: 09:00 – 17:00

**Two Oceans Restaurant**
09:00 – 18:00

**Curio Stores**
09:00 – 18:00

*one Point, a million points of view*

For more information contact the Visitor Centre Management:
Tel +27 (0)21 780 9010/11, Fax: +27 (0)21 780 9203, E-mail: capepoint@concor.co.za, Website: www.capepoint.co.za
Cape Point is a member of Cape Town's Big Six tourism icons, Website: www.capetownbig6.co.za

welcoming of buildings from the outside but do venture in; you'll feel dwarfed by the vast ceilings entirely unsupported by pillars. Note the enclosed pews with their own latched doors. The pulpit, carved by master sculptor Anton Anreith and carpenter Jan Graaf, consists of a pair of sculpted gaping lion jaws. The organ has almost 6,000 pipes and is one of the largest on the African continent.

## Houses of Parliament
*Parliament Street; tours unit on Upper Ground Floor, 90 Plein Street (021 403 2266/021 403 2201/www.parliament.gov.za)*. **Open** *Tours* 9am, 10am, 11am, noon Mon-Fri. Booking essential at least three days in advance. **Admission** free. **Map** p274 G4.

The parliamentary offices consist of a complex of interlinking buildings, a hangover from the apartheid era when there were three separate legislative complexes to cater to the different races. Besides being the spot where many a racially repressive law was passed, this is also where Hendrik Verwoed, the architect of apartheid, met his match in the form of Dimitri Tsafendas, an unhinged parliamentary messenger who stabbed the former president because, as he explained, 'a tapeworm ordered me to do it'. Watch parliamentary sessions in the National Assembly or take an hour-long tour through the debating chambers, library and museum. You'll need to buy a separate ticket if you want to listen in on the debating sessions when ministers are quizzed by MPs. Sittings take place at 2pm when parliament is in session (Jan-Mar; May-June; Aug-Nov), but always phone ahead. Overseas visitors must fax their passport numbers. **Photo** *p64.*

## Iziko South African Museum
*25 Queen Victoria Street (021 481 3800/www.iziko. org.za/sam)*. **Open** 10am-5pm daily; closed Christmas Day & Good Friday. **Admission** R10; R5 concessions. **Credit** DC, MC, V. **Map** p274 G4.
Home to more than half a million specimens of scientific importance, South Africa's natural history museum provides an authoritative account of the country's past. Check out artefacts from the early Iron Age, including Africa's earliest artworks the Lydenburg Heads – dioramas of dinosaur-like reptiles which lived in the Karoo region 250 million years ago, or listen to the song of the humpback whale and marvel at the massive blue whale skeleton hanging from the ceiling. The 700 million-year-old fossils and stone tools made by people 120,000 years ago should put your life into perspective.

## Iziko South African National Gallery
*Government Avenue (021 467 4660/www.iziko.org.za/ sang)*. **Open** 10am-5pm Tue-Sun. **Admission** R10; R5 concessions. **No credit cards**. **Map** p274 G4.
Reclining gracefully above the fishponds in the City Gardens, the Iziko SA National Gallery is as much a part of this peaceful setting as the tableau of Table Mountain. Inside, stuffy colonial portraits jostle for

Iziko South African Museum.

attention with contemporary graphics, beadwork and video installations in a permanent collection that spans several centuries. The gallery regularly mounts innovative and important exhibitions, and judiciously invests in new pieces. Shows range from the massively popular *Picasso in Africa* retrospective to photographer Guy Tillim's evocative studies of inner-city life in Jo'burg. An on-site coffee and gift shop provides respite between rounds.

## Planetarium
*25 Queen Victoria Street (021 481 3900/ www.iziko.org.za/planetarium)*. **Open** 10am-5pm daily. *Shows* 2pm Mon-Fri (excl first Mon of mth); 8pm Tue; noon, 1pm, 2.30pm Sat, Sun. **Admission** R20; R6 children. **Credit** MC, V. **Map** p274 G4.
Spend too much time in the city and it's easy to forget that there's an entire universe out there. So plonk down in a comfy chair for an hour of audio-visual entertainment (without the associated couch potato guilt). An array of ever-changing shows are projected on to the domed ceiling and tailored to make stargazing fun for little 'uns too.

## Cathedral Church of St George the Martyr
*1 Wale Street (021 424 7360/www.stgeorges cathedral.com)*. **Services** 7.15am, 1.15pm Mon-Fri; 8am Sat; 7am, 8am, 9.15am, 11pm last Sun of mth. **Admission** free. **Map** p274 G4.
Never bring up religion and politics at a dinner party? You'd best not mention St George's Anglican Cathedral then. Dubbed the 'People's Cathedral', the

# Table Mountain uncovered

Everything you need to know to make the most of our mountain.

## Table manners

There is a network of over 500 hiking routes on Table Mountain, and maps are available from the Info Centre at the V&A Waterfront, Cape Nature Conservation and the National Botanical Gardens. Here are a few tips before you set off:

● Never attempt a hike on your own.
● Getting lost is always a possibility, so familiarise yourself with your chosen hiking trail beforehand. Shortcuts are a definite no-no.
● No matter how stable the weather seems to be before the ascent, always hike with a waterproof windbreaker, map, compass, torch, spare food and enough water.
● During spring and autumn, gale force south-easterly winds can cover the mountain in thick mist. It is very easy to lose your way and become disorientated.
● Take only pictures and leave only footprints. Always carry all your litter off the mountain.
● Give Tip of Africa Walking Trails & Tours (084 716 8020, www.tipofafrica.co.za) a call. This is the best way to get to the top without getting lost. Small groups of no more that eight are taken on the six-hour hike up Table Mountain via Platteklip Gorge, returning to Kirstenbosch Gardens.

## AKA

Situated at the foot of Devil's Peak in the suburb of Vredehoek are three residential tower blocks officially know as Disa Park. They do, however, have some other names, most notably Pepper Pot Towers or Tampon Towers. They're not the favourite landmark the city has, but at least the 250-odd residents have uninterrupted views over Cape Town.

## Blown away

Legend has it that Table Mountain's tablecloth (the white cloud that spills over the mountain when the south-easterly wind blows in the summer) resulted from a smoking match that took place between the retired 18th-century pirate Van Hunks and a hooded stranger on a mountain top. After two days a tremendous gust of wind blew off the stranger's hat and revealed a pair of horns. Van Hunks and the Devil both went up in a puff of smoke. The mountain on which the match took place is known today as Devil's Peak.

Table Mountain's tablecloth is actually a meteorological occurrence that is caused by the hot and moisture-rich south-easterly wind that blows up against the mountain and rapidly cools down near the top, to form thick clouds. These clouds roll back over the mountain and form the characteristic tablecloth.

## Up, up & away

Table Mountain towers 1,086m (3,563ft) above Cape Town. Maclear's Beacon is the highest point.

## Birds, bees & trees

● There are over 1,470 different plant species growing on Table Mountain.
● The Table Mountain ghost frog is found nowhere else in the world.
● When Table Mountain was first formed it was below sea level and the cap was 1,700m thick. Since then, successive periods of geological uplift and erosion have both elevated the table top above sea level and eroded it down to a hard cap about 600m thick.
● Should your path cross unexpectedly with a creature that closely resembles a reanimated version of your grandmother's mink stole, fear not. It is merely a wee dassie (or hyrax); also known as the closest living relative to the African elephant.

## By a thread

The Table Mountain Cableway transports an average of 800,000 passengers to the summit each year, and has transported well

over 17 million passengers since its inception. In 1913 a vote was held by Cape Town's residents to build a funicular railway up Table Mountain at an estimated cost of £100,000. The project was cancelled when World War I broke out.

### Mountain lore

● In the early days of seafaring, the first sailor to spot Table Mountain was given ten Dutch Guilders and a bottle of wine.
● Long before the arrival of European seafarers, the Khoikhoi had named it *Hoerikwaggo*, meaning Sea Mountain.
● One of the most remarkable ascents up Table Mountain was accomplished in 1829 by Royal Navy Officer James Holwan, who climbed the mountain on horseback despite the fact that he was blind.

### Hear me roar

Lion's Head is so called because it looks like a reclining lion, facing Table Mountain. If you can see the resemblance, you've earned your status as a true Capetonian.

### Big bang

Cape Town's Noon Gun is situated on Signal Hill and has been operational since 1806. It was originally situated in the city centre, but was moved to its current spot when residents started complaining about the noise. The gun has been fired automatically since 1864 by a signal it receives from South Africa's master clock at the South African Astronomical Observatory in Sutherland. The gun actually consists of two guns that are fired on alternate days – they are the oldest guns in daily use in the world.

church was open to all races throughout the apartheid years and its members openly opposed the government's segregation policies. Its pews were regularly packed with protesters, addressed by Nobel laureate and first black archbishop of Cape Town Desmond Tutu. The church is worth a visit even if it's simply to rest weary limbs and bask in the glow of the beautiful Rose Window. Pop in at the cathedral's second-hand bookshop next door, where all books are donated.

### St George's Mall

*St George's Street.* **Map** p275 H3.
This pedestrian walkway runs northwest from Wale Street to Thibault Square. It's a good way to access Greenmarket Square and Museum Mile, as well as the Cape Town Tourism Centre (one block up on the corner of Castle and Burg Streets, 021 487 6800). It's a lively walk, crammed as the mall is with street traders, buskers, drummers, dancers and the odd choir or two. The area is patrolled by mounted police, so feel free to enjoy the entertainment with just one hand on your wallet instead of two. Some characterful cafés line the strip, if your rumbling tummy begins to drown out the music.

### Slave Lodge Museum

*Corner Wale & Adderley Streets (021 460 8200/ www.iziko.org.za/slavelodge).* **Open** 10am-4.30pm Mon-Sat. **Admission** R10; R5 concessions. **No credit cards**. **Map** p275 H4.
The Slave Lodge is the second-oldest building in Cape Town (built in 1679) and for almost 200 years housed up to 9,000 slaves owned by the ruling Dutch East India Company. With no windows (except tiny slits with bars) and a stream running beneath the lodge, living conditions were wet, dank and dark. Perhaps not surprisingly, the lodge was also the local brothel – open to men between 8pm and 9pm every evening, the going rate was a three-inch piece of tobacco. The slavery exhibition is a work in progress. At present visitors are introduced to the history of slavery at the Cape, exploring their enslavement and voyages from Africa and South East Asia. Experience the cramped conditions aboard a slave ship as well as the oppressive conditions inside the lodge. The building also houses the Cultural History Museum, showcasing artefacts from around the world and including examples of Chinese Tang (618-907) dynasty ceramic grave goods, as well as local early 20th-century South African ceramics.

## Table Mountain

### Noon Gun

*Military Road, Bo-Kaap, follow signs from corner of Bloem & Buitengracht Streets (021 787 1257).* **Map** p274 F3.
How do you tell a Capetonian from a tourist? When a daily blast rocks the city, the locals aren't looking skywards but checking their watches to confirm that it is indeed noon already. For those not immune to

Cape Town from **Signal Hill**.

the sound, the noon gun, which thunders through the city every day (except Sundays and public holidays), can sound not dissimilar to a bomb blast. The source of the blast is one of two 18-pound cannons located at Lion Battery in the Bo-Kaap. Back in the 1800s it was used to tell passing ships the time and not much has changed … although captains are more likely to consult their digital watches these days. Get to the battery by 11.30am to join the motley crew of enthusiasts and explosives junkies who watch the guns get loaded with a 3.1kg (8.3lb) bag of gunpowder and then fired.

### Signal Hill & Lion's Head
*Follow directions to Signal Hill from the top of Kloof Nek Road.* **Map** p274 D5.
Be sure to wear sturdy walking shoes rather than flip-flops (it's been known to be attempted in heels), because although relatively gentle, the hike up to the top of Lion's Head takes around 45 minutes and there's a tricky bit near the summit to navigate with chain ropes and metal ladders – although those with vertigo can circumvent this. Once at the top you'll be rewarded with sensational views over the City Bowl and Atlantic Seaboard. To the east lies Signal Hill, and a road winds along the mountain past the sacred Muslim *kramat* to the parking lot. This is a favourite spot for picnickers who dig into dips while the entire Atlantic Seaboard lies spread-eagled before them. Be aware that the popularity of these spots with tourists has made them equally popular with muggers, so don't come here alone or at night.

### Table Mountain Aerial Cableway
*Lower Cable Station, Tafelberg Road (021 424 8181/www.tablemountain.net).* **Open** *Summer* first cable car goes up at 8am, last one comes

down at 10pm. *Winter* first cable car goes up at 8.30am, last one comes down at 6pm (weather permitting). **Admission** R60 single, R120 return; R65 return concessions; free under-4s. **Credit** AmEx, DC, MC, V.
With all 1,086m (3,563ft) of it hulking up behind or in front of you, it's fairly difficult to ignore the landmark which has helped many a local artist put the kids through school. Remember that on cloudless, sunny days, you and every other tourist in Cape Town has decided today's the day to ascend the mount, so be prepared for snaking queues – and, if you're driving, a bit of a walk from your car. The line moves quickly, though, as the hordes are ferried up like clockwork. The floor of the spherical car revolves, meaning there's no need to make a mad dash for the space opposite the open window. The view can get quite dizzy from on high but the cheery commentary from the driver should help quell the vertigo. At the top, take a stroll along one of the pretty paths. After a few minutes' walk you'll find you're practically on your own, the majority of people tending to mill about near the entrance. Look out here for dassies – furry little creatures that are, surprisingly, the closest living relative to the elephant. If you've remembered to pack a picnic you won't have to search far to find the perfect vantage point, or there's a pricey (unsurprising considering its captive audience) restaurant.

## Bo-Kaap

### Bo-Kaap Museum
*71 Wale Street (021 481 3939/www.iziko.org.za/bokaap).* **Open** 9am-4pm Mon-Sat. **Admission** R5; R2 concessions; free under-6s; free Sat. **No credit cards. Map** p274 G3.
If you want to uncover the rich history of the Cape Malay community and are partial to a poke around a typical 18th-century home while you're at it, this intimate museum should be circled on your map. Built in the 1760s, it's the oldest house in the area and still has its original Cape Dutch façade intact. Inside the restored home, black-and-white photographs dating back to 1910 follow the colourful history of the Cape Malays of the area. Interviews with Muslim women (shop owners, academics and social workers) bring us to the present day, while a photographic exhibition upstairs offers further visual insights into the contemporary cultural and thriving business life of the area.

### Owal Masjid
*Dorp Street.* **Admission** no admission unless by special appointment. **Map** p274 G4.
Nobody seems to agree on when South Africa's first official mosque sprang into existence (dates range from 1785 to 1798). What is agreed upon is that Tuan Guru, a prince from the Indonesian island of Tidore, founded this first organised school to teach the Koran. It is also held to be the place where the Afrikaans language was first studied.

# Atlantic Seaboard

Pumped up house prices, pristine beaches and parky waters.

The sweep of shore extending from the V&A Waterfront to Cape Point offers up some sensational coastline and it's not difficult to see why it has become such prime real estate. Monolithic monstrosities begrudgingly share space with far subtler creations, but while no two look alike, one thing the homes on this stretch have in common is the price tag – hefty.

Starting from the **V&A Waterfront** (*see below*) the coast road heads west through Mouille Point, **Green Point** (*see p74*) and on into **Sea Point** (*see p75*) with its mix of seediness and gentility. From here the road climbs (as do the house prices) into Bantry Bay, past trendy **Clifton** (*see p74*), **Camps Bay** (*see p73*) and Bakoven before stretching out of town and on towards hilly **Llandudno** (*see p75*).

Settled on your beach of choice, you'll find the only people in the water this side of the peninsula (fed as the waters are by the Benguela current straight from Antarctica) are elephant-hided locals and tourists who don't know any better. Showers are provided, though, if you need to cool off after a game of frisbee or volleyball.

As the sun sets over the Atlantic in summer you'll get the feeling that there is nowhere else in the world you'd rather be, and you'll find plenty of locals happy to agree.

## V&A Waterfront

### Clock Tower Precinct
**Map** p275 H1.
Reach the Clock Tower Precinct via a swing bridge from Victoria Wharf – it swings aside to let boats pass into the marina – and you'll be greeted by the quirky-looking Victorian-Gothic Clock Tower. Built as the Port Captain's office in 1882, the octagonal, red-brick, three-storey structure has a mirror room which enabled the Port Captain to check out the goings-on in the harbour without having to leave his room. Recent excavations in the area have revealed part of the Chavonnes Battery, one of the oldest European structures in South Africa – built between 1714 and 1725. You'll also find a small shopping mall which houses the very useful Cape Tourism Office, packed with brochures and helpful staff. The departure point for trips to Robben Island (*see below*) is nearby too. You can buy your tickets at the Robben Island Exhibition & Information Centre and have a stroll around the museum while you wait to embark.

### Robben Island
*Ferries depart from the Nelson Mandela Gateway (021 413 4220/1/www.robben-island.org.za).*
**Departures** 9am, 10am, 11am, noon, 1pm, 2pm (weather permitting). **Admission** R150; R75 concessions; free under-4s. **Credit** AmEx, DC, MC, V. **Map** p275 H1.

Clock Tower Precinct.

Camps Bay. *See p73.*

A place of exile and imprisonment for 400 years, Robben Island is known chiefly as the place former South African president Nelson Mandela called home for 18 years. The island lies just a few kilometres from the shores of Cape Town and, despite being a place intended to crush the human spirit, has turned into a symbol of just the opposite. Declared a UN World Heritage Site in 1999, it's now a museum offering tours run by ex-prisoners. Board the ferry which takes you across the bay to this flat, desolate island, where tours will take you past the house where Robert Sobukwe (leader of the Pan Africanist Congress) was held in solitary confinement for nine years. You'll also visit the lime quarry where inmates endured hours of hard labour, as well as Nelson Mandela's cell in B-section of the Maximum Security Prison. You'll discover first-hand that tales of books written in code on scraps of toilet paper and smuggled out via sympathetic visitors were not the workings of overactive imaginations, but the beginnings of autobiographies by heroes of the struggle.

## Scratch Patch

*Dock Road (021 419 9429/www.scratchpatch.co.za).* **Open** 9am-5.30pm daily. **Admission** free. *Cave Golf* R8. *Scratch Patch* R10. **Credit** AmEx, DC, MC, V. **Map** p274 G1.

The opportunity to crawl through a colourful mound of semi-precious stones, plopping them into a little bag clutched in your paws, should never be passed up. If getting down on all fours is problematic these days (and getting up is even worse), or you simply can't be bothered, there's more fun inside the Cave with a spot of mini golf. The kids will love it.

## South African Maritime Museum

*Union Castle Building, Dock Road (021 405 2880/ www.iziko.org.za/maritime).* **Open** 10am-5pm daily. **Admission** R10 (includes a visit to the SAS Somerset); R5 concessions; free under-5s. **No credit cards**. **Map** p274 G1.

Being a port city, it's only natural that there should be a museum dedicated to the Cape's watery heritage. Insights into whaling, some of the shipwrecks in the area and the history of Table Bay Harbour are all on offer, as is the largest collection of model ships in the country. Check out a wooden-hulled yacht, as well as the original Penny Ferry that operated in the harbour. Outside in the dock you can snoop around the naval vessel SAS Somerset and a coal-fired steam tug.

## Two Oceans Aquarium

*Dock Road (021 418 3823/www.aquarium.co.za).* **Open** 9.30am-6pm daily. **Admission** R65; R30-R50 concessions; free under-4s; **Diving** R400. **Credit** AmEx, DC, MC, V. **Map** p275 H2.

Over 8,000 living creatures slip, slither, slide and swim around this watery paradise. You can watch Cape fur seals zig-zagging beneath the water, though you may want to keep your nostrils firmly pinched when you reach their rocky sunning spot – ditto for the penguins. The predator exhibit is open to the ocean and is home to ragged-tooth sharks, loggerhead turtles and shoals of yellowtail. If you're not big on the nasties, though, the kelp forest is a more meditative experience. Beams of light shoot down through the water, and shoals of silver fish shimmer as they dart among the dense strands. If you have

Green Point Market. *See p74.*

your Open Water 1 diving qualification, you can dive with the raggies (ragged-tooth sharks) or cosy up to the kelp. There's also a touch pool where kids can prod and poke a variety of seaweeds, anemones and sea urchins.

### V&A Waterfront

*Dock Road (021 408 7600/www.waterfront.co.za).* **Open** 9am-9pm Mon-Sat; 10am-9pm Sun. **Credit** AmEx, DC, MC, V. **Map** p275 H1.

Even those who tend to avoid shopping centres while on holiday will be hard pushed to give the tourist-friendly V&A Waterfront a wide berth. Never mind the fact that it's home to the Two Oceans Aquarium and the departure point for Robben Island, it's also packed with a vast array of restaurants from top-notch to takeaway, cinemas (both arty and mainstream), clothing boutiques and chainstores, souvenir shops, coffee bars, craft markets and a wellness centre. **Photo** *p74.*

### Camps Bay

**Map** p277 A8.

Right beneath Table Mountain's Twelve Apostles and overlooked by Lion's Head lies the stretch of creamy Camps Bay beach. Look up and chances are you'll see a brightly coloured paraglider wafting on the breeze (they land on a playing field nearby). It's described as the Cape Riviera thanks to its palm tree-lined strip, yachts that anchor in the bay, and the stylish restaurants and bars. The beach is peopled by an eclectic bunch – from families who tend to congregate near the southern end (there are picnic spots

# It's all kicking off

When Nelson Mandela hoisted the World Cup trophy to millions of viewers around the world, signifying South Africa's role as the host of the 2010 World Cup, South Africans let out a collective cry of joy. But in the months that have passed since the joyous occasion, the reality of the task facing the government has proved to be a daunting one.

In Cape Town itself the proposed refurbishment of the landmark Green Point Stadium from a suburban space to one that can accommodate 68,000 soccer fans is causing waves among soccer bodies and city residents alike. The R1.5 billion proposal includes building a new state-of-the-art stadium on a par with some of the world's finest football grounds. Features will include a weather-proof sliding roof.

The proposed new development also involves the building of an entirely new housing development. This has sparked controversy among city councillors, not least because the land around the current stadium (known as Green Point Common) was ceded to the council by King George V in 1923 for use as a recreational and sports common area. Many residents are concerned about the influx of more people into an already congested suburb.

Before any building work is undertaken, though, the city has some way to go. A number of impact studies – from traffic to environmental and heritage implications – as well as the views of the residents' associations have to be considered. Factors such as noise and light pollution, congestion on match days (during and after the tournament) as well as the loss of the common, effectively the only green belt for miles around, are all major concerns. Green Point also has no train service to alleviate traffic stress on the area.

Another important question that has come from the city's two home football clubs (*see p197*) is why the proposed stadium is not being built closer to the people and communities who will benefit from and make use of it after the tournament is over. A stadium of note in one of Cape Town's soccer-mad communities could do much to boost interest in the sport.

near the rocks) to models taking time out from their shoots to brush up on their tans. They may even be working – it's a common sight to find tousled camera crews beavering away while the rest of the city chills. Be aware that there's no resident lifeguard here and the current can be strong, so be careful when venturing into the water. If you want to stay clear of the crowds but close enough to the bars to enjoy a balmy evening cocktail, simply stroll around the rocks at the northern end. You'll find Glen Beach less crowded – most of its locals are on the water awaiting the perfect wave. **Photo** *p72.*

# Secret beaches

### Beta Beach, Victoria Road
**Map** p277 A9.
There are two sides to Bakoven's Beta Beach, reached by turning into Beta Road. The northern enclave is the smallest and is hidden away at the bottom of a steep flight of concrete steps. The secluded cove, carpeted with crushed seashells, is perfect for catching a tan without prying eyes, and looks directly at Lion's Head.

### Clifton 5th, Clifton
**Map** p277 A6.
Unbeknown even to most locals, there is a tiny patch of beach to the south of Clifton's Fourth beach. It's more rocky than sandy, but it's a secluded spot where you can enjoy a romantic sundowner picnic minus the masses.

### Diaz Beach, Cape of Good Hope Nature Reserve
Secluded and very beautiful, you may even have the beach to yourself. Because of this it's best not to go alone and do beware that baboons are common in the area – they should not be fed. Head to the parking lot at the end of Cape Point Road. Take the path down to the right-hand side, which will take you to the beach. It takes about 20 minutes but the walk is well worth the effort.

### Glen Beach, Camps Bay
**Map** p277 A7.
Easily missed, this small enclave of sand lies to the north of Camps Bay. Here you can give the preening of Camps Bay a skip, but still have easy access to the bars and restaurants lining the strip. This is a popular spot for surfers – but be warned, they can be as territorial out of the water as in.

## Clifton

Map p277 A6.
Divided neatly into four beaches by smooth, rounded boulders, Clifton is the place to go to show off those finely toned abs. Reached from the road by steep steps (fine on the way down, a little less so on the way up), you'll find yourself making a mental note to snap up one of the seaside bungalows here when you make your first R10 million. Each beach has its own set of steps from the road, but it's also easy enough to walk across them once you're down on the sand. First beach is the biggest, making it the sporting choice for volleyball or soccer players. Second beach is for those who love to pose in their Prada sunnies and whack a ball about with a beach bat. Third beach is popular with Cape Town's gay community and perfect for a bit of eye-candy. Meanwhile Fourth beach, being furthest south and closest to the parking lot, is the families' choice. There's no need to descend the vertiginous steps laden with supplies: vendors sell cool drinks, water, crisps and sandwiches on the beach. Do bring some candles with you, though, to stake out your spot when the sun goes down.

## Green Point

### Green Point Market
*Parking lot, Green Point Stadium.* **Open** 8.30am-6pm Sun (weather permitting). **Map** p274 F1.
Every Sunday the usually lifeless parking lot of the Green Point Stadium revs into gear with the shouts of traders enticing shoppers with their 'once-in-a-lifetime' bargains. If you're prepared to do a bit of

V&A Waterfront. *See p73.*

digging, they may in fact be right, otherwise you'll probably find yourself leaving with a great deal of tat. You'll find everything you never thought you needed – from pirated DVDs (complete with the crunch of moviegoers' popcorn), knock-off shoes and bags to 'unique' African masks and sculptures mass-produced in a factory outside Durban. It's worth a trawl for last-minute souvenirs, though, if you don't mind crowds. **Photo** *p73*.

### Mouille Point Lighthouse

*100 Beach Road (021 449 5171).* **Open** 9am-3.30pm Mon-Fri. **Admission** R12; R8 concessions. **No credit cards**.

Officially known as the Green Point Lighthouse, this picture-perfect Victorian structure is painted in red and white diagonal stripes. Pronounced 'Moo-ley Point', it's the oldest lighthouse on South Africa's coastline and was erected back in 1824. This is a great point from which to begin a stroll along the Sea Point Promenade (*see below*).

## Llandudno

*Victoria Road.*

Nestled between boulders (providing shelter from the south-easterly wind) and reached through a shaded little forest, Llandudno is a laid-back beach haven. Bushy areas above the sand provide the perfect surfer hangout, which leaves the beach for the rest of the sun-loving throngs. With a fish-eye view of some of the tacky palatial homes rising up behind, you'll see first-hand the architectural offspring of money and bad taste. Prepare yourself for a bit of a walk from your car in summer because the small parking lot fills up very quickly.

## Sandy Bay

*Follow signs from Llandudno off Victoria Road.*

After the 20-minute walk from Llandudno towards the dunes of Sandy Bay, you'll understand why this is Cape Town's unofficial nudist beach. Secluded from prying eyes, the Cape's naturists feel free here to derobe and soak up the rays. If you're up for joining, remember to bring along any essentials because you're a long way from the nearest shop, and snack-selling vendors have proven themselves unwilling when it comes to selling nibbles to nudists. There's a good walk straight across the beach if you're game for a nonchalant peek. It's advisable not to go alone, as it can become a bit desolate out of season.

## Sea Point

### Sea Point Promenade

*Beach Road, Sea Point.* **Map** p273 C2.

A great way to get an eyeful of the cultural microcosm of Cape Town, and some fresh salty sea air while you're at it, is to take the 6km (3.7-mile) seaside walk from the Mouille Point Lighthouse to the Sea Point public swimming pool (021 434 3341, open summer 7am-7pm daily, winter 8.30am-4.30pm daily, admission R9.50). You'll meet all sorts of characters along the way, from Lycra-clad joggers and helmet-wearing rollerbladers to self-involved lovers, pooper-scooping dog walkers and walking stick-wielding old timers. The wooden benches dotted along the route are sandwiched up against the railings, but patches of green grass line the promenade. So feel free to fling yourself down with a blanket, book and ice-cream from one of the vendors.

Llandudno.

# Southern Suburbs

Beer, balls and botanica in the 'burbs.

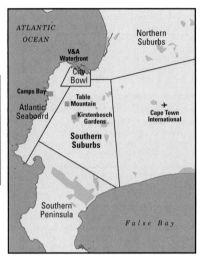

The Southern Suburbs run along the eastern slopes of Table Mountain and out towards False Bay, ending just before Muizenberg. Here, among the burglar-barred family homes, you'll find the usual suburban necessities like shopping centres complete with food courts and cinemas, but you'll also come across some noteworthy gems which are often overlooked. The **Irma Stern Museum** (*see p81*) is one. Regarded as a pioneer in South African art, this was Stern's home for 36 years and is definitely worth a visit for its collection of African artefacts collected on her travels, as well as her own Gauguin-esque paintings.

**Mostert's Mill** (with its quaint thatched roof; *see p81*) gets driven past any number of times a day with not a second glance from time-strapped commuters. The **Kirstenbosch Gardens** (*see below*), though, don't get overlooked quite so easily. During the summer months the gardens play host to a diverse range of music concerts and the rolling lawns are crammed with locals jostling for picnic hamper space. Just five minutes away the Constantia winelands, boasting award-winning labels like **Buitenverwachting** (*see p78*) and **Klein Constantia** (*see p79*), spread themselves out despite being hemmed in by suburbia. And rightly so – they were here first after all, this

being the oldest grape-growing region in the Cape. Stop off for wine tastings and a bite at one of the top restaurants.

Leave 30 minutes or so (longer if you fancy tea and scones) to drive up to the stately neo-classical **Rhodes Memorial** (*see p82*) that sits on the slopes of Devil's Peak. It overlooks the **University of Cape Town** (*see p82*), and the land on which the university sits was actually donated by Cecil himself. Rhodes fan or not, it's worth the short journey just to take in the sweeping views over the Southern Suburbs and out north towards the mountains of Du Toit's Kloof.

Sports fans will feel the inexorable pull of the **Newlands Cricket Ground** and the **Rugby Stadium** (for both, *see p80*); there's a museum as well for fans, but be wary of visiting on match days, as the roads get jammed with cars desperate for a parking spot.

## Constantia & surrounds

### Kirstenbosch National Botanical Gardens

*Rhodes Drive, Newlands (021 799 8783/021 799 8620/www.kirstenbosch.co.za).* **Open** Sept-May 8am-7pm daily. June-Aug 8am-6pm daily. **Admission** R27; R5-R15 concessions. **Credit** AmEx, DC, MC, V. Kirstenbosch is the third most popular tourist attraction in Cape Town (the Waterfront comes in second and Table Mountain an unsurprising first). And it's not difficult to see why. Neatly tended lawns tumble down the eastern slopes of Table Mountain, punctuated by flowering gardens, ponds and indigenous trees all knitted together by paved pathways. Created by Cecil John Rhodes in 1895, the oldest plant is actually a wild almond hedge planted by Jan van Riebeeck to form the border of the colony back in the 1600s. Within its borders, Kirstenbosch grows around 9,000 of the 22,000 plant species indigenous to South Africa. Some of the most interesting spots to head for are the Fragrance Garden, which consists of raised beds filled with indigenous aromatic plants (don't be shy to break off a leaf to rub between your fingers) and the Braille Trail which runs through natural forest and *fynbos*, with plants all clearly labelled in braille and large print. The gardens blend seamlessly with wilder vegetation at the base of the mountain, from where two popular (but strenuous) hiking routes up the mountain – Skeleton Gorge and Nursery Ravine – begin. Don't attempt this hike alone: the lower region can be a lucrative spot for

Mostert's Mill.

much (and please don't ask him or her to sign any body parts) – tours are run on the proviso that visitors remain low-key.

## Observatory

### Mostert's Mill
*Rhodes Avenue (021 762 5127).* **Open** 10am-2.30pm Sat when milling in progress. **Admission** R5; R10 family. **No credit cards**.
This Dutch windmill built in 1796 looks a little out of place, poking as it does out of the side of the M3 highway. It wasn't always like this, of course. The area was once covered in wheat fields and one Sybrandt Mostert used to grind his wheat here before both farm and mill were snapped up by Cecil John Rhodes. The mill is run by volunteers and isn't always open, so make sure you call ahead.

### Transplant Museum & Groote Schuur Hospital
*Groote Schuur Hospital, Old Main Building, Main Road, Observatory (021 404 5232/www.gsh.co.za).* **Open** 9am-2pm Mon-Fri. **Admission** R10; R5 concessions. **No credit cards**.
The world's first heart transplant, by Dr Christiaan Barnard in 1967, was performed in the very spot where this museum now stands. Models recreate scenes from the operation, and the heart in question, which passed from donor Denise Darall to Louis Washkansky (who lived for 18 days beyond the surgery), is also on display.

## Rondebosch

### Baxter Theatre Complex
*Main Road, Rondebosch (021 685 7880/www. baxter.co.za).* **Open** box office 9am-1hr before start of show. **Credit** AmEx, DC, MC, V.
The gaudy orange bowls hanging from the roof – once the height of 1970s glamour – retain a hint of retro chic and serve to give this rather vacuous and chilly theatre (the design of which was inspired by Moscow's train station) a healthy dose of character. Expect to catch anything from ballet and opera to stand-up comedy (the annual comedy festival is held here too).

### Groote Schuur Estate
*Klipper Road, Rondebosch (021 689 5741).* **Tours** (by appointment only, 1 week in advance) R60 per person, incl tea break. **No credit cards**.
Built by Sir Herbert Baker in typical Cape Dutch Revival style, this mansion has been handsomely renovated and houses a wonderful private collection of books, Batavian and Cape Dutch furniture, porcelain, paintings and tapestries which belonged to Cecil John Rhodes.

### Irma Stern Museum
*Cecil Road, Rosebank (021 685 5686/www.irma stern.co.za).* **Open** 10am-5pm Tue-Sat. **Admission** R10; R5 concessions. **No credit cards**.

Wonka's chocolate factory, where bottles of beer replace slabs of chocolate on the conveyor belt for the salivating masses. Tours finish with that much-anticipated tasting.

### Sports Science Institute of South Africa
*Corner Boundary Road & Dean Street, Newlands (021 659 5600/www.ssisa.com).* **Tours** Gateway to Newlands R20; R10-R15 concessions (021 686 2151/ www.newlandstours.co.za). **No credit cards**.
Come here for a workout and you may just find yourself sharing treadmill space with some of the country's top sportsmen. High-tech equipment and a team of scientists, nutritionists and coaches make war on love handles and beer bellies. The excellent tours take sports enthusiasts through the institute providing insight into the trends keeping the country's athletes at the top of their game. If you do spot a sporting great, do your best not to gawk too

Sightseeing

Irma Stern (1894-1966) was regarded as one of South Africa's pioneering artists of the 20th century and a visit to her home reveals a great deal about the woman and artist. Her love of the exotic prompted trips to Zanzibar, the Congo and the East and resulted in the collection of African, Oriental and ancient artefacts on display in the house. You'll find some of her own German Expressionist work on display too, while the upstairs area is used as a gallery space by contemporary South African artists.

### Rhodes Memorial

*Groote Schuur Estate, above UCT (Rhodes Memorial Restaurant & Tea Garden 021 689 9151).* **Open** 9am-5pm daily. **Credit** AmEx, DC, MC, V.

The site for the memorial was Rhodes's favourite spot in the Cape and was chosen by pal Rudyard Kipling and the architect Sir Herbert Baker. It comprises a giant granite staircase (the stone plucked from Table Mountain itself) leading up to a Greek-style temple façade, the entire structure flanked by huge bronze lions. Herds of wildebeest and zebra roam the surrounding grassy slopes, unperturbed by the honking on the M3 highway below. Monument aside, the real reason you'll want to visit is the magnificent view out over the Cape Flats and beyond. You can almost see Rhodes's Cape to Cairo railway stretching ahead of you, as you sip a cuppa in the tea room and ponder your next imperial takeover. The monument is fairly isolated with lots of nooks and crannies, so it's best not to come up here alone or at night.

### University of Cape Town

*Slopes of Devil's Peak, Rondebosch (021 650 9111/ www.uct.ac.za).*

Students buried in their books may not be aware of it, but this is one of the most beautiful university settings in the world. Buildings are cloaked in creeping ivy and brick-red tiles cover the roofs. Founded in 1829, it is the oldest university in South Africa and widely regarded as one of the best. Take a breather on Jamie Steps overlooking Table Bay and eavesdrop on the students' conversations.

## Zeekoevlei

### Rondevlei Nature Reserve

*1 Fisherman's Walk Road, Zeekoevlei, at the end of Perth Road (021 706 2404/www.rondevlei.co.za).* **Open** 7.30am-5pm daily. **Admission** R5; R2-R2.50 concessions; free under-3s; **Tours** Imvubu Nature Tours (021 706 0842). **No credit cards**.

This large wetland is overlooked by coastal dunes and, besides the 230 species of birds found here, the *vlei* is also home to the only five hippos left in the Cape – unfortunately, the hunting habits of the early European settlers have rendered the population virtually non-existent. If birds are your thing, perch at one of the bird hides and use the telescopes to observe white pelican, greater flamingo and African spoonbill. There's a snake house filled with slithering beasties and a freshwater aquarium.

Rhodes Memorial.

# Southern Peninsula

Swap Cape Town's urban sprawl for penguins, sharks and stunning coastlines.

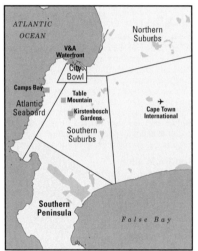

Table Mountain's craggy Twelve Apostles drop down towards the ocean to create one of South Africa's most spectacular coastlines. The peninsula comes to a halt at the crooked finger of Cape Point before swooping back in a gentle arch to form False Bay. Fed by the warmer Indian Ocean currents, beaches this side of the peninsula are less inclined to numb the extremities than their ice-cold counterparts on the Atlantic side.

A day trundling up and down both sides of the peninsula should begin with the coastal road over Llandudno which drops down into **Hout Bay** (*see p85*). The beach here is a hit with families and dog walkers, while fish-and-chip lovers head straight to Snoekies fish factory (Quay 4, 021 790 3330) at the harbour for their fix.

A drive along **Chapman's Peak** (*see p86*) is thrilling – but make sure you stop off at the viewpoints dotted along the edge so you can take a good gander without causing a pile-up. The drive will deposit you in **Noordhoek** (*see p86*) – if you have time make the hour-long walk to the 1900s wreck of the Kakapo, and on into Kommetjie, where the surf is always up. Scarborough, with its feel of a secret summer holiday spot, lies beyond Misty Cliffs, after which you'll find the deserted beaches and wildlife of the **Cape of Good Hope Nature Reserve** (*see p84*). Be on the lookout here for baboons, clawless otters and water mongoose among the larger herds of zebra and antelope. Winding up the other side of the peninsula, the proud naval base of **Simonstown** (*see p87*) welcomes you with a salty salute before you head through **Fish Hoek** (*see p84*) with its great family-friendly beach.

Grab some fresh fish at **Kalk Bay** harbour (*see p85*) where the fishermen bring in their catch of the day. Carry on past the stately homes once owned by wealthy mining magnates who bought up a stretch of coastal summer homes to form a 19th-century 'Millionaires' Mile', and enter the seaside suburb of **Muizenberg** (*see p85*). Plans to restore and develop many of the art deco buildings are finally underway and, with any luck, the sense of faded opulence will be kept intact. The beachside town is a great spot to try a bit of surfing.

Leave a day to complete this route, but if you wither at the thought of all that driving, consider boarding the train that runs from Cape Town station along the coast and right on through to Simonstown. It's a scenic trip but can be marred by the need to stay vigilant. Muggings have occurred on the line, so be sure to get a ticket in first class, keep your camera out of sight and leave your bling behind.

**Kalk Bay**. *See p85*.

## Cape of Good Hope

### Cape of Good Hope Nature Reserve

*Cape Point, turn off the M65 (021 780 9204/www.
tmnp.co.za). Open Apr-Sept 7am-5pm daily. Oct-Mar
6am-6pm daily.* **Admission** R50-R55. **Credit**
AmEx, DC, MC, V.

Tourists bussed in by their thousands head lemming-
like for the funicular up to the old lighthouse, buy a
postcard or two from the curio shop and are bussed
straight back out again. Only they miss the point,
as it were. The landscape, which at first glance may
look a little drab, is home to a huge array of indigenous plants and flowers (look out for the protea,
South Africa's national flower), through which wild
animals, including the cape mountain zebra, roam.
If you're game for a bit of a trek, hiking routes will
take you to shipwreck sites in the area, or take a
stroll along one of the windswept beaches; you may
bump into an African penguin. If you're planning a
picnic on the rocks, be aware that baboons do roam
the area and will make a beeline for your sandwiches. Remember that they are wild animals and
can get aggressive, so don't feed them.

### Cape Point Ostrich Farm

*Plateau Road, off the M65, opposite the entrance
to Cape Point (021 780 9294/www.capepoint
ostrichfarm.com). Open 9.30am-5.30pm daily.*
**Admission** free; R10-R30 guided tours. **Credit**
AmEx, DC, MC, V.

A breeding ground for the gangly, beady-eyed bird,
this is a stop-off for all things ostrich. Broody?
Watch the chicks hatch in spring. Hungry? Buy an
ostrich egg for breakfast; there'll be more than
enough left over for lunch and dinner. In search of a
little something to fill the gap on your mantelpiece?
A découpage ostrich egg, of course.

## Fish Hoek

### Fish Hoek Beach

What Fish Hoek lacks in the looks department
(buildings are a tad down-at-heel), it makes up for in
the family-friendly department. This beach is lapped
by warm waters, with waves big enough to catch
with a boogie board, but not so large they'll knock
the wind out of you. It's a great snorkelling spot too.
And with a playground thoughtfully provided for
the kids, everyone is catered for. Don't expect to pick
up a bottle of vino on the way through, though –
a bylaw makes it illegal to sell booze in the area.

### Jaeger Walk

*Start at Fish Hoek Beach or Sunny Cove on the way
to Simonstown.*
This pathway between Fish Hoek and Simonstown
runs right along the sea edge, offering a superb
spot for whale watching. It's paved as far as Sunny
Cove, from where it turns into a dusty track all the
way to Simonstown.

Submarine dream: check out life below the waves at **Fish Hoek Beach**.

## Hout Bay

### Circe Launches to Seal Island
*Hout Bay Harbour (021 790 1040/www.circe launches.co.za).* **Trips** 9.30am, 10.15am daily; 12.30pm, 2.30pm Sat, Sun (weather permitting). **Cost** R35; R10 concessions. **No credit cards**.
Circe's value-for-money trips to the seal colony of Duiker Island take around 40 minutes. Not only do you get to watch as the seals flip-flap on land, but you can also observe the goings-on beneath the water, from two glass viewing ports on the bottom of the boat. Take to the water on the weekend and you'll be whisked off on the scenic route to the island around the base of the mountain. Expect to gain a bit of perspective as Chapman's Peak rises up behind you and the pointy peak of the Sentinel, which overlooks the entrance to the bay, pierces the clouds in front.

### World of Birds
*Valley Road, Hout Bay (021 790 2730/www.world ofbirds.org.za).* **Open** 9am-5pm daily. **Admission** R50; R32-R40 concessions. **Credit** AmEx, DC, MC, V.
For birdwatching minus the binoculars, this is the place to perch. The largest bird park in Africa features over 4,000 species, from buzzards to vultures (including South Africa's national bird, the elegant blue crane), all preening, prancing and pecking in walk-through aviaries. The centre also cares for injured birds and breeds endangered species. Watch out for the mischievous squirrel monkeys, the pick-pockets of the primate world.

## Kalk Bay

### Kalk Bay Harbour
As the Sunday queues outside local delis and the renewed building work in the area testify, Kalk Bay, once the sole domain of salty surfers, hippies and fishermen, is now very firmly on the map. Thankfully though, no queuing is necessary at the harbour (although a pointy elbow wouldn't hurt) where fishermen return from the sea at 1pm every day to offload their catch. You'll be able to haggle over an array of local snoek, dorado or kabeljou and they'll do all the filleting for you – all you've got to do is season, squeeze on the lemon and bung it on the *braai*. **Photo** *p83*.

## Kommetjie

### Imhoff Farm
*Kommetjie Road (021 783 4545/www.imhofffarm. co.za).* **Open** 9am-5pm Tue-Sun & public holidays. **Admission** free. *Camel rides* R20. *Snake & Reptile Park* R15. *Donkey rides* R5. **Credit** varies.
Within spitting distance of the main road, a couple of camels hunch outside Imhoff Farm. Let them take you for a jaunt or leave them to dream of desert dunes while you take yourself for a potter around the eclectic mix of shops, where you can pick up local

Hout Bay's **World of Birds**.

arts and crafts, hand-made organic cheeses and even surfboards. Kids will love the farmyard and snake park and won't rest until they get a go on Greedy Guts the donkey.

## Muizenberg

### The Catwalk
*Starts at the Corner at Muizenberg, ends at St James.*
This level pathway runs along the rocky coast and is a great spot from which to take in the magnificent False Bay coastline and get up close and personal with a whale or two in season. It takes 40 minutes to walk each way but factor in more time if you've got kids – they'll love exploring the rock pools and will be fascinated by the brightly coloured sea anemones lurking inside.

### Muizenberg Beach
*From Main Road turn into Atlantic Road and pass under the bridge. Take the second right to park at the mountain end, or keep going to the big parking section.*
Warm waters keep the families flocking, and good breaks make it a popular surfing spot, while the kite-surfers have made it home too. Muizenberg is refreshingly attitude-free (unless you swipe someone else's wave), but it does lack the effortless beauty of

Chapman's Peak Drive.

the sandy Atlantic shores. For generations, kids have been magnetically pulled to the super-tube (giant waterslide) and the miniature golf green next door – resistance is futile. **Photo** *p89*.

### Rhodes Cottage Museum

*42 Main Road (021 788 1816).* **Open** *Apr-Sept* 9.30am-4.30pm. *Oct-Mar* 10am-4pm. **Admission** R5. **No credit cards**.

Cecil John Rhodes, revered by some for his contribution to the South African mining industry and education, maligned by others who regard him as an imperialist and the founding father of the oppressive migrant labour system in South Africa, was prime minister of the Cape Colony from 1890-1895. He built this house in 1899, only to die here three years later from tuberculosis, aged 49. Walls are lined with photographs, newspaper clippings, cartoons and caricatures which depict the life of the man labelled 'Europe's Greatest Businessman'.

### Silvermine Nature Reserve

*Off Ou Kaapse Weg, Silvermine, nr Muizenberg (021 780 9002/www.tmnp.co.za).* **Open** 8am-6pm daily. **Admission** R10; R5 concessions; free with a SANParks Wild Card. **No credit cards**.

A typically Capetonian misnomer, the area was never a silver mine, although shafts were sunk in the 1600s. Walking trails criss-cross the reserve and offer views over Noordhoek and Hout Bay on the Atlantic side, or Muizenberg and Fish Hoek on the False Bay side. Give yourself four hours to hike the well-trodden path to Elephant's Eye Cave which offers views over False Bay. Then reward yourself with a *braai* at one of the pretty picnic spots.

### Yokohama

*210 Main Road.*

A house made of papier mâché? This you've got to see. Built 100 years ago by a woman named Grace Tozer, it's still a private home so unfortunately you can't go snooping around.

## Noordhoek

### Chapman's Peak Drive

*Toll road between Noordhoek and Hout Bay (021 790 9163).* **Cost** R23 cars; R15 motorcycles. **Credit** AmEx, DC, MC, V.

With sheer cliffs stretching down sharply towards the sea, winding along this coastal stretch can feel precarious at times but is all the more exhilarating for it. View sites have been thoughtfully dotted along the drive, so take your pick. Depending on where you park your car, you'll enjoy views of the

# Just when you thought it was unsafe…

Don't let the memory of late-night *Jaws* reruns keep you from taking a dip in the warm waters of False Bay. An increase in great white shark attacks and sightings in the last four years (there were nine attacks between 2000 and 2005; three fatal) has prompted the decision to introduce official shark spotters to areas along the False Bay coastline.

Initially these spotters were either car guards paid by the community to keep an eye out during surfing competitions, or local fishermen on the lookout for shoals of fish, but in the past two years they have become a permanent feature. With sponsorship from the World Wide Fund for Nature, the shark spotters (all previously unemployed) have received first-aid training and plans are afoot to provide them with marine education and driver's licences.

There are always two spotters on duty at Muizenberg beach, kitted out with polarised sunglasses and binoculars, one sitting high above the surf on Boyes Drive, the other patrolling the beach. Both carry walkie-talkies, so if a shark is seen, the message is relayed to the beach. The siren is then sounded, signalling for people to get out of the water. A flag system keeps those surfside in the loop too:

 Black flag = poor visibility; no shark has been spotted.

 Green flag = good visibility; no shark has been spotted.

 Red flag = a shark has been seen in the area and has moved off; be careful.

 White flag with a black silhouette of a shark = shark in the area; get out of the water now.

A total of 132 sharks were spotted at Muizenberg during 2005 – so clearly something's working.

white specks of boats in Hout Bay harbour or the sands of Noordhoek beach stretching south towards Kommetjie. Keep this spectacular drive for a clear, blue-sky day and the toll fee will be more than worth it.

## Noordhoek Farm Village
*Corner Noordhoek Main Road & Village Lane (021 789 1317/www.noordhoekvillage.co.za).* **Open** *Shops* 8.30am-5.30pm daily summer; 9am-5.30pm daily winter. *Restaurants* 8am-late daily. **Credit** AmEx, DC, MC, V.
At the southern end of Chapman's Peak Drive lies this family haven where parents can rest while the kids run riot. There are restaurants to grab a bite, pubs for a post-walking pint, a playground for the kids, plus a farm stall and organic nursery. There's a tourist information office too.

## Slangkop Lighthouse
*Lighthouse Road, Kommetjie (021 783 1717/www.npa.co.za).* **Open** 10am-2pm Mon-Fri. **Admission** R12; R6-R8 concessions. **No credit cards**.
The tallest cast iron tower on the African coast, the Slangkop (meaning 'snake's head') Lighthouse has been lighting the way for ships rounding the Cape coast since 1918. Too late, unfortunately, for the Kakapo which ran aground on nearby Noordhoek

beach in 1900. The walkway to the lighthouse offers a great vantage point for spotting offshore birds like the albatross, best seen after winter storms.

## St James

### St James Pool
The cheerily painted Victorian-style beach huts overlooking the small, sheltered beach of St James wink at you from every postcard rack in town. The tidal pool is a favourite with families with little ones needing to splash about and can get desperately overrun, so if it's a secluded spot you're after, you're better off taking a short stroll south to Danger Beach. An offshore reef means waves are consistently good here, but do heed the warning in the beach's name – there is a powerful undertow.

## Simonstown

### Boulders African Penguin Colony
*Accessed from Seaforth or Boulders beaches, follow brown signs from Simonstown (021 786 2329/www.tmnp.co.za).* **Open** *Feb-May, Oct-Nov* 8am-6.30pm daily; *June-Sept* 8am-5pm daily; *Dec-Jan* 7am-7.30pm daily. **Admission** R20; R5 concessions. **Credit** AmEx, DC, MC, V.

# Boat trips

### Braai cruise

Tigger 2 Charter (021 790 5256, www.tiggertoo.co.za) offers luxurious cruises from Hout Bay harbour. Routes vary depending on weather conditions, but expect to round the Sentinel and cruise out to Seal Island, with a visit to the Maori shipwreck too. The three-course *braai* is served back in Hout Bay. R450 per person, minimum of six.

### White-knuckle ride

Atlantic Adventures, Pierhead, V&A Waterfront (021 425 3785, www.atlanticadventures.co.za) offers high-speed rubber duck boat rides across Table Bay. The 12-seater boat ride leaves from the V&A Waterfront and a standard trip takes you around the coast to Clifton and Bakoven or to Robben Island (R300). If your stomach can take it, a two-hour cruise to Hout Bay will cost you R500.

### Whale watching cruise

The Waterfront Boat Company (021 418 5806, www.waterfrontboats.co.za, R350 adults, R175 children) makes three- to four-hour cruises to Hout Bay or Robbesteen during the whale season from June to November. Keep your eyes peeled for whales, penguins, seals, dolphins, basking sharks, sunfish and Cape birdlife.

### Shark spotting

African Shark Eco Charters (021 785 1947, wwww.ultimate-animals.com) run shark-viewing trips from October to May. Head out from Simonstown and around Cape Point in search of blue and mako sharks. The predators are attracted using high-tech sound equipment. Watch the razor-toothed creatures swimming around the boat and, if you're lucky, catch one leaping out of the water. The R1,300 you pay helps to fund shark research.

Unfortunate name aside, you can't help but be charmed by the jackass penguins of Boulders. Named for their distinctive donkey-like honk, they have made themselves well and truly at home on the tiny, sheltered beach – under brush, over boulder, the friendly little flappers get absolutely everywhere and today there are well over 3,000 living here. Calm, warm-ish waters and the opportunity to swim with wild animals make this beach a very popular spot with tourists and locals alike.

### Bronze Age Art Foundry

*King George's Way (gallery 021 786 5090/foundry 021 786 1816/www.bronzeageart.com).* **Open** 10am-5pm Tue-Thur; 10am-4pm Fri; 10am-3pm Sat, Sun. **Admission** free.

If the sight of liquid metal all aglow gets you going, a stop-off at this foundry housed in an early 19th-century stables is a must. Molten bronze castings are done in the cool of the night to compensate for the scorching 1,200°C heat of the liquid metal. You can pick up signed, limited-edition bronze work from local and international artists in the adjoining gallery or wander through the inspiring sculpture garden next door which overlooks the Simonstown yacht basin.

### Heritage Museum

*Amlay House, King George Way (021 786 2302).* **Open** 11am-4pm Tue-Fri; 10am-5pm Sun. **Admission** R5 adults; R2 concessions. **No credit cards**.

Forcibly removed from Simonstown in the mid 1970s, the Amlays returned to their family home 20 years later to open this unique museum which offers a glimpse into the rich Muslim culture of the area. Zainab Davidson (née Amlay), a treasure trove of local information, will happily take you round her home, explaining the apartheid-era history to the uninitiated. Black-and-white family photographs (dating from the 1800s to the present day) paper the walls and jostle for attention with newspaper cut-outs describing the forced removals in the area. A bridal room showcases the traditional matrimonial suite while cookery books divulge the secret to making *koeksisters*, a sickly sweet local delicacy. Walking tours of the area are offered on Wednesday and Thursday mornings.

### Just Nuisance's Grave

*Off Redhill Drive, look for a sign just past Pine Haven, Simonstown.*

A Great Dane by the name of Just Nuisance, the story goes, would accompany British World War II seamen on their pub crawls through Cape Town, alerting the inebriated when the final train was heading back to Simonstown. He was rewarded with a free train pass and the rank of able seaman. Just Nuisance died an honourable death in 1944 and was given a full military burial at Klaver Camp on Red Hill, overlooking False Bay. It's not like the Navy to get all sentimental, but this lonely, quiet spot and the fact that it is open to the public in an otherwise restricted-access area, is an indication of just how great this Dane was.

### Mineral World & Topstone

*Dido Valley Road (021 786 2020).* **Open** 8.30am-4.45pm Mon-Fri; 9am-5.30pm Sat, Sun. **Admission** free. **Credit** AmEx, DC, MC, V.

You're never too old to rootle about for semi-precious stones. It's the thrill of the unexpected – you never quite know what you're going to find, and what if they left a nugget of gold in there by accident?

**Muizenberg Beach**. *See p85*.

Mineral World is an Aladdin's cave of semi-precious stones, from rose quartz to obsidian, with a selection of fossils to boot. And take a peek at the topstone factory – during the week you can watch the process of tumbling (where the stones are cleaned and polished) and see the craftsmen at work.

### Simonstown Boat Trips
*Depart from jetty by the waterfront (021 786 2136).* **Trips** 11.30am, 2.30pm daily. **No credit cards**.
Choose from a variety of cruises to fit your timetable and wallet. If you've only got 40 minutes to spare, take a potter around Simonsbay and sneak a peek at the South African Navy ships and submarines in dock. Keep your eyes peeled for seals along the way (R30; R15 under-12s). Two-hour voyages take you to Seal Island, the hunting ground for the great white shark. From August to December you'll sail past majestic southern right whales (R200). Depending on how late you were out the night before, you may or may not fancy the early riser special. Your punctual 7am arrival will be rewarded with a trip to Seal Island (R200) where chances are high you'll see the magnificent great white sharks breaching right out of the water and nabbing unsuspecting seals for breakfast. If it's more of a leisurely jaunt you're after, take the 2hr 30min trip around Cape Point (R250), where you'll discover the rich birdlife in the area and learn about the number of shipwrecks lying beneath you. You'll get to explore an ocean cave too.

### Simonstown Museum
*Court Road (021 786 3046/www.simonstown.com).* **Open** 9am-4pm Mon-Fri; 10am-1pm Sat; 11am-3pm Sun, public holidays. **Admission** R5 adults; R1-R2 concessions. **No credit cards**.
This former winter residence of Cape Governor Simon Adriaan van der Stel (Simonstown is named after him) was also a slave quarters and one-time town brothel. It has been a museum since 1977 and provides an extremely thorough cultural history of the area from hunter-gatherers to the present day. There's a lot of information crammed in and there's no test at the end, so head straight for the interesting bits such as artefacts from the Anglo-Boer War POW camp and the collar of celebrated Great Dane 'Just Nuisance' (*see p88*).

### Warrior Toy Museum
*Main Road, next to the Town Hall (021 786 1395).* **Open** 10am-4pm daily. **Admission** R3. **Credit** MC, V.
One warrior short of a war? You'll find the Zulu army here complete with animal hide shields and pointy *assegais*. You can also pick up the full British contingent. Shelves, in this candy store for kids and collectors, sport obsessively neat rows of dinky toy cars, trucks, trains, aeroplanes, houses and toy soldiers shipped in during the past 40 years from all over the world by owner and toy connoisseur Percy van Zyl.

# Northern Suburbs

Welcome to Pleasantville.

**Milnerton Flea Market**. *See p92.*

Stretching along the N1 highway and the N7 coastal road, the Northern Suburbs offer up a slice of suburbia in all of its 'just out of the box' splendour. Perfectly manicured lawns, well-tended rose gardens and wide, child-friendly roads perfect for biking or kicking a ball about are overlooked by the towering Tygerberg Hills which run perpendicular to the highway.

You'll find nothing jars here, but then nothing grabs your attention particularly either. The area boasts two large shopping malls, Canal Walk and Tygervalley, which, although not on a par with the Waterfront in terms of aesthetic appeal, are still packed with all the usual shops and brands. The newly opened Willowbridge Mall has injected a bit of glam into the area with excellent homeware stores, boutiques and trendy cafés.

The stretch of beach running alongside the coastal highway is called Blouberg and it's here that you'll get that picture-perfect shot of Table

Mountain. The beach is also a favourite haunt for surfers, windsurfers and kite-surfers. Although at first glance there may appear to be nothing much here to satisfy a tourist's taste, there are certainly some attractions that are well worth a visit. Take a day to trawl the lesser-frequented **Durbanville Wine Route** (*see p91*), wander the **Tygerberg Hills** (*see p92*) with sensational views across to Table Mountain or look a grizzly bear in the eyes at Cape Town's only **Zoo** (*see p92*).

## Durbanville

### Durbanville Nature Reserve
*Racecourse Road (021 970 3097).* **Open** 8am-4.30pm daily. **Admission** free.
Head to this little reserve if you'd like some down time from the madding crowd. Located in the endangered *renosterveld* next to Durbanville Race Course, it's the perfect hideaway for a lazy picnic lunch with the Sunday papers.

### Durbanville Rose Garden

*Durban Road (021 948 1744).* **Open** 8am-sunset daily. **Admission** free.

A rose garden just as rose gardens should be – civilised and proper. Poke your nose into the 500 varieties of roses which bloom in the thick clay under the area's topsoil. And if you pop by on a Sunday (Oct-May) you'll find cream tea on offer.

### Durbanville Wine Route

*021 915 4080/www.durbanvillewine.co.za.*

Durbanville is one of the coolest wine-producing areas in the Cape, and the fertile soil and chilly winds brought in from the Atlantic Ocean provide the perfect environment for the production of award-winning Sauvignon Blanc. Visitors can take their pick from the nine active wine farms dotted along this less popular (but by no means less worthy) Cape wine route, which range in age from 300 years old to under 20. The estates on the route are: **D'Aria** (021 975 5736); **Ntida Estate** (021 976 1467); **Hillcrest Estate** (021 975 2346); **Durbanville Hills Winery** (021 558 1300); **Bloemendal Wine Estate** (021 976 2682); **Altydgedacht** (021 976 1295); **Diemersdal** (021 976 3361); **Meerendal** (021 975 1655); and **De Grendel Estate** (021 558 6280).

# March of the penguins

The white sands that stretch out along Cape Town's salty, windy West Coast are populated by some strange characters. The wackiest of the West Coast's oddballs are found on the beaches, pecking at mussel shells, doddling through the surf and picking bugs out of their wings.

These coastal birds are a peculiar bunch, whether it's the sings-like-a-drunken-uncle-at-a-wedding Cape gannet (*Morus capensis*), the luminous-orange-socks-with-a-black-suit African oystercatcher (*Haematopus moquini*) or the chicken-in-a-tuxedo jackass penguin (*Spheniscus demersus*).

The penguins bray like donkeys, walk like Charlie Chaplin, eat anchovies by the shedload and are fiercely monogamous. It's no wonder, then, that Hollywood's animators have such a fascination with these funny fellows (witness *Madagascar* and *Happy Feet*).

And like all good Hollywood stars, Cape Town's penguins need a rehab centre. In their case, though, it's mostly for rehab from oil spills. SANCCOB, the South African Foundation for the Conservation of Coastal Birds, has responded to every oil spill along the South African coast since 1968, and has helped to treat more than 80,000 oiled, sick, injured and orphaned seabirds over the past four decades.

SANCCOB HQ is located in Table View, near the Rietvlei wetland on the way to Bloubergstrand, the beach with that famous postcard view of Table Mountain. On any given day (SANCCOB is open every day of the year) you'll find washed-up seabirds being cleaned and cared for by SANCCOB's employees – many of whom are kind-hearted volunteers who don't mind getting their hands pecked.

In a quiet year SANCCOB can treat as many as a thousand birds. Although there have been no major oil spills during the past five years, they treated a total of 4,453 penguins between 2001 and 2005. Recent research by the bird-counters at the University of Cape Town's Avian Demography Unit showed that the penguin population is 19% higher today than it would have been without SANCCOB's efforts.

The foundation's biggest challenge to date came on the Black Friday of 23 June 2000, when the iron ore tanker MV Treasure sank between Robben Island and Dassen Island, 8km (5 miles) off Table Bay, releasing 1,300 tonnes of fuel into the sea and critically endangering 19,000 penguins – more than 41% of the species. Another 19,500 un-oiled penguins had to be removed from Dassen Island as SANCCOB grappled with one of the world's worst ever coastal bird crises.

The rehabilitation project involved tens of thousands of volunteers, and took more than three months to complete. In the end more than 91% of the penguins were successfully cleaned and released.

While the coast has been clear for the past five years, SANCCOB continues to draw on volunteer support. One of their more popular projects is their Adopt a Penguin initiative, which allows donors to sponsor the rehabilitation and release into the wild of a wounded bird for R500. It's worth it… if only to watch your penguin waddle off into the sunset.

### SANCCOB

*22 Pentz Drive, Table View (021 557 6155/ www.sanccob.co.za).* **Open** 8am-5pm daily. **Penguin feeding** 10am, 3pm daily. **Admission** free.

Get up close and personal at the **West Coast Ostrich Show Farm**.

### Tygerberg Nature Reserve

*Travelling on the N1 from Cape Town, take Exit 20 (Jip de Jager Road) and follow the signs (021 913 5695).* **Open** 8am-4pm Mon-Fri; 9am-6pm Sat, Sun. **Admission** free.

The nature reserve lies at the top of the Tygerberg Hills, above the suburb of Welgemoed. Leave an hour or two to wander the trails which slice through the endangered vegetation, boasting over 400 species of indigenous plant species. Visit during spring and you'll be greeted by a carpet of brightly coloured flowering bulbs. Also keep your eyes peeled for the 125 bird species, including peregrine falcons and rock kestrels, and animals such as grysbok, rheebok and bat-eared foxes. If you missed your obligatory shot of Table Mountain from Blouberg beach, the reserve offers great views over the Cape Peninsula towards the mountain.

### Tygerberg Zoo

*Exit 39, Klipheuwel-Stellenbosch off-ramp, N1 highway (021 884 4494/www.tygerbergzoo.co.za).* **Open** 9am-5pm daily. **Admission** R44 adults; R30 concessions. **No credit cards**.

While you won't find larger animals like elephants and rhino here, what you will find are seldom seen ones – the zoo is a breeding ground for rare and endangered animals. Look out for lions from Siberia, Bengal tigers from India, grizzly bears from America and African cheetahs. The zoo also specialises in mini-antelope (including red and blue duiker), but expect to see primates too, including marmosets and chimps, as well as walk-through aviaries and a well-stocked tortoise collection.

## Milnerton

### Milnerton Flea Market

*Otto du Plessis Drive, Paarden Eiland.* **Open** 7am-4pm Sun.

Anyone who finds large, noisy crowds problematic, but is quite partial to a flea market find or two, should give Greenmarket Square and Green Point Market the runaround and head up to Milnerton instead. More car boot sale than flea market, sellers appear passionate about their wares. You get the feeling that you really could stumble across something special here.

## Table View

### West Coast Ostrich Show Farm

*Van Schoorsdrif Road, Philadelphia, nr Table View (021 972 1955/021 972 1669/www.ostrich ranch.co.za).* **Open** 8.30am-5pm daily. *Tours* every half-hour, on the hour. **Admission** R35 adults; R28 concessions; free under-6s. **Credit** AmEx, DC, MC, V.

From as far back as the 1600s, ostriches have been farmed in the Cape. Take a visit to the semi-rural area of Philadelphia and you'll find the tradition continues, albeit with a modern twist. Guided tours take you on a 45-minute trail through the breeding enclosures from where you'll be whisked off, with macabre synchronicity, to the leather factory. The relaxed environment in which the birds are reared makes for better quality leather. There are a variety of ostrich breeds here to get friendly with, as well as emus, rheas and peacocks.

# Eat, Drink, Shop

**Story**. *See p149.*

**The Victoria & Alfred Waterfront**
is located within the breathtaking
setting of a dynamic working harbour and includes
over 400 specialist stores, more than 80 restaurants,
coffee shops, pubs and take-aways, an aquarium, boat and helicopter
charters, art and craft markets, a variety of leisure attractions
as well as a choice of world-class
conference and hotel facilities.

The V&A Waterfront offers a range of cultural
landmarks including museums,
historic buildings and exclusive access to one of South Africa's
essential heritage sites; Robben Island. All of
this, coupled with ongoing events and entertainment,
within a vibrant cosmopolitan atmosphere,
ensures that the V&A Waterfront
is the heart of your visit.

# The Warm Heart of Africa

VICTORIA & ALFRED WATERFRONT CAPE TOWN SOUTH AFRICA
For further details please contact Waterfront Information on 021 408 7600,
email info@waterfront.co.za or visit www.waterfront.co.za

favourites, presented and prepared in a thoroughly modern manner – from confit of salmon with anchovy caviar to Japanese marinated quail, this is definitely one for the foodie's memory bank.

### Jardine

*185 Bree Street (021 424 5640/www.jardineonbree. co.za).* **Open** 11am-late Tue-Sat. **Main courses** R80. **Credit** MC, V. **Map** p274 G4 ⓩ
A simply stylish setting provides the backdrop for award-winning chef George Jardine's seasonal, contemporary cuisine. Sophisticated palates head upstairs to observe the chef in action and feast on 'epicurious' delights, while those in the mood for something unfussy mingle in the comfortably cool lounge-bar area downstairs. **Photo** *p102.*

### Manna Epicure

*151 Kloof Street (021 426 2413).* **Open** 8am-6pm Tue-Sat; 8am-4pm Sun. **Main courses** R60. **Credit** DC, MC, V.
A magnet for models and creative types, Manna does a brisk trade in designer breakfasts (the creamiest eggs imaginable), oh-so-stylish lunches (including a wholesome buffet and fantastic salmon) and delicious smoothies. The in-store bakery also offers pretty cakes for tea. **Photo** *p100.*

### Manolo

*30 Kloof Street (021 422 4747/www.manoloeat. co.za).* **Open** noon-3pm, 6pm-late Tue-Sun. **Main courses** R70. **Credit** AmEx, DC, MC, V. **Map** p274 G4 ⓯

# Meaty treats

South Africans are not known as meat and potato lovers for nothing, but thankfully their manner of serving it up has become decidedly more sophisticated over the years. Though steakhouse chains certainly offer tasty fare, smaller establishments that specialise in carnivorous cuts have a passion for their meat, ensuring it is hung for a minimum of three weeks, a non-negotiable in steak appreciation terms. For taste, rump is always your best bet, with sirloin combining flavour and tenderness in a solid cut, and the ever-popular fillet offering subtle flavour and melt-in-the-mouth tenderness.

### Barristers

See p115.
A Southern Suburbs steak stalwart of note – their ribs are finger-licking good too.

### Bayside Café

51 Victoria Road, Camps Bay, Atlantic Seaboard (021 438 265).
One of the most popular meaty restaurants on the Camps Bay strip. Don't forget to order their light-as-a-feather onion rings.

### Brad's Grill

69 2nd Avenue, Claremont, Southern Suburbs (021 671 2527).
Don't let the suburban interior get you down – owner Brad Steele really knows his stuff.

### Den Anker

Pierhead, V&A Waterfront, Atlantic Seaboard (021 419 0249).
Hollandse biefstuk and steak tartare are just two of the specialities at this Belgian landmark in the Waterfront.

### Famous Butcher's Grill

See p115.
A chain that really takes its grain-fed beef seriously. Choose your cut from the ageing room or have some vacuum-packed to take home and enjoy.

### Hussar Grill

10 Main Road, Rondebosch, Southern Suburbs (021 689 9516).
This old-school Southern Suburbs steakhouse still has it – be sure to smother your beef or game cut with any one of the speciality sauces on offer.

### Khaya Nyama

See p97.
Touristy as anything but their game cuts are in a class of their own. Try everything from warthog to kudu and springbok cuts – you'll understand why it lives up to its name (House of Meat in Zulu).

### Nelson's Eye

See p103.
This is the oldest steakhouse in Cape Town and there's a reason that people have been eating here for over 50 years. Their steaks are superb.

### Pirates Grill

160 Main Road, Plumstead, Southern Suburbs (021 797 5659).
It really doesn't get any cheesier than this jovial suburban steakhouse, and that's how the regulars love it. Expect your cut of meat (the rump is fab) to come with chips and sauce and not much else – the perfect venue for a meaty feast.

A glam eaterie with an established reputation for good food and great service. Deciding which of the three themed dining areas (ranging in style from minimalist chic to baroque drama) you want to sit in is easy compared with the task of having to choose between the enticing selection of Asian, European and South African dishes on offer. They also have an extensive wine list, and you will be tempted to linger long after you've finished your trio of crème brulée.

## 95 Keerom

*95 Keerom Street (021 422 0765).* **Open** noon-2.30pm, 7-10.30pm Mon-Sat. **Main courses** R85. **Credit** AmEx, DC, MC, V. **Map** p274 G4
This ultra-stylish restaurant is frequented by the city's cool set. Owner/chef Giorgio Nava presents a simple menu of northern Italian classics alongside an excellent wine list. Try the classic carpaccio or risotto, which are both superb.

## Relish

*70 New Church Street (021 422 3584).* **Open** noon-late Mon-Fri; 5pm-late Sat, Sun. **Main courses** R65. **Credit** AmEx, DC, MC, V. **Map** p274 F4 ⓱
This designer glass and brick industrial-chic space features a busy bar and sundowner deck as well as a small, sophisticated restaurant. The bar menu is peppered with a tempting selection of hearty snacks and light meals (like steak sandwich with bacon, avocado, brie and cranberry sauce), while the downstairs restaurant has a more elegant selection – the likes of seared Norwegian salmon on asparagus or gooseberry jus-drenched ostrich fillet.

## Savoy Cabbage Restaurant & Champagne Bar

*101 Hout Street (021 424 2626).* **Open** noon-2.30pm, 7-10.30pm Mon-Fri; 7-10.30pm Sat. **Main courses** R95. **Credit** AmEx, DC, MC, V. **Map** p274 G3 ⓲
A slick and sexy space with an interior neatly sandwiched between the past and the present. The food here is undoubtedly European albeit with plenty of nods to local flavours and produce – including loin or shank of everything from warthog to zebra. If you're dining in summer it's essential to try the now famous tomato tart, voted by the *New York Times* as one of the ten things to try before you die.

## Shoga

*121 Castle Street (021 426 2369).* **Open** 7pm-late Mon-Sat. **Main courses** R95. **Credit** AmEx, DC, MC, V. **Map** p274 G3 ⓳
The upstairs sibling to cult foodie landmark Ginja, Shoga is a more laid-back set-up with an out-and-out Asian influence evident on the menu. From peanut sauce-smothered teriyaki beef fillet to twice-cooked barbecue duck and a host of wok-fried main courses, this is a chic option for a city dinner.

## Tank

*Cape Quarter, 72 Waterkant Street (021 419 0007/ www.the-tank.co.za).* **Open** noon-3pm, 6pm-late daily. **Main courses** R80. **Credit** AmEx, DC, MC, V. **Map** p274 G3 ⓴
This swish spot adds a touch of glam to the Cape Quarter and is a great bet for cocktails. They also serve really well-priced sushi and a host of fusion-inspired meat and fish dishes.

**Manna Epicure.** *See p99.*

# Gourmet

## Antique

*31st Floor, ABSA Centre, Riebeeck Street (021 419 0672).* **Open** 7.30-11pm daily. **Main courses** R90. **Credit** AmEx, DC, MC, V. **Map** p275 H3 ㉑
A Hollywood-style setting makes this spot and its adjoining Butterfly Bar the stuff of fantasies – and so is the food. Recline on a lavish daybed and take in the view from the top of one of the city's tallest high-rises as you feast on Italian, French and Pacific Rim-inspired cuisine. A hefty bill is the price you'll have to pay for such decadence, so save your visit for a special occasion.

## Cape Colony

*Mount Nelson Hotel, 76 Orange Street (021 483 1850/www.mountnelsonhotel.co.za).* **Open** 6.30-10.30pm daily. **Main courses** R90. **Credit** AmEx, MC, DC, V. **Map** p274 G5 ㉒
Situated in the famous Mount Nelson Hotel, the Cape Colony offers fine dining with a twist. Opt for the special African Experience menu where the chef serves up local specialities with flair. Service is predictably superb and the wine list is fabulous. Pricey, but worth it.

## Chef

*3 Rose Street, De Waterkant (021 419 6767).* **Open** noon-2pm, 7-10.30pm Tue-Fri; 7-10.30pm Sat. **Main courses** R70. **Credit** AmEx, MC, V. **Map** p275 H3 ㉓
If you're a gourmand then no visit to the Mother City would be complete without booking a table at Chef. Owner-chef Nicolai Bareti offers an unbeatable personal dining experience, talking you through his specials of the day before retiring to work his magic in the kitchen. This is an all-evening occasion – and be warned, you might have to wait a while for your meal.

# Mediterranean

## Carlyle's on Derry

*17 Derry Street (021 461 8787).* **Open** 4.30-10.30pm Tue-Sun. **Main courses** R50. **Credit** MC, V.
The epitome of a local joint, where everybody knows everyone's name – pop in here alone and you're bound to leave with a friend or three. Social advantages aside, Carlyle's also does fantastic thin-based pizzas with excellent toppings, flavourful salads and wonderful seared tuna.

## Castle Hotel

*Corner Canterbury & Constitution Streets (021 461 6306).* **Open** noon-3pm, 7-10.30pm Mon-Fri; 7-10.30pm Sat. **Main courses** R70. **Credit** AmEx, DC, MC, V. **Map** p275 H5 ㉔
Hearty Portuguese fare doesn't get better than this. Mano Coulentianos (of Mano's fame) has transformed the upstairs section of a once rundown hotel in one of the city's most up-and-coming precincts into an inviting space in which to enjoy finger-

'Contemporary tapas' at **Fork**. *See p98.*

licking prawns and succulent calamari. Order a few of each for the table, and don't leave without sampling a custardy *pastéis de nata*.

## Col'cacchio

*Shop 2, Spearhead, 42 Hans Strijdom Avenue (021 419 4848).* **Open** noon-11pm Mon-Fri; 6.30-11pm Sat, Sun. **Main courses** R40. **Credit** AmEx, DC, MC, V. **Map** p275 H3 ㉕
Good service, great pizzas and a buzzing atmosphere ensure a memorable meal. And if you can't make up your mind, they're happy to make up half-and-half pizzas to get the best of both worlds.

## Limoncello

*8 Breda Street (021 461 5100/www.limoncello.co.za).* **Open** noon-3pm, 6-11pm Mon-Fri; 6-11pm Sat, Sun. **Main courses** R60. **Credit** AmEx, DC, MC, V. **Map** p274 G5 ㉖
An excellent choice if a low-key authentic Italian meal is what you're after. Pizza forms the basis of the menu, although they also do a mean seared tuna and, if you're lucky, the lamb shank might be on the specials board. If mussels are on the menu, don't think twice.

## Maria's Greek Restaurant

*31 Barnet Street, Dunkley Square (021 461 8887).* **Open** 10am-11.30pm Mon-Fri; 10am-11pm Sat. **Main courses** R60. **Credit** AmEx, DC, MC, V. **Map** p274 G5 ㉗

The food here is authentic and tasty. Choose a selection of meze to share, wash it all down with tumblers of cheap and cheerful red wine, then move on to flavourful mains like slow-roasted Greek lamb or garlicky mussels.

### Mesopotamia

*Corner Long & Church Streets (021 424 4664).* **Open** 6pm-late daily (lunch can be pre-booked). **Main courses** R60. **Credit** AmEx, DC, MC, V. **Map** p275 H4 **28**

Whether you go for dinner à deux or an en masse experience, an evening here is sheer entertainment. Waiters bearing massive trays of authentic meze talk you through the selection before you make your choice. Though they serve main courses, it's a better and tastier idea to simply fill up on more meze. Be warned: you are likely to reek of garlic for at least a day after.

### Nonna Lina

*64 Orange Street (021 424 4966).* **Open** 10am-midnight Mon-Fri; 6.30-10.30pm Sat. **Main courses** R65. **Credit** DC, MC, V. **Map** p274 G5 **29**

Perched on the corner of two of the city's busiest streets, this eaterie focuses on authentic Italian (Sardinian) fare. A simple, contemporary space with a buzzing atmosphere, the restaurant is a very pleasant lunchtime venue (the salads and antipasti are excellent) while dinnertime sees the throngs arrive for wood-fired pizzas (the Nonna Lina with Parma ham, tomato, rocket, basil and pecorino is fabulous) and inspired pastas.

### Porcini

*Heritage Square, Shortmarket Street (021 422 1300).* **Open** noon-10.30pm Mon-Thur, Sun; noon-11.30pm Fri, Sat. **Main courses** R65. **Credit** DC, MC, V. **Map** p274 G3 **30**

Perfectly placed in the heart of the city at Heritage Square and with ample safe parking available, Porcini fulfils the needs of Italian food-loving urbanites. Expect a rowdy atmosphere complete with well-clad Capetonians and heaving plates of authentic Italian food (unsurprisingly, porcini play a supporting role in a number of the dishes on offer). Though South African fare features, it's best to opt for a hearty pasta or any of the gourmet pizzas which come with suitably crispy bases.

## Seafood & sushi

### Miller's Thumb

*10B Kloof Nek Road (021 424 3838).* **Open** 6.30-10.30pm Mon, Sat; 12.30-2pm, 6.30-10.30pm Tue-Fri. **Main courses** R75. **Credit** AmEx, DC, MC, V. **Map** p274 F5 **31**

This neighbourhood joint has withstood the onslaught of trendy eateries and stuck to its hands-on guns with aplomb. Focusing on seafood with zing (though they also do fantastic steaks), be sure to try the famous blackened linefish or owner-chef Solly's seafood, chicken and chorizo studded jambalaya.

**Jardine.** *See p99.*

If you're really hungry, opt for the chicken and prawn 'Curry of Joy'. Once bitten, you'll definitely be back for more.

## Steakhouses

### Nelson's Eye

*9 Hof Street, Gardens (021 423 2601).* **Open** noon-2pm, 6-10.30pm Mon-Fri; 6-10.30pm Sat, Sun. **Main courses** R95. **Credit** AmEx, DC, MC, V. **Map** p274 G5 ❸❷

When it comes to steak, the Nelson's Eye has it sorted. The undoubted leaders in their field, this original steakhouse has held on to its crown for over 50 years and though the decor hasn't changed in all that time, it's all part of the charm. Granted it's not cheap, but when your plate of perfectly seared sirloin, rump or fillet arrives at the table and you take your first bite, you too will be smitten.

## Vegetarian

### Lola's

*228 Long Street (021 423 0885).* **Open** 8.30am-midnight daily. **Main courses** R30. **Credit** MC, V. **Map** p274 G4 ❸❸

Packed with backpackers, locals taking it slow and a host of interesting folk in between, Lola's focuses on simple vegetarian fare and a small selection of delicious home-made cakes. **Photo** *p105.*

## Cafés & casual eating

### Afro Café

*48 Church Street (021 426 1857).* **Open** 8am-6pm Mon-Fri; 8am-3pm Sat. **Main courses** R35. **Credit** DC, MC, V. **Map** p274 G4 ❸❹

Deliciously authentic African food and a super-cool interior beckon locals and visitors alike. Try some Afro coffee for a perk, and take home some local tea in a funky tin.

### Andiamo

*Shop C2, Cape Quarter, Waterkant Street (021 421 3687).* **Open** 9am-11pm daily. **Main courses** R60. **Credit** AmEx, DC, MC, V. **Map** p274 G3 ❸❺

Always busy, Andiamo is a shiny version of an authentic Italian deli in the heart of the Cape Quarter. The outside terrace area does a roaring trade in pizzas, tramezzini and light eats while inside sees shoppers stock up on their cured meats, imported and local cheeses and dried and tinned ingredients from all over the world.

### Birds

*127 Bree Street ( 021 426 2534).* **Open** 8am-4pm Mon-Thur; 8am-10pm Fri. **Main courses** R32. **Credit** MC, V. **Map** p274 G3 ❸❻

An avian theme permeates this entire café experience – from a soundtrack of birdcalls to posters on the walls and menus presented in field guides, the owners of this charming city spot have a distinct design vision. Happily their food is excellent too, specialising in wholesome, organic fare. Stop in for a generous sandwich served on home-baked whole-wheat bread with a salad, or try any of the flavoursome rustic casseroles. Their breads, cakes and strudels are fantastic and their lattes are the stuff of caffeine dreams. **Photo** *p110.*

### Café Gainsbourg

*64 Kloof Street (021 422 1780).* **Open** 7.30am-11pm Mon-Fri; 8.30am-midnight Sat; 9am-3.30pm Sun. **Main courses** R60. **Credit** AmEx, DC, MC, V. **Map** p274 F5 ❸❼

A new interior has breathed a sense of chic into this little urban spot. A simple menu tempts hungry city types with offerings like tomatoey meatballs and very tasty chopped salads. A good wine list ensures an enjoyable all-round eating experience.

### Café Manhattan

*74 Waterkant Street (021 421 6666/www. manhattan.co.za).* **Open** 10am-midnight daily. **Main courses** R50. **Credit** AmEx, DC, MC, V. **Map** p274 G3 ❸❽

Much loved by the city's glamorous gay boys, Café Manhattan is famous for serving up man-sized burgers, though their newly refurbished menu offers a good selection of home-style choices too. Crammed from early morning (for breakfast) to well after midnight, the outside section is the best place to sit and admire the view – it's a popular haunt for the pre-clubbing crowd.

### Dutch

*34 Napier Street (021 425 0157).* **Open** 8am-5pm Mon-Fri; 8am-3pm Sat. **Main courses** R40. **Credit** AmEx, MC, V. **Map** p274 G3 ❸❾

A slice of European café culture in the heart of the trendy De Waterkant neighbourhood, Dutch specialises in tasty treats all day. Try *uit-smijters* (toast topped with cheese, ham and egg) or ham and pea soup served with a slice of ham on rye.

### Frieda's Café

*15 Bree Street (021 421 2404).* **Open** 8am-4pm Mon-Fri. **Main courses** R36. **No credit cards**. **Map** p275 H3 ❹⓿

This gem of a café is situated downtown, sandwiched among office space and workshops. The lofty interior is an exercise in industrial chic (it used to be the Harley Davidson workshop) and is scattered with oversized communal raw wood tables and some of owner Frieda's own retro collectables. Simple café food features here – including home-made pies, a dish of the day and a great selection of oversized sandwiches. An unpretentious place to soak up the city vibe.

### Greens on Park

*5 Park Road (021 422 4415).* **Open** 8am-5pm Mon; 8am-11pm Tue-Sun. **Main courses** R55. **Credit** AmEx, DC, MC, V. **Map** p274 F4 ❹❶

Exactly what one expects from an urban café – consistently tasty all-day fare (breakfasts, burgers,

**Eat, Drink, Shop**

# A Tide of Pure Style...

*Experience...*

*the best classical and*

*contemporary cuisine,*

*rare wine vintages,*

*breathtaking views,*

*unsurpassed service,*

*the finest cultivars...*

*A combination so*

*refreshingly satisfying,*

*it should be savoured,*

*every day...*

Laid-back Long Street vegetarian at **Lola's**. *See p103*.

pizzas, seafood and steaks) served in a modern environment. Greens is also a popular place for early evening drinks.

## Home Again Restaurant

*Derry Street (021 465 8463).* **Open** 5pm-midnight Mon, Sat; noon-2pm, 5pm-midnight Tue-Fri. **Main courses** R55. **Credit** AmEx, DC, MC, V.

This restaurant and bar is a popular stop for regulars who come in for a post-work drink, mid-week meal or rowdy birthday celebration – if you're dining alone, you'll never feel lonely. Stars on the menu include burgers, garlicky *espetada* and tasty tapas to share.

## Lazari

*Corner Upper Maynard Street & Vredehoek Avenue (021 461 9865).* **Open** 7.30am-5pm Mon-Fri; 8am-4pm Sat; 8.30am-3pm Sun. **Main courses** R35. **Credit** AmEx, MC, V.

This is the quintessential neighbourhood joint – its owner Chris Lazari can't help making everybody feel at home. He and his congenial team bustle about, filling up coffees and serving a great selection of wholesome café food. From gigantic breakfasts to home-made soups, excellent Greek lamb (Chris's mother's secret recipe), bangers and mash and a whole host of toasted treats, this is the kind of place where you'll pop in for a cuppa and leave much, much later. **Photo** *p112*.

## M Café

*Metropole Hotel, 38 Long Street (021 424 7247/ www.metropolehotel.co.za).* **Open** 6.30am-8pm daily. **Credit** AmEx, DC, MC, V. **Map** p275 H3 ㊷

If the Metropole Hotel's Veranda restaurant and its ever fabulous M Bar cater for the after-dark glam crowd, then its newly opened M Café is the perfect daytime pit stop. This coffee bar and easy eaterie is a stylish place to rest your weary legs after a morning's browse on Long Street, and a great place for a quick cake and cappuccino. A range of beautifully packaged foodie gifts to take home adds zest and colour to this cosmopolitan city spot.

## Melissa's

*94 Kloof Street (021 424 5540/www.melissas.co.za).* **Open** 7.30am-8pm Mon-Fri; 8am-8pm Sat, Sun. **Main courses** R30-R60. **Credit** AmEx, DC, MC, V. **Map** p274 F5 ㊸

The original Kloof Street branch of what is now a five-store chain, Melissa's is the hallmark for quality wholesome fare packaged and presented with flair. Part deli (with plenty of gourmet meals to take home), they also serve a daily buffet of quiches, casseroles and salads all made with trademark dedication to quality. Be sure to fill up a basket with the biscuits, meringues and famous nougat as gifts for foodie friends.

**Other locations**: Portside Centre, Main Road, Green Point (021 434 1719).

## Origin

*28 Hudson Street (021 421 1000/www.origin roasting.co.za).* **Open** 8am-7pm Mon-Thur; 7am-6pm Fri, 8am-2pm Sat. **Main courses** R20. **Credit** AmEx, DC, MC, V. **Map** p274 G3 ㊹

The secret to really good coffee is in the beans. Owners David Donde and Joel Singer share a passion for caffeine and dedicate time to educating customers on everything from coffee roasting to the appreciation of latte art (the owners are highly skilled at both). Buy beans and other coffee paraphernalia before settling down with what is arguably the best cappy in Cape Town.

### La Petite Tarte

*Shop 11A, Cape Quarter, Waterkant Street (021 425 9077).* **Open** 8am-5pm Mon-Fri; 8am-3pm Sat. **Main courses** R42. **Credit** MC, V. **Map** p274 G3 ⓸⑤

Take a seat at this Parisian-inspired spot and watch the fashionistas pass by. Imported speciality teas and authentic French tarts and pastries help to fill a mid-morning or afternoon gap. **Photo** *p107*.

### Rick's Café Américain

*2 Park Street (021 424 1100).* **Open** noon-11.30pm Mon-Sat. **Main courses** R65. **Credit** DC, MC, V. **Map** p274 F4 ⓸⑥

In no time at all, Rick's has become a favourite haunt of city locals. With a cosy *Casablanca* theme, fireplaces, comfy lounge areas and a moreish array of tapas, you can easily spend a night here. If your hunger is more intense, try the linefish or a subtly spiced tagine. **Photo** *p108*.

### Royale Eatery

*273 Long Street (021 422 4536).* **Open** noon-11.30pm Mon-Sat. **Main courses** R45. **Credit** AmEx, DC, MC, V. **Map** p274 G4 ⓸⑦

This funky Long Street stop heaves with hungry punters from lunch till late, and with 20 types of gourmet burger (including beef, chicken and veggie options) it's easy to see why trendy twentysomethings use it as their social stomping ground. The American-style milkshakes are a must-try.

### Sundance Gourmet Coffee Co

*59 Buitengracht Street (021 424 1461/www. sundancecoffeeco.com).* **Open** 6.30am-6.30pm Mon-Fri; 6.30am-3.30pm Sat, Sun. **Main courses** R30. **Credit** DC, MC, V. **Map** p274 G3 ⓸⑧

Warm chocolate- and vanilla-toned interiors and the alluring aroma of coffee make celeb chef Conrad Gallagher's coffee emporiums hard to resist – choose a cuppa (espresso, latte, mocha or granita – they're all fabulous) and max your order with an oversized muffin, panino or chocolate treat.

**Other locations**: 21 Adderley Street (021 465 9990).

### Vida e Caffè

*Shop 1, Mooikloof, 34 Kloof Street (021 426 0627/ www.caffe.co.za).* **Open** 7am-5pm Mon-Sat; 8am-5pm Sun. **Credit** AmEx, DC, MC, V. **Map** p274 G5 ⓸⑨

It doesn't get any slicker than this design-tastic city coffee spot. The house blend keeps caffeine junkies buzzing all day long, while simple rolls filled with home-cured meats and cheeses and melt-in-the-mouth *pastéis de nata* fill the hunger gap. Great for getting a glimpse of the city's glamour set who swear by the place.

**Other locations**: Shop 2, Vogue House, Thibault Square (021 421 3974/www.caffe.co.za). Shop 6100, Victoria Wharf (021 425 9440/www.caffe.co.za).

### Yum

*2 Deer Park Drive (021 461 7607).* **Open** 5pm-midnight Tue; 9.30am-midnight Wed-Fri; 9am-midnight Sat; 9am-9pm Sun. **Main courses** R50. **Credit** AmEx, DC, MC, V.

Much loved by Vredehoek locals, Yum is exactly the place to go to when you don't feel like cooking and are up for a relaxed evening. The extensive menu features plenty of no-fuss options, including some

**Eat, Drink, Shop**

# Bargain bites

When your budget is limited but your taste isn't, there are plenty of fabulous and not-so-costly culinary options.

The city's visiting Taiwanese fishermen have called the **Jewel Tavern** (Vanguard Road, Cape Town Harbour, City Bowl, 021 448 1977) their home from home for years – expect authentic Asian cuisine in an equally authentic atmosphere.

Join the throngs of city workers as they pick up supper for their families from **Texies Fish & Chips** (Darling Street, City Bowl, 021 461 4817), an inner-city institution.

Ease into the week at the classic movie and pizza night on Mondays at the **Independent Armchair Theatre** (135 Lower Main Road, Observatory, Southern Suburbs, 021 447 1514). The delicious thin-crisp pizzas come from neighbouring Café Diva

and are the perfect accompaniment to the cult movies screened here.

Join **Perima** (Corner Belvedere & Lansdown Roads, Claremont, Southern Suburbs, 021 671 3205) at her eponymous restaurant in Claremont. A seemingly never-ending buffet of flavoursome Hindu food will keep your tastebuds on their toes.

Seriously authentic Chinese food is to be had at the Sunday night buffets at **Yellow River** (94 Monte Vista Boulevard, 021 559 3177) in Monte Vista. Eat all you can for well under R100.

One of the country's finest restaurants, **La Colombe** (*see p113*), makes its exquisite food available to all with the La Colombe Winter Special, which runs from May to October – prices start at R195 for three courses including a carafe of wine.

fabulous filled pastas (try the crispy bacon with sage and cream), a mean burger and very tasty wraps. The bar next door is the perfect place to retire and finish your bottle of wine. This is also a great choice for weekend breakfasts.

### Zucca
*84 Kloof Street (021 423 7331).* **Open** 9am-10.30pm daily. **Main courses** R50. **Credit** DC, MC, V. **Map** p274 F5 🐵
Conveniently located in the middle of bustling Kloof Street, Zucca offers quick pizza or pasta, or more substantial dishes such as oxtail or karoo lamb chops. The deli section is the perfect place to grab a quick antipasti bite.

## Atlantic Seaboard

## Contemporary

### Beluga
*The Foundry, Prestwich Street, Green Point (021 418 2948).* **Open** 9am-11pm Mon-Fri; 6.30-11pm Sat, Sun. **Main courses** R100. **Credit** AmEx, DC, MC, V. **Map** p274 G2 🐵
This inner-city restaurant plays host to a fabulously moody bar and an industrial chic restaurant that serves up a modern mix of steak, seafood and imaginative vegetarian dishes.

### Paranga
*Shop 1, The Promenade, Victoria Road, Camps Bay (021 438 0404/www.paranga.co.za).* **Open** 9.30am-11pm Wed-Sun. **Main courses** R100. **Credit** AmEx, DC, MC, V. **Map** p277 A8 🐵
This sexy space might make you feel you're in Miami or even St Tropez, but the menu is Cape Town all the way. Prices here are steep, though, so it might be wise to fill up on their wicked cocktails and opt for a simple plate of calamari to eat.

### Salt Restaurant & Bar
*The Ambassador Hotel, 34 Victoria Road, Bantry Bay (021 439 7258/www.saltrestaurant. co.za).* **Open** noon-3pm, 7-11pm daily. **Main courses** R90. **Credit** AmEx, DC, MC, V. **Map** p273 A4 🐵
One of the Atlantic Seaboard's hotel landmarks, the Ambassador in Bantry Bay has had an injection of cool thanks to the opening of Salt Restaurant & Bar. With glass walls that let in a stupendous view of turquoise waters and a subtly sophisticated interior, it's no surprise that people are singing its praises. View and setting aside, the food is excellent, with a surprisingly laid-back menu and, even more surprisingly, excellent prices. Globally inspired offerings are the order of the day, but rather than overpowering diners with his culinary prowess, chef David Winton opts to keep it simple, letting the flavour and superb produce do the talking. From the simplest of salads to perfectly seared cuts of meat and seafood, a meal here is bound to be memorable.

La Petite Tarte. *See p106.*

**Rick's Café Américain.** *See p106.*

## German

### Paulaner Brauhaus & Restaurant
*Shop 18/19, Clock Tower Square, V&A Waterfront (021 418 9999/www.paulaner.co.za).* **Open** 11am-1am daily. **Main courses** R60. **Credit** AmEx, DC, MC, V. **Map** p275 H1 ⑤④
This slice of Germany in the heart of the Waterfront serves Bavarian beers along with hearty fare like bratwurst, goulash and particularly tasty pork knuckle. A good bet if you're all seafooded out.

## Gourmet

### Azure
*12 Apostles Hotel, Victoria Road, Camps Bay (021 437 9029/www.12apostleshotel.com).* **Open** 6.30-10.30am, 12.30-3.30pm, 6-10.30pm daily. **Main courses** R100. **Credit** AmEx, DC, MC, V.
This five-star hotel is perfectly perched on the Atlantic Ocean – offering stupendous views from the bar area, outside terrace and swanky restaurant. Food is Afro-European with a heady mix of *fynbos* incorporated into many of the dishes. Wines are expensive but excellent.

### The Showroom
*10 Hospital Street, Harbour Ridge, Green Point (021 421 4682).* **Open** noon-3pm, 7-10.30pm Mon-Fri; 7-10.30pm Sat. **Main courses** *Lunch* R55; *Dinner* R70. **Credit** AmEx, DC, MC, V. **Map** p275 H3 ⑤⑤

The name of chef Bruce Robertson's sophisticated restaurant says it all. Everything is on show, from the slick white interior to the beautifully crafted cuisine. Select a main dish and match it with one of 20 precocious-sounding sauces for a delicious yet ever so slightly gimmicky gastronomic experience.

## Mediterranean

### Mano's
*39 Main Road, Green Point (021 434 1090).* **Open** noon-11pm Mon-Sat. **Main courses** R65. **Credit** AmEx, DC, MC, V. **Map** p274 G2 ⑤⑥
This laid-back venue comes to life after 5pm when the city's cool crowd drop by for a post-work bite. The calamari, penne al salmone and chicken kebabs are popular options. Get there early, or be prepared to wait at the bar.

### La Perla
*Corner Church & Beach Roads, Sea Point (021 434 2471).* **Open** 10.30am-midnight daily. **Main courses** R75. **Credit** AmEx, DC, MC, V. **Map** p273 B3 ⑤⑦
One of Cape Town's first restaurants, this is where many Sea Point families congregate on a weekly basis. The food is Italian with some consistently tasty favourites (tagliata with porcini mushrooms and parmesan is out of this world). Perfect for a lazy, sun-splashed Saturday lunch, although the service tends to be on the surly side unless you can impress the waiters.

### Posticino
*3 Albany Mews, 323 Main Road, Sea Point (021 439 4014).* **Open** noon-11pm daily. **Main courses** R50. **Credit** AmEx, DC, MC, V. **Map** p273 C2 ⑤⑧
Arguably the best Italian on the Main Road strip, drop by any night of the week and you'll find this spot overflowing with regulars tucking into perfectly crisp, thin-based pizzas and hearty pastas. Owners Jack and Eric encourage guests to choose their pasta sauce ingredients themselves, making it a popular option for fussy eaters.

### Sloppy Sam
*51A Somerset Road, Green Point (021 419 2921).* **Open** 6.30-10.30pm Mon-Sat. **Main courses** R65. **Credit** AmEx, DC, MC, V. **Map** p274 G2 ⑤⑨
Don't let the name deter you – the food, ambience and service here are anything but sloppy. Owner Hooman Saffarian's family-run trattoria is a home away from home that serves up heart-warming comfort food. The spicy calamari and slow roasted lamb shank are legendary.

## Seafood & sushi

### Blues
*The Promenade, Victoria Road, Camps Bay (021 438 2040/www.blues.co.za).* **Open** noon-11pm (10.30pm winter) daily. **Main courses** R90. **Credit** AmEx, DC, MC, V. **Map** p277 A8 ⑥⓪

Eat, Drink, Shop

This institution on the Camps Bay promenade is still a favourite with glam visitors from abroad. Expect a smattering of fusion dishes, a host of seafood options and classic burgers.

### The Codfather

*37 The Drive, Camps Bay (021 438 0782/www. thecodfather.co.za).* **Open** noon-late daily. **Main courses** R65. **Credit** AmEx, DC, MC, V. **Map** p277 A8 ⑤

Seafood maniacs are right at home at this very popular sushi and seafood restaurant. Take a seat at the revolving belt for sushi on the run or make an evening of it in the restaurant – guests choose their own cut of fish (sold by weight), indicating how they would like it prepared. Although it's a bit pricey, it makes for a great meal.

### Jimmy's Killer Prawns

*103 Regent Road, Sea Point (021 434 4643).* **Open** 11.30am-10.30pm daily. **Main courses** R70. **Credit** AmEx, DC, MC, V. **Map** p273 B3 ⑥

Don't expect slick service and trendy decor here. This everyday seafood spot offers family fare at

# Tops for tea

### Afro Café

*48 Church Street, City Bowl (021 426 1857).*
This bright and buzzy Afro-chic café (*pictured*) is the perfect host for steaming cups of chai and java harvested on the continent. They may not have scones but you have to try the *vetkoek* (deep fried dough balls) with cheddar and jam.

### Cape Grace Hotel

*West Quay Road, V&A Waterfront, Atlantic Seaboard (021 410 7100).*
One of the world's finest hotels also serves up a mean high tea in the library. Expect monstrous slices of just-baked cakes, as well as a selection of mouthwatering scones and decadent toppings.

### Kirstenbosch Restaurant

*Botanical Gardens, Kirstenbosch, Southern Suburbs (021 762 9585).*
Kirstenbosch is consistently voted one of the best botanical gardens in the world, and the tearoom also offers plenty of rewards after an hour or two's stroll among the indigenous flora.

### Mount Nelson Hotel

*76 Orange Street, City Bowl (021 483 1000).*
Voted the best high tea in the world by an ever-growing number of publications, tea in the sun-splashed conservatory or lounge is an epicurean feast.

### Rhodes Memorial Restaurant

*Groote Schuur Estate, Southern Suburbs (021 689 9151).*
A view second to none and scones with all the trimmings make this the perfect way to spend a lazy afternoon.

### Tea & Tarot

*102 Main Road, Lakeside, Southern Suburbs (021 788 8883).*
Let the resident clairvoyant see into your future when she analyses your tea leaves at this quaint Bohemian set-up.

### Tibetan Teahouse

*2 Harrington Road, Seaforth, Simonstown, Southern Peninsula (021 786 1544).*
Serving up chai tea rather than Ceylon, this is a restful haven far from the madding crowd.

### Winchester Mansions Hotel

*221 Beach Road, Sea Point, Atlantic Seaboard (021 434 2351).*
For tea by the sea in a suitably colonial environment, you can't go wrong with this grand old dame situated right on the Sea Point Promenade.

**Birds.** See p103.

Birds

affordable prices, and has made a name for itself with an all-you-can-eat prawn night and a host of other budget-friendly options. Stick to the prawns and leave the more adventurous seafood dishes to classier establishments.

### Pigalle
*57A Somerset Road, Green Point (021 421 4848).* **Open** noon-3pm, 7pm-late Mon-Sat. **Menu** R100-R230 per head for 3 courses. **Credit** AmEx, DC, MC, V. **Map** p274 G2 ⑥③
The combination of live music in the form of a swing band, OTT decor and a menu that's crammed with fancy surf 'n' turf options makes for a glamorous and fun night out.

### Saul's Sushi @ Vegas
*118 Main Road, Sea Point (021 433 2287).* **Open** 11am-11pm daily. **Main courses** R40. **Credit** AmEx, DC, MC, V. **Map** p273 C3 ⑥④
Blink and you'll miss this tiny venue on slightly seedy Main Road. Japanese sushi chefs churn out all the regulars like maki rolls and nigiri, as well as more innovative South African combos. Try the biltong sushi or even the ostrich if you're feeling brave. Great prices and specials keep locals coming back for more.

### Tuscany Beach Café
*41 Victoria Road, Camps Bay (021 438 1213).* **Open** 7.30am-midnight daily. **Main courses** R80. **Credit** AmEx, DC, MC, V. **Map** p277 A8 ⑥⑤
This ever busy, buzzing bar is the ideal 'I'm on holiday' spot. Serving up trays of Daiquiris to sun-kissed beachgoers, they also have a large menu crammed with seafood in every guise. Prices match its glamorous position but it's a great choice for seafood-loving party people.

### Wakame
*1st Floor, corner Surrey Place & Beach Road, Mouille Point (021 433 2377/www.wakame.co.za).* **Open** noon-3pm, 6-10.30pm Mon-Thur; 12.30-3.30pm, 6-11pm Fri-Sun. **Main courses** R80. **Credit** AmEx, DC, MC, V.
Wooden floors and a jaw-dropping view take care of the picture perfect setting, while the excellent sushi and fusion seafood menu takes care of the rest. You'll quickly notice that this is a popular haunt for the Atlantic Seaboard fash-pack. **Photo** *p114.*

### Willoughby & Co
*Shop 6132, Victoria Wharf (021 418 6115).* **Open** noon-10.30pm daily. **Main courses** R70. **Credit** AmEx, DC, MC, V. **Map** p275 H1 ⑥⑥
It may be situated slap bang in one of Cape Town's largest malls, but the throngs who gather here for the superb sushi and generous portions of seafood and grills put paid to the thought that location is everything. Willoughby & Co is widely regarded as one of the better seafood restaurants south of the equator. Dig into overflowing pans of linefish with chunky potato wedges, or grab a chair at the sushi counter and watch the chefs weave their magic.

## Steakhouses

### Buz-bey Grill
*14 Three Anchor Bay House, Three Anchor Bay
Road, Three Anchor Bay (021 439 5900).* **Open**
6-11.30pm Tue-Sun. **Main courses** R70. **Credit**
AmEx, DC, MC, V. **Map** p274 F2 ⑰
This meaty institution has been here for what seems
like aeons. Expect monstrous hunks of meat straight
off the grill smothered with delicious sauces and
accompanied by perfectly prepared chips.

### Theo's
*163 Beach Road, Mouille Point (021 439 3494).*
**Open** noon-4pm, 6-11pm Mon-Fri, Sun; 6-11pm Sat.
**Main courses** R70. **Credit** AmEx, DC, MC, V.
If you're a meat eater then Theo's is a must-visit.
Giant steaks in every shape and form, enormous
burgers and an alphabet of grills ensure carnivores
are very well fed.

Other locations: Shop 2, The Promenade, Victoria
Road, Camps Bay (021 438 0410).

## Cafés & casual eating

### Caffe Neo
*South Seas Building, 129 Beach Road, Mouille Point
(021 433 0849).* **Open** 7am-7pm daily. **Main
courses** R40. **Credit** AmEx, DC, MC, V.
Michael Elias's bright and breezy deli-style café is
an appealing destination for a lazy weekend brunch
or lunch on the go. Make your selection from the
fresh salad and meze counter, and take some time to
enjoy it on the sunny deck outside. The baklava is
the best in town.

### Carlucci's
*29 Victoria Road, Bantry Bay (021 439 6476).*
**Open** 7.30am-8pm daily. **Main courses** R25.
**Credit** AmEx, DC, MC, V. **Map** p273 A4 ⑱

# Something fishy

You want your fish fresh from the sea, so the
best bet is to stay as close to the harbour
as possible – here are some of our spots
for a bit of fish shopping or for the freshest
fish on your plate.

### Cape Town
After a hard morning's shopping on Long
Street, nothing beats sitting out in the sun
at any one of the V&A Waterfront's buzzing
waterside eateries. **Quay 4** (Pierhead, Quay 4,
021 419 2008) is situated right down on
the water's edge, so diners can happily tuck
into their calamari and chips while watching
the boats go by. **Baia** (Shop 6262, 021
421 0935) is one of the most exclusive
restaurants at the Waterfront – a superb
view of the water and mountain make this
a memorable must-do.

### Hout Bay
Home to a busy yacht basin, fishing boats
and fish factories galore, this is as good
a place as any to sample seriously fresh
fish. **Snoekies** seafood restaurant (Harbour
Road, 021 790 1867) is a perennial
favourite and their fish and chips really
hits the spot. They're also famous for their
fresh fish and lobster sales. **Mariner's
Wharf**'s (*see p116*) open-air eaterie
is packed with gleeful day-trippers noshing
down fish and chips after a walk on the
beach. **Fish 4 Africa** (Grey's Marine, Hout
Bay Harbour, 021 791 4110) sells just-
caught cuts to the public.

### Kalk Bay
Kalk Bay is arguably the quaintest harbour in
the Cape, and happily there are four eateries
to choose from. Try **Kalky's** (021 788 1726)
for seriously good, no-frills fish and chips
(they also do fab pan-fried prawns and fresh
fish cuts for home cooking). Visit **Livebait**
(021 788 5755) for a more upmarket, but
no less tasty seafood experience – the fresh
blue and white interior will have you thinking
of faraway islands. **Polana** (*see p116*)
celebrates Mozambican-Portuguese food with
flair and the spicy seafood offerings are
perfect washed down with an ice-cold beer.
**Harbour House** (*see p116*) is the undoubted
glamour spot on the harbour – its enviable
view and excellent seafood make it a very
special dining experience.

### Simonstown
This naval harbour is a pleasant 40-minute
drive down the peninsula from the city
and is located in the heart of a charming
village. Breakfast at **Berthas** (1 Wharf Street,
Simonstown, 021 786 2138) on a wind-
free day is definitely worth the drive. The
**Quarterdeck** (Jubilee Square, Simonstown,
021 786 3825) offers elevated views of the
harbour – you may even see one of the navy's
new submarines emerging from the water.
**Just Sushi** (Quayside Centre, Simonstown
Waterfront, 021 786 4340) serves just
that – sushi and sashimi in delightfully
unpretentious surroundings.

**Eat, Drink, Shop**

**Lazari.** *See p105.*

Eat, Drink, Shop

Much loved by the Gucci-clad baby boomer set, Carlucci's fills the gap on a deli- and coffee shop-starved stretch of the city. Italian meals fill the fridges along with gourmet staples, while the coffee bar sends out cappuccinos at an alarming rate from early till late. **Photo** *p117*.

### Cedar Café
*The Courtyard, 100 Main Road, Sea Point (021 433 2546).* **Open** noon-late daily, Sun reservations only. **Main courses** R75. **Credit** MC, V. **Map** p273 C2 ⑥⑨

Affordable and authentic Levantine food is the order of the day at this no-frills café. It's family-run, and the owner/chef is usually on hand to talk you through the specials of the day. Be sure to order plenty of mezze to share, but remember to leave space for house specials like rosemary roasted lamb.

### Newport Deli
*47 Beach Road, Mouille Point (021 439 1538).* **Open** 7.30am-8pm daily. **Main courses** R30. **Credit** DC, MC, V.

This large deli and café is a popular stop for post-promenade coffees and light meals. Build your own salad or sandwich or choose from their menu of wholesome favourites. A good stop for gourmet goods and fresh produce too. **Photo** *p116*.

### Societi Bistro
*Shop 6155, V&A Waterfront (021 418 9483).* **Open** 9am-11pm daily. **Main courses** R75. **Credit** AmEx, DC, MC, V. **Map** p275 H1 ⑦⓪

A haven of comfortable sophistication in the busy Waterfront area of the city, Societi Bistro offers up tasty brekkies (the eggs Benedict are brilliant) and excellent French bistro fare. The friendly service is another bonus.

### Wafu
*1st floor, corner Beach Road & Surrey Place, Mouille Point (021 433 2377/www.wakame.co.za).* **Open** noon-10.30pm daily. **Main courses** R50. **Credit** AmEx, DC, MC, V.

If Wakame (*see p110*) is where the city's beautiful people settle down to eat, its upstairs cocktail and Asian tapas bar Wafu is where they take a seat to drink and nibble on exotic treats and meals to share. Undoubtedly one of the best sundowner spots near the city, it's not difficult to see why patrons are seduced: there's that view, a tropical minimalist interior and terrace and a menu of share-and-share-alike treats that range from mouthwatering wontons to stir-fries, satays and skewers.

## Southern Suburbs

### African

#### Cape Malay Restaurant
*The Cellars-Hohenhort, 93 Brommersvlei Road, Constantia (021 794 2137/www.collectionmcgrath.com).* **Open** 7-9.30pm Tue-Sat. **Set menu** R150. **Credit** AmEx, DC, MC, V.

If a taste of the Cape with a fancy twist is what you're after then look no further than this top-notch restaurant. Traditional Cape cuisine cooked with flair and served with aplomb (and superb wines) will ensure you return the next time you're in town.

## Asian

### Chai Yo
*65 Durban Road, Mowbray (021 689 6157).* **Open** noon-2.30pm, 6-10.30pm daily. **Main courses** R70. **Credit** AmEx, DC, MC, V.
A Victorian two-storey dwelling on Mowbray's high street plays host to this popular Thai restaurant that serves up consistently tasty, well-priced food. From spring rolls to satays and seriously good curries, this is a relatively cheap and cheerful good bet.

## French

### Pastis
*Shop 12, High Constantia Centre, Groot Constantia Road, Constantia (021 794 8334/www.pastis brasserie.co.za).* **Open** 8am-10pm daily. **Main courses** R70. **Credit** AmEx, DC, MC, V.
Bistro food hits Constantia in the form of this authentic venue. The bar area features a blazing fireplace in winter and is the ideal place for pre-dinner drinks, while the main restaurant is packed with couples and families enjoying everything from French Dip (a jus-drenched steak roll) to bouillabaisse.

## Gourmet

### Buitenverwachting
*Klein Constantia Road, Constantia (021 794 3522/ www.buitenverwachting.co.za).* **Open** Apr-Oct noon-3.30pm, 7-9.30pm Tue-Sat; Nov-Mar noon-3.30pm, 7-9.30pm Mon-Sat. **Main courses** R130. **Credit** AmEx, DC, MC, V.
This fine dining restaurant is situated in the historic Buitenverwachting wine estate and features a distinctive Euro-centric menu with global twists. Prices are steep but you're guaranteed a memorable meal.

### La Colombe
*Constantia Uitsig, Spaanschemat River Road, Constantia (021 794 2390/www.lacolombe.co.za).* **Open** 12.30-2.30pm, 7.30-9.30pm daily. **Main courses** R120. **Credit** AmEx, DC, MC, V.
If you're serious about food then La Colombe, situated on the picturesque Constantia Uitsig wine farm, is a must. Plates of beautifully presented, carefully conceptualised dishes put a smile on even the most critical of foodies' faces. The pan-fried duck liver with red wine-poached pear is superb, as is the crumbed karoo lamb with gorgonzola, grappa and pine nut sauce. Details such as outstanding service, seasonal-only produce and an in-house sommelier make this one of the top ten restaurants in the country. They also serve prix fixe winter menus starting at under R200.

### Constantia Uitsig
*Uitsig Farm, Spaanschemat River Road (M42), Constantia (021 794 4480/www.uitsig.co.za).* **Open** noon-2.30pm, 7.30-9.30pm daily. **Main courses** R115. **Credit** AmEx, DC, MC, V.
The fact that Constantia Uitsig is fully booked almost every day and night of the week should be enough to persuade gourmets to go. The style is Mediterranean with a few global twists. Try the tagliata on rocket and tomato *concasse* – heavenly.

## Mediterranean

### Diva Caffè Ristorante
*88 Lower Main Road, Observatory (021 448 0282).* **Open** 10am-11.30pm daily. **Main courses** R45. **Credit** AmEx, DC, MC, V.
This cheap and cheerful café is a slice of Italy in the heart of Observatory. Perfect for a relaxed romantic evening – its pizzas are divine and the salads are pretty tasty too. **Photo** *p119*.

### Greek
*78 Durban Road, Mowbray (021 686 4314).* **Open** 9am-late Mon-Sat; 9am-3pm Sun. **Main courses** R60. **Credit** DC, MC, V.
The authentic interior and menu will have you reminiscing about that holiday spent island hopping in Greece, and the menu is crammed with plenty of meze choices (perfect for sharing with the table). Crowd-pleasers include the slow-roasted, garlicky Greek lamb and superb moussaka.

**Eat, Drink, Shop**

Picture perfect: sumptuous views and seafood at **Wakame**. *See p110.*

## Magica Roma

*8 Central Square Shopping Centre, Pinelands (021 531 1489).* **Open** noon-2pm, 6-10pm Mon-Fri; 6-10pm Sat. **Main courses** R80. **Credit** AmEx, DC, MC, V.

This old-school hub of suburban life is the site of an incredibly consistent Italian eating experience. Hosts Ezio and Franco flit around the room greeting old faces and welcoming new ones. Whatever style of Italian you're in the mood for, be it pizza, pasta, meat or seafood, you're bound to walk away satisfied.

## South American

### Fat Cactus Café

*47 Durban Road, Mowbray (021 685 1920).* **Open** 11am-11pm daily. **Main courses** R50. **Credit** AmEx, DC, MC, V.

This Southern Suburbs spot is wildly popular with students and exuberant twentysomethings intent on eating and drinking their way through the night. Perennial favourites include the feta-stuffed and deep-fried jalapeño chilli peppers, while the tacos and enchiladas are stuffed with tasty ingredients.

## Steakhouses

### Barristers Grill Room & Café on Main

*Corner Kildare & Main Streets, Newlands (021 674 1792).* **Open** 9am-late daily. **Main courses** R75. **Credit** AmEx, DC, MC, V.

From its beginnings as a meat-only restaurant, Barristers has happily evolved into serving seafood. There's also a café and bar for lunch and light meals. The steaks and ribs are among the best in the city.

### The Famous Butcher's Grill

*7 Main Road, Newlands (021 674 7186).* **Open** 11am-10pm daily. **Main courses** R70. **Credit** AmEx, DC, MC, V.

At the Famous Butcher's Grill they take their meat very, very seriously. No steak that hits your plate will ever be aged for anything less than 21 days and they also serve grillroom favourites like baked mushrooms and spicy chicken livers to start (and fabulous onion rings too).

## Cafés & casual eating

### Capers

*Black River Park North, Link Road, Observatory (021 448 4038).* **Open** 8am-4pm Mon-Fri. **Main courses** R45. **Credit** MC, V.

This light and bright café-style restaurant sticks out in an otherwise ugly business park. It's a great spot for a casual meal or business lunch. Food is seasonally inspired – gourmet salads and pastas in summer, hearty fare in winter – and the prices are good.

### Queen of Tarts

*213 Lower Main Road, Observatory (021 448 2420/www.queenoftarts.co.za).* **Open** 8am-5pm Tue-Fri; 8am-1pm Sat, Sun. **Main courses** R35-R40. **Credit** AmEx, DC, MC, V.

# 360° dining

**Polana** (*see p116*) is a wonderfully exotic-looking Mozambican-Portuguese lounge bar and restaurant with views sweeping across False Bay – the perfect way to end a day exploring the coastline.

For an all-time high, have dinner at **Antique** restaurant (*see p101*) then make your way to the Hemisphere nightclub (021 421 0581) – at 31 floors above Riebeeck Street, views don't come much better than this in the Mother City.

You might have to fight the throngs of twentysomethings (on a Sunday anyway) but the sunset from **La Med** (Glen Country Club, Victoria Road, Clifton, Atlantic Seaboard, 021 438 5600) is worth the effort.

It doesn't get much cheesier than the **Top of the Ritz** (21st Floor, Ritz Hotel, Main Road, Sea Point, Atlantic Seaboard, 021 439 6010), Cape Town's only revolving restaurant situated on the top of the formerly glam Ritz Hotel in Sea Point. Though the food is nothing to write home about, the 360° views of the city make popping up here for a drink worthwhile.

A bastion of inspired seafood in Simonstown, the **Black Marlin**'s (*see p116*) outside terrace and lawns provide unspoilt sea vistas and the perfect perch for whale spotting in the late winter months.

At Blowfish (*see p120*) in Table View (table + view – get it?), the views of Table Mountain and the bay might make it difficult to focus on your food. Happily the menu has enough to tempt you to peel your eyes away.

Not only is **Contstantia Uitsig** (*see p113*) home to some of the best cuisine in the country, they also produce some of the finest wines around. An afternoon spent under the oaks drinking in the verdant estate surrounds will calm even the most stressed out soul.

**@ The Hills** (*see p118*), based at the ultra modern Durbanville Hills Winery, serves Cape Cuisine under the watchful gaze of Table Mountain in the blue yonder.

**Eat, Drink, Shop**

When asked to sum up her new-kid-on-the-block corner café, Tina Bester says it's 'gourmet home cooking'. This chic, comfortable wonderland churns out yummy tarts, cupcakes, omelettes, quiches and salads, all served in signature enamelware.

### The River Café
*Constantia Uitsig Farm, Spaanschemat River Road, Constantia (021 794 3010/www.uitsig.co.za).* **Open** 8.30am-5pm daily. **Main courses** R65. **Credit** AmEx, DC, MC, V.
The Spaanschemat's wholesome country-style fare with flair ensures a steady stream of regulars. Great breakfasts and tasty salads make up for the sometimes lacklustre service.

## Southern Peninsula

## African

### Cape Courtyard
*Kronendal Estate, Main Road, Hout Bay (021 790 5837).* **Open** 7-11pm Tue-Sat. **Main courses** R100. **Credit** AmEx, DC, MC, V.
Championing that quintessential South African meal, the *braai*, the Cape Courtyard is set in an historical building in Hout Bay. Though they serve an

à la carte Cape menu during the week, the family-friendly Sunday *braais* are what they're known for. With chunky *mielie* (corn)-studded bread with guacamole and potfuls of mussels to start, followed by lamb and spicy chicken for mains, this is as good a way as any to get a taste of local tradition.

## Seafood & sushi

### Black Marlin
*Main Road, Miller's Point, Simonstown (021 786 1621/www.blackmarlin.co.za).* **Open** noon-4pm Mon, Wed, Sun; noon-4pm, 6-9pm Tue, Thur-Sat. **Main courses** R75. **Credit** AmEx, DC, MC, V.
This popular seafood haunt goes all out to tempt tastebuds with an inspired, varied seafood and shellfish menu. A 40-minute drive from the city centre, it is a popular stop on the tourist trail in summer, and booking a table on the outside, sea-facing terrace is well worth the effort.

### Chapman's Restaurant
*Chapman's Peak Hotel, Chapman's Peak Drive, Hout Bay (021 790 1036).* **Open** noon-10pm Mon-Sat; noon-9pm Sun. **Main courses** R70. **Credit** AmEx, DC, MC, V.
Watch the breakers on Hout Bay beach from the comfort of the sun-splashed terrace at this Cape Town institution. Famous for their pans of calamari and perfectly crispy battered fish and chips, they also serve a number of delicious Portuguese specialities in a pan. One of the great weekend bets.

### Harbour House
*Kalk Bay Harbour (021 788 4133/www.harbourhouse.co.za).* **Open** noon-4pm, 6-10pm daily. **Main courses** R95. **Credit** AmEx, DC, MC, V.
This picturesque clapboard and glass restaurant has arguably the best uninterrupted view across False Bay. As befits its prime harbour position, seafood is king here and the sophisticated café menu offers everything from an excellent prawn, avocado and tomato tian to spicy chermoula calamari and succulent panfried linefish.

### Mariner's Wharf
*Harbour Road, Hout Bay Harbour (021 790 1100/www.marinerswharf.co.za).* **Open** 9am-9.30pm daily. **Main courses** R60. **Credit** AmEx, DC, MC, V.
The downstairs dockside restaurant offers no-frills fish and chips, while upstairs at the Wharfside Grill you'll see a brisk trade in platters of crayfish and seafood. Though the maritime theme might get you down, you're guaranteed fresh-from-the-sea fare.

### Polana
*Kalk Bay Harbour, off Main Road (021 788 7162/www.harbourhouse.co.za/polana).* **Open** 4pm-3am Mon-Fri (including bar hours); noon-3am Sat; 8am-3pm Sun. **Main courses** R90. **Credit** AmEx, DC, MC, V.
This Mozambican-Portuguese restaurant is a moody venue for romantic trysts involving spicy prawns, fiery chicken livers and pans of garlicky sardines.

**Newport Deli.** *See p112.*

Carlucci's, the one-stop gourmet shop for Bantry Bay's well-heeled locals. *See p111.*

An adjacent bar and laid-back lounge has huge windows that open to let in the sights and smells of the ocean. It's also a popular venue for Sunday night Afro-jazz events.

## South American

### Cape to Cuba

*Main Road, Kalk Bay (021 788 1566/www. capetocuba.com).* **Open** noon-10.30pm Mon-Sat; 10am-10.30pm Sun. **Main courses** R65. **Credit** AmEx, DC, MC, V.
Situated as close to the water as you can get, this colourful space is a reflection of the owners' love of all things Cuban. Ornate furniture (all for sale) sets the faded Havana tone, while the spiced menu is peppered with tasty seafood (try the sardines) and meaty eats (the chocolate and sundried tomato-smothered strips of beef are fabulous). **Photo** *p120.*

## Cafés & casual eating

### Bertha's

*1 Wharf Street, Simonstown (021 786 2138).* **Open** 7am-11pm daily. **Main courses** R65. **Credit** AmEx, DC, MC, V.

Take a table on the outside deck and drink in the sights and sounds of the tranquil harbour setting. A Cape-inspired menu with some interesting seafood variations provides plenty to stave off hunger.

### Café des Artes

*20 Main Road, St James (021 788 5270).* **Open** 8am-3pm Tue; 8am-late Wed-Sat; 8am-4pm Sun. **Main courses** R40-R90. **Credit** AmEx, DC, MC, V.
This sliver of a restaurant does a steady trade in fresh and light breakfasts seven days a week, while Wednesday to Saturday evenings see it take on a more intimate candle-lit persona. The chalkboard menu changes daily but always features fresher-than-fresh linefish, inspired salads and one or two interesting pastas. There's a tiny but very well priced wine list. The restaurant shares a space with a wonderful ceramics gallery featuring work by some of the city's most talented artists.

### La Cuccina Food Store

*Shop 10, Victoria Mall, corner Victoria & Empire Roads, Hout Bay (021 790 8008/021 790 0808).* **Open** 8am-5pm daily. **Credit** AmEx, DC, MC, V.
This open, light-filled space bustles with hungry Hout Bay locals from morning till night. From breakfast to their inspired and wholesome buffet lunches (from South African favourites to Asian-

inspired curries and casseroles), this is a sight for tired eyes and tastebuds. There's also a great catering list for parties and some fabulous French pastries and tarts.

### Empire Café
*11 York Road, Muizenberg (021 788 1250).* **Open** 7am-4pm Mon-Wed, Sun; 7am-4pm, 6-8pm Thur-Sat. **Main courses** R55. **Credit** AmEx, DC, MC, V.
A picture-perfect position in sight of the breakers at Muizenberg's legendary Surfer's Corner ensures you'll be relaxed in no time. The menu here features everything from breakfast staples to more wholesome and sophisticated lunchtime choices, including pastas or lamb rump on wilted spinach. Service is as laid-back as it gets.

### Flukes
*Southern Right Hotel, 12-14 Glen Road, Glencairn (021 782 0314/www.southernright.info).* **Open** 8am-10pm daily. **Main courses** R65. **Credit** AmEx, DC, MC, V.
The outdoor terrace at the Southern Right Hotel in Glencairn plays host to the ever popular Flukes restaurant. Fancy pub grub with a strong seafood slant is the order of the day, and the consistency in flavour and price (along with a killer ocean view) make it easy to see why it's a perennially popular lazy lunch bet.

### Fogeys Railway House
*177 Main Road (above the old railway station), Muizenberg (021 788 3252/www.railwayrestaurant. co.za).* **Open** noon-10pm Tue-Sat; 10am-4pm Sun (live music 6pm-late). **Main courses** R85. **Credit** AmEx, DC, MC, V.
This jazz, live music and tango (on Thursdays) venue, based in the old Railway House on Muizenberg Station, has a menu that matches the glamour of times gone by. An extensive choice of mains spans all appetites with diners able to choose from the bistro (sardines, linefish and a very tasty seafood curry) or speciality menu that features three-course choices of European-style cuisine. Great for Sunday buffets overlooking the ocean.

### The Meeting Place
*98 St George's Street, Simonstown (021 786 1986).* **Open** 9am-4pm Mon; 9am-9pm Wed-Sat; 9am-5pm Sun. **Main courses** R40. **Credit** AmEx, DC, MC, V.
A bustling and sometimes chaotic café stop based in a picturesque seaside village, the Meeting Place looks out across the docks and to the sea. Fresh breads and pastries abound as do shelves of pretty packaged gourmet goods while the menu is crammed with something for every type of hunger. Great vegetarian salad choices, huge burgers and famous eggs Florentine keep regulars coming back.

### The Olive Station
*165 Main Road (off the parking lot across from Blue Bottle Liquors), Muizenberg (021 788 3264).* **Open** 8am-5pm Mon-Wed; 8am-9pm Thur-Sat; 9am-5pm Sun. **Main courses** R50. **Credit** AmEx, DC, MC, V.

Specialising in flavoursome Lebanese fare, the Olive Station is the ideal foodie pick-me-up. The menu offers plenty of flavour sensations – from home-made meze to slow-cooked lamb and a great selection of vegetarian treats. As good for a cup of tea with a pastry as a lazy, wine-fuelled lunch. **Photo** *p95.*

### Olympia Café & Deli
*134 Main Road, Kalk Bay (021 788 6396).* **Open** 7am-9pm daily. **Main courses** R70. **Credit** AmEx, DC, MC, V.
A favourite haunt of gourmets, artists and poets, Olympia is well deserving of its café crown. Authentically grubby with an utterly laid-back charm (and no reservations system), the food here is absolutely superb. Breakfasts include the usual suspects as well as a smattering of specials (spicy kidneys on toast) while the daily lunch and dinner menus always feature one or two fish options (if tuna is on, it's a must), hearty meat choices with tasty sauces and accompaniments, and always a pasta or two. Weekends are crazy, so if you're in the mood for a lazy lunch go there midweek.

## Northern Suburbs

## African

### @ The Hills
*Durbanville Hills Winery, Tygerberg Valley Road, M13, Durbanville (021 558 1300/www.durbanville hills.co.za).* **Open** noon-3pm Tue-Thur, Sun; noon-3pm, 6-9pm Fri, Sat. **Main courses** R65. **Credit** AmEx, DC, MC, V.
This beautifully designed winery affords incredible views of the farmlands and Table Mountain and its restaurant serves wholesome Cape fare. Designed to complement the winery's superb wines, expect locally inspired choices like smoked *kudu* salad, Malay chicken curry and delicious ostrich steak.

## Contemporary

### Meerendal
*Vissershoek Road, Durbanville (021 979 1958/ www.meerendal.co.za).* **Credit** AmEx, DC, MC, V.
A host of dining choices awaits at Meerendal Wine Estate. **Wheatfields** (021 975 1655, open noon-3pm, 6-11pm Tue-Sat, main courses R80) is the intimate fine dining restaurant ably manned by celeb chef David Higgs, while the **Bistro & Deli** (021 975 1655, open 8am-5pm, 6-10pm Mon, Sun, 6-10pm Tue-Sat, main courses R40) offers more laid-back choices with a Euro twist (from classic Caesar salad to cabernet-braised lamb shanks). The **Sunday Cape** table is a delightful buffet-style experience (021 975 1655, open Sun lunch, main courses R120).

### De Oude Welgemoed
*Pandoer Street, Welgemoed (021 913 4962/www. deoude.co.za).* **Open** noon-5pm, 7pm-late Mon-Sat. **Main courses** R85. **Credit** AmEx, DC, MC, V.

Mamma mia in the Mother City: pizza, pizza and more pizza at **Diva**. *See p113.*

Even the furniture's for sale at **Cape to Cuba**. *See p117.*

This handsome restaurant, in a 300-year-old manor, sets the scene for a sophisticated Cape menu. Expect a plethora of game dishes with subtle fruit and spice sauces, plus a good selection of seafood and pastas.

### Poplars

*D'Aria, Racecourse Road, M13, Durbanville (021 975 5736/www.daria.co.za)*. **Open** 7-10pm Mon-Sat; 9-10.30am, noon-3.30pm Sun. **Main courses** R75. **Credit** AmEx, DC, MC, V.

Poplars serves up a worldly lunch and dinner menu featuring dishes such as hearty lamb shank on mash or blueberry sauce-drenched venison steak.

## Seafood & sushi

### Blowfish

*Dolphin Beach, 1 Marine Drive, Bloubergstrand (021 556 5464)*. **Open** noon-10.30pm Mon-Fri; 7-10pm Sat, Sun. **Main courses** R85. **Credit** AmEx, DC, MC, V.

Superbly positioned on the sea, Blowfish is a trendy, popular spot for seafood lovers. From sushi to shellfish, and a plethora of Asian-inspired wok fries and noodle dishes, this is as good as it gets. An interactive experience awaits for fish lovers who can pick their cut and decide how they'd like it prepared.

### Blue Peter

*Blue Peter Hotel, 1 Popham Road, Bloubergstrand (021 554 1956/www.bluepeter.co.za)*. **Open** 7-10am, noon-3pm, 7-10pm Mon Sat; 7-10am, noon-3pm, 7-9pm Sun. **Main courses** R80. **Credit** AmEx, DC, MC, V.

The upstairs restaurant at this landmark can be forgiven for its rather staid interior when you see the stupendous ocean view. Specialising in Cape cuisine and seafood, they also offer a curry buffet on Wednesdays and traditional Sunday lunches. The downstairs bistro is your best bet and plays host to pizza- and seafood-eating barefoot locals. A perennially popular weekend sundowner spot.

# Pubs & Bars

Drink yourself under the Table Mountain.

Drink in the awesome views from the comfort of **Relish**. *See p124*.

For over 300 years Cape Town has been known as the tavern of the seas, and as you would expect from a city with a port heritage, you will not have to stumble far to find a watering hole.

There is a bewildering array of venues, and where you are in the city normally dictates the kind of bars you'll find. In a nutshell, if you fancy a swish, overpriced cocktail with a view, head for the Atlantic Seaboard. If you're after an old-fashioned pint, then the leafy Southern Suburbs is your playing ground. For something more earthy, slide into the city centre. Fancy an arty party with hordes of students? Then hit Long Street.

Many of the most engaging bars are hidden away in the most intriguing haunts, from the back of boutique hotels to old churches. As always the fun is in the finding; locals here are

pretty friendly and if you are lucky they might let you in on some secrets and introduce you to the Jaegerbomb, Cape Town's most dangerous cocktail. Just make sure you take a taxi home afterwards (*see p246* **Getting Around**); walking drunk can be hazardous.

## City Bowl

### Asoka Son of Dharma

*68 Kloof Street (021 422 0909/www.asokasonof dharma.com).* **Open** 5pm-late daily. **Credit** AmEx, DC, MC, V. **Map** p274 F5 ❶

This Eastern-themed lounge with its serious mystical leanings attracts a thirtysomething urban crowd. The Eastern motif is a tad overdone but it does have a real tree in the middle of the bar and overall it is a very elegant space to chill.

Camps Bay

## Café Vespa

*108 Kloof Street (021 426 5042/www.cafevespa. com).* **Open** noon-midnight Mon-Thur; 11am-midnight Fri, Sat. **Credit** AmEx, DC, MC, V. **Map** p274 F5 ❷

Sitting in this cheeky little café you can pretend you're in Milan. Drink fine coffee, gesticulate at the locals and even hire a moped – not after you've had a few, though.

## Carlyles on Derry

*7 Derry Street (021 461 8787).* **Open** 4.30pm-late Tue-Sun. **Credit** MC, V.

City dwellers and media types like to unwind in this quaint but functional spot. The place serves up great pizzas too.

## Caveau Wine Bar & Deli

*92 Bree Street (021 422 1367).* **Open** 7am-10.30pm Mon-Sat. **Main courses** R80. **Credit** AmEx, DC, MC, V. **Map** p274 G3 ❸

This city joint is full from morning till night, and with good reason. Essentially a wine bar (a very good one), wine buffs who love food are in good hands too. The menu seems to favour carnivores and features excellent game dishes. If you're not so hungry, choose from the tapas menu. **Photo** *p123.*

## Fireman's Arms

*25 Mechau Street, Corner of Lower Buitengracht Street (021 419 1513).* **Open** noon-2am Mon-Sat. **Credit** AmEx, DC, MC, V. **Map** p275 H3 ❹

This wonderfully old-fashioned pub is named after the fire-fighters who used to drink here. It has been around for 140 years and doesn't look like it has

changed much in the interim. Great for a pint and always packed out for big sporting events. Don't forget to pat the pub's enormous cat, appropriately called Piss Cat.

## Gallery Café

*172 Long Street (021 426 6119/www.urbanchic. co.za).* **Open** 9am-2am daily. **Credit** AmEx, DC, MC, V. **Map** p274 G4 ❺

The latest addition to Long Street is a cut above the clutter that surrounds it. Swish, swanky and sexy, this intimate cigar bar has become the venue of choice for the Johnnie Walker Black Label crowd. Great menu, great service and a really great terrace overlooking Long Street.

## Jo'burg

*218 Long Street (021 422 0142).* **Open** 5pm-4am Mon-Fri; 2pm-4am Sat; 7pm-late Sun. **Credit** AmEx, DC, MC, V. **Map** p274 G4 ❻

The bar that started the phenomenon that is Long Street is still going strong. A motley crew of art terrorists, car guards, backpackers, students and assorted creatures of the night lurk here till the early hours of the morning. No fake, franchised decor here, just a slightly risqué feel, lately appearing to verge on the somewhat dodgy. But some will say that's just how a real bar should feel.

## Kennedy's & The Dubliner

*251 Long Street (021 424 1212/www.kennedys. co.za).* **Open** 10.30am-3am Mon-Sat. **Credit** AmEx, DC, MC, V. **Map** p274 G4 ❼

This upmarket, beautiful jazz venue now shares an address, rather uncomfortably, with an Irish theme

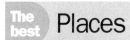

Caveau Wine Bar & Deli. See p122.

pub. The jazz is upstairs and the Irish folk band is downstairs, but no matter how you tart it up, an Irish theme bar is still an Irish theme bar.

### Marvel
*236 Long Street (021 426 5880)*. **Open** 8pm-4am daily. **Credit** DC, MC, V. **Map** p274 G4 ⑧
Marvel is a little underground, a little dark and a little dingy, but that does not stop it being packed out nightly with the mostly street-smart urban crowd who call it home. It can get very hot and uncomfortable, but for those in the know it is as cool as it comes.

### Miam
*196 Long Street (021 422 5823)*. **Open** 9am-10pm Mon-Fri. **Credit** AmEx, DC, MC, V. **Map** p274 G4 ⑨
Newly revamped into a restaurant/bar, Café Miam has a distinctly cutting-edge, loungey feel. Grab a plate of something extravagant to nibble on while you sip the night away. DJs spin funky tunes on Friday nights.

### Nose Restaurant & Wine Bar
*Cape Quarter, Dixon Street (021 425 2200/www. thenose.co.za)*. **Open** 9am-late daily. **Credit** AmEx, DC, MC, V. **Map** p274 G3 ⑩
Cape Town's friendliest wine bar. No airs and graces here, just fine quality plonk available by the pretty huge glass. Educational and entertaining, the venue has a nutty old aunt feel where the proprietor has no qualms about offering her two cents' worth (*see p127* **My kind of town**). But don't let the frivolity fool you: the Nose has one of the best wine lists in the city and some seriously tasty snack platters.

### Rafiki's
*13B Kloof Nek Road (021 426 4731)*. **Open** noon-2am daily. **Credit** AmEx, DC, MC, V. **Map** p274 F5 ⑪
This supremely chilled beach bar has the longest wraparound balcony in the city. On any given night it is packed with students and backpackers who are just, well, chilling. Rafiki means 'friend' in Swahili and it's a pretty fitting title for this popular place.

## The best Places

### For killer cocktails
**Alba Lounge** (*see p125*); **Cubana** (*see p126*); **Relish** (*see p124*).

### For a pint
**Fireman's Arms** (*see p122*); **Mitchell's Scottish Ale House** (*see p125*); **Paulaner Brauhaus** (*see p126*); **Peddlars on the Bend** (*see p126*).

### For sundowners
**Baraza** (*see p125*); **Lower Deck at Blue Peter** (*see p127*); **Sand Bar** (*see p126*).

### For wines by the glass
**Caveau Wine Bar & Deli** (*see p122*); **Nose Restaurant & Wine Bar** (*see p123*).

Alba Lounge. *See p125.*

## Relish

*70 New Church Street (021 422 3584).* **Open** noon-
late Mon-Fri; 5pm-late Sat, Sun. **Credit** AmEx, DC,
MC, V. **Map** p274 F4 ⑫
The urban factory-style decor here can be pretty off-
putting. But once you've had a few of their happy
hour cocktails and climbed the bare concrete stairs
to the top you'll see why it's packed – the views of
Table Mountain are awesome. **Photo** *p121.*

## The Shack

*25B De Villiers Street (021 461 5892).* **Open** 1pm-
4am Mon-Fri; 4am-4am Sat; 6pm-4am Sun. **Credit**
DC, MC, V. **Map** p275 H5 ⑬
This easygoing pool bar can become pretty lively
as night heads towards morning. The place seems
to attract more than its fair share of students and
late-night revellers who like a bit of drunken

debauchery. The multi-roomed nature of the place
gives it an exciting labyrinthine feel.

## Tank

*Shop B15, Cape Quarter, 72 Waterkant Street
(021 419 0007/www.the-tank.co.za).* **Open** noon-
3pm, 6pm-late daily. **Credit** AmEx, DC, MC, V.
**Map** p274 G3 ⑭
You should really know what you are in for when
there is a bar attached to a sushi bar replete with
huge exotic fish tank. It's all sooo coolly ironic and
sumptuously understated. But once the delicious
deep house DJs come on deck, you quickly forget the
pretences and slide into a cool, comfortable state
of mind. Situated in the wonderful Cape Quarter,
Tank has become the closest thing Cape Town has
to a New York 'in' spot. The excellent restaurant (*see
p100*) is just a jump to the left.

### Waiting Room
*273 Long Street, above Royale (021 422 4536).*
**Open** 6pm-late Mon-Sat. **Credit** AmEx, DC, MC, V.
**Map** p274 G4 ⑮
It was inevitable that Cape Town's trendiest
burger joint, Royale, would have to expand again.
Cape Town's hip and happening new media crowd
just don't like to hang in the street (still big up for
the Royale no reservation policy), so now they can
wait upstairs in the funky, comfortable Waiting
Room with an array of wonderful sofas to squeeze
into, electro beats and ad hoc live performers.

## Atlantic Seaboard

### Alba Lounge
*1st Floor, Pierhead Building, V&A Waterfront
(021 425 3385/www.albalounge.co.za).* **Open**
5pm-2am daily. **Credit** AmEx, DC, MC, V.
**Map** p275 H1 ⑯
This slick, stylish Waterfront spot has developed a
major following among the after-work, pre-party
brigade. Appealing more to the style-aware than the
style-conscious, its classy couches, subtle decor and
restrained vibe give off a kind of arrogant under-
statement. No need to flaunt it when you know you
don't need to any more. Chilled, live music every
Sunday and great views. **Photo** *p124.*

### Baraza
*The Promenade, Victoria Road, Camps Bay (021
438 2040).* **Open** 5pm-2am daily. **Credit** AmEx,
DC, MC, V. **Map** p277 B8 ⑰
Sit back, shake the sand from your shoes, settle into
the couch and feel the sea breeze caress your face.
Let one of the serving nymphs bring an exotic con-
coction while you gaze across the ocean. This
bar is indeed the picture postcard cliché of a cocktail bar and it is all the better for it. On hot, balmy
evenings the DJ kicks in, adding a little touch of Ibiza
to the mix.

### Buena Vista Social Café
*First floor Exhibition Building, 81 Main Road,
Green Point (021 433 0611/www.buenavista.co.za).*
**Open** noon-2am daily. **Credit** AmEx, DC, MC, V.
**Map** p274 F2 ⑱
This Cuban-themed bar was one of the first in town
and has a definite air of authenticity about it, with
a great cigar and food menu and an original old-
school Latino soundtrack. It can become crowded so
claustrophobics should give it a miss.

### Café Caprice
*37 Victoria Road, Camps Bay (021 438 8315).*
**Open** 9am-2am daily. **Credit** AmEx, DC, MC, V.
**Map** p277 B8 ⑲
Models, trust fund brats and Eurotrash all jostle for
attention at this trendy sundowner bar on the Camps
Bay strip. The setting is simply stunning and the
service is pretty slick, but the main reason anyone
goes to Caprice is to be seen. At the height of summer the bar spills out on to the street.

# Queen of shebeens

The township hangout of Mzoli's is
certainly unique. It started as a butchery
and still is, but here you pick your meat
and the staff *braai* on the spot and then
bring it to your table. The place is a
magical melting pot, and on any given
night you are just as likely to bump into a
young captain of industry, a *kwaito* star or
sporting hero. Add ad hoc deep house DJs
and spontaneous dancing and you have
one jumpin' spot. There are some other
fantastic watering holes in the townships
and it is something that should be
experienced by any visitor, although sadly
it is still not safe to go gallivanting off by
yourself. Have a local take you or join one
of the many evening township tours.
Coffeebeans (www.coffeebeans.co.za) and
Thuthuka Café (082 979 5831/021 638
7766) both offer tours.

### Mzoli's
*Shop 3, corner NY115 & NY108,
Gugulethu (021 638 1355).* **Open**
9am-6pm daily. **No credit cards.**

### Ice Lounge
*North Wharf, V&A Waterfront (072 919 0358/
www.icelounge.co.za).* **Open** 5pm-late daily. **Credit**
AmEx, DC, MC, V. **Map** p275 H1 ⑳
Ice has hit Africa in a big way. Don a poncho and
sip a chilly cocktail in this new spot, which turns
into a bar after 5pm. It's only here for four months
of the year (Nov-Feb). **Photo** *p126.*

### La Med
*Glen Country Club, Victoria Road, Clifton (021 438
5600/www.lamed.co.za).* **Open** 3pm-1am Mon-Fri;
noon-late Sat, Sun. **Credit** AmEx, DC, MC, V.
**Map** p277 A7 ㉑
La Med has been a Cape Town institution for years
and claims that this is 'where the world meets
Cape Town'. It is certainly true that almost every
Capetonian has been here at some time. No need to
dress up as board shorts and bikinis abound, and
punters settle down to watch the sunset over the
rim of a fruity fantasy. As night falls and the drink
kicks in it can get pretty wild. Sundays especially
are a madhouse.

### Mitchell's Scottish Ale House
*East Pier Road, V&A Waterfront (021 419 5074).*
**Open** 11am-2am daily. **Credit** AmEx, DC, MC, V.
**Map** p275 H1 ㉒

**Eat, Drink, Shop**

Sadly they don't even sell any Scottish beer on tap here any more, but they do still offer a handful of good, traditional ales and it is one of the only places in town where you can get a decent pint of Guinness. The Ale House itself has a great atmosphere with a wooden bar and an upstairs attic.

### Paulaner Brauhaus

*Shop 18/19, Clocktower Square, V&A Waterfront (021 418 9999/www.paulaner.co.za).* **Open** 11am-1am daily. **Credit** AmEx, DC, MC, V. **Map** p275 H1 ㉒
Beer, bratwurst and buxom serving wenches. This little bit of Bavaria in the heart of Cape Town has warmed the soul of many a local. The reasonably priced beer, which is brewed on the premises, is the best in Cape Town, bar none. Only the very brave should try the Salvatore brew. Line your tummy with hearty meat offerings such as *eisbein*.

### Sand Bar

*31 Victoria Road, Camps Bay (021 438 8336).* **Open** 9.30am-late daily. **Credit** AmEx, DC, MC, V. **Map** p277 A8 ㉓
This great little pavement bar has all the charm, plus the same great views, but none of the pretension or exorbitant prices of some of its trendy neighbours. The strawberry Daiquiris are definitely worth stopping off for, as are the cheesy nachos.

### Zep Tepi

*2nd floor, The Promenade, Victoria Road, Camps Bay (021 438 0055).* **Open** 9pm-2am Wed-Sun. **Credit** MC, V. **Map** p277 A8 ㉔

Chill out at the **Ice Lounge**. *See p125.*

Camps Bay's restaurant and cocktail bar strip has been given a serious injection of sex appeal in the form of Zen Tepi. A sun-kissed crowd of gorgeous guys and gals (no surprise really, considering half of the space is occupied by a model agency by day) make the most of its perfect position in the heart of the beachside action. Daytime trade sees smoothies, salads and wraps being enjoyed in the plush comfort of this beautifully designed interior, but come sundown, the slew of wicked cocktails and the sounds of guest DJs bring people back for more.

## Southern Suburbs

### Cubana

*3 Aska House, Main Road, Newlands (021 683 4040/www.cubana.co.za).* **Open** 8am-2am daily. **Credit** AmEx, DC, MC, V.
This stylish bar is always full of nubile young things, and due to the proximity to Newlands you are always likely to happen upon a drunken Springbok or two.

### Foresters Arms

*52 Newlands Avenue, Newlands (021 689 5949).* **Open** 11am-11pm daily; 11am-midnight Fri; 10am-11pm Sat; 10am-6pm Sun. **Credit** AmEx, DC, MC, V.
This olde English village pub is situated in the most English of Cape Town's suburbs, Newlands. Its wood panelling interior and leafy beer garden make it the perfect spot to relax with a pint in the sun.

### Oblivion Wine Bar & Restaurant

*22 Chichester Road, Harfield Village (021 761 8522/www.oblivion.co.za).* **Open** 11am-2am daily. **Credit** AmEx, DC, MC, V.
This funky little suburban wine bar is a favourite haunt of the after-work commuter crowd. It starts off slow and sophisticated, but by closing time it can get pretty lively. Tables have been known to be danced upon.

### Peddlars on the Bend

*3 Spaanschemat River Road, Constantia (021 794 7747).* **Open** 11am-11pm daily. **Credit** AmEx, DC, MC, V.
Peddlars on the Bend is the venue of choice for the mink-and-manure brigade – very Home Counties, very English, very refined. In the evening the older after-work pint crowd quickly makes way for the rich young things.

### Touch of Madness

*12 Nuttal Road, Observatory (021 448 2266/www.cafeatom.co.za).* **Open** noon-late Mon-Sat; 7pm-late Sun. **Credit** AmEx, DC, MC, V.
Lewis Carroll would feel right at home in this Victorian converted house. They have kept the original house's structure so that each room has its own unique charm. It's a bustling little bar with an open-plan café area and, best of all, an exquisite sitting room complete with sofas, antiques and original knick-knacks.

# My kind of town Cathy Marston

Cathy, along with husband Kevin, trekked across the equator to establish the popular Nose Restaurant & Wine Bar (*see p123*) in the heart of Green Point. They only sell wines that they enjoy drinking themselves, and this approach has brought them rave reviews from wine connoisseurs and quaffers alike.

**Cape Town makes me...** happy to be living here and not in the cold, wet flatness of East Anglia.

**I treat myself at...** Cape Town Fish Market (King's Warehouse, V&A Waterfront, City Bowl, 021 418 5977, www.ctfm.co.za).

**I dine at...** 96 Winery Road, Somerset West (Zandberg Farm, Winery Road, off the R44, 021 842 2020).

**I get takeaways from...** Tom Yum (72 Regent Road, Sea Point, Atlantic Seaboard, 021 434 8139). The crispy duck is great.

**I drink sundowners at...** Harvey's at Winchester Mansions (221 Beach Road, Sea Point, Atlantic Seaboard, 021 434 2351; *see p183*).

**I wake up to...** the sound of the fire station opposite testing their sirens.

**I go to sleep in...** next to no time at all.

**I love...** *Fawlty Towers*, *Blackadder* and *Men Behaving Badly* DVDs.

**I buy presents at...** Exclusive Books (011 803 3773, www.exclusivebooks.com).

**I have fun at...** my friends' houses.

**I hide from the world at...** Atlantic Express (1B Regent Road, Sea Point, Atlantic Seaboard, 021 439 3038). Breakfast with dark glasses, no make-up and the Sunday papers makes for pure indulgence.

## Southern Peninsula

### Brass Bell
*Kalk Bay Station, Main Road, Kalk Bay (021 788 5456).* **Open** 11am-11pm daily. **Credit** AmEx, DC, MC, V.
On stormy days the waves wash right up on to the outside terrace at this convivial, old-school seafront tavern. Locals have been drinking here ever since they left Noah and tourists flock here in summer. If the sun becomes too much you can cool off in the tidal pool next door.

### Polana
*Kalk Bay Harbour, Main Road, Kalk Bay (021 788 7162).* **Open** 4pm-3am Mon-Fri; noon-3pm Sat; 8pm-3am Sat. **Credit** AmEx, DC, MC, V.
This bar/restaurant boasts one of the best views around – you're literally on the rocks. Bag a leather couch, nurse a bottle of chilled white and watch the sea do its thing for an entire afternoon. And if you're hungry, dig into tasty snack platters or garlicky Portuguese fare.

### Skebanga's Beach
*Upstairs, Corner of Beach & Pine Roads, Noordhoek (021 789 1783).* **Open** 11am-midnight daily. **Credit** AmEx, DC, MC, V.
They named the pub after a dog that used to be a local, so it's salt of the earth stuff here, friendly and full of character. A must-stop sundowner spot on the Chapman's Peak Drive (*see p86*).

## Northern Suburbs

### Cubana
*92 Edward Street, Durbanville (021 910 4963/ www.cubana.co.za).* **Open** 8am-2am daily. **Credit** AmEx, DC, MC, V.
Edward Street is the epicentre of entertainment in the Northern Suburbs, with bars, clubs and restaurants all competing for the young professionals who congregate here. With its classy ambience and delectable cocktails, this is probably the best jumping off point to go bonkers in Durbanville. They've opened a huge new branch at 9 Somerset Road, Green Point (021 421 1109) – suitably comfy and inviting.

### Forum Grand Café
*82 Edward Street, Bellville (021 910 4458/www. theforumgrandcafe.co.za).* **Open** 4pm-2am Mon-Sat. **Credit** AmEx, DC, MC, V.
Belgians make great beer and this place probably sells a greater array than anywhere outside Flanders – 350 to be exact. When it's bustling, it has the buzzing bonhomie of a good, old-fashioned beer hall.

### Lower Deck at Blue Peter
*1 Popham Road, Bloubergstrand (021 554 1956/ www.bluepeter.co.za).* **Open** 10am-11pm daily. **Credit** AmEx, DC, MC, V.
This unassuming hotel bar offers only one thing – the view. But what a view it is. To sit on the lawn gazing at majestic Table Mountain towering over the shimmering bay, you'll think you are in heaven.

Eat, Drink, Shop

# The Sparkling Tour

A WORLD CLASS JEWELLERY EXPERIENCE

DIAMOND CUTTING TOUR
JEWELLERY MANUFACTURING
TANZANITE BOUTIQUE
WINNING DESIGNS
WALL OF FAME
INTERNET CAFE

**THE DIAMOND WORKS**

Southern Africa Tourism
Services Association

7 Coen Steytler Ave, Foreshore, Cape Town
Tel:  27 21 425 1970  Web:  www.thediamondworks.co.za
Email:  info@thediamondworks.co.za

Hours:  Mon-Sun 09h00-17h00
Extended hours on request

# Shops & Services

Serious retail therapy – from mega malls to tribal crafts.

Shopping central: **Victoria Wharf**. *See p130.*

Part of the joy of visiting any big city is discovering that special something that just has to come home with you. In Cape Town you really are spoilt for choice – from superior wines to cutting-edge local fashions, excellent crafts and a slew of artworks by young, upcoming talents. It's almost impossible not to be seduced at every turn.

If you're short of time, hitting the malls is your best bet. Whether you choose to shop at bigger set-ups like Canal Walk and the Waterfront or smaller designer sites like Portside on Green Point Main Road or Willowbridge in Durbanville, you're bound

to enjoy the host of international labels on offer, as well as some of the bigger names on the South African fashion and lifestyle scene.

Of course, if you have a little more time, you'll do well to leave the mayhem of the mall behind and take to the streets, where small and sometimes unassuming shopfronts belie a world of bargains and discoveries. Long Street and Cape Town's answer to the King's Road, Kloof Street, remain the main offbeat shopping arteries of the city, with plenty of caffeine stops dotted along the way for regular refuelling – a pilgrimage along this route is a must and you are bound to be energised by the eye candy that presents itself on almost every block.

Further away from the city, the more suburban addresses of Claremont and Newlands are equally enticing, offering up quality boutiques, luxury home stores and a sophisticated mall too. Travel further down the line and along the coast and you'll eventually hit Kalk Bay, where the hordes descend at weekends – scrounge around here and you too will leave with that telltale 'I found what I was looking for' smile on your face.

If bargain hunting is up your alley, buy the annual *A-Z of Factory Shops* guide by Pam Black – it lists every kind of factory outlet your heart can desire.

## Malls

### Canal Walk
*Century Boulevard, Century City, Milnerton, Northern Suburbs (021 555 4444/www.canal walk.co.za).* **Open** 9am-9pm daily. **Credit** AmEx, DC, MC, V.
This mock Italianite mall is arguably the largest in Cape Town and filled to the brim with shopping, eating and entertainment options for the whole family. All the major retail chains have stores here, as do the major players in the SA fashion game.

### Cavendish Square
*Dreyer Street, Claremont, Southern Suburbs (021 657 5600/www.cavendish.co.za).* **Open** 9am-6pm Mon-Thur, Sat; 9am-9pm Fri; 10am-4pm Sun. **Credit** AmEx, DC, MC, V.
Where the city's monied suburban set hang out, this popular mall is a stylish option for a fashion-fuelled shopping day. Glossy boutiques cater for fashion-savvy guys and gals and there are plenty of coffee shops and a clutch of quality restaurants for refuelling along the way.

Dressing up the suburbs: the designer-led **Willowbridge Lifestyle Centre**.

### Gardens Centre

*Mill Street, City Bowl (021 465 1842).* **Open** 9am-6pm Mon-Fri; 9am-3pm Sat. **Credit** AmEx, DC, MC, V. **Map** p274 G5.

With plenty of parking available, this city shopping centre is a convenient one-stop for urban dwellers. Whether you need a quick haircut, some milk and bread, a gift for a friend or an outfit for the evening, it's all available here.

### Portside

*1 Upper Portswood Road, Green Point, Atlantic Seaboard (021 419 0440).* **Open** daily 9am-5pm. **Credit** AmEx, DC, MC, V. **Map** p274 G2.

This newly completed centre is situated right on Green Point's main drag and plays host to a handful of ultra-cool retailers, including some of the top clothing designers in the country, a seriously cool gift shop and the buzzing Melissa's Food Shop.

### Victoria Wharf

*V&A Waterfront, Atlantic Seaboard (021 408 7600/www.waterfront.co.za).* **Open** 9am-9pm Mon-Sat; 10am-9pm Sun. **Credit** AmEx, DC, MC, V. **Map** p275 H1.

This monstrous shopping, eating and entertainment space has an enviable perch overlooking the water, a view of Table Mountain and enough to keep you busy for days. Open until late seven days a week, you'll find a host of international names holding court among SA's own leading retailers. A good bet for tourists as there are plenty of stylish curio, jewellery and diamond stores, plus some of the city's best restaurants. **Photo** *p129*.

### Willowbridge Lifestyle Centre

*39 Carl Cronje Drive, Tyger Valley, Northern Suburbs (021 914 7218/www.willowbridge.co.za).* **Open** 9am-8pm Mon-Sat; 9am-6pm Sun. **Credit** AmEx, DC, MC, V.

This design destination has turned the Northern Suburbs shopping scene on its head. An open piazza is lined with stylish fashion and home retailers as well as trendy coffee shops. The new Woolworths lifestyle store is a major force and combines a restaurant and state-of-the-art retail solutions – from an in-house fabric and paint service to an Apple electronics store and the W Collection of designer homeware accessories.

## Antiques

### Backyard

*148 Main Road, Muizenberg, Southern Peninsula (021 788 6890).* **Open** 9am-6pm Mon-Fri; 10am-4pm Sat, Sun. **Credit** DC, MC, V.

Remarkably well-priced vintage kitchenalia is a popular feature here, as are the piles of galvanised buckets (perfect for potting plants), rickety ladders and larger pieces like farm-style tables and dressers. The owner has a good eye for cheap and cheerful goodies like wooden blocks and toy boats – perfect retro gifts for the kids.

### Bruce Tait Antiques & Kitsch Collectables

*4 Buitenkloof Centre, 8 Kloof Street, City Bowl (021 422 1567).* **Open** 10am-6pm Mon-Fri; 9.30am-2pm Sat; 10am-2pm Sun. **Credit** AmEx, DC, MC, V. **Map** p274 F5.

This cornucopia of craziness is a Kloof Street institution. As is Leonard, the shop's extremely pierced manager. From beaten-up old shop mannequins to old records, once-loved chairs (they seem to have a thing for chairs), movie posters and kitsch *tchochkes* (think naked-lady ashtrays and glow-in-the-dark rubber skeletons), there's a veritable feast of interesting goodies and garbage to mull over.

## Burr & Muir
*82 Church Street, City Bowl (021 422 1319).*
**Open** 9.30am-4.30pm Mon-Fri; 9.30am-1pm Sat.
**Credit** AmEx, MC, V. **Map** p274 G4.
A den of divine antique finds, especially for lovers of good glass and art deco pieces. Lalique and Murano pieces are constant features, while Clarice Cliff-ites are in good hands.

## CDS Junk Store
*239 Main Road, Diep River, Southern Suburbs (021 712 6584).* **Open** 9.30am-5.30pm Mon, Wed, Fri; 9.30am-5pm Tue, Thur. **No credit cards.**
One of the city's original junk stores, this is where you really have to sift through the chaff to find the wheat. Sort your way through old wooden crates and dented enamel buckets – if you're lucky, you may find a set of old school chairs or a cult piece from the 1950s in need of a little love.

## Farriers
*53 Constantia Main Road, Plumstead, Southern Suburbs (021 761 4767).* **Open** 9am-5pm Mon-Fri; 9am-2pm Sat. **Credit** AmEx, DC, MC, V.
A happy mix of sophisticated antiques and revamped vintage pieces, this is fast becoming a hotspot in the Southern Suburbs. Look out for pretty dressing tables given a new lease of life, beautiful dining room pieces and smaller silverware items.

## Long Street Antique Arcade
*127 Long Street, City Bowl (021 423 3585).* **Open** 9am-4.30pm Mon-Fri; 9am-2pm Sat. **Credit** AmEx, DC, MC, V. **Map** p274 G4.
This mini 'mall' of antiques dealers and stallholders plays host to loads and loads of pieces waiting to be discovered. Look out for brooches, bracelets and cult ceramics from the turn of the 19th century.

## Plush Bazaar
*30 Somerset Road, City Bowl (021 419 8328).* **Open** 8.30am-4.30pm daily. **Credit** AmEx, DC, MC, V. **Map** p274 G2.
Owner Andre Crouse always has his ear to the ground, managing to snap up vintage treasures way before some of the other dealers in town. Nostalgic style is king at his busy store and you can expect to be greeted by masses of kitchenalia, as well as excellent glassware and a host of French wares such as monogrammed linens and antique cushions.

## Books

### Biblioteq
*41 Kloof Street, City Bowl (021 422 0774/www.biblioteqbooks.com).* **Open** 10.30am-6.30pm Mon-Fri; 11am-3pm Sat. **Credit** MC, V. **Map** p274 F5.
This über-stylish spot is the ideal lair for graphic designers, art lovers and people who appreciate beautiful imagery bound in equally enticing books. Specialising in high-end imported books devoted to visual imagery, owner and ex-advertising pro Rotem Sachar has designed a space that puts her much-loved books on equally stylish pedestals. Near to some of the city's favourite coffee spots, the shop also boasts striking contemporary artworks by renowned talent Julian Opie and a number of collectable book offerings, some of which are signed by their creators.

### Clarke's
*211 Long Street, City Bowl (021 423 5739/www.clarkesbooks.co.za).* **Open** 9am-5pm Mon-Fri; 9am-1pm Sat. **Credit** AmEx, DC, MC, V. **Map** p274 G4.
You can't help but leave Clarke's with a feeling that you've had something of an education. Owner Henrietta Dax is the bibliophile's bibliophile and she carries an impressive range of biographies on local

# To market

## Church Street Antique Market
*Church Street, City Bowl.* **Open** 9am-4pm Mon-Sat. **No credit cards.** **Map** p274 G3.
Vintage costume jewellery is always a good bet here, as are the interesting ceramics.

## Greenmarket Square
*Corner Shortmarket & Berg Streets, City Bowl.* **Open** 9am-4pm Mon-Sat. **No credit cards.** **Map** p275 H4.
One of the Mother City's most famous landmarks, Greenmarket Square is home to vendors from all over Africa selling their authentic crafts.

## Green Point Flea Market
*Bill Peters Drive, Green Point Stadium parking lot (021 439 4805/082 845 5580).* **Open** 9.15am-5pm Sun & public holidays. **No credit cards.** **Map** p274 F1.
A cacophony of noise greets you at this colourful market that's part authentic (African curios) and part made in China.

## Hout Bay Craft Market
*Hout Bay Village Green, Main Road, Hout Bay, Southern Peninsula (021 790 3474).* **Open** 10am-5pm Sun. **No credit cards.**
This family-friendly market is held on the village green in Hout Bay. Expect a plethora of home-made produce and crafts lovingly created by the eclectic mix of stallholders.

## Milnerton Flea Market
*Racecourse Road, Milnerton, Northern Suburbs.* **Open** 7am-5pm Sat, Sun. **No credit cards.**
The maxim 'one man's junk is another's gold' certainly rings true at this delightfully varied market.

**Eat, Drink, Shop**

political players as well as excellent books on the history of South Africa. Take time to pop upstairs and marvel at the collection of rare Africana too.

## Exclusive Books

*Shop 6160, Victoria Wharf, Atlantic Seaboard (021 419 0905/www.exclusivebooks.com).* **Open** 9am-10.30pm Mon-Thur; 9am-11pm Fri, Sat; 9am-9pm Sun. **Credit** AmEx, DC, MC, V. **Map** p275 H1.

The country's most ubiquitous chain of bookshops, this is where to come to stock up on bestsellers and excellent coffee table choices. There's a particularly comprehensive section for local authors, as well as all the overseas magazines and newspapers you need to keep up on international trends (especially in the bigger stores). There are also regular author readings and the free Fanatics Club membership cards offer great cash vouchers.

## Reader's Den

*Shop G10, Stadium on Main, Main Road, Claremont, Southern Suburbs (021 671 9551/www.readersden.co.za).* **Open** 10am-5pm Mon-Fri; 9am-3pm Sat. **Credit** DC, MC, V.

For many, graphic novels and cult comics are the way forward and at Reader's Den they certainly seem to agree. Stock up on Marvel comics and keep your eye out for the owner's latest Japanese finds.

# Love thy neighbour

The latest trend to take funky and good-living Capetonians by storm is the weekly Neighbour Goods Market (*pictured*). The brainchild of the guys behind the What if the World creative (www.whatiftheworld.com), this Saturday market is definitely making organic ultra-cool.

Buy a Belgian waffle to munch on while you browse and taste your way through stalls overflowing with cheese, bread, wine, honey and olives. There are also funky jewellery and clothes to buy – all design work is cutting-edge and very wearable. Best of all are the central trestle tables that have been set up where you can sit back, enjoy fabulous salads, dips, cheeses, breads and quiches bought on the premises, and watch the world go by.

If the future is all about buying exceptional, fresh produce, hanging out with your friends and enjoying a lazy day's marketing, then the future is most definitely here.

## Neighbour Goods Market

*Old Biscuit Mill, Albert Road, Woodstock, Southern Suburbs (021 448 1438).* **Open** 9am-4pm Sat. **No credit cards**.

Chic urban jewels at Phillippa Green and Ida Elsje's **Olive Green Cat**. *See p134.*

## Traveller's Bookshop

*Shop 2, King's Warehouse, Victoria Wharf, Atlantic Seaboard (021 425 6880).* **Open** 9am-9.30pm Mon-Sat; 10am-9pm Sun. **Credit** AmEx, DC, MC, V. **Map** p275 H1.

This store is staffed with globetrotters galore who will help you make the best book buy according to your travel needs (stock ranges from extensive reference books to pocket city guides and foldaway maps). All the major guide publishers are featured here and the section devoted to local South African travel is comprehensive.

## Wordsworth Books

*Shop 1, King's Warehouse, Victoria Wharf, Atlantic Seaboard (021 425 6880).* **Open** 9am-10pm Mon-Sat; 10am-9.30pm Sun. **Credit** AmEx, DC, MC, V. **Map** p274 G5.

This chain of intimate bookshops prides itself on being staffed by people who actually read the books they recommend. Sales pitch aside, the service here really is unparalleled and they will go out of their way to help you choose a book that suits or find the one you want.

## Electronics

### Apple Centre Waterfront

*Shop 101, Lower Level, Victoria Wharf, Atlantic Seaboard (021 425 1942/www.apple.com/za/buy/applecentre).* **Open** 9am-9pm Mon-Sat; 10am-9pm Sun. **Credit** AmEx, DC, MC, V. **Map** p275 H1.

This design-tastic official Apple megastore has all the latest Apple gear. From iPods in their various sizes and guises to iBooks, desktops and all the paraphernalia in-between. There's also an excellent after-sales and troubleshooting service.

## Audiovision

*Shop 6124, Lower Level, Victoria Wharf, Atlantic Seaboard (021 421 1055/www.audiovision.co.za).* **Open** 9am-9pm Mon-Sat; 10am-9pm Sun. **Credit** MC, V. **Map** p275 H1.

This stalwart on the home electronics scene stocks everything from top-of-the-range video and DVD players to all the latest home entertainment system components. They also stock a range of Mecer PCs, with knowledgeable staff to advise you on all your software requirements.

## Bang & Olufsen

*1st Floor, Weylandts Home Store, Corner Alfred & Hospital Streets, Green Point, Atlantic Seaboard (021 418 1385/www.bang-olufsen.co.za).* **Open** 9am-5.30pm Mon-Fri; 9am-2pm Sat; 10am-2pm 1st Sun of mth. **Credit** AmEx, MC, V. **Map** p275 H3.

The Danish über-brand of home entertainment options has a welcome home here in the city. Their beautifully designed wares are sheer inspiration and will have you hatching plans to turn your space into a contemporary haven of superb sound in no time.

## Caldis Sound & Furnishers

*57A Long Street, City Bowl (021 423 6747).* **Open** 8.30am-5.30pm Mon-Fri; 8.30am-1pm Sat. **Credit** AmEx, DC, MC, V. **Map** p274 G4.

Whether you're in the market for a top-of-the-range amp, high-tech vacuum cleaner or the best plasma screen money can buy, the enthusiastic team at

**Eat, Drink, Shop**

Caldis is there to advise you. Though they sell high-end goods, they also have excellent options for budget-conscious shoppers.

### Hi-Fi Corporation
*34 Klipfontein Road, Rondebosch, Southern Suburbs (021 689 3880/www.hificorp.com).* **Open** 9am-6pm Mon-Fri; 8.30am-5pm Sat; 9am-2pm Sun. **Credit** AmEx, DC, MC, V.
Probably the city's best known cut-price electronics store, with everything from dictaphones to the latest plasma screens and home theatre systems. The knowledgeable service ensures you leave with exactly what you're looking for, while the after-sales guarantees will put your mind at rest too.

## Fashion

## Accessories

### Accessorize
*Shop 202, Victoria Wharf, Atlantic Seaboard (021 425 7701).* **Open** 9am-9pm daily. **Credit** AmEx, DC. MC, V. **Map** p275 H1.
Seasonal displays of bracelets, beaded necklaces, brooches, hair accessories, scarves, hats and purses are co-ordinated according to colour, helping you to make the right choice for your outfit or mood.

### Bead Centre of Africa
*223 Long Street, City Bowl (021 423 4687/www. beadafrica.com).* **Open** 8.45am-5pm Mon-Fri; 9am-2pm Sat. **Credit** AmEx, DC, MC, V. **Map** p274 G4.
Discover your inner jeweller at this wholesale store where you pick up a plastic tray and fill the compartments with piles of colourful beads waiting to be strung into something special. The new Swarovski section helps you create your own Austrian crystal masterpieces at a fraction of retail prices.

### Charles Greig
*Shop U6224, Victoria Wharf, V&A Waterfront, Atlantic Seaboard (021 418 4515/www.charles greig.co.za).* **Open** 9am-9pm Mon-Sat; 10am-9pm Sun. **Credit** AmEx, DC, MC, V. **Map** p275 H1.
This world-class store is situated in a discreet corner of the V&A Waterfront and offers an excellent selection of their own cutting-edge design pieces – from chandelier earrings to whopping diamond pieces, as well as beautiful creations for men. The shop is also an official Rolex retailer.

### Diamonds International
*Shop 122, Ground Floor, Clock Tower Centre, V&A Waterfront, Atlantic Seaboard (021 421 1888).* **Open** 9am-8.30pm Mon-Sat; 10am-8.30pm Sun. **Credit** AmEx, DC, MC, V. **Map** p275 H1.
If you're in the market for carats, this is an excellent bet. Skilled staff are on hand to help you make your choice and advise you on the importance of cut, clarity, colour and carat size. They also stock ready-to-wear jewellery items and can make up designs in just 24 hours.

Homegrown glam at **Big Blue**. *See p138.*

### Glare
*Shop 2, Gardens Centre, Mill Street, City Bowl (021 461 6335).* **Open** 9am-6pm Mon-Fri; 9am-3pm Sat. **Credit** AmEx, DC, MC, V. **Map** p274 G5.
Glare specialises in small and exclusive collections by big names – you're likely to find the statement-making sunglasses you've been searching for here. They also stock Roberto Cavalli silk scarves and a range of impossibly soft kidskin driving gloves.

### Olive Green Cat
*79 Kloof Street, City Bowl (021 424 1101/www. olivegreencat.com).* **Open** *Workshop & showroom* 8am-5pm Mon-Fri; by appointment Sat. **Credit** AmEx, MC, V. **Map** p274 F5.
If you're looking for something with urban edge, you can't go wrong at this city store. It's a collaboration of two young talents, Phillippa Green and Ida Elsje. Shop for perspex-embroidered cuffs and 'situ' rings that feature suspended diamonds in resin. They also make customised pieces. **Photo** *p133.*

### Peter Gilder Jewellery
*Shop 40, Constantia Village, Constantia, Southern Suburbs (021 794 2116/www.petergilder.com).* **Open** 9am-6pm Mon-Fri, 9am-5pm Sat; 10am-1pm Sun. **Credit** AmEx, DC, MC, V.

Eat, Drink, Shop

A perennial favourite with the Constantia yummy mummies, expect a range of contemporary classics in a warm and welcoming environment. Peter's daughter Mandy has her own Mandy G range for the younger fashion set.

### Sandy McCormack

*Durban House, 34 Durban Road, Wynberg, Southern Suburbs (021 762 9179/www.sandy mccormack.com).* **Open** 9am-5pm Mon-Fri; 9am-1pm Sat. **Credit** AmEx, DC, MC, V.
The trend towards eclectic pieces of jewellery that incorporate crystals, beadwork and charms is still going strong at this intimate boudoir-esque store. Browse the glass-fronted cabinets or book a consultation with the designer herself; she'll happily create something that has your name written all over it.

### Scarab

*Shop LG45, Cavendish Square, Claremont, Southern Suburbs (021 683 4646/www.scarabct.co.za).* **Open** 9am-6pm Mon-Thur, Sat; 9am-9pm Fri; 10am-4pm Sun. **Credit** AmEx, DC, MC, V.
Scarab has been around for years and is well known for its classic style. Semi-precious stones feature strongly in the small collection of striking earrings, bracelets and necklaces.

### Sea Weeds

*Shop 48B, Constantia Village. Constantia, Southern Suburbs (021 794 8233).* **Open** 9am-5.30pm Mon-Fri; 9am-5pm Sat; 10am-1pm Sun. **Credit** AmEx, DC, MC, V.
One of the best stockists of quality swimwear in the city, Sea Weeds is great for form-flattering choices that'll last for seasons to come. Staff are spot on with suggestions for what flatters your figure best.

### Shimansky Collection

*Shop 210-212, Clocktower Precinct, V&A Waterfront, Atlantic Seaboard (021 421 1488/ www.shimansky.co.za).* **Open** 9am-9pm Mon-Sat; 10am-9pm Sun. **Credit** AmEx, DC, MC, V. **Map** p275 H1.
This sophisticated set-up specialises in uncut diamond and platinum jewellery. You can take your pick from an impressive collection of ready-cut diamonds and up your knowledge of the world of bling at the diamond museum and polishing workshop.

### Storm in a G Cup

*4 Cavendish Street, Claremont, Southern Suburbs (021 674 6629).* **Open** 10am-6pm Mon-Fri; 9am-2pm Sat. **Credit** DC, MC, V.
Where fashion-conscious, well-endowed women shop for sexy underwear that keeps everything in place. This specialist store helps you make the most of your assets by offering a measuring service, as well as advice on fit and style.

### Tanzanite International

*Shop 118, Clock Tower, V&A Waterfront, Atlantic Seaboard (021 421 5488).* **Open** 9am-9pm Mon-Sat; 10am-9pm Sun. **Credit** AmEx, DC, MC, V. **Map** p275 H1.

The tanzanite stone has taken the world by storm and this store is dedicated to it. The only one of its kind in the world, expect to be blown away by the array of tanzanite in all its brilliant blue hues. The shop sells individual stones as well as jewellery.

### Temptations

*Shop 577, Upper Level, Canal Walk, Century City, Milnerton, Northern Suburbs (021 551 9731).* **Open** 9am-9pm daily. **Credit** AmEx, DC, MC, V.
Shop for fabulously sexy underwear (from satin numbers to pretty cotton ensembles) at excellent prices. You'll also find come-to-bed sleepwear and a host of special occasion teddies and bra-and-knickers sets that'll get temperatures soaring.

### Uwe Koetter

*Shop 14, V&A Arcade, V&A Waterfront, Atlantic Seaboard (021 421 1039/www.uwekoetter.co.za).* **Open** 9am-9pm Mon-Sat; 10am-9pm Sun. **Credit** AmEx, DC, MC, V. **Map** p275 H1.
One of the big names in the local diamond jewellery game, this store is a real Aladdin's cave of quality pieces. You can work with one of the consultants for your ultimate bespoke piece or select something from their latest collections of precious metal and gemstone creations.

## Childrenswear

### Crazy About Cape Town

*Shop 132, Victoria Wharf, Atlantic Seaboard (021 419 9474/www.kushnerkids.com).* **Open** 9am-9pm daily. **Credit** AmEx, DC, MC, V. **Map** p275 H1.
What to get the far-flung niece, nephew or grandchild that has everything? A souvenir T-shirt of Cape Town, of course. Funky designs to fit kids of all ages are the order of the day here.

### Earthchild

*Shop 112, Victoria Wharf, Atlantic Seaboard (021 421 5033/www.earthchild.co.za).* **Open** 9am-9pm Mon-Sat; 10am-9pm Sun. **Credit** AmEx, DC, MC, V. **Map** p275 H1.
Earthchild is the offshoot of the nature-inspired Earth Addict range for adults, and you'll find comfy leisurewear items for kids made from 100% natural fibres. Caters for newborns and upwards.

### Fairy Shop

*311 Main Road, Kenilworth, Southern Suburbs (021 762 1546).* **Open** 9am-5.30pm Mon-Fri; 9am-1.30pm Sat. **Credit** DC, MC, V.
Every little girl dreams of tripping around in sparkling ballet shoes and a tutu, wings on her back and wand in hand, and at this delightful little store you can make those fantasies a reality. A great stop for fairy parties and gifts for aspiring Tinkerbells.

### Farriers Baby

*49 Constantia Road, Plumstead, Southern Suburbs (021 761 2212).* **Open** 9am-5pm Mon-Fri; 9am-1pm Sat. **Credit** DC, MC, V.

*Eat, Drink, Shop*

# SHIMANKSY
## "It's the way you make me feel"

Christina Aguilera wearing Shimansky at the Unite the Stars 2005 concert

The splendour and beauty of a superior quality well-cut diamond lies not only in its exquisite outward appearance. It's the way it makes you feel that makes it priceless.

**THAT SPECIAL FEELING**
A diamond says so much. It's a salute to the precious moments in our lives. It's a dazzling reminder of somebody's love, a reward for a great accomplishment, and enduring symbol to be treasured and celebrated. This is something Yair Shimansky, the founder of Shimansky - a leading jewellery manufacturing company - understands very well. "A diamond is something exceptional, it's something that will always remind you of the special moments in your life and the milestones it represents," he says passionately.

**THE STARS' CHOICE**
Given the Shimansky commitment to integrity and of course the superior expertise of the diamond-cutting workshop, it is no surprise that Charlize Theron, the South African-born Oscar winner, chose a 47ct D Flawless Emerald Cut Diamond on her visit to South Africa. Even Bill Clinton, one of the most loved American Presidents, thanked Shimansky with a personal letter after his visit. Collectors and buyers from across the globe are ordering diamonds to their hearts' desire. From unique and patented Shimansky cuts of diamonds to rare and sought-after colours such as the Blue-White Flawless, Fancy Yellow or Pink Diamond Shimansky makes dreams come true. After all, any thing is possible when you are in love...

> The most sought after diamond ring in South Africa - the Shimansky Millennium Diamond Ring

Oscar winner Charlize Theron wearing a 47ct D Flawless Shimansky Diamond

Intense Fancy Yellow Diamonds - a Shimansky speciality

Tanzanite with Micro-set Diamonds - from Shimansky's Ayanda Collection

Superbly cut Shimansky Diamonds - set in handcrafted Platinum designs

## PERSONALLY SELECTED

A Diamond's journey from the earth may take up to two billion years. So in Yair Shimansky's opinion, there is little need to rush the process of sourcing and buying quality diamonds. This thinking is applied during his regular expeditions to Kimberley, the Orange River, and the West Coast, where he personally selects diamonds of the finest quality from the most trustworthy sources. This guarantees you, the discerning buyer, a truly South African, conflict-free diamond. Shimansky diamonds are then cut and polished to perfection at their main showroom situated at The Clock Tower, V&A Waterfront, Cape Town. It is here in the luxurious showroom that you can experience the same unhurried philosophy that lets you treasure the moment of discovering your own perfect diamond.

WORKSHOPS AND SHOWROOM

The Clock Tower, Waterfront, Cape Town
Tel: (021) 421 2788 Other retail outlets:
CAPE TOWN: V&A Waterfront; Canal Walk
GAUTENG: Sandton City, Johannesburg;
Brooklyn and Menlyn Park, Pretoria
DURBAN: The Pavilion, Westville
www.shimansky.co.za

Mandela and Bill Clinton - Shimansky captures the moment

Yair Shimansky - founder and CEO

❛ Diamonds are the perfect way to celebrate life's special moments ❜

# SHIMANSKY

Farriers Baby offers beautiful linens for nursery or bedroom in the palest shades. Quality finishes and attention to detail ensure they will be handed down from generation to generation.

### Seven Ounce
*Shop 111, Lower Level, Victoria Wharf, Atlantic Seaboard (021 425 8006/www.sevenounce.com).* **Open** 9am-9pm Mon-Sat; 10am-9pm Sun. **Credit** AmEx, DC, MC, V. **Map** p275 H1.
Need to stock up on the coolest gear for fashion savvy kids? Look no further than this ultra hip store. Their laid-back, durable basics will become firm wardrobe favourites.

---

## Ladieswear

### Alternative Designs
*128 Long Street, City Bowl (021 424 2883).* **Open** 9am-5.30pm daily. **Credit** AmEx, MC, V. **Map** p274 G4.
The perfect stop for fashion-savvy gals who like to think and dress out of the box, this is something of a Long Street staple and plays host to rail upon rail of colourful and detailed one-off designs, jewellery and accessories by some of the city's most talented fashion whizzes. You'll find plenty of feminine offerings but none that make a wilting flower out of any girl. A small range of gothic and fetish labels inspire those who like to live a little closer to the edge.

### Big Blue
*47C Somerset Road, Green Point, Atlantic Seaboard (021 425 1179/www.bigblue.co.za).* **Open** 9am-5pm Mon-Fri; 9am-1pm Sat. **Credit** AmEx, DC, MC, V. **Map** p274 G2.
This haven of homegrown design stocks an ever changing and eclectic selection of skirts in modern ethnic styles, deconstructed tops and funky bags that scream Afro chic. This is definitely the place to shop if you are serious about looking glam – the local way. **Photo** *p134.*

### Callaghan Collezioni
*Shop G7, Cavendish Square, Claremont, Southern Suburbs (021 683 1716).* **Open** 9am-6pm Mon-Sat; 10am-4pm Sun. **Credit** AmEx, DC, MC, V.
For styles that reflect current international ready-to-wear trends, this is the place to come. Prices reflect the international origins but the choice of clothing from the likes of Diane von Furstenburg and Donna Karan is impressive.

### Christiaan Gabriel Du Toit & Klûk
*Portside Centre, Corner Main & Upper Portswood Roads, Green Point, Atlantic Seaboard (083 377 7780).* **Open** 9.30am-5.30pm Mon-Fri; 9.30am-2pm Sat. **Credit** AmEx, DC, MC, V. **Map** p274 G2.
Two of the city's fashion It Boys share this sophisticated space in the swanky new Portside Centre. Browse the rails of gorgeously feminine items in impossibly delicate fabrics.

**Sun Goddess.** *See p140.*

### Cigar Clothing
*10 Cavendish Street, Claremont, Southern Suburbs (021 683 3582).* **Open** 9am-5pm Mon-Sat. **Credit** AmEx, DC, MC, V.
French big names like Tara Jermon and famous linen brand Zyga are on display at this sexy new store. Sisters Kerry and Debbie Taylor offer carefully considered collections of contemporary Parisian styles for a grateful Cape Town audience.

### Frock
*Shop 25, 50 Kloof Street, City Bowl (021 424 5993/www.frock.co.za).* **Open** 9am-5.30pm Mon-Fri; 9am-3pm Sat. **Credit** AmEx, DC, MC, V. **Map** p274 F5.
City gal Nathalie Becker knows how to make clothes to flatter every woman's figure – from wide-legged pants to floaty tops, plus a host of pretty accessories.

### Habits
*1 Cavendish Close, Cavendish Street, Claremont, Southern Suburbs (021 671 7330/www.habits.co.za).* **Open** 9am-5.30pm Mon-Fri; 9am-1.30pm Sat. **Credit** AmEx, DC, MC, V.
Jenny Le Roux has a seemingly never-ending ability to bring new styles and classics in the making to her grateful customers. Hands-on service (including cappuccinos), a welcoming atmosphere and something to suit every shape and figure ensure you'll never leave empty-handed. Great handbags and shoes too.

### Hip Hop
*12 Cavendish Street, Claremont, Southern Suburbs (021 674 4605/www.hiphopfashion.co.za).* **Open** 9am-6pm Mon-Fri; 9am-5pm Sat; 10am-2pm Sun. **Credit** AmEx, DC, MC, V.
This is the home of superbly crafted evening gowns, sparkly party dresses and stylish occasional wear. The City Bowl store carries end-of-season items. **Other locations**: 35B Buitenkant Street, City Bowl (021 465 0352).

### India Jane

*Station Building, Main Road, Kalk Bay, Southern Peninsula (021 788 3020/www.indiajane.com).*
**Open** 9.30am-5pm daily. **Credit** AmEx, DC, MC, V.
A kaleidoscopic collection of local and imported designs, just perfect for the girl with a gypsy soul. Loads of glorious colour options, out-there fabrics and interesting cuts.

### Jenni Button

*Shop L74, Cavendish Square, Claremont, Southern Suburbs (021 683 9504/www.jennibutton.co.za).*
**Open** 9am-6pm Mon-Thur, Sat; 9am-9pm Fri; 10am-4pm Sun. **Credit** AmEx, DC, MC, V.
This place is always recommended when you find yourself in one of the two bigger malls in Cape Town. Look out for heavily beaded evening gowns, cut-to-the-waist suits and sparkly tops that promise a good night out at this much-loved, über-fashionable store. There's also a great range of swimwear and impossibly comfortable skyscraper shoes.
**Other locations**: Shop 550A, Upper Level, Canal Walk (021 552 8844).

### Lulu Tantan

*Shop 7, Kildare Centre, Main Street, Newlands, Southern Suburbs (021 683 8148/www.lulu tantan.com).* **Open** 9am-5pm Mon-Fri; 10am-2pm Sat. **Credit** AmEx, DC, MC, V.
Like stepping into a Chinese jewellery box, this all-red salon is a favourite among the city's style cognoscenti. Rails of imported and local designs feature feminine creations for any occasion. Look out for the Sensai coats made from antique kimonos – each is a timeless work of fashionable art.

### Lunar

*Kildare Centre, 62 Main Street, Newlands, Southern Suburbs (021 674 6871).* **Open** 9am-4.45pm Mon-Fri; 9am-2pm Sat. **Credit** DC, MC, V.

Designer Karen Termorshuizen has a knack for clean-lined classics that are bound to become wardrobe staples for many seasons to come. Her raw silk party dresses (in flirty 1950s styles), elegant linen shifts and wide-legged pants have the ability to make you feel on top of the world.

### MeMeMe

*279 Long Street, City Bowl (021 424 0001).*
**Open** 9.30am-5pm Mon-Fri; 9.30am-3.30pm Sat.
**Credit** AmEx, DC, MC, V. **Map** p274 G4.
When you're tired of the same old styles in the bigger stores, it's time to head for MeMeMe, award-winning artist Doreen Southwood's quirky store. Look for multi-length skirts, wrap-over dresses and tops that allow you to wear your edgy personality with pride.

### Misfit

*287 Long Street, City Bowl (021 422 5646).* **Open** 10am-5.30pm Mon-Fri; 10am-2pm Sat. **Credit** DC, MC, V. **Map** p274 G4.
Saskia Köner combines international catwalk trends with her own innate style and understanding of the South African scene. From curiously cut dresses to longer than long pants, this is the place to visit for statement-making stuff. Look out for cutting-edge accessories that'll get your friends talking.

### Monsoon

*Shop G41, Cavendish Square, Claremont, Southern Suburbs (021 671 9687).* **Open** 9am-6pm Mon-Thur, Sat; 9am-9pm Fri; 10am-4pm Sun. **Credit** AmEx, DC, MC, V.
This slip of a store is stocked with small collections of classic co-ordinates updated on a weekly basis. From the perfect wraparound black dress to elegant denims and smart pants, this has been a favourite for stylish Southern Suburbs women for years. It's also popular for party dresses at excellent prices.

Trendy designs for trendy teens at **YDE** (Young Designers Emporium). *See p141.*

## Nicci Boutiques

*Shop G47, Cavendish Square, Claremont, Southern Suburbs (021 683 9458).* **Open** 9am-6pm Mon-Thur, Sat; 9am-9pm Fri; 10am-4pm Sun. **Credit** AmEx, DC, MC, V.

Glamazons race here whenever they have an important do. The rails of sexy, sophisticated co-ordinates mean you'll always be dressed to kill.

## Pure Solid

*Shop 6248A, Second Level, Victoria Wharf, Atlantic Seaboard (021 421 9556).* **Open** 9am-9pm Mon-Sat; 10am-9pm Sun. **Credit** AmEx, DC, MC, V. **Map** p275 H1.

Home to a host of Asian-inspired fashions, expect out-of-the-ordinary hemlines, oversized collars and batwing sleeves in hardy cottons and denims. The printed T-shirts featuring dragons and *anime* graphics are great for everyday wear too. **Other locations**: LG84A, Cavendish Square, Claremont (021 671 8121).

## Riga

*8 Cavendish Street, Claremont, Southern Suburbs (021 674 4394).* **Open** 9am-5pm Mon-Sat. **Credit** DC, MC, V.

This space is much loved by local fashion divas. Various Maxmara ranges form the backbone of the store, while sophisticated knitwear and co-ordinates from famous French labels offer more dressy options.

## Secret Room

*14 Cavendish Street, Claremont, Southern Suburbs (021 683 7607).* **Open** 9.30am-5pm Mon-Fri; 9.30am-4pm Sat. **Credit** AmEx, DC, MC, V.

Sister to the India Jane stores, this decadent shop offers sophisticated imported apparel for dressy occasions. Loved by local TV celebs, it's the perfect pitstop for slinky dresses, embroidered and embellished blouses and the latest in fashionable shawls and jackets.

## Slate

*Shop 232, Victoria Wharf, Atlantic Seaboard (021 421 2554).* **Open** 9am-9pm daily. **Credit** AmEx, DC, MC, V. **Map** p275 H1.

Slate sells a great mix of local and international trendy clothing with an undeniably feminine feel. Great coats, plus a host of slinky skirts, dresses and party tops. They also stock a limited range of must-have accessories.

## Sun Goddess

*Shop 230, Victoria Wharf, Atlantic Seaboard (021 421 7620/www.sungoddess.co.za).* **Open** 9am-9pm daily. **Credit** AmEx, DC, MC, V. **Map** p275 H1.

This Afro chic label has devotees scattered around the globe and with good reason – it celebrates a new South African design consciousness. You'll find gloriously modern interpretations of classic African style, embellished with tongue-in-cheek beading and embroidery details. A must-visit for a taste of the new South African creative revolution. **Photo** *p138*.

### Taxi

*15 Bloem Street, City Bowl (021 422 3669).* **Open** 10am-5pm Mon-Fri; 10am-2pm Sat. **Credit** MC, V. **Map** p274 G4.

Karen van Huysteen seems to have an unending source of energy and her new store certainly reflects the urban spirit of its location. Shop for originally styled and off-the-wall clothing items, as well as a host of accessories that reflect the spirit of the city.

### Vertigo

*Shop 27, Upper Level, Cavendish Square, Main Road, Claremont, Southern Suburbs (021 683 9930/www.vertigoclothing.co.za).* **Open** 9am-6pm Mon-Thur, Sat; 9am-9pm Fri; 10am-4pm Sun. **Credit** AmEx, DC, MC, V.

Preppy is the order of the day at this urban store, from combats with pretty detailing to no-nonsense button-up shirts, cardigans and jackets.

### YDE

*Shop F50, Cavendish Square, Claremont, Southern Suburbs (021 683 6177/www.yde.co.za).* **Open** 9am-6pm Mon-Thur; 9am-9pm Fri; 9am-6pm Sat; 10am-4pm Sun. **Credit** AmEx, DC, MC, V.

The leading force in championing local talent, Young Designers Emporium is a funky feast of fashionable choices at affordable prices. Exceedingly popular with fashion-conscious teens and twenty-somethings, they also stock loads of accessories to glam up any outfit. **Photo** *p140*.
**Other locations**: Shop 225, V&A Waterfront (021 425 6232); Shop 432, Canal Walk (021 555 2090).

## Menswear

### Aca Joe

*Shop F68, Cavendish Square, Claremont, Southern Suburbs (021 671 3334).* **Open** 9am-6pm Mon-Thur, Sat; 9am-9pm Fri; 10am-4pm Sun. **Credit** AmEx, DC, MC, V.

Preppy cuts meet hip hop style at this über-urban clothing store. From combats and jeans to oversized hoodies, T-shirts and button-down shirts, this is the ideal stop for weekend wear.

### Cape Storm

*Shop 108, Canal Walk, Milnerton, Northern Suburbs (021 555 0655/www.capestorm.co.za).* **Open** 10am-9pm Mon-Fri, Sun; 9am-9pm Sat. **Credit** AmEx, DC, MC, V.

The trend towards good-looking outdoor gear is on the rise and nobody knows this better than the Cape Storm crew. Though much loved as a leisure wear brand, their goods are also respected for the sophisticated fabrics and finishes.

### Cape Union Mart

*Far Ocean Marine Building, Quay Four, V&A Waterfront, Atlantic Seaboard (021 425 4559/www.capeunionmart.co.za).* **Open** 9am-9pm Mon-Thur, Sun; 9am-11pm Fri, Sat. **Credit** AmEx, DC, MC, V. **Map** p275 H1.

This outdoor and adventure store also carries an excellent range of comfy menswear – perfect for weekends spent fishing, watching the rugby or just plain mooching around. Their combat pants are perennial favourites while their in-house brand polar fleeces are perfect for keeping off winter chills. Look out for the hemp-only T-shirts too.

### Diesel Stylelab

*Shop 6277, Victoria Wharf, Atlantic Seaboard (021 425 5777).* **Open** 9am-9pm Mon-Sat; 10am-9pm Sun. **Credit** AmEx, DC, MC, V. **Map** p275 H1.

Prices that match the out-there styles are guaranteed at this bastion of super-coolness. More affordable are the well-cut jeans, while the suits and casual jackets add flair to any man's wardrobe.

### Due South

*Shop 514, Canal Walk, Milnerton, Northern Suburbs (021 529 3140/www.duesouth.co.za).* **Open** 10am-9pm daily. **Credit** AmEx, DC, MC, V.

International and local outdoor garb by the likes of North Face, Columbia and Cape Storm are the watchword at this rugged store. They also sell paraphernalia for adventure seekers – from the latest hiking boots to sleeping bags that will keep you warm on camping trips.

### Fabiani

*Shop 272, Victoria Wharf, Atlantic Seaboard (021 425 1810).* **Open** 9am-9pm Mon-Sat; 10am-9pm Sun. **Credit** AmEx, DC, MC, V. **Map** p275 H1.

An excellent one-stop shop for the man about town. Famous for their exquisitely cut suits in imported fabrics, shirts in a kaleidoscope of colours and G-star jeans that hug all the right places, this is a must-visit for any guy wanting to add an injection of sophistication to his wardrobe.

### Hugo Boss

*Shop 6267, Upper Level, Victoria Wharf, Atlantic Seaboard (021 421 3052).* **Open** 9am-9pm Mon-Sat; 10am-9pm Sun. **Credit** AmEx, DC, MC, V. **Map** p275 H1.

From beautifully designed wallets and stylish ties to perfectly cut jeans and suits, you'll walk out of this famous name store looking and feeling like a million bucks.

### Lacoste

*Shop 6205, Upper Level, Victoria Wharf, Atlantic Seaboard (021 421 8836).* **Open** 9am-9pm Mon-Sat; 10am-9pm Sun. **Credit** AmEx, DC, MC, V. **Map** p275 H1.

The famous crocodile logo has never really gone out of fashion, but in recent years Lacoste collared shirts have enjoyed something of a resurgence. Make your selection from a candy coloured display of up-to-the-minute colours. They also stock a small selection of the latest seasonal jackets and knits to top off the look.

### Markham

*Shop 235, Upper Level, Victoria Wharf, Atlantic Seaboard (021 418 5518/www.markham.co.za).* **Open** 9am-9pm Mon-Sat; 10am-9pm Sun. **Credit** AmEx, DC, MC, V. **Map** p275 H1.

This chain of male-oriented clothing stores offers affordable and fashionable choices. As well as top-to-toe selections of great casual wear, they also stock more serious garb.

### Metrosexual

*Shop 554, Canal Walk, Milnerton, Northern Suburbs (021 418 5518/www.markham.co.za).* **Open** 10am-9pm Mon-Fri, Sun; 9am-9pm Sat. **Credit** AmEx, DC, MC, V.

As the name suggests, this Northern Suburbs store is the place for making the most of one's metrosexuality. All the latest leisure-wear styles, as well as sleek three button suits, can be found with a great range of shirts to match.

### Queenspark for Men

*Shop 526, Canal Walk, Milnerton, Northern Suburbs (021 552 3575).* **Open** 10am-9pm Mon-Fri, Sun; 9am-9pm Sat. **Credit** AmEx, DC, MC, V.

Long a favourite with businessmen, this stand-alone store offers everything from suits and co-ordinating shirts and ties to chinos and casual shirts for non-boardroom get-togethers.

### Uzzi

*Shop 269, Upper Level, Victoria Wharf, Atlantic Seaboard (021 418 0334).* **Open** 9am-9pm Mon-Sat; 10am-9pm Sun. **Credit** AmEx, DC, MC, V. **Map** p275 H1.

This is the perfect place to grab a party shirt. They also stock a great selection of own-label jeans and fashionable shoes to finish off the look.

## Shoes

### Footgear

*Shop C15/16, Access Park, Kenilworth, Southern Suburbs (021 683 3308/www.footgear.co.za).* **Open** 8.45am-5.45pm Mon-Fri; 8.45am-3.45pm Sat; 9.30am-1.30pm Sun. **Credit** AmEx, DC, MC, V.

From Reebok to Adidas, Nike and Asics running shoes, sporty types are spoilt for choice here. Staff are on hand to advise on your special shoe needs and the excellent prices mean that you'll be kitted out to conquer the road, tennis or squash court in affordable style.

### New Balance Factory Outlet

*Shop G22, Longbeach Mall, Sunnydale Road, Noordhoek, Southern Peninsula (021 785 3530/ www.newbalance.co.za).* **Open** 10am-5.30pm Mon-Thur; 9am-6pm Fri; 8.30am-5pm Sat; 9am-2pm Sun. **Credit** AmEx, DC, MC, V.

The popular US brand has a small outlet store in the heart of Noordhoek. Here you'll find a good range of last season's stock at excellent prices as well as a handful of goods that are currently on mainstream shop shelves. They also stock a range of New Balance exercise clothing.

### Nine West

*Shop 252, Victoria Wharf, Atlantic Seaboard (021 418 7164/www.ninewest.com).* **Open** 9am-9pm Mon-Sat; 10am-9pm Sun. **Credit** AmEx, DC, MC, V. **Map** p275 H1.

Fashionable shoes and bags with a quality edge are the watchword at this international store on the V&A Waterfront. Invest in a pair of heels and look out for the high fashion choices that finish any outfit off perfectly.

### Planisphere

*Shop 6178, Victoria Wharf, Atlantic Seaboard (021 418 8719/www.universalfootwear.co.za).* **Open** 9am-9pm Mon-Sat; 10am-9pm Sun. **Credit** AmEx, DC, MC, V. **Map** p275 H1.

Planisphere is a real local success story that ended the shoe drought in this country. Copies of high-street winners and a host of own-design heels at great prices are on offer, as well as a great range of sparkly sandals for summer and great boots for the winter months.

### Queue Shoes

*Shop 48C, Constantia Village, Main Road, Constantia, Southern Suburbs (021 794 8687).* **Open** 9am-6pm Mon-Fri; 9am-5pm Sat; 9am-1pm Sun. **Credit** AmEx, DC, MC, V.

This chain of boutique-style stores seems to be mushrooming, and when you check out the prices and considerable selection you'll understand why. From cheap and cheerful must-haves in the hottest colours to sophisticated heels from the likes of Steve Madden and Nine West, you'll always find something to suit.

### Shoe City

*Shop A7, Access Park, Kenilworth, Southern Suburbs (021 683 5687).* **Open** 9am-5pm Mon-Fri; 8.30am-3pm Sat; 9am-1pm Sun. **Credit** AmEx, DC, MC, V.

This giant store is stocked from floor to ceiling with cheap-as-chips footwear for both young and old. Surprisingly fashionable finds are a boon, and at prices that more often than not stay below the R100 mark you'll be forgiven for buying more than your fair share.

### Tsonga Shoes

*Shop 48, Constantia Village, Constantia, Southern Suburbs (021 794 8827/www.tsonga.com).* **Open** 9am-5.30pm Mon-Fri; 9am-5pm Sat; 10am-1pm Sun. **Credit** AmEx, DC, MC, V.

This SA brand specialises in leather and suede shoes that effortlessly combine supreme comfort with classic style. Look out for their loafers that are perfect teamed with jeans.

## Vintage clothing

### Déjà Vu

*278 Main Road, Kenilworth, Southern Suburbs (021 797 7373).* **Open** 9am-4.30pm Mon-Fri; 9am-1pm Sat. **No credit cards.**

# Bright young things

These four fashion designers are on the lips of those in the know:

## Stephen Quatember

**Label**: Stephen Quatember.
**Available**: V&A Waterfront (021 415 3411).
This line is cutting-edge – literally. Quatember's raw edges and unprocessed seams wend their way up and down the catwalks of Cape Town Fashion Week. Part of a new wave of southern African chic.

## Tasleem Bulbulia

**Label**: Funeka.
**Available**: Blackbeard & Dare, Willowbridge Lifestyle Centre, Durbanville (021 914 5777). Funeka means 'wanted' in Xhosa and once you lay eyes on Tasleem Bulbulia's unique Afro-chic clothes, you too will have her garments on your most wanted list. Tasleem describes her style as 'using global trends but giving them a definite South African flavour'.

## Malcolm Klûk & Christiaan Gabriel du Toit

**Label**: KLûK & CGDT.
**Available**: KlûK & CGDT, Portside Centre, Main Road, Green Point (083 377 7780). Though they each have a label, these two designers work together on each other's collections. Malcolm's classic feminine designs in striking fabrics have cult status. Christiaan specialises in edgy 'couture for every day' with colours and fabrics that push the boundaries of ultra-feminine designs.

## Chloe Townsend

**Label**: Missibaba.
**Available**: Stefania Moreland, 153 Kloof Street, City Bowl (021 422 2609). In just a short time, Chloe has found herself in the South African accessories spotlight with her hand-tooled leather handbags, 'flower' scarves and belts, bird earrings and exquisitely detailed stitchwork patterns.

## Flowers

### Aspen

*113 Long Street, City Bowl (021 424 6511/www. aspenflowers.co.za).* **Open** 8am-4.30pm Mon-Fri. **Credit** AmEx, DC, MC, V. **Map** p274 G4.
Style diva Nicci Scholtz is the queen of crazy colour combinations. Her inspiring store is a visual treat and she also sells garden- and flower-inspired paraphernalia such as colourful wellies and designer Tord Boontje's flower cut-out paper lampshades.

### Chart Farm

*Klaasens Road, Wynberg, Southern Suburbs (021 761 0434).* **Open** 9am-4pm daily. **No credit cards**.
One of Cape Town's not-so-hidden gems, Chart Farm is home to row upon row of gloriously blooming roses waiting to be picked. Sold by the stem, selecting your roses and enjoying a cup of tea after is a wonderful way to spend a morning.

### Lush

*13A Kloof Nek Road, City Bowl (021 423 5503).* **Open** 9am-5pm Mon-Fri. **Credit** DC, MC, V. **Map** p274 F5.
The host who has everything will never say no to a stylish bouquet of blooms from this designer florist.

## Hairdressers

### Boygirl

*4 Mooikloof Centre, 34 Kloof Street, City Bowl (021 422 4755).* **Open** 9am-6pm Tue-Sat; by appointment Sun. **Credit** MC, V. **Map** p274 F5.
This swish new salon hasn't taken long to carve its niche on the Kloof Street scene. Hairstylist Gunther churns out funky, fresh hairdos for all ages and genders. The vibe is packed with energy.

### Frank Fowden

*Shop 201, Upper Level, Victoria Wharf, Atlantic Seaboard (021 419 3186).* **Open** 10am-8pm Mon-Thur; 9am-5pm Fri; 9am-7pm Sat; 10am-6pm Sun. **Credit** MC, V. **Map** p275 H1.
This trendsetting salon offers excellent cuts and an impressive arsenal of colouring options. Staff offer great advice for maintaining your do at home too.

### Partners for Men

*58A First Floor, Gardens Centre, Mill Street, City Bowl (021 465 7253/www.partnershair.co.za).* **Open** 9am-6pm Mon-Fri; 8.30am-4pm Sat; 9am-1pm Sun. **Credit** MC, V. **Map** p274 G5.
Specialising in men's hair, this is a great spot for quick trims or for indulging in a brand new look in a comfortable environment.

### Peter the Haircutter

*201 Upper Buitenkant Street, Vredehoek, Southern Suburbs (021 462 3100).* **Open** 9am-5pm Tue-Sat. **Credit** AmEx, DC, MC, V.
Long loved by city trendsetters, Peter's ultra-cool exterior belies his softly spoken, affable nature. His haircuts are guaranteed to make the most of you.

Sustainable beauty: **Ecoco**. *See p146.*

Still going after all of these years, this is the place to pick up a vintage Chanel bag or stock up on some designer jeans that have already been worn in.

### Secondhand Rose

*Cavendish Close, Warrick Street, Claremont, Southern Suburbs (021 674 4270).* **Open** 9.30am-5pm Mon-Fri; 9.30am-1.30pm Sat. **Credit** DC, MC, V.
The owner has an excellent eye for 1950s dresses and coats, plus a host of classic bags and accessories looking for a new home.

### Second Time Around

*196 Long Street, City Bowl (021 423 1674).* **Open** 9am-5pm Mon-Fri; 9am-2pm Sat. **No credit cards**. **Map** p274 G4.
Crammed with clothing from the 1920s up to a few years ago, an hour spent here really is like playing dress-up. Stock up on spangly jumpsuits from the '60s or go glamorous with a Dallas-inspired satin number – this is the perfect place for renting party costumes too.

### Stock Exchange

*116 Kloof Street, City Bowl (021 424 5971).* **Open** 10am-5pm Mon-Fri; 10am-1pm Sat. **No credit cards**. **Map** p274 F5.
A strict policy of designer-only labels means you don't have to sift too long before you find a gem. From Missoni to Prada, the well-preserved and cared for garments fly out of the store. Pop in and browse the seasonal shoe selection too.

## Tylers

*First Floor, 87 Kloof Street, City Bowl (021 426 5700).* **Open** 8.30am-5pm Tue, Thur; 8.30am-7.30pm Wed, Fri; 8am-3pm Sat. **Credit** AmEx, DC, MC, V. **Map** p274 F5.

Owner Tanya Tyler holds court at her hipper than hip salon in the city. An excellent option for coloured or highlighted hair.

## Health & beauty

### Body Shop

*Shop G54, Ground Floor, Cavendish Square, Claremont, Southern Suburbs (021 671 1082/*

*www.thebodyshop.co.za).* **Open** 9am-6pm Mon-Thur, Sat; 9am-9pm Fri; 10am-4pm Sun. **Credit** AmEx, DC, MC, V.

This cornucopia of fruity smells and beautifully packaged products is the ideal spot for a pick-me-up.

### Denise Beauty & Skincare

*LG014, Lower Ground Floor, Cavendish Square, Claremont, Southern Suburbs (021 674 2980).* **Open** 9am-6pm Mon-Thur, Sat; 9am-9pm Fri; 10am-4pm Sun. **Credit** AmEx, DC, MC, V.

Conveniently situated in the heart of one of the city's most popular mall. Schedule in a treatment before, during or after a shopping spree.

# Music to your ears

## African Music Store

*134 Long Street, City Bowl (021 426 0857).* **Open** 9am-6pm Mon-Fri; 9am-2pm Sat. **Credit** MC, V. **Map** p274 G4.

A must-visit for those wanting to discover the wealth of music that rocks the continent. Switched-on staff are ready and willing to help you make your selection.

### Look & Listen

*Shop F14, Cavendish Square, Claremont, Southern Suburbs (021 683 1810/www. lookandlisten.co.za).* **Open** 9am-10.30pm daily. **Credit** AmEx, DC, MC, V.

This well-stocked store features a great selection of dancefloor winners, all the latest chart releases and some of the more obscure one-hit wonders.

### Mabu Vinyl

*Shop 2, Rheede Centre, Rheede Street, Gardens, Southern Suburbs (021 423 7635).* **Open** 9am-5pm Mon-Fri; 10am-2pm Sat. **No credit cards.**

This champion of local music is the ideal destination for a taste of the sounds that are putting South Africa's talent in the spotlight. They also stock vinyl.

### Musica

*Shop 214, Upper Level, Victoria Wharf, Atlantic Seaboard (021 418 4722/ www.musica.co.za).* **Open** 9am-11pm Mon-Sat; 10am-11pm Sun. **Credit** AmEx, DC, MC, V. **Map** p275 H1.

South Africa's original music store packs an impressive punch, with a great selection of local musical talent.

### Musica Megastore

*Dock Road Complex, V&A Waterfront (021 425 6300/www.musica.co.za).* **Open** 9am-9pm Mon-Thur, Sun; 9am-10pm Fri, Sat. **Credit** AmEx, DC, MC, V. **Map** p275 H1.

As the name implies, this is an enormous space filled with thousands of music and DVD options. Each section is manned by someone passionate about their genre, while the jazz lounge is a must-visit. Saturday morning concerts are a big draw too.

Eat, Drink, Shop

### Ecoco

*86 Loop Street, City Bowl (021 424 3339/www.*
*ecoco.co.za).* **Open** 9am-5pm Mon-Fri; 10am-1pm Sat.
**Credit** AmEx, DC, MC, V. **Map** p274 G4.
Most countries have beauty brands for which they
are famous and thankfully South Africa is no exception. Ecoco (the Ecological Cosmetics Company) has
its flagship store in the heart of the city, and it's a
beautifully designed space bursting with prettily
packaged, gorgeously scented bath, face and body
products. In keeping with their company ethos, local
and imported sustainable ingredients form the basis
of each of the products. **Photo** *p144.*

### Human Nature

*Shop 32, Constantia Village, Constantia, Southern*
*Suburbs (021 794 5078).* **Open** 8.30am-6pm Mon-
Fri; 9am-5pm Sat; 9am-3pm Sun. **Credit** AmEx,
DC, MC, V.
Your one-stop shop for homeopathic remedies, aro-
matherapy oils and other such goodies.

### MAC Cosmetics

*Shop 6140, Ground Floor, Victoria Wharf, Atlantic*
*Seaboard (021 421 4886/www.maccosmetics.com).*
**Open** 9am-9pm Mon-Sat; 10am-9pm Sun. **Credit**
AmEx, DC, MC, V. **Map** p275 H1.
This stand-alone store is dedicated to the cult cos-
metics brand favoured by international make-up
artists and models in the know. Trendy staff are
always on hand to help you reveal your best assets.

### Mr Cobbs the Barber Shop

*Shop 279, Upper Level, Victoria Wharf, Atlantic*
*Seaboard (021 418 2427/www.shavingshop.co.za).*
**Open** 9am-9pm Mon-Sat; 10am-9pm Sun. **Credit**
MC, V. **Map** p275 H1.
This charming, old-fashioned shaving shop has a
huge original barber's chair ready and waiting for
an authentic hot towel shave. The staff will also
advise on what animal bristle brushes are best for
shaving and they have an excellent selection of
shaving paraphernalia – shaving stands, mirrors
and their ever popular own-brand shaving cream in
a variety of delicious flavours.

### Parfums de France

*Shop 22, Constantia Village, Constantia, Southern*
*Suburbs (021 794 3327).* **Open** 9am-6pm Mon-
Fri; 9am-5pm Sat; 10am-2pm Sun. **Credit** AmEx,
DC, MC, V.
This store specialises in many of the big names in
cosmetics and perfumes and many of the lesser
known ones too. Parfums de France also has an in-
store beauty salon and stocks a good selection of
imported handbags.

### s.k.i.n.

*Dock Road, V&A Waterfront, Atlantic*
*Seaboard (021 425 3551/www.skinonline.co.za).*
**Open** 9am-9pm Mon-Fri; 9am-6pm Sat; 10am-
5pm Sun. **Credit** AmEx, DC, MC, V.
**Map** p275 H1.

# Tribal trends

If you wander round Cape Town, you'll soon
notice the assortment of crafts available
on every street corner, at the main markets
and in many of the stores in and around
the city. Here are a few pointers to help
you get the most out of your curio or local
craft experience:
● When you buy from street vendors, you
know you're buying relatively straight from
the source. Good things to look out for are
beaded wire decorative objects and quirky
animals made form recycled plastic. These
are also easy to store in your luggage and
make great gifts for family and friends.
● When you wander through any of the
African craft markets based in and around
the city, don't buy from the first place you
come across. Invariably you'll find the same
mask or carving at a nearby stall for a lower
price. That said, don't expect bargaining to
be as prolific as it is in many Asian countries.
Good buys are masks, carvings and
inexpensive jewellery items.
● If you're looking to buy something that will
take pride of place in your home, it is

advisable to visit one or two retailers who
should give you a background of the object
(age and origin), care advice (especially if it
is wood and will be taken to a foreign clime)
and whether or not they can ship it for you.
These retailers do make an impressive
mark-up, so ask about discounts.

### African Art Factory

*Block E, Old City Hospital Complex,*
*2 Portswood Road, V&A Waterfront, Atlantic*
*Seaboard (021 421 9910/www.african*
*artfactory.co.za).* **Open** 8.30am-4.30pm
Mon-Fri. **Credit** MC, V. **Map** p274 G1.

### African Image

*52 Burg Street, City Bowl (021 423 8385).*
**Open** 9am-5pm Mon-Fri; 9am-1pm Sat.
**Credit** AmEx, DC, MC, V. **Map** p275 H3.

### Out of This World

*Shop 6147, Ground Floor, V&A Waterfront,*
*Atlantic Seaboard (021 419 3246).*
**Open** 9am-8.45pm Mon-Sat; 10am-8pm
Sun. **Credit** AmEx, DC, MC, V.
**Map** p275 H1.

Much loved by visiting celebs, this all-white, utterly serene space offers excellent facials and pedicures, including a men-only programme and an alphabet soup of massage and relaxation therapy treatments.

## Household & design

### African Image

*52 Burg Street, City Bowl (021 423 8385).* **Open** 9am-5pm Mon-Fri; 9am-1.30pm Sat. **Credit** AmEx, DC, MC, V. **Map** p275 H3.

This Cape Town institution eschews curio stalls and chichi boutiques in favour of an authentic experience where you can pick up everything from antique artifacts worth tens of thousands of rands to cheap and cheerful pink pigs made out of recycled plastic.

### Africa Nova

*Shop 3A, Cape Quarter, 72 Waterkant Street, City Bowl (021 425 5123).* **Open** 10am-5pm Mon-Sat. **Credit** AmEx, DC, MC, V. **Map** p274 G3.

One of the first promoters of trend-conscious African crafts, here you'll find everything from potato print fabrics to cute African Christmas tree decorations and jewellery by local craftspeople.

### @Home

*Shop 6135, Victoria Wharf, Atlantic Seaboard (021 408 9000/www.home.co.za/for other branches 021 938 1911).* **Open** 9am-9pm daily. **Credit** AmEx, DC, MC, V. **Map** p275 H1.

This popular retail chain is crammed with great contemporary objects – from kitchenalia for budding chefs to great bedroom choices and an excellent range of delicious bath goodies.

### Bright House

*97 Bree Street, City Bowl (021 424 9024/www.bright house.co.za).* **Open** 9am-5pm Mon-Fri; 9am-1.30pm Sat. **Credit** AmEx, DC, MC, V. **Map** p274 G4.

You're spoilt for choice at this furniture shop, with clean lines and innovative ideas to funk up any home. Great smaller must-haves too. **Photo** *p149.*

### Cape to Cairo

*125 Waterkant Street, City Bowl (021 421 3518).* **Open** 9.30am-5.30pm Mon-Fri; 9.30am-2pm Sat. **Credit** AmEx, DC, MC, V. **Map** p274 G3.

This sister store to the Kalk Bay original is twice the size of its sibling and filled to the brim with trademark avant-garde objects found in some of the far-flung corners of the globe. Larger reworked pieces from Cuba and Russian crafts are popular. **Other locations**: 100 Main Road, Kalk Bay (021 788 4571).

### Carrol Boyes Shop

*Shop 6180, Victoria Wharf, Atlantic Seaboard (021 418 0595/www.carrolboyes.com).* **Open** 9am-9pm daily. **Credit** AmEx, DC, MC, V. **Map** p275 H1.

This is possibly one of South Africa's most famous creative exports – there's even a sister store in New York. Pick up pewter and silverware in Carrol's distinctive designs.

**Imagenius**. *See p148.*

**Wallflower**. *See p149.*

### Congo Joe

*Shop LG191 Lower Ground, Cavendish Square, Claremont, Southern Suburbs (021 671 2714).* **Open** 9am-6pm Mon-Thur, Sat; 9am-9pm Fri; 10am-4pm Sun. **Credit** AmEx, DC, MC, V.
This whimsical store features locally crafted crockery, patchwork quilts and crocheted blankets, and an enticing range of bath and beauty products.

### Hadeda

*Dunkley Square, 3 Wandel Street, City Bowl (021 465 8620).* **Open** 9am-5pm Mon-Fri; 9am-1pm Sat. **Credit** AmEx, DC, MC, V. **Map** p274 G5.
Walk into this colourful lair and leave feeling a little like Frida Kahlo. Great vintage-inspired paraphernalia – trays and glasses, plenty of religious icons and related goodies and a host of worm lanterns and mirrors. **Photo** *p150.*

### Heartworks

*98 Kloof Street, City Bowl (021 424 8419).* **Open** 9.30am-5.30pm Mon-Fri; 9.30am-2pm Sat. **Credit** AmEx, DC, MC, V. **Map** p274 F5.
This store, devoted to the appreciation of southern African craft, just gets it so right. Whether you walk away with a hand-crafted ceramic bowl or wire and bead serviette rings, you know you're taking a true taste of Africa with you.

### Helon Melon

*399 Main Road, Sea Point, Atlantic Seaboard (021 434 4282/www.helonmelon.co.za).* **Open** 9am-5pm Mon-Fri; 9am-1pm Sat. **Credit** AmEx, DC, MC, V. **Map** p273 C2.

This Sea Point store is filled with gloriously decadent linens by local talent Helen Gibb. Stock up on competitively priced sets for the boudoir of your dreams. She also stocks smalls – from bags and aprons to baking kits.

### Imagenius

*117 Long Street, City Bowl (021 423 7870).* **Open** 9am-5pm Mon-Fri; 9am-1pm Sat. **Credit** AmEx, DC, MC, V. **Map** p274 G4.
This eclectic store features a constantly changing array of local and imported products, including printed hanging lampshades, locally made jewellery and the Dirty Girl range of bath products from the US. Look out for the own-label baby clothes – the cutest souvenir of Cape Town ever. **Photo** *p147.*

### LIM

*86A Kloof Street, City Bowl (021 423 1200).* **Open** 9am-5pm Mon-Fri; 9.15am-1pm Sat. **Credit** AmEx, DC, MC, V. **Map** p274 F5.
This boutique-style store features a small range of custom-made contemporary furniture. They also stock beautiful ceramics and an enticing range of colourful perspex storage options.

### Loads of Living

*Shop 482, Upper Level, Canal Walk, Century City, Milnerton, Northern Suburbs (021 552 0297/ www.loadsofliving.co.za).* **Open** 9am-10pm daily. **Credit** AmEx, DC, MC, V.
This local success story features loads of products for the contemporary home, from brightly coloured cushions covered in striking graphics to gorgeous

bedlinen. Look out for the Rhubarb and Typhoon ranges of fun and frivolous kitchenalia.

### Loft Living

*122 Kloof Street, City Bowl (021 422 0088/ www.loftliving.co.za).* **Open** 9.30am-5.30pm Mon-Fri; 9.30am-1.30pm Sat. **Credit** AmEx, DC, MC, V. **Map** p274 F5.

Filled to the rafters with an eclectic selection of goodies from here and further afield. Expect to find brightly coloured cabinets from exotic climes, own-design contemporary furniture and a host of stuff that can only make you smile – from pot-bellied Buddhas to loud and proud flower-bedecked melamine tableware.

### Mr Price Home

*Shop 651, Upper Level, Canal Walk, Century City, Milnerton, Northern Suburbs (021 551 4439/ www.mrpricehome.co.za).* **Open** 10am-9pm Mon-Fri; 9am-9pm Sat. **Credit** AmEx, DC, MC, V.

As cheap and cheerful as it gets in South Africa, Mr Price (or Monsieur Prix as many refer to it) is crammed with affordable homeware that's both chic and contemporary. Look out for copies of design classics like Ant chairs or perspex nest tables.

### Nocturnal Affair

*Shop 38, Gardens Centre, Mill Street, City Bowl (021 461 7412).* **Open** 9am-6pm Mon-Fri; 9am-3pm Sat; 10am-2pm Sun. **Credit** AmEx, DC, MC, V. **Map** p274 G5.

Stop in for clean-lined ceramics, naturally scented soaps and a baby range of linen and clothing.

### Pa Kua

*55 Main Street, Newlands, Southern Suburbs (021 671 1553).* **Open** 9am-5pm Mon-Fri; 10am-1pm Sat. **Credit** AmEx, DC, MC, V.

This sophisticated Newlands store is stocked with a host of great imported glassware and local arts.

### Spirit

*Shop 41, Gardens Centre, City Bowl (021 462 4959).* **Open** 9am-6pm Mon-Fri; 9am-3pm Sat; 10.30am-2pm last Sun of mth. **Credit** AmEx, DC, MC, V. **Map** p274 G5.

Browse a modern mix of kitchenalia, tableware and gadgets galore at this chic little store. A great range of kiddies' things, excellent space-saving ideas and quirky gear to make you smile.

### Still Life

*229C Long Street, City Bowl (021 426 0143).* **Open** 10am-5pm Mon-Fri; 9am-1pm Sat. **Credit** AmEx, DC, MC, V. **Map** p274 G4.

This eclectic and friendly store is crammed with hand-sewn, vintage-inspired aprons and tea towels, quirky paintings for sprucing up your space and a host of cheerful homeware items.

### Story

*221A Upper Buitenkant Street, Vredehoek, Southern Suburbs (021 462 4889).* **Open** 9am-5pm Mon-Fri; 9.30am-1.30pm Sat. **Credit** DC, MC, V.

This gorgeous store is like stepping into a well-ordered dressing room. Expect a feminine selection of stuff from delicate ceramics to mirrors, sparkly beaded jewellery and rails of floaty dresses and skirts – perfect for champagne-fuelled soirées.

### Wallflower

*Shop 2, Portside Centre, Somerset Road, Green Point, Atlantic Seaboard (021 434 8265).* **Open** 9am-6pm Mon-Fri; 9am-5pm Sat. **Credit** DC, MC, V. **Map** p274 G2.

One of the most innovative lifestyle stores on the scene. Owner Stefan Blom works with each of his suppliers to create utterly unique, covetable products, from the jaw-dropping wooden carved wings that dominate one wall to his own range of bath and beauty products, quirky stationery, ice cream-coloured ceramics and miniature artworks by some of the city's most talented. **Photo** *p148.*

### Weylandts

*Corner Alfred & Hospital Streets, City Bowl (021 425 5282/www.weylandts.com).* **Open** 9am-5.30pm Mon-Fri; 9am-2pm Sat; 10am-2pm 1st Sun of mth. **Credit** AmEx, DC, MC, V. **Map** p275 H3.

This multi-level bastion of contemporary style has it all – from outdoor to indoor furniture. Bedroom, lounge and dining set-ups help you visualise the look in your own home.

Clean living: **Bright House**. *See p147.*

**Eat, Drink, Shop**

## Opticians

### Bauer

*Shop 34, Gardens Centre, Mill Street, City Bowl
(021 465 1260).* **Open** 9am-6pm Mon-Fri; 9am-3pm
Sat. **Credit** AmEx, DC, MC, V. **Map** p274 G5.
Owner-run, this Gardens Centre store offers everything from eye tests to contact lens fittings, frame
selections and a great after-sales service – they will
adjust your glasses or sunglasses for free.

### Extreme Eyewear

*Shop A18, Cape Quarter, 72 Waterkant Street,
City Bowl (021 421 1135).* **Open** 10am-6pm Mon-
Fri; 10am-5pm Sat. **Credit** AmEx, DC, MC, V.
**Map** p274 G3.
This design-tastic store is the perfect destination for
trendy eyewear, with ranges from the likes of Oliver
Peoples, Gucci, Chanel and Armani.

### Mullers

*Shop 5, Alfred Mall, V&A Waterfront, Atlantic
Seaboard (021 421 4980/www.mullers.co.za).*
**Open** 9am-9pm Mon-Sat; 10am-9pm Sun. **Credit**
AmEx, DC, MC, V. **Map** p275 H1.
The city's oldest opticians, they offer a superb
optometry service and carry a comprehensive selec-
tion of frames from the world's big fashion brands.

### Specsavers

*G39 Ground Floor, Cavendish Square, Claremont,
Southern Suburbs (021 674 3183/www.specstores.
co.za).* **Open** 9am-6pm Mon-Thur, Sat; 9am-9pm Fri;
10am-4pm Sun. **Credit** AmEx, DC, MC, V.
Cut-price frames are the order of the day here. They
also offer professional eye examinations and carry
the Transitions range of photo-sensitive lenses.

## Sports

### Bowman's Cycles

*153 Bree Street, City Bowl (021 423 2527).*
**Open** 7.30am-5.30pm Mon-Fri; 9am-1.30pm Sat.
**Credit** AmEx, DC, MC, V. **Map** p274 G4.
The city and its surrounds are a mountain biking
mecca and at Bowman's Cycles they will kit you out
with the latest gear.

### Cape Union Mart

*Shop 142, Victoria Wharf, Atlantic Seaboard (021
419 0019/www.capeunionmart.co.za).* **Open** 9am-
9pm Sun-Thur; 9am-11pm Fri, Sat. **Credit** AmEx,
DC, MC, V. **Map** p275 H1.
This enormously popular outdoor store is the first
port of call for many an adventurer – they stock
everything from sleeping bags to mini gas camping
stoves and high-tech gear. Staff are helpful.

**Hadeda.** See p148.

## Outdoor Warehouse

*Shop 1, Willowbridge Value Mall, Corner Old Oak Road & Carl Cronje Drive (021 914 1358/www. outdoorwarehouse.co.za).* **Open** 8.30am-5.30pm Mon-Fri; 8.30am-4pm Sat; 9am-1pm Sun. **Credit** AmEx, DC, MC, V.

Run by outdoor-crazy people for outdoor-crazy people, you'll find every single item you'll ever need for outdoor living right here.

## Toys & games

### Peggity's

*Shop 6126, Victoria Wharf, Atlantic Seaboard (021 419 6873).* **Open** 9am-9pm Mon-Sat; 10am-9pm Sun. **Credit** AmEx, DC, MC, V. **Map** p275 H1.

No matter what your age, you'll never fail to be delighted by the colourful displays at this Waterfront institution. Perfect for last-minute gifts, they also stock excellent learn-while-you-play games.

### Tinka Tonka Toys

*175 Buitenkant Street, City Bowl (021 461 1441).* **Open** 8.30am-6pm Mon-Fri; 8.30am-5pm Sat; 9am-3pm Sun. **Credit** AmEx, DC, MC, V. **Map** p274 H4.

This superb city store is crammed with every kind of toy imaginable. The staff really know their stuff and will advise you on the best toys to suit

various age groups. They also stock some beautiful wooden toys and train sets and have plenty of buckets filled with everything from rubber animals to joke items and stationery.

### Toi Toy

*Victoria Wharf, V&A Waterfront, Atlantic Seaboard (082 320 2236/www.toytoi.co.za).* **Open** 9am-9pm daily. **Credit** AmEx, DC, MC, V. **Map** p275 H1.

This teeny little toy store (barrow, really) in the Waterfront caters for enthusiasts and collectors of vinyl toys. Imported limited production figurines from the US and Japan feature heavily but the real stars of the show are the Zolos – hand-made (from recycled material) South African vinyl toys.

## Wine

### Caroline's Fine Wine Cellar

*15 Long Street, City Bowl (021 419 8984/www. carolineswine.com).* **Open** 9am-5.30pm Mon-Fri; 9am-1pm Sat. **Credit** AmEx, DC, MC, V. **Map** p274 G4.

This bastion of wines champions the best the Cape has to offer at competitive prices. The service is what sets this shop apart, with tastings and advice offered at every turn. They ship all over the world. **Other locations**: Shop 8, King's Warehouse, Victoria Wharf, V&A Waterfront (021 425 5701).

So many bottles, so little time: **Vino Pronto** stocks fine wines and friendly staff.

## Manuka Wine Boutique

*The Cellars, Shop 9, Chapman's Peak Drive, Noordhoek Farm Village, Noordhoek, Southern Peninsula (021 789 0898/www.manuka.co.za).* **Open** 10am-6pm Mon-Fri; 9am-5pm Sat; 10am-5pm Sun. **Credit** AmEx, MC, V.

Manuka has built a name for itself as a store with impeccable and knowledgeable hands-on service. The extensive selection caters for all budgets and palate preferences, and they also offer extra services like delivery (locally and abroad), regular wine tastings and popular dinners with guest winemakers.

## Vaughan Johnson's Wine & Cigar Shop

*Dock Road, V&A Waterfront, Atlantic Seaboard (021 419 2121).* **Open** 9am-6pm Mon-Fri; 9am-5pm Sat; 10am-5pm Sun. **Credit** AmEx, DC, MC, V. **Map** p275 H1.

Cape wine doyen Vaughan Johnson rules the roost at this top-notch wine shop. From top-of-the-range limited edition vintages to easy-drinking palate pleasers, it's impossible to leave not feeling better educated about wine. Shipping all over the world can be arranged and they also offer an excellent online sales service.

## Vino Pronto

*42 Orange Street, City Bowl (021 424 5587/ www.vinopronto.co.za).* **Open** 10am-8pm Mon-Fri; 10am-5pm Sat. **Credit** DC, MC, V. **Map** p274 G5.

This deceptively hole-in-the-wallish dealer houses an enormous variety of some of the best wines available in the city. The staff really have a nose for what they're doing and are full of helpful recommendations should you need some guidance navigating your way around their stash. If you're a regular, they even keep a look-out for new blends they think you might enjoy.

## Wine Concepts on Kloof

*Shop 15, Lifestyles on Kloof Centre, 50 Kloof Street, City Bowl (021 426 4401/www.wineconcepts.co.za).* **Open** 10am-7pm Mon-Fri; 9am-5pm Sat. **Credit** AmEx, DC, MC, V. **Map** p274 F5.

Conveniently situated and stocked from floor to ceiling with delicious, carefully selected wines, Wine Concepts on Kloof is a shop run by buffs for buffs. Take your dinner party menu along and they'll ably recommend a wine to accompany each course. They also have a good national and international delivery service available.

# Arts & Entertainment

# THE CAPE GALLERY, 60 CHURCH STREET

*deals in fine art reflecting
the rich cultural diversity of South Africa.*

---

*Gallery Hours:* **Mon to Fri:** 9h30 to 17h00 | **Sat:** 9h00 to 13h00
**tel:** 27 21 423 5309 **fax:** 27 21 424 9063
**e-mail:** cgallery@mweb.co.za **web:**www.capegallery.co.za

*American express, Mastercard, Visa and Diner cards are accepted.
Reliable arrangements can be made to freight purchases to foreign destinations.*

THE CAPE
GALLERY

# Festivals & Events

Even the penguins get a festival in South Africa.

No set designer needed at **Kirstenbosch Botanical Gardens**. *See p156.*

From the start of the 'green season' in winter through to the major summer festivities, Cape Town is a city that's big on culture. The social calendar is crammed with must-see events, from rock concerts and cycle races to penguin festivals and minstrel carnivals.

Deciding what to see and do on your travel itinerary might be a tough choice, but the city is well prepared to help you make up your mind. You can drop into one of the local tourist offices (021 487 6800/www.tourismcapetown.co.za), check out the local press or simply ask a friendly Capetonian for tips on what you should do.

## Spring

### Cape Town International Comedy Festival

*Baxter Theatre Complex, Rondebosch, Southern Suburbs (021 417 5949/www.comedyfestival.co.za).* **Date** Sept.
The world's leading stand-up comics share the stage with South Africa's finest to give you their latest hilarious takes on sex, politics and anything else they feel like poking fun at. There's something for all comedy tastes, from good family fun to the slightly more risqué.

### Simonstown Penguin Festival

*Jubilee Square, Simonstown (021 786 1758/021 786 5798/www.simonstown.com/penguinfestival).* **Date** mid Sept.
First held in 2004, the Simonstown Penguin Festival has become a firm fixture on Cape Town's conservation calendar. In honour of the area's feathered friends, the festival aims to raise funds for penguin conservation. Each year the town dresses up in black and white and comes alive with sounds, culture, sport and fun to support this worthy cause.

### Hermanus Whale Festival

*Hermanus, Whale Route (028 313 0928/www.whalefestival.co.za).* **Date** late Sept.
A bit further afield, but a definite drawcard for any visitor. At any other time during the year you could be forgiven for thinking of Hermanus as just a sleepy town in the Western Cape. But during the Whale Festival locals and tourists alike are promised spectacular sightings of these magnificent creatures alongside flea markets, music and outstanding South African cuisine.

### Cape Argus Sanlam Cycle Tour

*Starts from Bellville Velodrome, Bellville, Northern Suburbs (021 949 2537/8/www.argussanlam.co.za).* **Date** mid Dec.

The 118km Argus Sanlam Cycle Tour is a gruelling race through some of Cape Town's most picturesque scenery and a premier event on the local cycling calendar. The challenging route attracts some of the world's top cyclists among the 10,000 entrants.

### Carols by Candlelight at Kirstenbosch

*Kirstenbosch Botanical Gardens, Rhodes Drive, Southern Suburbs (021 799 8783/www. kirstenbosch.co.za).* **Date** mid Dec.

The already festive Cape Town atmosphere is made all the merrier by the Carols by Candlelight services at Kirstenbosch. It's a great evening out for the family but bring a blanket to sit on and a jumper for later when it gets chilly – and do get there early to stake your patch of grass. **Photo** *p155.*

### Vodacom/Good Hope FM Clifton Beach Challenge

*Clifton Beach, Atlantic Seaboard.* **Map** p277 A6. **Date** mid Dec.

Set on Clifton's cosmopolitan 4th Beach, this fitness challenge is a sure-fire crowd pleaser between former and current Springboks and the Clifton Beach lifesavers. To date, players like Corné Krige, Breyton

**Mother City Queer Costume Party.**

Paulse and Percy Montgomery have taken part in the event to raise funds for the Clifton Lifesavers. There is also the ever-popular Clifton New Face Search competition.

### Mother City Queer Costume Party

*Ratanga Junction, Milnerton, Northern Suburbs (021 426 5709/www.mcqp.co.za).* **Date** mid Dec.

Now in its 12th year, Cape Town's Mother City Queer Costume Party is well known for attracting the most diverse crowd of local and international gays, lesbians and friends, all dressed in some of the most outlandish attire imaginable. It all adds up to one of the city's most raucous 24-hour parties.

### Cape Town Minstrel Carnival

*City Bowl.* **Date** 1-2 Jan.

When the Cape Minstrels come out to do their thing, everyone else stands back and watches. Their passion for having a party and getting the New Year off to a rowdy start is infectious. The parade gets underway in District Six and marches its way to Green Point Stadium, and there's plenty to keep you entertained en route. The carnival is such a tradition that it's hardly publicised, but ask around and you'll be sure to find out where and when it's going down.

### J&B Metropolitan Handicap

*Kenilworth Racecourse, Kenilworth, Southern Suburbs (021 700 1621/www.jbmet.co.za).* **Date** late Jan.

The J&B Met is a big date on Cape Town's social calendar with the glitterati turning out en masse for this annual horse-racing event. But you don't have to don the latest Valentino or Gucci to attend. Just as long as you're dressed smartly, you can live it up alongside Cape Town's finest.

### Cape Town Pride Festival

*City Bowl (021 425 6461/www.capetownpride.co.za).* **Date** late Feb.

The ten-day Gay and Lesbian Pride Festival features some really wild events. It's not just about having a party; it's about making a statement of friendship and unity. The whole shindig reaches its peak with a Mardi Gras-like festival and Pride Parade (complete with floats and top DJs) on the last day.

### Cape Argus Pick 'n' Pay Cycle Tour

*Cape Peninsula (021 685 6551/www.cycletour.co.za).* **Date** early Mar.

Over 35,000 cyclists from all over the globe line up for one of the most beautiful races in the world – a gruelling 109-kilometre (68-mile) ride across the Cape Peninsula.

### KFM Symphony of Fire

*V&A Waterfront, Atlantic Seaboard (www.symphony offire.co.za/www.kfm.co.za).* **Map** p275 H1. **Date** mid-late Mar.

Behold the sky turning into a captivating kaleidoscope of colour to a soundtrack of dramatic musical

**KFM Symphony of Fire.**
*See p156.*

scores. Taking place at the V&A Waterfront, with internationally renowned pyrotechnics companies representing their countries, this is the largest event of its kind on the continent.

### Old Mutual Two Oceans Marathon
*Cape Town (021 671 9407/www.twooceans marathon.org.za). Date early Apr.*
The Two Oceans, known as 'the most scenic ultra-marathon in the world' is also one of the toughest, with the route taking runners over some of Cape Town's most gruelling hills. Even if you don't harbour any ambitions of running the full 56 kilometres (35 miles), there's a great vibe among spectators.

### Cape Times Waterfront Wine Festival
*V&A Waterfront, Atlantic Seaboard (021 408 7600/www.waterfront.co.za).* **Map** p275 H1.
**Date** early May.
If you enjoy fine wine, the Cape Times Waterfront Wine Festival will save you the trouble of having to hunt it out. This annual event brings almost all of the Western Cape's most celebrated wineries together under one roof. There's also a great selection of cheeses, olive oils and olives to taste and buy.

### Cape Gourmet Festival
*Cape Town International Convention Centre, City Centre (021 797 4500/www.gourmetsa.com).* **Map** p275 I3. **Date** late May.
This gastronomic feeding frenzy is Africa's largest food exhibition and culminates in the four-day Good Food & Wine Show, where South Africa's culinary elite gather to cook up a storm.

## Winter

### Hobby-X
*Cape Town International Convention Centre, City Bowl (011 478 3686/www.hobby-x.co.za).*
**Map** p275 I3. **Date** early June.
From archery to woodwork, Hobby-X is an A-Z of anything and everything that can entertain you. Browse the stands or enrol for one of the workshops.

### Encounters: South African International Documentary Film Festival
*Cinema Nouveau, V&A Waterfront, Atlantic Seaboard (021 426 0405/021 465 4686/ www.encounters.co.za).* **Map** p275 H1. **Date** July.
Encounters is South Africa's only film festival dedicated exclusively to documentaries.

### Cape Wow Festival
*City Bowl (021 447 9108/www.capewow.co.za).*
**Date** early Aug.
WOW stands for Woman of the World and it's fitting that the Mother City gets to host the Cape WOW festival – a celebration that coincides with National Women's Day. Join some of South Africa's leading ladies to celebrate what it means to be a woman.

### Cape Town Fashion Week
*Cape Town International Convention Centre, City Bowl (021 422 0390/www.capetownfashion week.com).* **Map** p275 I3. **Date** late Aug.
Cape Town is the fashion capital of Africa. Every year, South Africa's top designers come to the city to put on a show of unashamed haute couture.

**Arts & Entertainment**

# Children

The perfect spot for Cape crusaders.

Cape Town seems designed to create childhood memories – a trip down to the dark, dingy dungeons of the Cape of Good Hope Castle or up to the top of towering Table Mountain is sure to be remembered for a very long time. But while the Mother City is very child-friendly, some local operators aren't great at advertising their junior options, so make sure you phone before you visit.

Cape Town Tourism's Visitor Centre (021 487 6800/www.tourismcapetown.co.za) can help with activities to keep the kids entertained and on the go during their weekend, holiday or stopover in the city. For pre-packaged tour options, contact Kid About Tours (021 715 8387/www.kidabouttours.co.za) or Cape for Kids (021 790 6067/www.capeforkids.com).

## Activities

### Indoors

#### City Rock

*Corner of Anson & Collingwood Streets, Observatory, Southern Suburbs (021 447 1326/www.cityrock. co.za).* **Open** 11am-9pm Mon-Fri; 10am-6pm Sat, Sun. **Admission** R55; R35 concessions. **Credit** MC, V.
Big kids can get to grips with the bouldering cave and the three climbing walls, while five- to ten-year-olds can tackle a specially designed section with the help of instructors, good grips and gentler slopes.

#### GrandWest Casino & Entertainment Centre

*1 Vanguard Drive, Goodwood, Northern Suburbs (021 505 7777/www.grandwest.co.za).*
**Magic Company** *(021 534 0244).* **Open** 10am-11pm Mon-Thur, Sun; 10am-1am Fri, Sat.
**Ice Station** *(021 535 2260/www.icerink.co.za).* **Open** 10am-12.30pm, 2-4.30pm Mon-Wed; 10am-12.30pm, 2-10.30pm Thur; 10am-2.30pm, 4.30pm-midnight Fri, Sat. **Admission** R25.
**Credit** AmEx, MC, V.
Gambling seems like an annoying distraction at the casino's entertainment complex, where the Magic Company offers games, rides, go-karting and mini-golf, while the Ice Station keeps kids happy with two ice rinks.

#### Iziko South African Museum

*25 Queen Victoria Street, City Bowl (021 481 3800/ www.iziko.org.za/sam).* **Open** 10am-5pm daily. **Admission** R10; R5 concessions; free under-5s; free to all Sat. **Credit** MC, V. **Map** p274 G4.

The Iziko South African Museum offers loads of detailed, interesting, up-to-date exhibits. The whale well is always a popular place for kids, while at least one entire generation of Cape Town children has been haunted by the bloodthirsty dinosaur displays.

#### Kenilworth Karting

*Corner Warrington & Myhof Roads, Kenilworth, Southern Suburbs (021 683 2670/www.karting. co.za).* **Open** 1-11pm Mon-Thur; 11am-11pm Fri; 10am-7pm Sat, Sun. **Admission** R35/10 laps.
**Credit** MC, V.
Cape Town's road ragers earn their racing stripes by zooming their go-karts around the laps of the city's indoor Grand Prix circuits. The most popular is this Southern Suburbs track.

#### Laserquest

*Lower Level, Stadium on Main, Main Road, Claremont, Southern Suburbs (021 683 7296/ www.laserquest.co.za).* **Open** 10.30am-11pm daily. **Admission** R30/35mins; R40/45mins.
**Credit** MC, V.
What better way for would-be warriors to spend a day than running around in the dark shooting laser guns at their buddies? Their energy will run out long before their ammunition.

#### Let's Go Bowling

*Lower Level, Stadium on Main, Main Road, Claremont, Southern Suburbs (021 671 1893/ www.letsgobowling.co.za).* **Open** 9am-midnight Mon-Sat. **Admission** R25 per game before 4pm; R35 after 4pm. **Credit** MC, V.
Let's Go Bowling offers enough crazy lighting and pumping music to keep pretty much any amateur ten-pinner happy.
**Other locations**: N1 City, Goodwood (021 595 2100). Tygervalley Centre, Durban Road, Bellville (021 914 8217). Somerset Mall, Somerset West (021 850 0254).

#### MTN ScienCentre

*407 Canal Walk, Century City, Entrance 5, Milnerton, Northern Suburbs (021 529 8100).*
**Admission** R24; R22 concessions. **Open** 9.30am-6pm Mon-Thur; 9.30am-8pm Fri, Sat; 10am-6pm Sun. **Credit** AmEx, DC, MC, V.
The MTN ScienCentre in Century City features over 280 interactive displays, plus an auditorium, camera obscura, computer rooms, laboratories and an exhibition hall.

#### Planetarium

*South African Museum, 25 Queen Victoria Street, City Bowl (021 481 3900/021 481 3900/www. iziko.org.za/planetarium).* **Screenings** 2pm Mon,

Wed-Fri; 2pm, 8pm Tue; noon, 1pm, 2.30pm Sat, Sun. **Admission** R20; R6-R8 concessions. **No credit cards**. **Map** p274 G4.
Tilt back in your reclining seat and watch the heavens appear around you. The interactive Twinkle show will appeal to younger kiddies, while the Sky Tonight shows the older ones what they'll find in Cape Town's night sky. **Photo** *p160*.

### Scratch Patch
*Dock Road, V&A Waterfront, City Bowl (021 419 9429/www.scratchpatch.co.za).* **Open** 9am-5.30pm daily. **Stones** *per bag* R10-R65. **Credit** AmEx, DC, MC, V. **Map** p274 G1.
Purchase a small plastic bag or container, and go scratching for multi-coloured rocks and tumble-polished semi-precious stones. With stones like tiger's eye, amethyst, rose quartz and agate filling the 'patch', it's like going on a mini treasure hunt.

### South African Astronomical Observatory
*Observatory Road, Observatory, Southern Suburbs (021 447 0025/www.saao.ac.za).* **Tours** 8pm 2nd Sat of mth. **Admission** free.
Stay up past your bedtime and take a look into the night skies at the historic observatory.

### Stadium on Main
*Main Road, Claremont, Southern Suburbs (021 671 3665/021 683 9061).* **Open** 8.30am-2am Mon-Fri; 8am-5pm Sat, Sun. **Credit** MC, V.

This complex near Cavendish Square features a selection of action cricket, action netball, action soccer and action beach volleyball – complete with sand.

## Outdoors

### Action Paint Ball
*Tokai Forest, Tokai, Southern Suburbs (021 790 7603/www.actionpursuit.co.za).* **Open** 9.30am-1pm, 1.30-5pm daily. **Rate** R90 incl paintball gun, 100 paintballs, neck protector and bush jacket. Additional paintballs R35/100. **No credit cards**.
The minimum age for paintball is 11, but trigger-happy teens are more than welcome.

### Boulders Beach
*South of Simonstown, Southern Peninsula (021 786 2329).* **Open** 8am-5pm daily. **Admission** R15; R5 concessions.
Few sights are more amusing than watching a penguin waddling up the beach at the end of a long day's fishing. And few are more heart-warming than watching your toddler waddling behind.

### Cape Point Ostrich Farm
*Plateau Road, opposite entrance of Cape of Good Hope Nature Reserve, Southern Peninsula (021 780 9294/www.capepointostrichfarm.com).* **Tours** R25; R10 concessions. **Credit** AmEx, DC, MC, V.
You won't get to ride on one of these large, flightless birds, but you will get to see their long necks, huge eggs and proud feathers.

**Boulders Beach.**

**Arts & Entertainment**

**Planetarium**. *See p158.*

## Chart Farm
*Claasens Road, Wynberg Park, Wynberg, Southern Suburbs (021 761 0434).* **Open** 9am-4pm daily. **No credit cards**.
The last surviving farm in suburban Wynberg has orchards, vineyards, and chestnut and walnut groves where small, eager hands can pluck away.

## Downhill Adventures
*Shop 10, Overbeek Building, Junction Kloof, Long & Orange Streets, City Bowl (021 422 0388/www. downhilladventures.com).* **Open** 8am-5pm Mon-Fri. **Credit** MC, V. **Map** p274 G4.
Cape Town's one-stop adventure shop arranges packages for sandboarding, surf schools, kiteboarding, shark diving, quad biking, tandem skydiving – more than enough to get young (and old) daredevils' hearts beating.

## Honeybee Education Centre
*Corner Parow & Milner Roads, Maitland, Northern Suburbs (021 511 4567/www.beekeeping. com/honeybee-africa).* **Open** 8am-4.45pm Mon-Thur; 8am-4pm Fri; 8am-noon Sat. **Admission** R15. **No credit cards**.
This bee-keeping centre lets kids watch what happens in the hive from behind the sting-free safety of a glass window. Book in advance if you want to see the honey show.

## Imhoff Farm
*Kommetjie Road, Kommetjie, Southern Peninsula (021 783 4545/083 753 5227/www.imhofffarm. co.za).* **Open** 9am-5pm Tue-Sun. **Admission** varies. **Credit** MC, V.
Fancy getting up close and personal with a snake? Admiring a peacock's feathers? Exploring a working farmyard? Riding a camel on the beach? Riding a horse? It's all possible at the child-friendly Nature Park at Imhoff Farm.

## Kirstenbosch National Botanical Gardens
*Rhodes Avenue, Newlands, Southern Suburbs (021 761 4916/www.sanbi.org.za).* **Open** Apr-Aug 8am-5pm daily; Sept-May 8am-7pm daily. **Admission** R25; R5-R15 concessions; free under-6s. **Credit** AmEx, DC, MC, V.
These famous botanical gardens have a great deal to offer the little ones – whether they're running after the wild geese, exploring the Touch Garden or simply enjoying the traditional summertime Sunday sunset concerts.

## Monkey Town
*Mondeor Road, Somerset West (021 858 1060/ www.monkeys.co.za).* **Open** 9am-5pm daily. **Admission** R50; R2-R35 concessions; free under-3s. **Credit** MC, V.
This primate paradise is home to 25 simian species, from big chimps to curious lemurs. Monkey Town offers supervised holiday programmes for school children in July and October, with guided field trips through the makeshift jungle.

## Ratanga Junction
*Century City Boulevard, Century City, Milnerton, Northern Suburbs (086 120 0300/group bookings 021 550 8504/www.ratanga.co.za).* **Open** 10am-5pm Fri, Sun; 10am-6pm Sat; 10am-5pm daily during school holidays. **Admission** Above 1.3m (4.2ft) tall R100 ; under 1.3m (4.2ft) tall R50. **Credit** DC, MC, V.
Cape Town's signature theme park seems to be constantly on the brink of closing down, so enjoy the fun rides like Monkey Falls, Diamond Digger and the Cobra while you can. The park is closed during the winter holidays.

## Two Oceans Aquarium
*Dock Road, V&A Waterfront, Atlantic Seaboard (021 418 3823/www.aquarium.co.za).* **Open** 9.30am-6pm daily. **Admission** R65; R30-R50 concessions; free under-4s. **Credit** AmEx, DC, MC, V. **Map** p275 H2.
This is a must-visit for anyone – with or without little ones in tow. Attractions include seals, penguins, a kelp forest and, of course, fish. There's a touch pool where kids can prod and poke a variety of seaweeds, anemones and sea urchins. The aquarium also offers holiday events that include sleepovers in the brilliant blue shadow of the shark tank.

## Tygerberg Zoo
*Exit 39, Klipheuwel-Stellenbosch off-ramp, N1 (021 884 4494/www.tygerbergzoo.co.za).* **Open** 9am-5pm Mon-Thur; 9am-4.30pm Fri. **Admission** R44; R28 concessions. **No credit cards**.
Come face to face with lions, tigers, cheetahs, chimps, zebras, bears, reptiles and antelope. There's also a children's farmyard and café.

## World of Birds
*Valley Road, Hout Bay, Southern Peninsula (021 790 2730/www.worldofbirds.org.za).* **Open** 9am-5pm daily. **Admission** R50; R32-R40 concessions. **Credit** AmEx, DC, MC, V.
Africa's largest bird park boasts walk-through aviaries containing more than 4,000 birds, plus monkeys, meerkats, marmosets and squirrels.

# Theatre

## Lilliput Children's Theatre Company
*Baxter Theatre & other venues (www.lilliputplayers. co.za).* **Tickets** R18 at Baxter, free in public areas like Cavendish Square. **Credit** varies.
This energetic theatre group performs interactive shows at the Baxter Theatre, shopping centres, schools, functions and birthday parties.

## Rainbow Puppet Theatre
*Constantia Waldorf School, Spaanschemat River Road, Constantia, Southern Suburbs (021 783 2063).* **Shows** 10am Sat. **Tickets** R15. **No credit cards**.
This puppet theatre, aimed at the under-sevens, changes its shows every month. Shows take place on Saturday mornings in the country setting of the Waldorf School.

**Arts & Entertainment**

### Stagecraft Drama Studio
*Based in Oranjezicht area, shows at Artscape, GrandWest & elsewhere (021 423 2675).* **Tickets** R25. **Credit** varies.
This drama studio, which is sponsored by the National Arts Council, offers educational shows throughout the year.

## Restaurants

### Barnyard Farmstall
*Steenberg Road, Tokai, Southern Suburbs (021 712 6934).* **Open** 9am-4.30pm Mon-Fri; 8.30am-4.30pm Sat, Sun. **Main courses** R40. **Credit** AmEx, DC, MC, V.
Located at the foot of Ou Kaapse Weg, this farmstall offers wholesome country fare and a setting that's straight out of a children's book: all straw bales, bouncing rabbits and strutting roosters.

### Deer Park Café
*2 Deer Park Drive, Vredehoek, City Bowl (021 462 6311).* **Open** 8.30am-4pm Mon, Tue, Sun; 8.30am-9pm Wed-Sat. **Main courses** R50. **Credit** AmEx, DC, MC, V.
This small restaurant opens on to a children's park in Vredehoek, on the outskirts of the City Bowl. The menu features healthy veggie options and free-range meat dishes… plus cappuccinos for Mum and Dad.

### Dunes Bar & Restaurant
*1 Beach Road, Hout Bay, Southern Peninsula (021 790 1876).* **Open** 9am-late. **Main courses** R70. **Credit** AmEx, DC, MC, V.
Probably the most child-friendly restaurant on the Cape Peninsula, Dunes has outdoor seating, a play park (complete with jungle gym) and the golden sands of Hout Bay beach.

### Spur Steak Ranches
*Shop 280, Victoria Wharf, V&A Waterfront, Atlantic Seaboard (021 418 3620/www.spur.co.za).* **Open** 9am-midnight Mon-Thur; 9am-1am Fri, Sat; 9am-11pm Sun. **Main courses** R50; R20 children. **Credit** AmEx, DC, MC, V. **Map** p275 H1.
With branches across the Cape the Spur chain remains a favourite with kids. And while grown-ups may scoff at the faux Native American decor, just about everybody who's grown up in South Africa knows the menu off by heart.
**Other locations**: Arthur Road near the Protea Hotel, Sea Point (021 439 5536). Main Road, Claremont (021 683 3860).

## Shops

### Naartjie
*Shop 117, Victoria Wharf, Atlantic Seaboard (021 421 5819).* **Open** 9am-9pm Mon-Sat; 10am-9pm Sun. **Credit** AmEx, DC, MC, V. **Map** p275 H1.
One of the first cool kid-friendly brands in the country, Naartjie continues to go from strength to strength. Cute prints in a seemingly never-ending

array of colours for boys and girls are the order of the day, ensuring your little ones always stand out from the crowd. The baby range is adorable too. There's a great factory shop in Hout Bay.
**Other locations**: Shop F62, Cavendish Square (021 683 7184); Shop 437, Upper Level, Canal Walk (021 551 6317); 46 Main Road, Hout Bay (021 790 30930).

## Babysitting & childcare

Some operators charge more for babysitting in hotels, so be sure to ask about rates (and experience) before you hire.

### Childminders
*(021 788 6788/083 254 4683/www.childminders.co.za).* **Open** 8.30am-5pm Mon-Fri. **Rates** R28-R55/hr. **No credit cards**.
Childminders' minders all have at least three years' experience, as well as first aid qualifications. The agency offers casual babysitting, au pairs and night nurses.

### Mary Poppins
*(021 674 6689/083 454 1282).* **Open** 8am-5pm Mon-Fri. **Rates** R25-R40/hr. **No credit cards**.
This au pair agency (not a babysitting service) does long- and short-term placements and requires a few days' notice.

Naartjie.

# Comedy

The Cape of good laughs.

Capetonians know their elbow from their funny bone, and fortunately most locals – despite being stressed-out Sarf Africans – do have a pretty good sense of humour.

Much of the credit for the current rude health of Cape Town's comedy scene goes to British stand-up Mark Sampson who, in the late 1990s, started a free local comedy workshop called the Comedy Lab, which grew from seven regulars to a small nation of 30 comedians known as the Cape Comedy Collective. The Collective has since reinvented itself as the smaller, modestly named Comedy All-Stars (www.comedyallstars.co.za), with many CCC alumni going solo to provide the Mother City with a mother lode of one-man (or one-woman) shows.

So what do Cape comedians joke about? Funnily enough, the local funny folk tend to leave politics and politicians alone (letting the facts speak for themselves), focusing instead on broader topics to appeal to the cosmopolitan Cape's broader audience.

For details of the annual Comedy Festival (growing in popularity every year) *see p155* or visit www.comedyfestival.co.za.

**Riaad Moosa**.
*See p164.*

Twakkie & Corné. *See p164.*

## Venues

### Armchair Theatre
*135 Lower Main Road, Observatory, Southern Suburbs (021 447 1514/www.armchairtheatre.co.za).* **Open** 9pm-2am show nights. **Tickets** R20-R50. **No credit cards**.
An old favourite in Cape comedy circles, the Armchair hosts the Comedy All-Stars every Sunday, with other acts in between.

### Baxter Theatre
*Main Road, Rondebosch, Southern Suburbs (021 685 7880/www.baxter.co.za).* **Box office** 9am-start of performance Mon-Sat. **Credit** AmEx, DC, MC , V.
While the acts may vary, the Baxter invariably has at least one comedy show on the go at any given time. Check local listings for details.

### On Broadway
*88 Shortmarket Street, City Bowl (021 424 1194/ www.onbroadway.co.za).* **Shows** 8.30pm Tue-Sun. **Tickets** R65. **Credit** AmEx, DC, MC, V. **Map** p274 G3.
Comedy and cabaret combine at this deliciously over-the-top venue. The food's good and the comedy's even better, but the shows aren't ideal for a family audience.

## Comedians to watch

### Alan Committie
He's FUCT…. as in, Formerly University of Cape Town. And he can't help it. Committie's comedy is coloured by a range of madcap characters, including his dentally handicapped alter-ego Johan van der Walt.

# My kind of town Kurt Schoonraad

A born performer, Kurt Schoonraad joined the Creative School of Speech and Drama at the age of ten, and hasn't looked back since. His off-kilter brand of comedy has made him one of the most popular comedians in South Africa.

**Cape Town makes me...** happy.

**I treat myself at...** Rhodes Memorial Restaurant (Groote Schuur Estate, Southern Suburbs, 021 689 9151, www.rhodesmemorial.co.za; *see p82*).

**I dine at...** Sushi Minato (4 Buiten Street, City Bowl, 021 423 4712).

**I drink sundowners in...** my own backyard.

**I wake up to...** banging! My neighbour is renovating.

**I go to sleep in...** a T-shirt.

**I love...** dogs.

**I buy presents at...** Cavendish Square (Claremont, Southern Suburbs, 021 657 5600, www.cavendish.co.za; *see p129*).

**I drink coffee at...** Vida e Caffè (34 Kloof Street, City Bowl, 021 426 0627; *see p106*).

**The south-easter is...** nothing you can have as a double.

**I have fun at...** A Touch of Madness (12 Nuttall Road, Observatory, Southern Suburbs, 021 448 2266; *see p126*).

### Corné & Twakkie
Corné and Twakkie rose from very modest beginnings in a caravan park to become the hosts of the hugely successful TV series, *T\*M\*A\*S* (The Most Amazing Show), where they spread the universal gospel of the Good Vibe. **Photo** *p163*.

### Cokey Falkow
The highlights of Cokey Falkow's career so far have included stealing the show at the CTICF a couple of years ago and making an appearance in the recent Vinnie Jones Hollywood action film *Blast!*

### Tracy Klaas
She's a divorced, Jewish, single mum in the middle of a mid-life crisis, and she's working in an industry that's dominated by young males. You couldn't ask for better material to work with.

### Marc Lottering
Lottering is one of Cape Town's most popular comedians – largely because his material is good, clean fun, and because local audiences identify with his personalised caricature comedy.

### Riaad Moosa
A qualified doctor who started out as a 'pick a card, any card' comedy magician, Moosa is a young, post-9/11 Muslim who grew up in Cape Town. The material pretty much writes itself. **Photo** *p163*.

### Mark Sampson
Crazy hair, crazy guy. The blond, dreadlocked former Cape Comedy Collective chief may have mellowed in his middle age, but his razor-sharp improv skills and interactive stand-up style have kept him as popular as ever.

### Kurt Schoonraad
Like Lottering, Schoonraad bases much of his material on his memories of his Cape Flats childhood. Funny faces? Check. Silly voices? Check.

### Sky 189
His business card classifies him as a 'freestyle comedy rapper', but he's much funnier and more talented in real life.

### Stuart Taylor
Another Cape comedy magician, this suave, sophisticated Stellenbosch graduate is an expert at making things (not audience members, fortunately) appear and disappear.

### Pieter-Dirk Uys
This incisive, cross-dressing comedian (and his alter-ego Evita Bezuidenhout) somehow survived being an apartheid-era comedian, and is still South Africa's most famous funny man. A tireless crusader for HIV/AIDS awareness, s/he's practically become the mayor of the West Coast town of Darling.

Arts & Entertainment

# Film

Hollywood still rules OK, but homegrown talent is on the rise.

Civilised cinema: the Twelve Apostles Hotel's **Cine 12** screening room. *See p167.*

South African cinema-goers are not the most discerning bunch, if a look at any given week's 'Top Ten' box office takers is anything to go by. It's easier to find a screen showing the new Brad Pitt blockbuster than it is to track down one showing a South African-produced film.

In early 2005 rocketing ticket prices and plummeting audience numbers forced cinema chain Ster-Kinekor to slice ticket prices in half. An ugly price war broke out, and once the dust had settled, rival chain NuMetro had also cut its prices, Ster-Kinekor had rebranded some of its cinemas and people were watching movies again. Or, in *Variety* slanguage, the cheaper tix were boffo with local auds... and the distribs did whammo biz.

## Cinemas

The mainstream movie theatres belong to either of the two local distribution giants, **Ster-Kinekor** (0861 300 444/www.sterkinekor.com) and **NuMetro** (021 419 9700/www.numetro.co.za), and all the mainstream Hollywood features granted theatrical release hit their big

screens. Ster-Kinekor have hedged their bets, though, screening 'arthouse' movies at Cavendish Nouveau in Cavendish Square and at the Cinema Nouveau Waterfront. NuMetro countered that with their own Cinema Privé at Canal Walk, which boasts roomy seats with ample space for you and your glass of wine.

### Cavendish Nouveau

*Lower Ground Floor, Cavendish Square, Claremont, Southern Suburbs (Ticketline 082 16789/Bookings 0861 300 444).* **Tickets** R38. **Credit** AmEx, DC, MC, V.

The biggest non-mainstream cinema complex in Cape Town, Cavendish Nouveau has for years provided patrons with otherwise unavailable films. It has a proud history of screening films by Jim Jarmusch, David Lynch and the like – films hard to track down elsewhere. Cavendish Nouveau shows art films with all the technology usually reserved for mainstream multiplexes.

### Cinema Nouveau Waterfront

*Victoria Wharf, V&A Waterfront, Atlantic Seaboard (Ticketline 082 16789/Bookings 0861 300 444).* **Tickets** R38. **Credit** AmEx, DC, MC, V. **Map** p275 H1.

The mainstream face of arthouse cinema. If you're looking for a Resnais retrospective, you're going to be disappointed, but you will find more foreign accents on display than usual. Members can visit the VIP Lounge and pretend they're about to fly somewhere. It has, however, displayed a rather vexing tendency to favour European independent movies over their equally worthy Yankee counterparts.

## Cinema Privé

*Canal Walk, Century City, Milnerton, Northern Suburbs (021 555 2510/www.numetro.co.za).* **Tickets** R42. **Credit** AmEx, DC, MC, V. Cinema Privé is located at Canal Walk, the city's best shopping mall. While it does have a more rarified air than the cinemas across the hall, it shows pretty much the same stuff, which is a shame.

# Tsotsi's new wave

It picked the pockets of Palestine's Golden Globe winner *Paradise Now*, it robbed Germany's acclaimed *Sophie Scholl* and it fleeced France's *Joyeux Noël* and Italy's *La Bestia Nel Cuore*.

In March 2006 the relatively unfancied South African gangster flick *Tsotsi* (*pictured*) stole the show at the Academy Awards ceremony, winning the Oscar for Best Foreign Language Film. That 'language' was *tsotsitaal* (literally 'thug language'), a township slanguage spewed out by the thugs and bad-asses who run the streets of South Africa's crime-riddled shantytowns.

In accepting the Oscar, director Gavin Hood saluted his fellow nominees: 'We may have foreign language films, but our stories are the same as your stories.' And he's right. South Africa's stories are as poignant, relevant and tellable as anybody else's.

Why, then, have there been so few South African movies in the past? For years, local productions have been low-budget, low-quality, lowest common denominator fare, with the occasional gritty drama (*Sarafina!* and *Cry, The Beloved Country*) punctuating the slop of slapstick comedies. Then came *Tsotsi*.

Hood's Oscar-winner is surfing a new wave of decent-budget, decent-quality South African cinema. In 2005 South African-born actress Charlize Theron won the Best Leading Actress Oscar, while the isiZulu-language HIV/AIDS drama *Yesterday* was nominated for Best Foreign Language Film. *Yesterday* then became the first South African film to win a Peabody award in the US. Later in 2006 *Elalini* (filmed by Johannesburg film student Tristan Holmes) won the Honorary Foreign Film award at the 33rd Annual Student Academy Awards – this after *Forgiveness*, starring Arnold Vosloo (the bad guy in *The Mummy*), took two awards at the 2004 Locarno International Film Festival.

In the three years leading up to *Tsotsi*'s international release, the South African government issued a three-year, R35 million grant to the local film industry, which got the industry rolling on 26 feature films. That grant wasn't renewed, but two months after *Tsotsi* took the Oscar, culture minister Pallo Jordan signed an agreement with Britain that secured foreign funding for local films and paved the way for co-productions between South Africa and the UK.

The cash-injected, post-*Tsotsi* South African new wave is bringing in a tide of films made in South Africa, by South Africans, for South Africans – but often starring a cast of bankable international stars. Samuel L Jackson and Juliette Binoche are appearing in an adaptation of local author Antje Krog's *Country of My Skull*, Hilary Swank is starring in the post-apartheid drama *Red Dust*, and John Malkovich is starring in the film adaptation of JM Coetzee's *Disgrace*.

### Cinema Starz

*GrandWest Casino, 1 Vanguard Drive, Goodwood,*
*Northern Suburbs (021 534 0250/www.cinemastarz.*
*co.za).* **Tickets** R18 before 4pm; R25 after 4pm.
**Credit** MC, V.
Located at GrandWest Casino and owned by South
African film producer Anant Singh, Cinema Starz
offers crowd-pleasing flicks and an escape from the
roulette tables.

### Cine 12

*Twelve Apostles Hotel & Spa, Victoria Road,*
*Camps Bay, Atlantic Seaboard (021 437 9000/*
*www.12apostleshotel.com).* **Tickets** prices vary.
**Credit** AmEx, MC, V. **Map** p277 B8.
If you're looking for something more intimate, but
don't want to stay at home watching DVDs, the
Twelve Apostles Hotel offers this 16-seater screening room to guests and non-guests. Screenings are
complimentary for guests at the hotel but visitors
are welcome to a dinner and movie special at the
restaurant for R195 per person. **Photo** *p165.*

### Labia

*68 Orange Street, next to the Mount Nelson Hotel,*
*City Bowl (021 424 5927/www.labia.co.za).* **Tickets**
R25; R15-R20 concessions. **Credit** AmEx, MC, V.
**Map** p274 G5.
What the Labia lacks in technology it more than
makes up for in charm, and it remains the filmhouse
of choice for discerning city cinema-goers. You've got
to love the old skool vibe: the main cinema started
life as a theatre, while the tiny cinema upstairs has
a projector that rattles and clicks in your ears.

### Labia on Kloof

*Upper Level, Lifestyles Centre, Kloof Street, City*
*Bowl (021 424 5927/www.labia.co.za).* **Tickets** R25;
R15-R20 concessions; movie/meal specials R60-R70.
**Credit** AmEx, MC, V. **Map** p274 F5.
The Labia's newer, smarter sister shares its slightly
amusing name (they're named after an Italian
princess, OK?), but not its outdated equipment. This
one has new, first-rate equipment, and it's located
right on Kloof Street's restaurant strip. Among its
endearing features is the fact that they let you take
your wine in during screenings. Two thumbs up.

## Festivals

### Out in Africa: South African Gay & Lesbian Film Festival

*Cinema Nouveau, V&A Waterfront, Atlantic*
*Seaboard (021 461 4027/www.oia.co.za).* **Credit**
AmEx, DC, MC, V. **Date** Mar-Apr. **Map** p275 H1.
Cape Town's premier gay film festival is well organ-
ised, well attended and well worth checking out, as
it also screens locally made films.

### Encounters South African Independent Documentary Festival

*Nu Metro, Victoria Wharf Upper Level, V&A*
*Waterfront, Atlantic Seaboard (021 465 4686/*
*www.encounters.co.za).* **Date** July. **Map** p275 H1.

Labia.

Now in its ninth year, Cape Town's top documentary festival features anything and everything –
from nature documentaries to socio-political pieces.
Essential viewing.

### Three Continents Film Festival

*Cinema Nouveau, V&A Waterfront, Atlantic*
*Seaboard (021 788 5462/www.3continents*
*festival.co.za).* **Date** Sept. **Map** p275 H1.
Those three 'continents' being Africa, Asia and
Latin America. This festival showcases films from
developing nations – and it does so by arranging
rural, township and urban screenings.

### Molweni Township Film Festival

*Various locations around the townships*
*(www.rainbowcirclefilms.co.za).* **Date** Sept.
Cape Town's first township film festival began in
1999 and brings the movie biz to the township
streets, setting up impromptu screenings in places
where films seldom see the light of day. The festival
shows a wide mix of documentaries, short films and
feature films.

### Cape Town World Cinema Festival and Sithengi Film & TV Market

*Various cinemas around Cape Town (021 430*
*8160).* **Date** Nov.
When it was established back in 1995, Sithengi's aim
was to develop trade in African film products. Its
World Cinema Festival and Film & TV Market have
achieved this and more, screening features, shorts
and documentaries.

**Arts & Entertainment**

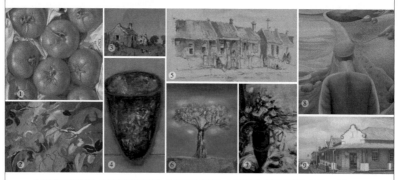

# Galleries

Let's fill this town with artists.

Cape Town is often accused of being an 'arty-farty' kind of place, and when one counts the number of galleries and exhibition spaces, it seems fair enough. From the Atlantic Seaboard right around the mountain to Simonstown, there are more art venues than public *braai* spots. Noted exclusions, however, are the Cape Flats and surrounding township areas which, between them, do not have one permanent gallery of note.

It helps that the artistic gene pool is kept replenished by the two reputable university art departments (Stellenbosch and Cape Town) and numerous independent art schools and collectives. It's also good that Capetonian artists and art lovers themselves are a fairly feisty bunch who like nothing better than a bout of intellectual fisticuffs, thus sustaining dynamic debate.

And the sheer scope of exhibition space – from a small ceramic showcase in a seaside village to a trendy loft space in the city – encourages an enthusiastic turnover of visitors. From works by South African masters to installations by indigenous young mavericks, the Cape Town gallery circuit has it all.

## City Bowl

### 34 LONG
*34 Long Street (021 426 4594/www.34long.com).* **Open** 9am-5pm Tue-Fri; 10am-2pm Sat; Sun, Mon & public holidays by appointment. **Credit** AmEx, DC, MC, V. **Map** p274 G4.
The century-old house at 34 Long Street has been beautifully renovated into a gallery housing South African and international contemporary art. Since its opening a couple of years ago the list of names featured has been consistently impressive, including local artists such as William Kentridge, Esther Mahlangu, Willie Bester and Zwelethu Mthethwa, and 'imports' such as Yoshitomo Nara, Tokyo's answer to Andy Warhol.

### 3rd I Gallery
*95 Waterkant Street (021 425 2266).* **Open** 9am-5pm Mon-Fri; 9.30am-1pm Sat. **Credit** MC, V. **Map** p274 G3.
This gallery rightly has a reputation for exciting, funky presentations by innovative modern artists. The turnover of talent – which ranges from installation artists to oil painters – is brisk and attracts a steady flow of punters. Poetry readings and live music are sometimes added to the mix.

## Association for Visual Arts

*35 Church Street (021 424 7436/www.ava.co.za).*
**Open** 10am-5pm Mon-Fri; 10am-1pm Sat. **Credit**
AmEx, DC, MC, V. **Map** p274 G4.
Opening nights at the AVA are very often raucous
affairs where penny-whistling buskers, dishevelled
art professors and nouveau bohemians rub shoulders over glasses of warm white wine. It's ideally
situated in arty Church Street, so one can pop in any
time for a quick art fix. As one of the city's oldest
non-profit art galleries, its list of exhibitors over the
years reads like a *Who's Who* of the Cape Town art
scene; it has also been a supportive space for the
city's more marginalised artists. With a three-week
turnover period and room for three artists all to
exhibit at the same time, the venue has found the
right formula for keeping things fresh.

## Atlantic Art Gallery

*25 Wale Street (021 423 5775).* **Open** 9.30am-
4.30pm Mon-Fri; 10am-1pm Sat. **No credit cards**.
**Map** p274 G4.
At the Atlantic Art Gallery, Riva Cohen will gladly
guide you through the ups and downs of art investment, with a particular focus on established South
African artists. With names like Robert Slingsby
and Cecil Skotnes on her books, she knows what
she's talking about and will happily point out the
good, the bad and the brilliant on the local scene.

## Bell-Roberts Gallery

*89 Bree Street (021 422 1100/www.bell-roberts.com).*
**Open** 8.15am-5.30pm Mon-Fri; 10am-1pm Sat.
**Credit** AmEx, DC, MC, V. **Map** p274 G4.

**Association for Visual Arts.**

The wife-and-husband team of Brendon and Suzette
Bell-Roberts is the creative force driving the Bell-
Roberts Gallery, the contemporary magazines *itch*
and *Art South Africa*, a thriving art consultancy,
and a publishing wing. The mags are a must for anybody interested in critical debate around arts and
culture issues; the gallery, with its emphasis on modern dynamics, is equally alluring. To date, hip hop
video loops, neo-pop sculptures, clay icons and
Kentucky Fried Chicken have all played their part.
Who knows what's next…

## The Bin

*105 Harrington Street (021 465 8314/www.
thebin.co.za).* **Open** 10am-4pm Mon-Fri; 10.30am-
2.30pm Sat, Sun. **Credit** DC, MC, V. **Map** p275 H4.
A spunky new venue that aims to give breathing
space to emerging artists wanting to explore an
alternative to mainstream galleries. Work is chosen
via an open call for submissions. Email info@
circuslab.co.za for details if you think you've got
what it takes. **Photo** *p174.*

## Cape Gallery

*60 Church Street (021 423 5309/www.capegallery.
co.za).* **Open** 9.30am-5pm Mon-Fri; 9am-1pm Sat.
**Credit** AmEx, DC, MC, V. **Map** p274 G4.
The small but vibrant Church Street mall has long
been a home for antique dealers, second-hand
traders, auctioneers, curio vendors and café owners.
You can spend a good few hours here, listening to
local street musicians, ordering frothy cappuccinos
and poking at archaic pieces. The Cape Gallery fits
right into this setting, offering a quiet retreat where
visitors can get lost in an extensive and engaging
inventory. The catalogue stretches from early Cape
nature artists up to contemporary names such as
Sipho Hlati, Kenneth Baker and Hylton Nel.

## Erdmann Contemporary

*63 Shortmarket Street (021 422 2762/072 356
7056/www.erdmanncontemporary.co.za).* **Open**
10am-5pm Tue-Fri; 10am-1pm Sat. **Credit** AmEx,
MC, V. **Map** p274 G3.
The Erdmann Contemporary and Photographer's
Gallery are housed in this double-volume space
founded by Namibian Heidi Erdmann. Works by
some of the country's finest photographers can be
found here, alongside graphic art and multimedia
installations. Jurden Schadeburg, Paul du Toit,
Conrad Botes and Roger Ballen are just some of
the drawcards.

## Joao Ferreira Fine Art

*70 Loop Street (021 423 5403/www.joaoferreira
gallery.com).* **Open** 10am-5pm Tue-Fri; 10am-2pm
Sat. **Credit** AmEx, DC, MC, V. **Map** p274 G4.
Where Joao leads, others follow. With a gift for
recognising potential and a reputation for backing
winners, it's not surprising dealers and collectors
keep an eye on Joao Ferreira's movements. Unafraid
to back unknown artists, he has seldom gone wrong
with a choice; at the same time, more established
names are often keen to be represented by him,

# The multimedia man

Nicholas Hlobo has an affinity for non-traditional materials such as rubber inner tubes, leather, ribbons and soap. They make frequent appearances in his works which explore Xhosa traditions, homosexuality and 'anything that people find embarrassing in society', as Hlobo himself puts it.

A true multimedia artist, he pushes boundaries and plays havoc with conventions while working with painting, video and installation. Sculpture is probably the medium closest to his heart, but he is also a performance artist and his sculptural pieces sometimes form part of his costumes for performances.

He has been described as 'a buoyant individual, possessing a unique spirit and the ability to eloquently convey his desires and visions'. However, despite the complex nature of his creative work, Hlobo's work is anything but elitist. 'Art should not always be difficult. It should be accessible because that is what freedom is,' he reckons.

Born in the Cape in 1975, Hlobo has a BTech degree under his multi-faceted belt and a number of interesting exhibitions to his credit, including participation in *A Decade of Democracy: Witnessing South Africa* at the Museum of the National Center for Afro-American Artists, Boston, and *Show Us What You're Made Of II* at the Premises, Johannesburg. In 2005 he spent three months in residence at the Thami Mnyele Foundation studios in Amsterdam, and in 2006 he picked up the prestigious Tollman Award for the Visual Arts, given annually to a young South African artist of exceptional ability. According to the criteria for the award, the artist 'must already have produced some striking work, to critical acclaim, but not yet be widely recognised'. Nicholas Hlobo fits the bill perfectly – but we predict that last bit will change.

resulting in an even stable of mature and new talent. He also cannot be faulted on his gallery manners, devoting as much attention to first-time buyers as established clients. Dorothee Kreutzfeld, Abrie Fourie and Deborah Bell are among his showcase of contemporary South African artists.

## Johans Borman Fine Art Gallery

*In-Fin-Art Building, Upper Buitengracht Street (021 423 6075/www.johansborman.co.za).* **Open** 10am-6pm Mon-Fri; 9am-2pm Sat. **Map** p274 F4.

If you're after works by South African masters – and have the financial resources to pay for them – then the Johans Borman Fine Art Gallery should be just up your boulevard. Paintings by greats like Irma Stern, JH Pierneef, George Pemba and Gregoire Boonzaier don't come cheap, but then again they don't come often either, so it all works out in the end. The gallery also features leading contemporary

artists such as Erik Laubscher. Even if you can't afford to buy your own Gerard Sekoto, a visit to this upmarket showcase of indigenous art history is well worth it.

## VEO Gallery, Frameworks & Warehouse

*8 & 28 Jarvis Street, off Dixon Street, De Waterkant (021 421 3278/www.veo.co.za).* **Open** 9am-5pm Mon-Fri; 10am-4pm Sat, Sun. **Credit** AmEx, DC, MC, V. **Map** p274 G3.

Take time out from browsing the trendy De Waterkant village shops to visit this user-friendly venue. Regular group and solo exhibitions, framing services and even art pieces for hire (especially for the film industry) are on offer. An easygoing approach to art buying makes the whole business that much easier, with both edgy and conventional pieces on view.

# Gender: right

Despite a constitution which prohibits discrimination against homosexuals, South African society still has a way to go in terms of tolerance. When a black teenage lesbian is stoned to death by a group of young boys because of her orientation, you realise just how radical Zanele Muholi's work is.

As a photographer and gender and sexual rights activist, Muholi has contributed to a series of exhibitions and released a book on the subject of black lesbians in South Africa. Her work challenges the notion that lesbians are 'unAfrican' and offers an empathetic and often very sensual view of black female sexuality.

'I am personally involved in my photographic projects. I cannot take your piece of flesh without being involved. Most of the time, it's outsiders looking at us, taking our pictures. I am very much involved with the people I portray; I am one of them,' she says.

Muholi currently works for the Forum for the Empowerment of Women (FEW), a black lesbian organisation, and has previously worked as a photographer and reporter for *Behind the Mask*, an online magazine on lesbian and gay issues in Africa. She has participated in many conferences and exhibitions, including the Gender & Visuality and Doing Gender conferences at the University of the Western Cape, Sexual Rights & Moral Panics at the International Association for the Study of Sexuality, Culture and Society in California, and the South African group exhibition *Olvida Quien Soy/ Erase Me from Who I Am* at the Centro Atlantico de Arte Moderna in Las Palmas de Gran Canaria.

'I use photography as a means to communicate my issues and other people's issues. If it's not done, it will never be done,' says Muholi. 'I'll have images of two women kissing, and there will be people who won't like what they see. Even though we live in a democratic country, some people won't agree with our views. It's not that I want to provoke people; I'm doing something that I think is right.'

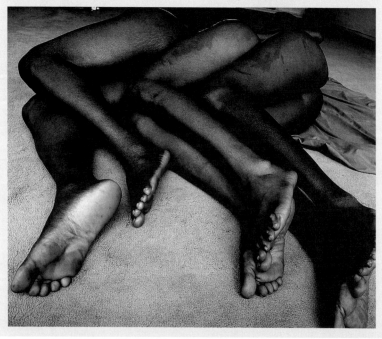

# Atlantic Seaboard

## Everard Read Gallery
*3 Portswood Road, Waterfront (021 418 4527/ www.everard-read-capetown.co.za).* **Open** 9am-6pm Mon-Fri; 9am-4pm Sat; by appointment only Sun. **Credit** AmEx, DC, MC, V. **Map** p274 G1.
The Cape Town branch of the country's oldest art dealership is all about classy aesthetics. Designer gates, courtyard sculptures and renovations by the ever-tasteful Revel Fox have combined to make this a space where fine art finds a comfortable home. With an emphasis on more mainstream works, rigorous interplay between the Jo'burg head office and Cape Town ensures a supply of valuable local works by the likes of Arabella Caccia, Sipho Ndlovu and Walter Meyer.

## The Framery
*64 Regent Road, Sea Point (021 434 5022).* **Open** 9.30am-5.30pm Mon-Fri; 9.30am-1pm Sat. **Credit** AmEx, DC, MC, V. **Map** p273 B3.
On Sea Point's busy shopping strip you can buy bagels and biltong, go to the gym, get your poodle groomed, and browse through Debby Grewe-Mbuyi's fine collection of contemporary South African, Zimbabwean and Congolese art at the Framery. Prices are reasonable, and the range is accessible and interesting. The gallery includes a framing consultancy.

## Die Kunskamer
*3 Portswood Road, Waterfront (021 419 3226/ www.kunskamer.co.za).* **Open** 8.30am-5pm Mon-Fri; 10am-1pm Sat. **No credit cards.** **Map** p274 G1.
Louis Schachat's art dealership is one of Cape Town's oldest. Housed on the Everard Read property, the respected consultancy places a strong emphasis on masters and important Africana, and can be of invaluable assistance when making art investment choices.

## Michael Stevenson Contemporary
*Hill House, De Smit Street, Green Point (021 421 2575/www.michaelstevenson.com).* **Open** 9am-5pm Mon-Fri; 10am-1pm Sat. **Credit** AmEx, DC, MC, V. **Map** p274 G2.
The Michael Stevenson gallery continues to impress with cutting-edge exhibitions and the production of high-quality catalogues, featuring leading contemporary South African artists. Allocation of space is divided fairly among photographers, painters, sculptors and the like, with the same democratic approach to featuring established names (think David Goldblatt or Wim Botha) and hot emerging talent (Zanele Muholi, Churchill Madikida). Art dealer and historian Michael Stevenson is at the helm, assisted by Sophie Perryer (editor of *10 Years/100 Artists: Art in a Democratic South Africa*), Kathy Comfort-Skead, previously the curator of photography and new media at the South African National Gallery, and experienced arts administrator Andrew da Conceicao. A formidable team and gallery.

## Rose Korber Art Consultancy
*48 Sedgemoor Road, Camps Bay (021 438 9152/021 438 9998/www.rosekorberart.com).* **Open** 9am-5pm Mon-Fri; by appointment Sat, Sun. **Credit** AmEx, DC, MC, V. **Map** p277 B7.
The genial and art-aware Rose Korber helps architects, interior designers, international art buyers and local collectors source appropriate contemporary South African art. As an independent art consultant, she has access to a broad spectrum of artists and can advise on most mediums, from pottery to photography. She'll source you a six-foot Louise Gelderblom original faster than you can say 'ceramic'. Her home, which can be visited by appointment, is a showcase of splendid South African artworks – clients have been known to wander for hours through the space, wine glass in hand. Korber is also responsible for the annual Art Salon at the Bay, held in December each year.

# Southern Suburbs

## Carmel Art
*66 Vineyard Road, Claremont (021 671 6601/ www.carmelart.co.za).* **Open** 9am-5pm Mon-Fri; 9am-1pm Sat. **Credit** AmEx, DC, MC, V. *Constantia Village Shopping Centre, Main Road, Constantia (021 794 6262).* **Open** 9am-6pm Mon-Fri; 9am-5pm Sat. **Credit** AmEx, DC, MC, V.
We're talking serious scale here. Literally hundreds of artworks are available via the Carmel Art website and database, and also through their two shops. Commercial works dominate, so if you're searching for upmarket pieces to complement your interior design, look no further.

# Southern Peninsula

## Albie Bailey A.R.T. Gallery
*20 Main Road, Kalk Bay (021 788 8718/www. clementina.co.za).* **Open** 10am-5pm daily. **Credit** AmEx, DC, MC, V.
Situated right opposite sparkling Dalebrook Pool, with a view of the surfers at Kalk Bay reef (if you stand on tiptoes), the A.R.T. Gallery definitely has one of the coolest settings in the Cape. Ceramicist Clementina van der Walt and her partner Albie Bailey have opened a gallery that adjoins the cosy Café des Arts coffee shop and restaurant, so you can relax after browsing the small but stylish art space. Exhibitions are fairly regular, featuring ceramics (of course) and also prints, paintings and sculptures.

## Bronze Age Sculpture House
*King George Way, Simonstown (021 786 5090/ www.bronzeageart.com).* **Open** 10am-5pm Tue-Thur; 10am-4pm Fri; 10am-3pm Sat, Sun. **Credit** AmEx, DC, MC, V.
This interesting workshop and gallery is tucked away near the Simonstown harbour, but it's well worth making the effort to find it. If you happen to walk past while a bronze casting is taking place,

Arts & Entertainment

you'll be immediately captured by the molten light and heat that emanate from this foundry. The venue features a sculpture garden and small exhibition space, and the beautiful works range in scale from very small to massive.

### Hout Bay Gallery

*71 Victoria Avenue, Hout Bay (021 790 3618/ www.houtbaygallery.co.za).* **Open** 9am-5pm Mon-Fri; noon-5pm Sat, Sun. **Credit** AmEx, DC, MC, V.
Good value and some pleasant surprises make a visit to Hout Bay Gallery worth the trip. It's not exactly the kind of place where you'll pick up a Kentridge or a Bester, but you will find a solid selection of contemporary work by local middleweights. It's mostly paintings and prints, but they also sell a good selection of furniture and hand-spun carpets.

### Kalk Bay Gallery

*62 Main Road, Kalk Bay (021 788 1674/www. farsa.co.za).* **Open** 9am-5pm Mon-Fri; 9.30am-5pm Sat, Sun. **Credit** AmEx, DC, MC, V.
Situated in the hub of bohemian, bustling Kalk Bay, this gallery cleverly displays paintings of the local scenery to lure punters into the shop. Once inside, however, it's not all seaside art – abstracts, portraits and prints make up the respectable bulk of the inventory. There are no exhibitions, but there is a pacy turnover of artworks.

### The Potter's Shop & Studio

*6 Rouxville Road, Kalk Bay (021 788 7030).* **Open** 9.30am-1pm, 1.30-4.30pm Mon-Sat; noon-4.30pm Sun. **Credit** MC, V.
Tiny and stylish, the Potter's Shop always has the most fabulous ceramics on show. Exhibitions range from rare pieces from the fantastic Ardmore collective to a Lisa Firer or Majolandile Dyalvane showcase. The cups, saucers and plates on sale are to die for and well worth the investment.

## Northern Suburbs

### Art.b Gallery

*Bellville Library Centre, Carel van Aswegen Street, Bellville (021 918 2301/www.artb.co.za).* **Open** 9am-8pm Mon-Thur; 9am-6pm Fri; 9am-1pm Sat.
Art.b, the Arts Association of Bellville, is described as an 'innovative, community-oriented organisation, sensitive to new ideas and supportive of established and emerging artists from all cultural backgrounds'. Which pretty much sums up what takes place at the Bellville gallery, regarded by many as one of the best in the Northern Suburbs for showcasing contemporary local works.

### Lindy van Niekerk Art Gallery

*31 Kommandeur Road, Welgemoed (021 913 7204/5/www.artpro.co.za).* **Open** 9am-5.30pm Mon-Fri; 9am-2pm Sat. **Credit** AmEx, DC, MC, V.
Conventional, colourful mainstream works can be found at Lindy van Niekerk's gallery, where the emphasis is on art that isn't necessarily challenging,

The Bin. *See p170.*

but is certainly cheerful. Don't expect any major signatures, but rather a hand-picked selection of neighbourhood names.

### Rust-en-Vrede Gallery

*10 Wellington Road, Durbanville (021 976 4691).* **Open** 9am-4.30pm Mon-Fri; 9am-12.30pm Sat. **No credit cards.**
A lively turnover of interesting exhibitions by both well-known and new talent makes the Rust-en-Vrede Gallery worth coming back to. It's a small but well-used space where you may find a Pieter van der Westhuizen or Jaco Benade on any given day.

### Sanlam Art Gallery

*2 Strand Road, Bellville (021 947 3359/www.sanlam. co.za).* **Open** 9am-4pm Mon-Fri. **Credit** AmEx, DC, MC, V.
A gallery with some heavyweight surprises – for instance, you may come across an exhibition on expressionist influences on South African art, featuring the likes of Tyrone Appollis, Gerard Sekoto, Irma Stern and William Kentridge.

# Gay & Lesbian

Paint the town pink.

South Africa has one of the most liberal constitutions in the world and outlaws homophobia (hate speech on the grounds of sexual orientation is illegal), diminishes former discriminatory practices – like the sodomy laws of more than 11 years ago – and protects the sanctity of same-sex relationships. It has also led to new legislation regarding the adoption of children, accessing state-funded housing and, in recent months, it has also taken relationships to the next level with the legalisation of same-sex marriages.

That said, it doesn't mean Cape Town is less African than the rest of the continent. It only means that laws have been put in place to protect its citizens. There are still those that carry unnecessary baggage in the city of the free, and here and there you will encounter the odd stare or burrowed frown. So don't let your guard down just because you're a visitor. At the end of the day, this is still a city in Africa.

The pinnacle of gay Cape Town has to be De Waterkant, the cottage-chic village in Green Point with its cosy cafés, multi-functional restaurants, exquisite guesthouses, dreamy designer shops and pulsating clubs.

But don't think that this is where the pink map of Cape Town ends: all along the Atlantic Seaboard you'll find quaint guesthouses and titillating tearooms that happily embrace the power of the pink.

Exclusively girl-on-girl establishments are, unfortunately, not yet a huge priority in the bigger pink picture, but lesbians are always welcomed with open arms into the jaunts of their male counterparts.

If you're one of the pleasure seekers who enjoy the seedier side of things, the best place to start is the **Hot House** (18 Jarvis Street, De Waterkant, 021 418 3888). Although it is a very busy sauna and steam bath, you should keep in mind that Africa is in the grips of an AIDS pandemic: wear a condom. There is also a chain of **Adult World** stores (36 Riebeeck Street, City Centre, 021 418 7455) that could help you in your endeavour.

### RESOURCES

The **Triangle Project** (Unit 29, Waverly B Park, Mowbray, Southern Suburbs, 021 448 3812) is an organisation working to eradicate discrimination against and within the lesbian, gay, bisexual and transgender community. It provides sexual health education, free weekly walk-in clinics, professional face-to-face counselling and a helpline (021 422 2500).

The **Gay & Lesbian AA Group** (021 510 2288) meets every Tuesday at 8pm at the Congregational Church Hall on the corner of Kloof Street and Eton Road, City Bowl. **Cocktail-tales**, an alcoholics support group for men only, meets every Wednesday at 6pm at the Sacred Heart Church in Somerset Road, Green Point, Atlantic Seaboard.

**Cape Info Africa** (32 Napier Street, De Waterkant, City Bowl, 021 425 6461) is a tourist's dream come true. If you need information on exploring the Atlantic Seaboard, this is your highway to a variety of travel and tourism answers.

**Friends of Dorothy Tours** (021 465 1871/www.friendsofdorothytours.co.za) makes it easy to explore the City Bowl, West Coast, Winelands, Cape Peninsula and the Garden Route with their exclusively gay tours.

For local news and information on lesbian events in Cape Town, call **Myrna** (082 565 6174/www.lushcapetown.co.za).

## Accommodation

### 4 on Varneys

*4 Varneys Road, Green Point, Atlantic Seaboard (021 434 7167/www.4onvarneys.co.za).* **Rates** R850. **Credit** AmEx, DC, MC, V. **Map** p274 F2.
Thierry and Philip's spacious and stylish rooms, heated pool and comfortable lounge and dining area are situated in a quiet corner of Greenpoint, around the corner from shops, restaurants, a gym and the V&A Waterfront. The first-floor covered balcony overlooks Signal Hill.

### Amsterdam Guest House

*19 Forest Road, City Bowl (021 461 8236/ www.amsterdam.co.za).* **Rates** R695. **Credit** MC, V.
This centrally located luxury guesthouse with its clothes-optional entertainment area – jacuzzi, sauna, steam room, solar heated pool and sundeck – is the ideal getaway spot. Apart from its four-star grading and exquisite views, it also serves a full breakfast till noon – so you can still sleep in after a long night out.

### Blackheath Lodge

*6 Blackheath Road, Sea Point, Atlantic Seaboard (021 439 2541/www.blackheathlodge.co.za).* **Rates** R500-R700. **Credit** DC, MC, V. **Map** p273 D2.

This is a no-nonsense, no-frills, spacious seven-room guesthouse. And with rates like these, it's no wonder people come back again and again.

### Colette's B&B for Women

*16 The Bend, Pinelands, Southern Suburbs (021 531 4830/083 458 5344/www.colettesbb.co.za).* **Rates** R200. **Credit** MC, V.

With secure parking and a rate that includes breakfast, this is a home away from home for all female travellers. It is close to shopping spots, near enough for wine-tasting afternoons and accessible for those in the mood to do a bit of mountain walking.

### De Waterkant Village

*1 Loader Street, De Waterkant, City Bowl (021 409 2500/www.dewaterkant.com).* **Rates** R1,000. **Credit** AmEx, DC, MC, V. **Map** p274 G3.

De Waterkant's luxurious rooms are a very short walk from the Cape Quarter and Somerset Road – the ideal place to stay and play while enjoying the best that Cape Town has on offer.

### O on Kloof

*92 Kloof Road, Bantry Bay, Atlantic Seaboard (021 439 2081/www.oonkloof.co.za).* **Rates** R500. **Credit** AmEx, MC, V. **Map** p273 A4.

If you're leaning towards the healthier habits in life, you will enjoy this boutique-style, five-room family house, with its indoor heated salt pool, juice bar and gym area to keep the circulation going.

## Beaches

### Bloubergstrand

*Follow signs off the R27.*

If you want to experience the live version of the famous postcard of Table Mountain and the ocean in the foreground, there is only one place to go: Bloubergstrand.

### Clifton Third Beach

*Victoria Drive, Atlantic Seaboard.* **Map** p277 B6.

A sheltered piece of heaven encrusted with beautiful bodies, giant granite boulders and pickled with picnic spots for perfect summer sundowners.

### Sandy Bay

*Follow the signs from Llandudno off Victoria Road, Atlantic Seaboard.*

Leave your hang-ups at home: all you need for this secluded gay nudist beach are a pair of sandals for the short walk from the parking area. Be warned: the stirring bushes in the area are not always the effect of the south-easter.

### Sea Point Promenade

*Along Beach Road, Sea Point, Atlantic Seaboard.* **Map** p273 C2.

The longest and oldest stretch in Cape Town for jogging, walking or enjoying scenic sunsets. It is also reputed to be one of the most famous pick-up spots in the city.

Enjoy the lip-smacking burgers (and views) at **Café Manhattan**. *See p178.*

# My kind of town Mince

Keiron Legacy and Lilly Slaptsilli of Cape Town's über-successful drag show, *Mince*, have been around the theatre block a few times. They have been entertaining audiences with their stellar singing and bitchy quips for over a decade, taking everything in their stiletto-heeled stride.

## Lilly Slaptsilli

**Cape Town makes me...** drip with excitement.

**I dine at...** Sloppy Sam (51A Somerset Road, Green Point, Atlantic Seaboard, 021 419 2921; *see p108*).

**I drink sundowners at...** Café Vespa (108 Kloof Street, City Bowl, 021 426 5042; *see p122*).

**I wake up to...** two hungry cats.

**I love...** blondes.

**I buy presents at...** Bright House (101 Bree Street, City Bowl, 021 423 5966; *see p147*).

**I drink coffee at...** Melissa's (Green Point, Atlantic Seaboard, 021 434 1719; *see p104*).

**I have fun at...** Cruz (21B Somerset Road, De Waterkant, City Bowl, 021 421 5401, www.cruzcapetown.co.za; *see p178*).

**I hide from the world at...** my house.

## Keiron Legacy

**Cape Town makes me feel...** alive and proud to be South African.

**I dine at...** Capella (21 Somerset Road, De Waterkant, City Bowl, 021 425 0439).

**I drink sundowners at...** Twelve Apostles Hotel (Victoria Road, Camps Bay, Atlantic Seaboard, 021 437 9000, www.12apostleshotel.com; *see p45*).

**I wake up to...** the sound of running water and birds talking.

**I go to sleep in...** a scent of my choice.

**I love...** a summer day in Camps Bay.

**I buy presents at...** Tam-Tam Trading (11 Auckland Street, Paarden Eiland, 021 462 3129).

**I drink coffee at...** Societi Bistro (V&A Waterfront, Atlantic Seaboard, 021 418 9483; *see p112*).

**I have fun at...** Almyra (37 Durban Road, Little Mowbray, Southern Suburbs, 021 685 5353).

**I hide from the world at...** a spa in a float tank (Medi-Spa, 99 Kloof Street, City Bowl, 021 426 1156).

Arts & Entertainment

# Pubs & bars

## Bar Code

*18 Corben Street, off Somerset Road, City Bowl*
*(021 421 5305/www.leatherbar.co.za).* **Open**
*Summer* 10pm-late daily. *Winter* 10pm-late
Wed-Sat. **Admission** R30. **No credit cards.**
**Map** p274 G3.

If you're looking for something out of the ordinary,
dressed up in leather and usually confined to the
darker corners of your imagination, you will probably find it here among the mazed darkrooms, slings
and outdoor deck.

## Bronx Action Bar

*35 Somerset Road, De Waterkant, City Bowl*
*(021 419 9216/www.bronx.co.za).* **Open** 8pm-
dawn daily. **Admission** free. **No credit cards.**
**Map** p274 G3.

Whether you're up for a drink or a dance, a snog or
a sly glance, this is the place where it all started. The
original gay and lesbian bar-cum-dance club caters
for everyone and anyone. Wall-to-wall bodies in all
shapes and sizes make it hard to move around.
Expect a packed dancefloor with a fine balance of
up-beat remixed golden oldies and some of the
hottest tracks on the radio. This is such an inclusive,
friendly venue, many non-gay folk love coming here
for a guaranteed great evening out – and it is still
the place to be (whatever your predilection).

## Cruz

*21B Somerset Road, De Waterkant, City Bowl (021*
*421 5401/www.cruzcapetown.co.za).* **Open** 8pm-4am
daily. **Admission** R20-R30. **Credit** AmEx, MC, V.
**Map** p274 G3.

This spot is the ideal place to start off your night on
the town. Join sexy masked dancers, shake your
booty on the raised dancefloor and be sure to visit
the bathroom with the wall-to-wall mirrors in the
back of the lounge area. The drinks are a bit overpriced and the crowd a bit pretentious, but then you
don't have to stay the whole night.

# Restaurants & cafés

## Andiamo

*Shop C2, Cape Quarter Centre, Waterkant Street,*
*City Bowl (021 421 3687).* **Open** 9am-11pm daily.
**Main courses** R60. **Credit** AmEx, DC, MC, V.
**Map** p274 G3.

Staff are so friendly at this quintessentially Italian
restaurant and deli-bar that you might like to eat in.
But with so many great offers (on the shelves in the
deli), you may just want to pick something up before
rushing home.

## Café Erte Internet Café
## & Cosmic Cocktail Bar

*265A Main Road, Sea Point, Atlantic Seaboard (021*
*434 6624/www.cafeerte.com).* **Open** 10am-4am daily.
**Main courses** R30. **Credit** AmEx, DC, MC, V.
**Map** p273 D2.

Treat yourself to an otherworldly experience by popping into this psychedelic café. Surf the speedy web
while sipping on a cosmic variety of cocktails, or
simply munch away on any number of tasty veggie
treats on the menu. Enjoy the company of Goth-like
lesbians, street-smart rent-boys or whatever the
forces of nature drag in.

## Café Manhattan

*74 Waterkant Street, De Waterkant, City Bowl (021*
*421 6666/www.manhattan.co.za).* **Open** 10am-late
daily. **Main courses** R50. **Credit** AmEx, DC, MC,
V. **Map** p274 G3.

This is one of the oldest and best-loved establishments of Cape Gay. With good wholesome food
(they're well known for their lip-smacking burgers
and super steaks) and a bar that is a safe and comfortable haven to meet and greet, it's no wonder
this place is a hive of activity at any given time.
Relationships are forged here in a relaxed environment where everyone feels like they could be your
best friend. There's also live entertainment on
Thursday and Sunday nights. **Photo** *p176.*

## Lazari Food Gallery

*Corner Upper Maynard Street & Vredehoek Avenue,*
*Vredehoek, Southern Suburbs (021 461 9865).*
**Open** 7.30am-5pm Mon-Fri; 8am-4pm Sat; 8am-3pm
Sun. **Main courses** R35. **Credit** AmEx, MC, V.

Say hello to Chris Lazari, the owner of this stylish
1950s, Formica-glam patisserie. Lunch and weekend
brunches are the defining dining times. Share your
choice of pastas and ciabattas with neighbourhood
regulars, suave actors and media moguls.

## Lola's

*228 Long Street, City Bowl (021 423 0885).*
**Open** 8.30am-midnight daily. **Main courses** R30.
**Credit** AmEx, DC, MC, V. **Map** p274 G4.

Vegetarian meals, 1950s-style furniture and delicious thirst quenchers are a few of the highlights at
this piece of Afro-Cubanism that spills on to the
pavement of vibey Long Street. **Photo** *p179.*

## Mustard Seed

*16 Bree Street, City Bowl (021 419 6666).* **Open**
7am-5pm Mon-Fri; 8.30am-1pm Sat. **Main courses**
R25. **Credit** AmEx, DC, MC, V. **Map** p274 G4.

If you want to experience the staggering contrasts
of Cape Town, this is where to find them: new and
traditional, gay and straight, Mediterranean but
Capetonian, from light meals to satisfying dishes.
Don't miss the *bobotie*.

## On Broadway

*88 Shortmarket Street, City Bowl (021 424 1194/*
*www.onbroadway.co.za).* **Credit** AmEx, DC, MC, V.
**Map** p274 G3.

Make a few new friends at this superb dinner-show
restaurant. The food is scrumptious, the drinks reasonable and the shows a variety of the best that
South Africa has to offer. The pleasant environment
will entice you to an encore. There is a strictly non-
negotiable no-smoking policy.

Lola's. *See p178.*

### Veranda
*1st Floor, Metropole Hotel, 38 Long Street, City Bowl (021 424 7247/www.metropolehotel.co.za).* **Open** 7am-late daily. **Main courses** R70. **Credit** AmEx, DC, MC, V. **Map** p275 H3.
Special occasions call for special treats. With a well-balanced menu of fusion dishes, a solid wine list and a minimalist (but sleek) approach to fine dining, this is definitely *the* uptown hotspot.

## Special events

### Cape Town Pride
*083 919 2525/www.capetownpride.co.za.*
**Date** mid Feb.
Pride unifies and celebrates the diversity of the local gay community. The streets of the city turn into a fabulous extravaganza with floats, delectable bodies and tiaras. But don't limit yourself to the cherry on the cake – the week before the parade is a feast of parties and celebrations continue with a variety of after-parties.

### Gat Party
*Theo Marais Park, off Koeberg Road, Milnerton, Northern Suburbs.* **Date** 1st, 2nd & last Sat of mth.
Come and experience *langarm* dancing to a mixed bag of beats that includes *boeremusiek*, bubblegum pop, *kwaito* and rave. The most diverse crowd in Cape Town can be found on the dancefloor: from lipstick lesbians and scene queens to dykes on bikes. The bar usually opens at 9pm. Tickets are R25. Call 082 821 9185 for more information.

### Mother City Queer Project
*www.mcqp.co.za.* **Date** mid Dec.
This is the biggest annual gathering of gays and lesbians (and everyone in between), and certainly the glitziest of circuit parties in Africa. Internationally known for its extreme fun factor, decadence and vibrant atmosphere, the hardest part is deciding who to go with and what to wear – a costume is a must. Themes from past years include the Shopping Trolley Project, Safari Camp, Heavenly Bodies, Farm Fresh and Kitsch Kitchen.

# Music

Enjoy the sounds of the Mother City, from Beethoven to boeremusiek.

**Melanie Scholtz**, one of the new stars of Cape Town's vibrant live music scene.

Whether you're into trip hop or Tchaikovsky, big bands or Beethoven, Cape Town generally has it covered. But the trick is knowing where to go, and how to find out what's on.

Jazz is one of the city's bigger exports. Cape Town is home to many jazz legends, as well as being the birthplace of several new jazz styles over the years. The city also hosts the **Cape Town International Jazz Festival** (*see p183*) at the International Convention Centre each year, undoubtedly the greatest jazz event on the continent, with artists flying in from around the world.

For the classically inclined we suggest you find the nearest Computicket outlet (there's one in most malls) and pick up the brochures advertising forthcoming productions. Alternatively, tune into Fine Music Radio or log on to www.cpo.org.za. For almost all other live music you'd do well to buy a copy of the

weekly *Mail & Guardian* and turn to the music listings section for details of upcoming events. Classical concerts are usually, but not always, listed here as well.

If it's summer, however, just head for the **Kirstenbosch Botanical Gardens** (Rhodes Drive, Newlands, Southern Suburbs, 021 799 8783, www.kirstenbosch.co.za) on a Sunday afternoon, regardless of who's playing. You're sure to be entertained with a family-friendly helping of the best of local talent. They've recently started winter concerts in one of the restaurants too, if you're in need of some musical cheer during the chillier months.

### Computicket
*083 915 8000/info 083 915 8100/ www.computicket.co.za.*

### Artscape Dial-a-seat
*021 421 7695/information 021 421 7839.*

# Classical & Opera

The basics are pretty simple: the most popular classical concerts take place on Thursday evenings in the City Hall (or occasionally at the Artscape), while recitals by visiting soloists and chamber ensembles take place at the Baxter Theatre and are hosted by what is informally called the **Concert Club** (www.ctconcerts.co.za). The Artscape also hosts performances by **Cape Town Opera** (www.capetownopera.co.za).

## Major venues

### Artscape Theatre Centre

*DF Malan Street, City Bowl (021 410 9800/021 421 7839/www.artscape.co.za/www.capetownopera.co.za/ www.capetowncityballet.org.za/www.jazzart.co.za).* **Open** box office 9am-5pm Mon-Fri; 9am-12.30pm Sat. **Tickets** R75-R350. **Credit** AmEx, DC, MC, V. **Map** p275 I3.

The Artscape is synonymous with ballet, opera and musicals. Previously known as the Nico Malan and still sometimes referred to as the Nico, the Artscape has reinvented itself and thrown off its image as the state-funded bastion of white performing arts. The views are good from every angle, and digital sur-titles are provided on an overhead screen for foreign-language operas. Take note that stalls are marked A-W and the seating on the balcony AA-GG. The Cape Philharmonic Orchestra accompanies all opera and ballet productions.

### Baxter Theatre Centre

*Main Road, Rondebosch, Southern Suburbs (021 680 3989/021 685 7880/www.baxter.co.za/www. ctconcerts.co.za).* **Open** box office 9am-start of performance Mon-Sat. **Tickets** R65-R150. **Credit** AmEx, DC, MC, V.

The Baxter is seen as the Artscape's little sister, and is one of the busier venues in Cape Town, offering an array of theatre, comedy and live music productions in the main theatre, concert hall and Sanlam studio centre. The Cape Town Concert Series hosts world-class chamber music performances and solo recitals here by renowned national and international artists. The Von Beckerath organ is a focal point in the concert hall and acoustics are superb. The Baxter is also wheelchair-friendly and offers facilities for those with impaired hearing.

### City Hall

*Darling Street, across from the Grand Parade, City Bowl (Cape Philharmonic Orchestra 021 410 9809/www.cpo.org.za).* **Tickets** R55, R90, R105, R115. **Credit** AmEx, DC, MC, V. **Map** p275 H4.

Thursday night in Cape Town sees the Cape Philharmonic Orchestra (CPO) whipping up a storm under the baton of Bernhard Gueller. City Hall is the permanent venue of the CPO and is over 100 years old, its quaint façade a feature on many of

the earliest pictures of Cape Town. The Cape Philharmonic is much in demand these days, boasting close to 130 performances each year. The best seats in the house are those situated up on the main balcony, but cheaper platform seats are available on the stage behind the orchestra where, although the seating isn't quite as comfortable, the volume is seriously impressive.

## Other venues

### Groote Kerk

*Adderley Street, City Bowl (021 461 7044).* **Tickets** prices vary. **No credit cards**. **Map** p275 H4.

The magnificent Pelz & Zoon organ in the oldest Dutch Reformed Church in South Africa makes for some of the best organ recitals you're likely to hear. The best seats are those on the organ gallery.

### Kirstenbosch Botanical Gardens

*Rhodes Drive, Newlands, Southern Suburbs (021 799 8783/www.kirstenbosch.co.za).* **Open** box office 8am-6.45pm daily. **Tickets** prices vary. **Credit** AmEx, DC, MC, V.

The setting is unparalleled and the very popular New Year's Eve Concert with the Cape Philharmonic, while you enjoy your picnic and bubbly, will make for a fabulous memory.

### St George's Cathedral

*1 Wale Street, City Bowl (021 424 7360/www. stgeorgescathedral.com).* **Admission** free. **No credit cards**. **Map** p274 G4.

One of the oldest and best-known landmarks in Cape Town, St George's Cathedral is a fully functional Anglican Church that sees the 11am mass on the last Sunday of every month dedicated to choir and orchestral music by Haydn, Mozart, Beethoven, Schubert and many more under the expert baton of Dr Barry Smith, the cathedral's renowned organist. Full choral evensong is performed on Sunday evenings. Needless to say, the acoustics alone are reason enough to go.

# Jazz

Cape Town has seen the rise of many jazz legends over the years, including the late Basil Coetzee and Dollar Brand, more commonly known as Abdullah Ibrahim since his conversion to Islam. These days most of the previously exiled African jazz musicians are gone, but a few of the greats are back and can occasionally be seen performing in and around Cape Town.

These include Miriam Makeba, Jonas Gwangwa and Hugh Masekela. Notable new stars include names such as vocalist Sibongile Khumalo, guitarist Jimmy Dludlu and pianist Paul Hanmer. Cape jazz, a subgenre of South African township jazz, was pioneered by

Winchester Mansions Hotel. *See p183.*

Adullah Ibrahim, and is still played regularly. Some of the bigger events can be booked through Computicket (*see p180*).

## Venues

### Baxter Theatre

*Main Road, Rondebosch, Southern Suburbs (021 685 7880/021 680 3989/www.baxter.co.za).* **Open** *box office* 9am-start of performance Mon-Sat. **Tickets** R50-R150. **Credit** AmEx, DC, MC, V.
With ties to the University of Cape Town's College of Jazz right next door, this venue sees some great performances from both visiting guests and students. See the website for upcoming events.

### Dizzy's Jazz Café

*39 The Drive, Camps Bay, Atlantic Seaboard (021 438 2686/www.dizzys.co.za).* **Open** 1pm-late daily. **Admission** R20. **Credit** AmEx, DC, MC, V. **Map** p277 B8.
Dizzy's is one of Cape Town's oldest and most respected jazz venues, with nightly bands featuring anything from African jazz to commercial background music. It can get quite rowdy, so if you're into stomping and jiving the night away, this is the place to be.

### Green Dolphin

*Victoria & Albert Arcade, V&A Waterfront, Atlantic Seaboard (021 421 7471/www.greendolphin. co.za).* **Open** noon-4.30pm, 6pm-midnight daily. **Admission** R20-R25. **Credit** AmEx, DC, MC, V. **Map** p275 H1.

The Green Dolphin is one of the bastions of local jazz, with great performances almost every night of the week (not to mention excellent food – it's also a restaurant). It holds the Guinness World Record for the highest number of consecutive nights of live jazz. The music usually starts around 8pm.

### Hanover Street Jazz Club

*GrandWest Casino, 1 Vanguard Drive, Goodwood, Northern Suburbs (021 505 7777).* **Open** 9pm-late Wed, Fri, Sat. **Admission** R30. **Credit** AmEx, DC, MC, V.
If you can find GrandWest Casino out in the suburb of Goodwood, and you don't mind wading your way through the drone of slot machines, then this two-storey club with its New Orleans vibe is well worth a visit. Jimmy Dludlu regularly graces the stage.

### Kennedy's Cigar Bar & the Dubliner

*251 Long Street, City Bowl (021 424 1212).* **Open** 10.30am-late Mon-Sat. **Admission** free. **Credit** AmEx, DC, MC, V. **Map** p274 G4.
Smack bang in the middle of the Long Street mayhem is this beautiful, laid-back venue with its leather couches and excellent restaurant – interesting fare on the menu includes crocodile. Cape jazz bands are a regular feature.

### Manenberg's Jazz Café

*Shop 102, Clock Tower Centre, V&A Waterfront, Atlantic Seaboard (021 421 5639/www.manenbergs jazzcafe.com).* **Open** 11am-late daily. **Admission** R40-R80. **Credit** AmEx, DC, MC, V. **Map** p275 H1.

Although some people say it lacks atmosphere, Manenberg's still manages to retain its reputation as one of the top upmarket jazz venues. It is also frequented by famous musicians.

## Marimba Restaurant & Cigar Bar

*Corner Heerengracht & Coen Steytler Avenues, Entrance 5, Cape Town International Convention Centre, City Bowl (021 418 3366/www.marimbasa. com).* **Open** noon-late Mon-Fri; 6pm-late Sat, Sun. **Admission** R30 Sun-Thur; R40 Fri; R50 Sat. **Credit** AmEx, DC, MC, V. **Map** p275 I3.

The Marimban Big Band on Tuesday nights is apparently the only one of its kind in the world, and the event is often sold out weeks in advance. You may need to book even to get a seat at the bar.

## West End

*College Road, Rylands, Southern Suburbs (021 637 9133).* **Open** 9pm-late Fri, Sat. **Admission** R40. **Credit** AmEx, DC, MC, V.

You're sure to hit the main nerve of great mainstream jazz at West End. The crowd is sophisticated and it's worth dressing up.

## Winchester Mansions Hotel

*221 Beach Road, Sea Point, Atlantic Seaboard (021 434 2351/www.winchester.co.za).* **Open** *jazz* 11am-2pm Sun. **Admission** R125 (incl lunch). **Map** p273 B2.

Sunday brunch with a side order of jazz has become something of a Cape Town ritual, and this hotel is one of the top spots. Booking essential. **Photo** *p182.*

## Festivals

### Jazzathon

*V&A Waterfront (021 683 2201/www.jazzathon. co.za).* **Date** Jan.

A mostly free jazz marathon that, judging by the incredible turnout, is here to stay. Get there early for a decent view.

### Cape Town International Jazz Festival

*CTICC, Convention Square, 1 Lower Long Street, City Bowl (021 422 5651/www.capetownjazz fest.com).* **Date** Late Mar. **Map** p275 H3.

# Cape beats

## Kwaito

Please, please know this: there's more to South African music than the penny whistle. The *isicathamiya* vocalising of Ladysmith Black Mambazo and the township jive of Mahlathini and the Mahotella Queens have now given way to the ubiquitous sounds of *kwaito*, the definitive sound of South Africa's urban black youth.

Ten years ago DJs discovered that township clubbers preferred imported house music slowed down from 45rpm to 33rpm. By adding a little experimentation, some South African melodies and liberal helpings of *tsotsi-taal* (gangster slang), *kwaito* was born. Artists worth a listen include the hooded Mzekezeke, Tokollo (ex-TKZee), and the rock-influenced Mandoza. Other notable groups include Bongo Maffin, Mafikizolo and the tuneful Malaika.

*Kwaito* is also having its influence on local hip hop with its more middle-class background and predominantly English lyrics, and the likes of Skwatta Kamp and Cashless Society certainly give 50 Cent a run for his money.

## Boeremusiek

Urban Afrikaners have long derided traditional Afrikaner *boeremusiek* (farmer's music), and found satisfaction instead in Karen Zoid and

the heavy rock of Fokofpolisiekar, all by way of the balladeer Koos Kombuis, Afrikanerdom's very own Bob Dylan and granddaddy of the alternative scene. But the sounds of modernised *boeremusiek* have now been readmitted on the retro ticket, and something quite unique and fun can be found in recordings by the Klipwerf Orkes or the psycho *vastrap* troupe Gramadoelas. These groups certainly give hope in the face of the disturbing up-country proliferation of *sokkie* techno and CDs like *Bosklong 4* – a chilling example of what can happen when a beatbox falls into the wrong hands.

## Afropop

Hundreds of English-speaking South African bands continue to replicate international sounds to good effect. Any number of a very long list of bands are likely to ensure a roaring night out, but since the break-up of Boo! and the Springbok Nude Girls (still nostalgically referred to as the Nudies), there seems to be very little that's new and different. At the same time the relocation of Just Jinger and Wonderboom has left a certain star-sized hole that has yet to be filled. Dave Matthews set the example, and it seems our best bands prefer to follow the money abroad. Heavy metal masters Seether even changed their name from Saron Gas to accommodate American sensibilities.

**Arts & Entertainment**

Look no further: this is by far the greatest jazz event on the continent, with the best of local and international performers making the full two-day pass a must for serious jazz fans.

# Rock

Although the suburbs present quite a sprawl, the fact is the city of Cape Town is pretty small. So when it comes to live music there's not much venue variety. However, on the assumption that predictability isn't exactly in keeping with the whole rock 'n' roll ethos, organisers often like to arrange something a little different to keep things fresh – whether it be a sports club, skate park, abandoned old brewery, burnt-out movie theatre, Kirstenbosch Botanical Gardens or even the Castle of Good Hope. So if you want to catch some of the better shows and bigger bands, it's well worth your while to keep an eye on the music listings in the weekend papers, most notably the Friday section of the weekly *Mail & Guardian* (www.mg.co.za), or visit www.zazone.com or www.powerzone.co.za.

Otherwise there are really only two rock-steady venues that see the best bands make a regular appearance: **Mercury Live & Lounge** (*see below*) in the District Six part of town, and the **Independent Armchair Theatre** out in the suburb of Observatory (*see below*). Slightly further afield one can also catch some good performances in Stellenbosch, or for international acts you'll have to head for the **Green Point Stadium** (*see below*). Some of the bigger events can be booked through Computicket (*see p180*).

## Major venues

### Bellville Velodrome
*Willie van Schoor Road, Bellville, Northern Suburbs (021 949 7450).*
When international acts do grace the city, they usually perform in this cycle track in Bellville.

### Green Point Stadium
*Fritz Sonnenburg Road, Green Point, Atlantic Seaboard (021 434 4510).* Map p274 F1.
The stadium recently saw Metallica and Fat Boy Slim strut their stuff, and it's conveniently easy to reach on foot from the centre of town. It could do with a facelift, though – luckily plans are underway for a major refurb.

## Clubs

### Cool Runnings
*92-96 Station Road, Observatory, Southern Suburbs (021 448 7656).* Open 10am-4am daily.
Admission free.

This Caribbean-themed bar hosts regular live bands and has an interesting layout, which is best enjoyed in summer. The outside section is covered in beach sand and sees fire-juggling on Wednesdays – head for the open-air bar upstairs for the best view.

### Hectic on Hope
*71 Hope Street, City Bowl (021 465 4918).*
**Open** 8.30pm-late Fri, Sat. **Admission** R20-R40.
**No credit cards.** Map p274 G5.
Weekends here offer experimental and themed parties where strange and sometimes international acts grace the stage. The vibe here is alternative.

### Independent Armchair Theatre
*135 Lower Main Road, Observatory, Southern Suburbs (021 447 1514/www.armchairtheatre. co.za).* **Open** 9pm-2am daily. **Admission** R10-R50.
**No credit cards.**
Originally opened as a small, independent and alternative movie theatre for the student crowd, this long-standing success began hosting good comedians and then live music. Despite its slightly cramped layout, some of the better live acts perform here and it's not unusual to find yourself embroiled in an impromptu mosh pit. Many bands play their first gigs here, and whether they can get the crowd dancing is usually a good measure of their future success.

### Jo'burg
*218 Long Street, City Bowl (021 422 0142).* **Open** 5pm-4am Mon-Thur; 4pm-4am Fri; 2pm-4am Sat; 7pm-4am Sun. **Admission** free. **Credit** AmEx, DC, MC, V. **Map** p274 G4.
Seen as the heart of the Long Street mayhem, Jo'burg feels a bit like a clogged aorta. It tends to get very crowded on Friday and Saturday nights, and attracts customers that are both clean-cut and deeply dodgy. Its live music offerings on Sundays, however, are often interesting, complemented by a more relaxed, chilled lounge atmosphere where you can imbibe your poison on the ruby-red couches and meet some locals, or play pool in the open-air courtyard out the back.

### La Med
*Victoria Road, Clifton, Atlantic Seaboard (021 438 5600/www.lamed.co.za).* **Open** noon-1am daily.
**Admission** free. **Credit** AmEx, DC, MC, V.
**Map** p277 A6.
La Med is a popular sundowner bar with awesome mountain and sea views and occasional live bands. It's very relaxed and many of its patrons come straight off Clifton beach, but it can get seriously packed on a balmy Saturday evening.

### Mercury Live & Lounge
*43 De Villiers Street, City Bowl (021 465 2106/ www.mercuryl.co.za).* **Open** 8pm-4am Mon-Sat.
**Admission** from R10. **No credit cards.**
**Map** p275 H5.
This is Cape Town's premier live music venue. On weekends Mercury's large upstairs space (Live) hosts larger bands from all over the country and

# Getting fresh

From Bo-Kaap jazz lovers and suburban housewives to bikers and trance-heads, Freshlyground (*pictured*) attracts an incredibly varied fan base, and the decision to launch their second album at Johannesburg's Constitution Hill and Cape Town's Huguenot Hall, venues each with a dubious history, showed that this seven-piece band seems out to dust away some cobwebs.

They are fast becoming the South African music industry's face of national reconciliation. They recently performed live on Ireland's most popular radio show as part of a feature on ten years of democracy in South Africa, and were asked to play at the Reconciliation Day Concert at Company Gardens in Cape Town alongside such legends as Jimmy Dludlu and Jonas Gwangwa, just six months after starting out.

Their second album, *Nomvula*, was produced by Joe Arthur and Victor Masondo. Says Joe Arthur: 'When I first heard Freshlyground play live I knew this was no ordinary pop group. For the first time I was

listening to the real new South African sound: a conglomerate of ages, experiences and cultures as diverse as the people themselves, yet incredibly homogenous and virulently interactive.'

The band manages to mix Afro-rock, jazz, reggae, soul, *kwela* and dance-hall with such musicality that it's hard to remain unmoved. Frontman Zolani Mahola also sings in three languages: Xhosa, English and Afrikaans.

The future must seem a far cry from the days when Freshlyground had to sell their debut album, *Jika Jika*, without the help of shops and major distributors (they still managed to sell over 2,000 copies in the first four months). 'We've called the album *Nomvula* (rain),' says flute and *mbira* player Simon Attwell, 'after a track written by our lead vocalist Zolani, which is a eulogy to her late mother. It's a really great album with a unique blend of fresh flavours.'

It could be argued that Freshlyground are bigger than themselves. They do more than make music. They represent.

abroad, while the more intimate downstairs venue (Lounge) often showcases smaller up-and-coming bands during the week. It's a come-as-you-are sort of place for both young and old. The Shack and Blue Lizard bars next door are fun to explore and offer good burgers from an all-night kiosk upstairs.

## Obz Café
*115 Lower Main Road, Observatory, Southern Suburbs (021 448 5555/www.obzcafe.co.za).* **Open** 7am-1am daily. **Admission** free. **Credit** AmEx, DC, MC, V.
This is more of a deli restaurant than a live music venue, but it has been known to showcase some

# My kind of town Miki Clarke

**I treat myself at...** Willoughby & Co (V&A Waterfront, Atlantic Seaboard, 021 418 6115; *see p110*) with sushi.

**I dine at...** Chef Pon's (12 Mill Street, City Bowl, 021 465 5846; *see p97*). The duck jungle curry is my favourite.

**I get takeaways from...** Naked on Kloof (51 Kloof Street, City Bowl, 021 422 0351). They have good wraps.

**I drink sundowners at...** work, usually Mojitos.

**I wake up to...** my gurgling son.

**I go to sleep in...** my bed.

**I love shopping for...** junk at Milnerton Flea Market (Racecourse Road, Milnerton, Northern Suburbs; *see p131*).

**I buy presents at...** Gardens Centre (Mill Street, City Bowl, 021 465 1842; *see p129*).

**I drink coffee at...** Vida e Caffè (34 Kloof Street, City Bowl, 021 426 0627; *see p106*).

**I have fun at...** Rafiki's (13B Kloof Nek Road, City Bowl, 021 426 4731; *see below*).

**I hide from the world at...** Olympia Café (134 Main Road, Atlantic Seaboard, 021 788 6396; *see p118*).

Miki Clarke's vision when he opened Rafiki's (*see below*) in 2000 was to offer Capetonians a laid-back place to hang out, with good food and a great atmosphere. Judging by the amount of City Bowl regulars who cross the threshold on a daily basis, it looks like he's succeeded.

good smaller acts. The food is good and the music is laid-back. Check out the website for information about upcoming events

## Purple Turtle
*Corner Shortmarket & Long Streets, City Bowl (021 423 6194/021 423 7366).* **Open** 10am-2am Mon-Sat. **Admission** R10-R30. **No credit cards**. **Map** p274 G4.

The Purple Turtle on Greenmarket Square is a Cape Town legend, attracting an alternative crowd to a grungy interior quite at odds with its shocking purple exterior. The live music is mostly of the hardcore variety – punk, alternative and metal, with the odd bit of ska thrown in. It's a nice enough place if you want to kick off the festivities early, and the balcony upstairs offers a decent central city vibe in the late afternoon.

## Rafiki's
*13b Kloof Nek Road, City Bowl (021 426 4731).* **Open** noon-late daily. **Admission** free. **No credit cards**. **Map** p274 F5.

This is an easy-going bar away from the hustle and bustle of the central city. The wrap-around outside balcony attracts a friendly crowd while the interior often hosts smaller live acts.

## Zula Sound Bar
*194 Long Street, City Bowl (021 424 2442/www. zulabar.co.za).* **Open** noon-late daily. **Credit** (restaurant & bar) MC, V. **Admission** R10-R40. **Map** p274 G4.

The attraction here is the balcony upstairs where you can safely gawk at the Long Street mayhem below while keeping half an ear on whatever live act is kicking up a storm inside.

# Nightlife

Trance nation.

**Chrome**. See p188.

After years of all-night madness Cape Town's clubland has finally calmed down. This is due primarily to the strictly enforced 4am licensing laws. For many it is maturing, having become less hands in the air and more hands on cocktails. Others, though, desperately cling to the eternal night, searching dive bars for that last party.

The trend is moving towards DJ bars where, after cocktail hour, decks are set up and the music kicks in. There is a small but loyal deep house posse, hordes of hardcore hip hop heads, breakbeat is well represented, there is a legendary once-a-month drum 'n' bass party, and electro, electro-clash and all underground styles in between can be found.

If you are after a larger, more in-your-face clubbing experience with all the electric bells and lighting whistles then you will have to prepare yourself for a soundtrack of commercial house, radio hits and R&B. Every now and again we still have flying visits from the club

world's über-brands and marquee names – the production is always good so they are worth checking out.

Cape Town is one of the world's hot spots for psychedelic trance. Every summer weekend sees thousands of tie-dyed ravers from all over the world ruining some farmer's field. The events are well organised and worth losing a weekend over. Illegal substances are readily available and are inconsistently enforced by the authorities, but the penalties are harsh, so be careful. Local jails are not holiday camps.

Capetonians across the board have two things in common – a love to party and the willingness to make room for one more.

## INFORMATION

Venues come and go in Cape Town – as always your best bet is word of mouth and flyers which can be found in bars, clothing shops and restaurants all over town. Otherwise try the following websites:

# Future sounds

Way down here in the slow south, you probably wouldn't expect to find a fully charged scene of independent local dance and electro producers. Well, think again. Thanks to YouTube and Myspace, Cape Town might as well be Detroit or Paris, and in a few short years we've started to make our presence heard.

Back in 2000, two slightly unstable DJs combined record boxes to form **Krushed & Sorted**, and the album *Acid Made Me Do It* was born. This deceptively simple mash of bass break beats, psychedelic squelches, African rhythms and loopy loops destroyed the status quo, and all preconceptions about local dance music were trashed. The success led them to create African Dope records (www.africandope.co.za) and its success has opened the door for every local beat freak and hip hop head to sample their MP3s on the world market.

The latest 'beat terrorists' to emerge from African Dope's murky cradle are the **Real Estate Agents**. Weird electronica meets scratch-tastic mayhem in a freaked-out, beeped-out, full-frontal collision. Not quite the kind of guys you would buy property from.

On a more atmospheric trip hop vibe is the otherworldly electronica of **Lark**. Opera- and jazz-trained vocalist Inga overlays swirls of meaning with edgy electro and dark beats. With a haunting, oppressive sound and stage presence, you will feel afraid, very afraid.

Lightening the mood is the tribal house-funk hybrid of showstoppers **Iridium Project** (www.iridiumprojectlive.com), who blend funky dancefloor beats with some radical percussion to create a unique Afro-samba sound. Add the super sex diva Lu Chase into the mix and you reach musical Viagra. We dare you not to dance.

Perhaps the most exciting breaking act to swim into the scene is **Goldfish** (www.goldfish live.com). With delicious concoctions of jazzy flavours, luscious loops and Afro-vibes incorporated into house tracks with a wasabi-like kick, this is one sushi you will not forget. These two jazz-trained innovators have broken down all the barriers on the scene, whether they are grooving in a club, schmoozing in a bar or jamming at a sold-out gig at Kirstenbosch Botanical Gardens.

What makes all these acts so vital is that they are not stuck in the bedroom or studio. On any given night you can find them testing their latest stuff in joints all over Cape Town. Live or on your iPod, these are the future sounds of Cape Town.

## General clubbing
www.thunda.com; www.e-vent.co.za; www.capetownnightlife.co.za.

## Drum 'n' bass, breaks, electro
www.algorhythm.co.za; www.africandope.co.za.

## Hip hop
www.rage.co.za; www.blacknoise.co.za.

## Trance
www.3am.co.za; www.aliensafari.co.za.

## City Bowl

### Chrome
*6 Pepper Street (083 700 6078/www.chromect.com).* **Open** 10pm-late Wed-Sat. **Admission** R50-R100. **Credit** AmEx, DC, MC, V. **Map** p274 G4.
This venue has gone through a stunning revamp and rebranded itself as an exclusive clubbing experience. The VIP Lounge – Platinum Privé – is especially lavish; here chandeliers are juxtaposed with plasma screens. As you would expect, the crowd is moneyed so it can get a bit snooty. **Photo** *p187*.

### Corner House
*Glyn Street (www.cornerhouse.co.za).* **Open** 9pm-4am Fri, Sat. **Admission** varies. **No credit cards.** **Map** p275 H5.
This den of iniquity opened 15 years ago and has not changed one iota. Same musical mix of rock, metal and ska, same dark dancefloor, same dodgy ambience and it probably still has the same paint job. But it is a formula that works, as every Saturday night it is packed with late-night revellers. It's so dark that you can't really see anyone else on the dancefloor. Remember: don't wear your prettiest Jimmy Choo shoes because they will get seriously messed up.

### Deluxe
*Unity House, Corner Long & Longmarket Streets (021 422 4832).* **Open** 10pm-4am Wed, Fri, Sat. **Admission** R40-R60. **Credit** AmEx, DC, MC, V. **Map** p274 G4.
This intimate dance club has a sophisticated European ambience. Deep, funky and French is the music *du jour* for the cute young things that schmooze, shake and shimmy here every weekend. Retire to the wood-panelled lounge if the dancefloor gets too hectic.

## Fashion Café

*114 Hout Street (021 426 6000/www.ftv.co.za).*
**Open** 10am-late. **Admission** free. **Credit** AmEx,
DC, MC, V. **Map** p274 G3.
Strike a pose. The fashionistas are in the house. As
part of the global FTV brand this venue seeks to
emulate the catwalks of Paris on the dancefloors of
Cape Town. If beautiful, strutting people are your
Prada, then this is the place for you. Stunning
plasma screens keep you entertained while the staff
swoon over you. Every night the dancefloor kicks in
with the latest R&B.

## Fiction

*226 Long Street (021 424 5709/www.fictionbar.
com).* **Open** *Summer* 8pm-4am daily. *Winter*
closed. **Admission** free. **Credit** AmEx, DC, MC, V.
**Map** p274 G4.
Fiction is a sweet lounge/DJ bar that promises to be
one of the coolest spots this summer. Already the
Long Street counter-culture crew of designers, DJs
and Diesel junkies are making this place their centre of operations. Ironic decor, different beats (a strict

Opium.

no commercial, no R&B policy) and cool balcony all
combine to make this place one of the hippest spots
in town.

## Hectic on Hope

*71 Hope Street (021 465 4918).* **Open** 8.30pm-late
Fri, Sat. **Admission** R20-R40. **No credit cards**.
**Map** p274 G5.
This old, run-down pool bar has rebranded itself into
an arty, alternative space. Every Friday it is home
to EVOL, a street fashion indie night frequented by
a sassy and sussed crowd. Saturdays vary between
goth and rock nostalgia, Arty Party (performance-
based) and Pink (gay) events.

## Hemisphere

*31st floor, Absa Building, 2 Riebeeck Street (021 421
0581/www.hemisphere.org.za).* **Open** 4.30pm-late
Tue-Fri; 9pm-late Sat. **Admission** *Women* R30.
*Men* R50. **Credit** AmEx, DC, MC, V. **Map** p275 H3.
Being 31 floors up certainly gives this venue a
unique feel, and the 180° views of the harbour and
Table Mountain are simply stunning. Once you get
used to the thrill of sky-clubbing, you quickly realise
that Hemisphere is still just a club. Retro and R&B
keep the thirtysomething suburban revellers that
flock here busy till the early hours.

## Liquid

*84 Sir Lowry Road (021 461 9649/www.liquid
online.co.za).* **Open** 9pm-8am Fri, Sat. **Admission**
R40-R50. **No credit cards**. **Map** p275 J4.
Hard dance central. Throw your hands in the air and
prepare to dance till dawn. The biggest promoters
in hard house, Tidy Tracks and Nucleus have been
known to make sorties here and top UK spinners like
Anne Savage and Lisa Lashes are regulars. Lasers,
surround sound and well-up-for-it ravers all make
this the best pre-dawn spot in town.

## Mercury Live & Lounge

*43 De Villiers Street (021 465 2106/www.mercuryl.
co.za).* **Open** 8pm-4am Mon-Sat. **Admission** from
R10. **No credit cards**. **Map** p275 H5.
This is a great double-decker venue. Downstairs the
intimate lounge is always jumpin' to a mixed bag of
1970s, '80s, and '90s classics. It is such a friendly
space that it's like having a party in your own living room. Upstairs is a live venue but often plays
host to an array of themed fancy dress parties that
always make for a legendary night out.

## Opium

*6 Dixon Street (021 425 4010/www.opium.co.za).*
**Open** 9pm-4am Wed-Sat. **Admission** R50. **Credit**
AmEx, DC, MC, V. **Map** p274 G3.
Certainly a firm favourite in the Cape Town
nightscape, three dancefloors, two lounges and an
outside terrace combine to give it a superclub feel –
especially on the big theme nights, when brands like
Buddha Bar and Pasha jet in. Intimacy is retained
by low ceilings and a labyrinthine feel. The mostly
commercial house policy is lapped up by a posse of
beautiful young things and preppy boys.

Loud and proud: feel the rhythm (and dance on the bar) at **Pulse**. *See p191.*

## Orchard Bank

*229B Long Street (021 423 8954/www.orchard*
*bank.co.za).* **Open** 4pm-4am daily. **No credit cards**.
**Map** p274 G4.
Another one of Long Street's left-of-centre DJ
dens. Upstairs the lounge area is funky and relaxing, but the downstairs dance area is decidedly
edgier. The music policy is a mix of hip hop, breaks
and electro.

## Rhodes House

*60 Queen Victoria Street (021 424 8844/www.*
*rhodeshouse.com).* **Open** *Winter* 10pm-4am Sat.
*Summer* 10pm-4am Thur-Sat. **Admission** *Winter*
R50. *Summer* R80. **Credit** AmEx, DC, MC, V.
**Map** p274 G4.
Serious style and classic charm are the order of the
day at this sumptuous converted mansion. The
building is actually a national monument as it used
to be the Cape Town residence of Cecil John Rhodes,
and many of the regular guests here have almost as
much moolah. A favourite haunt of models, millionaires and mannequins who glide constantly from
the elegant lounge to the intimate dancefloor until
they finally reach the hallowed grounds of the
upstairs VIP lounges.

## Roosevelt's

*60 Bree Street (021 433 0393).* **Open** times vary.
**Admission** Free-R50. **Credit** AmEx, DC, MC, V.
**Map** p274 G4.

This stylish club and bar comes close to being all
things to all people. Downstairs in the slick lounge
thirtysomethings lounge on opulent leather seats
and discuss the latest property prices. Upstairs the
young electro trash set preen, pose and pogo to '80s
electro and new indie delivered by edgy DJs and
irreverent bands. Arrive early as parking in this part
of town is problematic.

## Zula Sound Bar

*194 Long Street (021 424 2442/www.zulabar.co.za).*
**Open** noon-late daily. **Admission** varies. **Credit**
MC, V. **Map** p274 G4.
Breaks, beats and old skool hip hop are the perfect
accompaniment for this ethnic and earthy venue.
Often a live music venue, but as soon as the band is
done there is always a DJ on hand to play some eclec-
tic tracks. Great balcony.

## Atlantic Seaboard

## Blush Lounge

*43 Somerset Road, Green Point (021 425 0295/*
*www.blushlounge.co.za).* **Open** 10pm-late daily.
**Admission** *Women* R30. *Men* R50. **Credit** AmEx,
DC, MC, V. **Map** p274 G2.
Recently launched in the space of the old Bossa
Nova, this new nightclub is cool and contemporary
with crisp white floors and funky colour accents of
red and blue. There are salsa nights and music
varies from house to Latin.

Girls just wanna have fun at suburban superclub **Tiger Tiger**.

### Ignite

*Second floor, The Promenade, Victoria Road, Camps Bay (021 438 7717).* **Open** 6pm-2am Thur-Sat. **Admission** R30. **Credit** AmEx, DC, MC, V. **Map** p277 A8.

This funky DJ bar with stunning views over the Atlantic has a cool, comfortable lounge and large function room that can change from a catwalk for fashion shows to a delirious dancefloor. Best of all is the huge terrace where the sea breeze quickly cools you down. Thursday R&B nights are packed.

### Pulse

*23 Somerset Road, Green Point (021 425 4010/ www.pulsebar.co.za).* **Open** 5pm-late Wed, Thur; noon-late Fri-Sun. **Admission** R20. **Credit** AmEx, DC, MC, V. **Map** p274 G2.

Pulse is a student-oriented bar that pulsates every night of the weekend. Fuelled by drinks specials and blaring commercial blasts, the crowd here work themselves into a frenzy. Slick decor makes it a cut above your average student haunt and on a good night you will often see the luscious locals dancing on the bar. **Photo** *p190.*

## Southern Suburbs

### Barmooda

*86 Station Road, Observatory (021 447 6752).* **Open** noon-2am Wed-Sat. **Admission** R20 Fri, Sat after 11pm. **Credit** AmEx, DC, MC, V.

This trendy Obs groove den is proving to be very popular, with a friendly mix of University of Cape Town students and young professionals clogging up the dancefloor. Ladies night on Thursdays is always a winner.

### Galaxy

*Cine 400, College Road, Rylands (021 637 9132).* **Open** 9pm-5am Thur-Sat. **Admission** R40. **Credit** AmEx, DC, MC, V.

This clubland institution has been drawing in the punters every weekend since it was a resistance favourite during the darkest days of apartheid, and it's still going strong. Its pumping soundtrack of R&B, radio hits and commercial hits gives the Southern Suburbs space a very friendly, Cape Flats community feel, but visitors are always made to feel welcome.

### Tiger Tiger

*Stadium on Main, Main Road, Claremont (021 683 2220/www.tigertiger.co.za).* **Open** 8pm-4am Tue-Sat. **Admission** R20; R40 after 10.30pm. **Credit** MC, V.

Short skirts, sexy cleavages and striped shirts are the order of the night at this vast suburban superclub. The young, well-heeled crowd goes crazy to a mish-mash of radio hits and retro tunes. The custom-designed space with central sunken dancefloor is perfect for the mating rituals that this place is all about. Prince Harry has been known to drop in when he's in town.

**Arts & Entertainment**

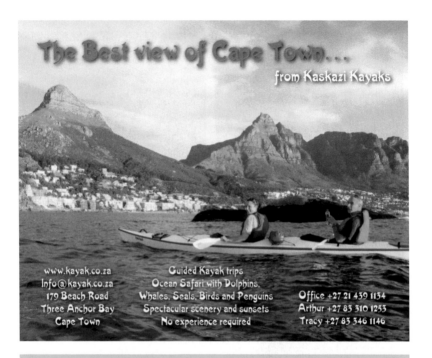

# Sport & Fitness

Action for all, from cricket to kiteboarding.

The Cape's best mountain biking spot is **Tokai Forest**. *See p201.*

Whether it's screaming unashamedly for the Stormers, jeering opposition fielders at the cricket at Newlands, or furiously blowing South Africa's trademark plastic trumpets (capable of making an extraordinary amount of noise), otherwise laid-back Capetonians are fanatical about their sport. The grounds aren't always full, certainly, but read the Monday paper or listen to talk radio station Cape Talk after the local rugby team has lost, and you'll quickly understand just how important sport is in the city.

And there's plenty of it – rugby test matches, a cricket World Cup, football internationals and golf's South African Open have all passed through the Mother City in recent years, along with assorted international tennis, beach volleyball and polo events, meaning you'll have a good chance of catching a game of one code or another while you're in town.

But it's not merely watching sport that gets the city going – there's a huge culture of participation, with events like the Cape Argus Pick 'n' Pay Cycle Tour, Old Mutual Two Oceans Marathon and Gun Run getting thousands of locals out competing en masse during the year. Club sport thrives, with hockey, cricket, soccer and rugby all enjoying plenty of support, and ensuring that sports fields are awash with varying levels of competition every weekend.

Water sports are also increasingly popular, from more traditional pastimes like yachting and windsurfing, to newer endeavours like kite-surfing. And the skies are frequently full of assorted hang-gliders and paragliders.

Cape Town's reputation for taking life easy isn't entirely unearned – and the gourmet qualities of the city lend themselves to good living – but it's still a city that gets out a great deal, with a love of sport extending beyond a seat in the stands.

## Participation sports

### Angling

Fishing boats can be chartered from Hout Bay and Cape Town – on these deep sea tuna trips expect longfin up to 30 kilogrammes, yellowfin up to 100 kilogrammes, as well as mako sharks and dorado. Further inshore, snoek and yellowtail are caught on light tackle and fly.

If the rod and reel is not your thing, another sumptuous delicacy that's easily and cheaply found is crayfish (or *kreef*, as it's known locally). Permits are available from most post offices for a small fee. The season lasts from mid-November to the end of January for daily crayfishing, and only on weekends and public holidays between February and April.

If you're a competent spearfisherman – and are prepared to risk the sharks of False Bay – you could hunt and shoot yellowfin tuna that match your own body in size.

### Cape Sea Safaris
*47 Berg Street, City Bowl (021 422 4611/www. capeseasafaris.com).* **Open** 9am-5.30pm daily. **Credit** AmEx, DC, MC, V.

### Hooked on Africa
*Departures from Hout Bay harbour, Southern Peninsula (021 790 5332/083 460 3963/www. hookedonafrica.co.za).* **Open** 6am-5pm Mon-Fri. **Credit** MC, V.

## Athletics

The beauty of Cape Town makes it a great city to go running in, and if you're of an athletic persuasion, the **Old Mutual Two Oceans Marathon** (021 671 9407/www.twooceans marathon.org.za) offers a magnificent 56-kilometre challenge. It attracts nearly 10,000 runners from around the world, with a strong Russian contingent usually challenging the locals; if 56 kilometres is a little far, there's a 21-kilometre event that runs on the same morning. There are also numerous events throughout the year, with several marathons running through the Winelands areas – give **Western Province Athletics** a call on 021 699 0611 to find out what's next on the calendar. You'll need a local race number to compete in most events, but you can usually acquire one at the race.

## Badminton

Although very much a fringe sport in Cape Town, there are devotees of the shuttlecock to be found. Call the **Western Province Badminton Association** (021 671 5233) if you're on the lookout for a game.

## Bowling

Armies of white-clad pensioners take to the greens every weekend, and South Africa has produced international class bowlers. And it's not a sport exclusively for senior citizens – younger players are involved as well. Try one of the following clubs to get going. Alternatively, try your hand at tenpin bowling at Stadium on Main (*see p158*) in Claremont.

### Milnerton Bowling Club
*Woodbridge Road, Milnerton, Northern Suburbs (021 551 6452).*

### Mowbray Bowling Club
*Upper Chapel Road, Mowbray, Southern Suburbs (021 689 1617).*

### Western Province Bowling Association
*(021 421 1894).*

## Cricket

There's a strong cricket culture in Cape Town, and ovals across the city offer the chance to play beneath Table Mountain. The club season starts in October, although early games often catch the tail end of the winter rain, and runs through to April. The **Western Province Cricket Association** (021 657 2003/www. capecobras.co.za) will point you in the direction of a club, and you'll find that joining in net sessions will quite often lead to the chance of a game over the weekend. Be prepared for competitive cricket, plenty of good-natured sledging, and a couple of beers with your new teammates after the match.

## Cycling

Cape Town's roads are awash with Lycra-clad cyclists, particularly in the first few months of the year, in the build-up to the highlight of the cycling calendar: the 109-kilometre **Pick 'n' Pay Cape Argus Cycle Tour** (www.cycletour.co.za/021 685 6551). About 35,000 cyclists make up the world's largest timed cycle race, a small slice of the peleton made up of professional riders, but the bulk of the field amateur enthusiasts. It's a glorious ride, although dealing with some of the climbs may offset your appreciation of the scenery.

If you want something even more challenging, try the **Cape Epic** (021 426 4373, www.cape-epic.com), an eight-day mountain bike stage race that starts off in Knysna and ends after more than 900 punishing kilometres in Stellenbosch.

## Golf

The country that has produced major winners Gary Player, Ernie Els and Retief Goosen is golf crazy, and courses across the country are usually busy. Weekdays are your better bet for getting a tee time, as members have right of way at weekends, but if you book in advance you can usually get on to the top courses – and the Cape has some of the best. Green fees for foreigners are steep, but caddies are comparatively inexpensive, and a good idea if you're playing in unfamiliar territory. Check out the dress regulations before playing, and if you need to hire clubs, it's also a good idea to phone ahead.

### Atlantic Beach Golf Club

*Birkenhead Drive, Melkbosstrand (080 465 3258/ www.atlanticbeachgolfclub.co.za).* **Credit** AmEx, DC, MC, V.
Situated on the West Coast, and looking out towards Robben Island, Atlantic Beach boasts splendid views, springbok on the course, fairways guarded by indigenous *fynbos*, and, when the wind blows, a brutal challenge that can get plain nasty. Steel yourself if conditions aren't mild – you've got a tough round ahead of you.

### Clovelly Country Club

*Clovelly Road, Clovelly, Southern Peninsula (021 782 1118/www.clovelly.co.za).* **Credit** AmEx, DC, MC, V.
Clovelly is a gem of a layout, a short but tricky design that gets very tough when the wind picks up. Make sure your driver is hitting nice and straight – accuracy is a premium here – and work your way around a swim or walk on the beach in Fish Hoek, a couple of minutes away, with warm water and gentle conditions.

### King David

*Palotti Road, Montana (021 934 0365).* **Credit** AmEx, DC, MC, V.
A slightly unkempt appearance masks a brilliant design, and a course which offers some delightful holes. Situated near the airport, it's often perceived as being on the wrong side of the golfing tracks, but that means price and accessibility are very reasonable for an under-rated course.

### Rondebosch Golf Club

*Golf Course Road, off Klipfontein Road, Mowbray, Southern Suburbs (021 689 4176/www.rondebosch-golf-club.co.za).* **Credit** AmEx, DC, MC, V.
Ten minutes from the centre of Cape Town, Rondebosch offers a pleasant parklands course that isn't overly testing, and provides great views of Table Mountain. The par-five 11th sees the occasional errant drive head off into traffic on the adjoining highway, so be careful.

### Hockey

Hockey is huge in South African schools, and the club scene is equally strong, with Cape Town providing a number of players for the men's and women's national teams every year. Try the **Western Province Hockey**

**Association** (021 448 2656) for details of local clubs. Training on both artificial (better sides) and grass (the more social teams) takes place during the week, with matches at weekends. Indoor hockey is also popular; the Hockey Association will point you in the right direction.

### Ice-skating

Cape winters can be downright unpleasant, but they're not quite arctic, and snow-dusted mountaintops are the closest you'll get to a

# Nature calling

Christoph Sauser, the Swiss professional mountain biking star (and winner of the 2006 Cape Epic, *see p194*), arrives in Cape Town at the beginning of each year to train for the international season ahead. An appreciation of local wine is one reason he keeps returning, but the main one is the quality of the region for cyclists – both professional and amateur. Unsurprisingly in a city that hosts a cycle race with 35,000 participants, there are plenty of bicycles on the road, taking advantage of a city that has plenty to attract the casual rider.

And much the same reasoning applies to runners: majestic scenery, generally pleasant weather and plenty of varied terrain to explore. So whether you're donning your trainers or jumping on the bike, you're in the right part of the world. For cyclists, the outskirts of Stellenbosch, Paarl and Franschhoek offer relaxed, scenic Winelands routes, while the Southern Peninsula, though a little more built-up, has great ocean views, particularly over Chapman's Peak. Take care with motorists – Cape Town's drivers have grudgingly accepted the idea that bicycles have a right to the road as well, but it's best to be extra vigilant just the same.

For joggers, the Tokai forest area offers cool, shaded running, although for safety be sure to run with at least one other person, while the route along the Sea Point promenade (and through to Camps Bay if you're feeling particularly fit) is popular with locals. Gyms and athletics clubs usually have a handful of informal running groups, so if you're looking for a group of like-minded souls and a little guidance on where to hit the road, ask around for some local advice.

**Arts & Entertainment**

Cape Argus Pick 'n' Pay Cycle Tour.

white winter. But there is an ice rink called the **Ice Station** (021 535 2260) at the GrandWest Casino if you're a skating enthusiast.

## Rugby

Rugby is religion in South Africa, the form of regional or national teams frequently determining the mood of the city. But as well as watching, there are plenty of devoted players, and the club rugby competition is very strong. Most clubs run a range of teams, from a tough first XV to older players who've lost a little pace and gained a little girth. The under-21 league is also very competitive; for information on how to get involved, call the **Western Province Rugby Union** (021 659 4500/www. wprugby.com). Also look out for the inevitable games of touch rugby on the beach during summertime – ask to join in, and enjoy a workout on the sand.

## Sailing

Yachting in South Africa has received enormous exposure with the success of the colourful Shosholoza, challenging for the America's Cup in 2007. Table Bay sees plenty of sailing – call **South African Sailing** (021 511 0929) or **Royal Cape Yacht Club** (021 421 1354) if you're keen to hit the ocean.

## Sports & leisure centres

Capetonians are a gym-conscious lot, and the city has plenty of options. Professional sportsmen work out at the **Sports Science Institute** in Newlands (021 659 5600), so expect to see a familiar face or two among the rowing machines and weights. **Virgin Active** (021 710 8500/www.virginactive.co.za) is the place to 'see and be seen', though you'll certainly work up a sweat – the spinning sessions are the stuff of legend. Alternatively, give **Planet Fitness** (021 683 3121/www.planetfitness.co.za) a spin. All offer daily, weekly and monthly packages.

## Tennis

League tennis in Cape Town is played to a reasonable level, and there are plenty of courts around the city, mostly of the all-weather or hard court variety. The **Western Province Tennis Association** (021 686 3055) will have details on where to get playing.

## Spectator sports

### Cricket

Players around the world agree that Cape Town's home ground is one of the finest on earth, and a day of international cricket under

spartan crowds, unless Kaizer Chiefs or Orlando Pirates, the big Soweto teams with massive national support, are the opponents. Tickets are inexpensive, and security at most matches is fine.

## Golf

The annual **Nelson Mandela Invitational** (www.nelsonmandelainvitational.co.za), hosted by Nelson Mandela and Gary Player, attracts celebrity names like Samuel L Jackson and Ronan Keating, as well as top golfers like Ernie Els and Retief Goosen, allowing you to combine golf viewing with a little spectator spotting. The South African professional tour, known as the **Sunshine Tour** 021 850 6500/www.sunshinetour.co.za), hosts a number of events in the Cape.

## Horse racing

There's racing throughout the year at the **Kenilworth Race Course** (021 700 1600) in the Southern Suburbs and the **Durbanville Race Course** (021 976 9690) in the outer Northern Suburbs.

## Motorsport

The city's rev heads visit **Killarney Motor Racing Circuit** (021 557 1639/www.wpmc.co.za) for racing in various formats – Cape Town's roads frequently offer something similar, especially when minibus taxis meet rush hour, but it's Killarney where more formal racing plays out.

## Rugby

International rugby is plentiful in Cape Town, with the Super 14 seeing teams from South Africa, New Zealand and Australia playing each other from February to May. The Stormers are the home team and crowds depend on how well they're doing; plenty of Springboks in the local side, plus the chance to see Wallaby or All Black stars, makes a day of rugby at Newlands a big attraction. Contact the **Western Province Rugby Union** (021 659 4500/www.wprugby.com) for details on Super 14 matches, as well as international fixtures, with a major test match played mid-year in Cape Town. There's also the Currie Cup, South Africa's prestigious domestic competition, with Western Province playing in their famous blue stripes. If you're fanatical about the game, club derbies are always passionate affairs, with the University of Cape Town-Stellenbosch clash hugely anticipated each year.

blue skies, with the mountain rising up above the stadium, will live long in the memory. Call the **Sahara Park Newlands ticket hotline** (021 657 2043/2089) or the **Western Province Cricket Association** (021 657 2003) for information on international fixtures, as well as domestic games featuring local team Cape Cobras, who pack in a reasonable crowd for limited overs matches.

## Cycling

Bicycles rule in the annual Cape Argus Pick 'n' Pay Cycle Tour in March, as 35,000 riders attempt the 109-kilometre gauntlet through the city. It's quite a sight to behold, and locals have become accustomed to spending the day at the side of the road, having a *braai* or a picnic and cheering on the riders. Visit **www.cycletour.co.za** to get an idea of the route, and the perfect point to watch the race unfold.

## Football

Soccer fever is bubbling along as the 2010 World Cup draws closer, and with Cape Town looking to host a number of matches, football culture is as strong as ever in the Mother City. Not that it always seems that way – watching Ajax Cape Town or Santos Cape Town's two sides in the Premier Soccer League involves

Arts & Entertainment

## Extreme sports

Take two rocky, beach-littered coastlines. Wrap them around a mountain chain. Add wind from both directions. Season with some of the most unique and diverse flora and fauna on the planet. Shake together and enjoy.

In some cities, 'extreme' is about taking your life into your own hands to escape a humdrum existence. In Cape Town, it's about embracing all the gorgeous natural beauty out there. Keep that in mind, and you'll have a blast. But if you're not ready to change your plans with the weather, you'll be miserable. This city has every adventure ingredient you could want, but you must be ready to mix it up a bit. So keep your humour and be flexible: want to go kite-surfing but there's no wind today? Go jump out of an aeroplane instead. Want to go diving but visibility is next to nothing? Hire a longboard and learn to surf the swells.

### ONE-STOP SHOPS

Truth is, Cape Town's a bit of an incestuous city, and the adventure industry even more so. There are a few one-stop shops that will book or tailor any kind of extreme outing for you, but do any adventure and that operator will more than likely know somebody who knows somebody who will hook you up with the adrenalin fix you want.

### Downhill Adventures

*Shop 10, Overbeek Building, Junction Orange, Kloof & Long Streets (021 422 0388/www.downhill adventures.com).* **Open** 8am-5pm Mon-Fri; 8.30am-1pm Sat. **Credit** MC, V. **Map** p274 G4.
Owner Axel Zander is the original sandboarding local who went on to win the World Champs. Now his company will offer you a whole host of off-the-shelf adventures. Just walk in and pick one.

### 180 Degrees Adventures

*19 Clare Street, City Bowl (021 462 0992/www. 180.co.za).* **Open** 8am-5pm Mon-Fri. **Credit** MC, V.
These guys organise all kinds of adventure sports events, and will tailor-make any package you dream of. The best in the business, but expect to pay.

## Abseiling/rappelling

### Abseil Africa

*1 Vredenburg Lane, off Long Street, City Bowl (021 424 4760/www.abseilafrica.co.za).* **Open** 9.30am-3.30pm daily (weather permitting). **Credit** MC, V. **Map** p274 G4.
Download the front page of www.abseilafrica.co.za and feel the grin on your face. H-U-G-E air. This is the biggest commercial abseil in the world – 112m, directly off Table Mountain, with Robben Island in the background. Even jaded, rappel-weary climbers don't snigger at this one.

## Climbing & mountaineering

There's no shortage of rock in Cape Town, but you need to be in the lee of the wind if it's pumping – some of the exposed faces on Table Mountain can get a bit precarious when the winds howl. The good news is that there's always the opposite side of the Peninsula to head for if it's not great on your side. The **Mountain Club of South Africa** (021 465 3412/http://cap.mcsa.org.za) owns large tracts of land as well as mountain huts for overnight stays, strictly available to members only.

### CityRock Indoor Climbing Gym

*Corner Collingwood & Anson Roads, Observatory, Southern Suburbs (021 447 1326/www.cityrock. co.za).* **Open** 11am-6pm Mon-Thur; 10am-6pm Fri-Sun. **Credit** MC, V.

### South African Mountaineering Development & Training Trust

*083 768 9021/www.mdt.za.org.*
With their mission of 'developing and maintaining nationally and internationally recognised training standards for organisations and individuals active in mountain related activities', these are good guys to contact if you're looking to qualify, or just want a reliable guide recommendation.

## Diving

Sure, it might not match the Red Sea or the Great Barrier Reef in scale, but Cape Town's cold waters have plenty of charm, with seals, kelp and wrecks particular highlights (not to mention great white sharks and southern right whales). Cape Town is also one of the cheaper places on the planet to learn to scuba. The basic open water course that qualifies you as a scuba diver usually requires six lectures, four pool sessions and five sea dives. This can be completed in one week. Expect to pay R1,695 for NAUI or R1,995 for PADI qualifications, both of which are international accreditations.

### Orca Industries

*3 Bowwood Road, Claremont, Southern Suburbs (021 671 9673/www.orca-industries.co.za).* **Open** 8.30am-5.30pm Mon-Fri; 8.30am-1pm Sat. **Credit** AmEx, DC, MC, V.

### Pro Divers

*Shop 88B, Main Road, Sea Point, Atlantic Seaboard (021 433 0472/082 934 8372/www.prodivers.co.za).* **Open** 8.30am-6pm daily. **Credit** AmEx, MC, V.
These guys offer good bang for your buck if you've never dived before: called 'Scubadrenalin', it's an introduction to scuba with a pool dive to learn the basics, then a kelp and seal dive on the Peninsula. The day finishes at the Two Oceans Aquarium with a dive in the shark tank.

**Sandboarding**. *See p203.*

### Scuba Shack Dive Centre

*289 Long Street, City Bowl (021 785 6742/021 424 9368/083 277 1843/www.scubashack.co.za).* **Open** 10am-6pm Mon-Fri. **Credit** MC, V. **Map** p274 G4.

## Hiking

Full moon up Lion's Head is the must-do classic. Don't get Capetonians started on this – they'll wax lyrical for hours, though most only get round to doing it once or twice in their lives. In the summer months, when the cable car on Table Mountain (*see p70*) is open till well into the evening, walking up one of the many routes to the top, enjoying sundowners up there and returning by cable car is unforgettable. (Get friends to go up in the cable car and meet you with the picnic – you'll be amazed how heavy a bottle of bubbly starts to feel halfway up.)

For those who don't mind a bit of pampering (little joys like porters and caterers), Table Mountain National Park's pride and joy, the new multi-day **Table Mountain Trail** (www.sanparks.org/parks/table_mountain/ht), showcases the city and mountain's virtues while creating much-needed employment for people who live in townships.

Alternatively, try some of the well-marked but seemingly wildly remote walks further south near Cape Point in the Cape of Good Hope Nature Reserve (*see p84*).

### Baboon Matters

*15 Glen Road, Southern Right Hotel, Glencairn, Southern Peninsula (021 782 2015/084 413 9482/ www.baboonmatters.org.za).* **Open** 8am or 4pm daily. **No credit cards.**
Less about the walking and more about the wild encounter, these guided tours will take you through mountain *fynbos* on a specialised two- or three-hour walking adventure to spend time with the last remaining Chacma baboons in the Cape Peninsula. A wonderful experience.

**Surfing.** *See p203.*

# A case of mild exhaustion

## Nordic walking

Currently one of the fastest growing recreational fitness sports in the world, Nordic walking started in the early 1930s in Finland as an off-season training method for competitive cross-country skiers. This exercise puts no pressure on joints and knees, loosens up the upper body and burns two-thirds more calories than normal walking. Arina Botha of the Dirtopia Trail Centre is now the first internationally accredited South African instructor.

### Dirtopia Trail Centre
*Delvera Farm, R44, Klapmuts (021 884 4752/www.dirtopia.co.za).* **Open** 8am-5pm daily. **Credit** MC, V.

## Pilates

Capetonians are sold on the concept of rock-solid core strength. All of the biggest gyms in the city offer an elementary form of pilates as one of their class options, and most physiotherapists can provide personal tuition. Your best bet, though, is to find a small professional studio.

Check out **www.pilatesafrica.co.za** for a list of studios in the Western Cape.

## Yoga

There might be over 100 types of yoga, but they do share underlying philosophies and poses. Cape Town offers pretty much the full range, with new studios popping up all the time.

### Moksha
*Thebe Hosken House, 3rd Floor, 16 Mill Street, City Bowl (021 465 1733/www. moksha.biz).* **Credit** AmEx, DC, MC, V.
Moksha specialises in Ashtanga, an aerobic, muscle-shaping, mind-sculpting, physically demanding workout in which students move from one posture to another to build strength, flexibility and stamina.

### Yogazone Cape Town
*10th floor Picbel Parkade, 58 Strand Street, City Bowl (021 421 8136/www.yoga zone.co.za).* **No credit cards.**
Gorgeously poised Jessika Munnel started Cape Town's Bikram craze. Follow her lead at Yogazone, but be prepared to sweat.

### Cape Nature
*CapeNature House, 14 Belmont Park, Belmont Road, Rondebosch, Southern Suburbs (021 659 3400/ www.capenature.org.za).* **Open** 7.30am-3.30pm daily. **Credit** AmEx, DC, MC, V.

### Mountain Club of SA
*97 Hatfield Street, City Bowl (021 465 3412/ http//:cap.mcsa.org.za).* **Open** 10am-2pm Mon-Fri. **Map** p274 G5.

### Real Cape Adventures
*Vineyard House, 3 Greenacres Close, Hout Bay, Southern Peninsula (021 790 5611/082 556 2520/ www.seakayak.co.za).* **No credit cards**.

### Washer
*(021 434 0517/083 953 3056/www.hikecapetown. co.za).* **No credit cards.**
Mountain guide Barry Washkansky is best known by his nickname and his website profiles all the best places to hike on the Cape Peninsula.

## Kiteboarding

Dolphin Beach at Bloubergstrand is one of the best places in the world for kiteboarders – it's known as 'kite beach' these days. False Bay

hotspots include Sunrise Beach near Muizenberg and Glencairn, and weekends away simply must be at Langebaan. Beginners can fast-track their progress with a bit of tuition: expect to pay R350 for a two-hour lesson, including equipment. Otherwise it costs R250 per day for a kite and the same for a board. **Photo** *p202.*

### Cabrinha Kitesurf SA
*Shop 5, Beach Centre, Blaauwberg Road, Table View, Northern Suburbs (021 556 7910/www. cabrinha.co.za).* **Open** 9am-6pm Mon-Fri. **Credit** AmEx, DC, MC, V.

### Windswept
*47 Antigua, Bratton Way, Table View, Northern Suburbs (021 554 1864/082 961 3070/www. windswept.co.za).* **Open** 10am-5pm daily. **Credit** AmEx, DC, MC, V.
In addition to rental and tuition, Windswept offers SA's only International Kiteboarding Association accredited training for instructors.

## Mountain biking

The best all-round mountain bike destination is Tokai Forest, which offers some good climbing as well as technical single track. Permits cost R20, payable at the picnic area en route to Tokai Manor House. Entrance is theoretically only during daylight hours, but a group meets every Thursday evening for an accident-prone night ride. The start and finish is the Alphen Hotel (Alphen Drive, Constantia) at 6.30pm.

Closer to the city limits, Grabouw has long been known to the mountain biking community as somewhat of a haven, with no shortage of mountains, *fynbos* and forest. Now acclaimed trail-maker Meurant Botha has expanded this to include trails from Thandi Kitchen – the restaurant on the adjacent wine farm.

### Daytrippers
*414 Voortrekker Road, Unit 8, Santos Park, Maitland (021 511 4766/082 807 9522/ www.daytrippers.co.za).* **Open** 7am-3pm daily. **Tours** R365 for mountain biking on the slopes above the City Bowl to the historic King's Blockhouse (incl hire of bike & guide). **Credit** AmEx, DC, MC, V.

### Pedal Power Association
*9 Hillpark Lane, Mowbray, Southern Suburbs (021 689 8420/www.pedalpower.co.za).* **Open** 9am-4.30pm Mon-Fri. **Membership** R160 per year, plus R80 for every family member. **Credit** AmEx, DC, MC, V.

## Paragliding

Cape Town offers plenty of good spots, but they're not all suited to the inexperienced. Many do, however, end near a pub. Most renowned, of course, is the classic launch off Lion's Head, with a flight along the Twelve Apostles of Table Mountain, and a neat landing on clipped lawns in front of La Med restaurant, Camps Bay. Good news for the non-qualified is that this can be done tandem. Expect to pay around R750 for the 20-minute flight.

### Birdmen Paragliding
*36 Champagne Way, Table View, Northern Suburbs (082 658 6710/www.birdmen.co.za).* **No credit cards**.

### Wallend-Air School of Paragliding
*368 Main Road, Wynberg, Southern Suburbs (021 762 2441/www.wallendair.com).* **Credit** MC, V.

## Rafting & canoeing

While the rivers might be seasonal, there's never a shortage of sea, so the oceans are increasingly the focus for those keen on

**Kiteboarding**. *See p201.*

anything paddling-related. Surfers' Corner, Muizenberg, is always a good option for whitewater enthusiasts, while the harbours dotted all along both sides of the Peninsula provide safe havens and easy entries for canoeists. If conditions are right, even beginners can paddle around Cape Point – the 'Cape of Storms'.

For commercial rafting trips on local rivers, the African Paddling Association has a lengthy list of safe and certified operators. Remember when you book with anybody that APA membership binds them to a code of conduct and safety and provides an assurance that the operator and/or guide is responsible and reputable. You'll be promoting good practice by asking for proof of membership before booking a trip.

### African Paddling Association
*21 Selous Road, Claremont, Southern Suburbs (021 674 1645/www.apa.org.za).*

### Gravity Adventure Group
*21 Selous Road, Claremont, Southern Suburbs (021 683 3698/www.gravity.co.za).* **Open** 8.30am-5pm Mon-Fri. **No credit cards.**

Gravity's trips in the Kogelberg Reserve near Gordon's Bay can be combined with hikes or abseils as a weekend adventure. Gravity has been awarded the sole rights to operate commercial sea kayaking trips in the beautiful West Coast National Park, with a wilderness beach camp for overnight stays.

### Real Cape Adventures
*Vineyard House, 3 Greenacres Close, Hout Bay, Southern Peninsula (021 790 5611/082 556 2520/ www.seakayak.co.za).* **No credit cards.**
Sea kayaking at Hout Bay, Simonstown, around the Peninsula and along the West Coast.

## Sandboarding

Sure this town has its fair share of sunshine and beaches, but in days gone by its inhabitants lamented the fact that it had no snowboarding. Then Axel Zander started pulling moves on the sand dunes, and Capetonians thought they might just have a substitute. When international travellers pointed out how much fun it was to board in baggies and bikinis, Capetonians woke up to the fact they had something cool on their hands. What they don't have is a single ski lift. **Photo** *p199*.

### Downhill Adventures
*See p198.*

## Skydiving

If you're looking for memorable moments, try this: hop out of a plane and check out Table Mountain and Robben Island from the air. If you're a beginner, your senses will be heightened by the thrill and every detail will be etched into your brain. If you're more experienced, you'll have a longer freefall to take in the view. Everybody wins.

### Skydive Cape Town
*Off the R27 West Coast Road, Melkbosstrand (082 800 6290/www.skydivecapetown.za.net).* **No credit cards.**

## Surfing

Coastlines in every direction mean decent summer and winter swells – the latter bringing some monster action at times. The Red Bull Big Wave Africa event sees some of the world's best big-wave surfers congregating at Dungeons, just off Hout Bay. At the opposite end of the scale, Muizenberg is the perfect beginners' playground. **Photo** *p200*.

### Gary's Surf Shop
*34 Beach Road, Muizenberg, Southern Peninsula (021 788 9839/083 324 5110/www.garysurf.com).* **Credit** DC, MC, V.

# Theatre & Dance

From alfresco Shakespeare to camp cabaret.

## Theatre

The definition of theatre in Cape Town is about as broad as the concept of snow in Iceland. It could mean Shakespeare declaimed under a proscenium arch, or a troupe of painted players slaughtering a chicken on a suburban stage. Perhaps a band of musicians paying tribute to Elvis, or a community group exploring a painful past.

It's all of these and a lot more besides. In post-apartheid South Africa, the range of cultural expression pretty much matches the diversity of the country. And while it's possible to experience world class interpretations of the Bard, Cape Town's stages are also very proudly local. Playwrights and directors are unafraid to tackle topical issues of the day – from HIV/AIDS to racism and homophobia – and are also keen to celebrate the possibilities of the future, reflected in dynamic forms of physical and visual theatre.

It's not all serious stuff either – there are plenty of productions that deal exclusively in fun entertainment. Musical tributes, dinner theatre, stand-up comedy and even circus shows are on offer. And the venues are often an atmospheric part of the package – a converted chicken coop, a former lion's den, a renovated post office and a national botanical garden are all included on the theatre circuit.

From stabbing satire to raunchy rock operas, dressed-up drama to minimalist mime, cutting-edge comedy to family fun, the city pretty much has it all.

Most tickets can be booked at theatre box-offices, either in person or by phone, or through Computicket or Dial-a-Seat (for both, *see p180*). Also log on to the website www.fdcawards.co.za – an excellent resource for listings, news and reviews.

### Major venues

### Artscape Theatre Centre

*DF Malan Street, Foreshore, City Bowl (021 421 7839/www.artscape.co.za).* **Open** *box office* 9am-5pm Mon-Fri; 9am-12.30pm Sat; 1hr prior to performance Sat, Sun. **Tickets** R100-R350. **Credit** AmEx, DC, MC, V. **Map** p275 I3.

Despite its imposing architecture, the Artscape Theatre Centre has managed to morph into a lively home for drama, opera, ballet and music productions, as well as fashion shows, charity balls and art exhibitions. Opened (to racially segregated audiences) in the early 1970s, it is now a much-transformed multi-stage venue that hosts an eclectic line-up of local and international shows. From *Cats* to *Sarafina!*, there's always something on the go. And for those who like entertainment that takes a walk on the improvised side, there's the irresistibly funny Theatresports, an improv 'reality drama' that's been resident here for 12 years. For pre-show meals and drinks visit Nino's (021 421 1425). Based in the complex are Cape Town Opera, Cape Town City Ballet, dance company Jazzart Dance Theatre and the Cape Philharmonic Orchestra.

### Baxter Theatre

*Main Road, Rondebosch, Southern Suburbs (021 685 7880/021 680 3989/www.baxter.co.za).* **Open** *box office* 9am-start of performance Mon-Sat. **Tickets** R50-R150. **Credit** AmEx, DC, MC, V.

Baxter Theatre.

Three stages, a bustling bar and a stark restaurant are all housed in this multistorey complex. The Baxter enjoys a reputation for staging original, challenging drama (such as works by Athol Fugard, Fiona Coyne and Mike van Graan, or the Handspring Puppet Company), and the boards have been trod by the likes of John Kani and Steven Berkoff. Musically, the Concert Hall gives equal weight to jazz and classical performances. The smaller Studio Theatre often features new works, and is also used for stand-up comedy and solo spots. The best place to be post-show is in the bar, where performers and audiences get to kick back among posters of previous productions.

### Theatre on the Bay

*1 Link Street, Camps Bay, Atlantic Seaboard (021 438 3301/www.theatreonthebay.co.za).* **Open** *box office* 9.30am-5pm daily; 9.30am-8pm performance days. **Tickets** R100-R250. **Credit** AmEx, DC, MC, V. **Map** p277 B8.

The lavish concrete curtains decorating the façade of the Theatre on the Bay have led to its affectionate nickname, the Shroud of Toerien. And for good reason. The theatre belongs to the hard-working Pieter Toerien, who has spent several decades importing top-quality scripts to South Africa. From farces to more serious fare, Toerien has largely focused on the work of international playwrights,

while his cast lists feature a roll call of respected South African thespians. The Act One Theatre Café (021 438 8818) offers à la carte dining, and you can take drinks into the performances.

## Other venues

### Barnyard Theatre

*Willowbridge Lifestyle Centre, Durbanville, Northern Suburbs (021 914 8898/011 280 4300/083 913 3434/www.barnyardtheatre.co.za).* **Open** *box office* 9am-5pm daily. **Tickets** R95. **Credit** MC, V.

Part of the incredibly popular Barnyard chain of theatres, this is the first branch to open in the Cape. The Barnyard franchise is run on simple but successful lines: punters bring their own supper, buy drinks at the in-house bar, and are treated to musical entertainment that mainly follows a tribute format – the Beatles, Elvis, etc. Songs are sing-along familiar, and the performers are usually super-slick and professional. Good, clean fun.

### Cape Town International Convention Centre

*Convention Square, 1 Lower Long Street, City Bowl (021 410 5000/www.capetownconvention.com).* **Tickets** R50-R250. **Credit** AmEx, DC, MC, V. **Map** p275 I3.

# My kind of town Gill Hockman

Gill Hockman owns one of Observatory's favourite nightspots, the Independent Armchair Theatre (see p206), and is also a member of the band Buckfever Underground.

**Cape Town makes me...** crazy.

**I treat myself at...** Vibes Vinyl (Stadium on Main, Main Road, Claremont, Southern Suburbs, 021 683 5676) and Mabu Vinyl (Shop 2, Buitenkloof Centre, 8 Kloof Street, City Bowl, 021 423 7635; see p145).

**I dine at...** Royale (273 Long Street, City Bowl, 021 422 4536; see p106) and Chef Pon's (12 Mill Street, City Bowl, 021 465 5846; see p97).

**I get takeaways from...** Diva (88 Lower Main Road, Observatory, Southern Suburbs, 021 448 0282; see p113) and the Engen Quick Shop (27 Annandale Street, City Bowl, 021 461 4320).

**I drink sundowners at...** balconies all over the city.

**I wake up to...** the eternal bliss of not having an alarm clock.

**I go to sleep in...** a Moroka Swallows football shirt.

**I love...** Fuzigish (a local band).

**I buy presents at...** The Bin (105 Harrington Street, City Bowl, 021 465 8314; see p170).

**I drink coffee at...** Mimi (107 Lower Main Road, Observatory, Southern Suburbs, 021 447 3316).

**The south-easter is...** my one never-ending step away from sanity.

**I have fun at...** Big Love parties (www.biglove.co.za, 082 666 6014).

**I hide from the world at...** Oppikoppi (012 346 2011, www.oppikoppi.co.za).

One of the biggest seated venues in the city, with space for 1,200 punters. The auditorium at the CTICC is a monstrously large space that is used for mega-scale international productions, such as the popular *Mamma Mia!* But be warned – some seats are restricted view, and the sound is not always up to par. Check before you book.

## Die Hoenderhok
*Langverwacht Farm, Kuilsriver (021 906 4636/ www.hoenderhok.co.za).* **Open** 7pm-late Tue-Thur. **Tickets** prices vary. **No credit cards.**
A refreshingly amusing website and answering-machine message (something like 'sorry we're not here, we're busy counting eggs') set the tone for this unusual theatre on a farm. The 80-seater venue is situated in the farm's original chicken coop (hence the name). During the week there's Afrikaans fare from the likes of Trix Pienaar and Chris Chameleon, ranging from local comedy to more edgy cabaret. Ticket prices include light refreshments (wine, juice, home-made soup).

## Independent Armchair Theatre
*135 Lower Main Road, Observatory, Southern Suburbs (021 447 1514/www.armchairtheatre. co.za).* **Open** 9pm-late daily. **Tickets** R20-R50. **No credit cards.**
Sagging couches and crusty cushions are all part of the Independent's charm. As is the clientele, which is as eclectic as the entertainment. Funky film-makers, punk rastas, skate rebels and hip hop god-desses lay claim to the space, which can get hecti-cally crowded. Stand-up comedy, cabaret, live bands, movies and drama productions all appear on the programme, with something going down nearly every night of the week. Very popular with the Obs student population.

## Kalk Bay Theatre
*52 Main Road, Kalk Bay, Southern Peninsula (073 220 5430/www.kbt.co.za).* **Open** 7-11pm Tue-Sat. **Tickets** R75 (R150 incl dinner). **Credit** MC, V.
If it's stylish intimacy you're after, treat yourself to an evening at the Kalk Bay Theatre. Situated in a

beautifully renovated church, the 47-seater theatre is on the first floor, with a wooden staircase leading up to a second-level restaurant. Begin here with a tasty two-course meal, meander down to the featured show, and then round off with dessert and coffee. See something as offbeat as Gaetan Schmid's *Incredible Beer Show* or as entertaining as a tribute to Pink Floyd. Booking essential.

### Lane Theatre
*Corner Port & Alfred Roads, V&A Waterfront, Atlantic Seaboard (021 418 4600/www.waterfront theatreschool.co.za).* **Tickets** R20-R50. **No credit cards**. **Map** p275 H2.
Theatre stalwarts Delia Sainsbury and Keith Galloway have been running the Waterfront Theatre School for many years, with a curriculum focused on musical theatre. The Lane Theatre is used to showcase student productions, most of which feature popular show tunes and fancy footwork performed by a young and enthusiastic cast.

### Little Theatre/Arena Theatre/ Intimate Theatre
*Hiddingh Campus, 37 Orange Street, City Bowl (021 480 7129/www.uct.ac.za/depts/drama).* **Tickets** R25-R40. **No credit cards**. **Map** p274 G4.
The UCT Drama Department – which celebrated its 75th birthday in 2006 – has three theatres to showcase student productions: the Arena, the Little and the Intimate. As is to be expected from a university campus, standards range from the excellent to the, um, interesting, but most performances are worth the effort. The department boasts some impressive alumni – Richard E Grant for one – and overall the campus forms a contemporary cultural hub, sharing space with the Michaelis Art School.

### Masque Theatre
*37 Main Road, Muizenberg, Southern Peninsula (021 788 6999/021 788 1898/www.muizenberg.info/masque.asp).* **Open** box office 9am-5.30pm Mon-Fri; 9am-noon Sat. **Tickets** R35-R50. **No credit cards**.
The Masque is something of an institution. For many years it was the only theatre on this stretch of the coast. Local amateur dramatic societies predominantly use the venue, with the programme varied in content and quality. A family-oriented space that's well supported by the local community.

### Obz Café
*115 Lower Main Road, Observatory, Southern Suburbs (021 448 5555/www.obzcafe.co.za).* **Open** 7am-1am daily. **Tickets** *theatre* R40-R60; *poetry & music* R20. **Credit** AmEx, DC, MC, V.
A concerted effort has gone into turning one half of the trendy Obz Café into a performance space where anything from flamenco to traditional African music can be enjoyed. The restaurant/bar/theatre is hugely supportive of local talent, and the frequent turnover of acts allows for both established artists and new talent on the block to get a shot.

### On Broadway
*88 Shortmarket Street, City Bowl (021 418 8338/021 424 1194/www.onbroadway.co.za).* **Tickets** R55-R75. **Credit** AmEx, DC, MC, V. **Map** p274 G3.
Cross-dressing lip-synchers, glam boy bands and singers with big hair are just a taste of what you can expect at On Broadway, where the show isn't over even when the fat ladies have sung – literally. Musical tribute shows, camp cabaret and the occasional piece of hip theatre contribute to a party formula that keeps punters coming back again and again. It usually starts with dinner and a show, but one never quite knows where it is going to end.

### Roxy Revue Bar
*1 Vanguard Drive, GrandWest Casino, Goodwood, Northern Suburbs (021 505 7777/www.grandwest.co.za).* **Open** 6pm-late Wed-Sat. **Tickets** R67. **Credit** AmEx, DC, MC, V.
Push through pinging slot machines to get to this unexpected site within the Cape's biggest casino complex. Once inside, kick back and enjoy a fun cabaret and musical menu. The programmes are slick, the performers pretty and you can always go gaming for extra fun after the show.

### Theatre @ the Pavilion
*BMW Pavilion, V&A Waterfront, City Bowl (021 419 7661/www.thepavilion.co.za).* **Open** box office 8am-5pm Mon-Wed; 8am-8pm Thur-Sat. **Tickets** R95, R180 with buffet dinner. **Credit** AmEx, DC, MC, V. **Map** p274 G1.
Situated on the quieter side of the V&A complex, this venue nevertheless rocks with high-volume musical tribute shows. With titles like *Myths & Legends*, and an emphasis on familiar rock and pop numbers, jovial audiences are usually singing along by half-time.

## Outdoor theatre
### Kirstenbosch Open-Air Theatre
*Kirstenbosch Botanical Gardens, Rhodes Drive, Newlands, Southern Suburbs (021 799 8783/021 761 2866/www.kirstenbosch.co.za).* **Tickets** prices vary. **Credit** AmEx, DC, MC, V.
Bryan Adams, the Soweto String Quartet and the Dalai lama have all had great gigs in the Kirstenbosch Gardens. The summer season always attracts thousands to loll and listen on the lush botanical lawns. But there's an even more unusual experience for those prepared to rise with the sun – the annual early-morning performance of Greek drama on the stairs of the stone amphitheatre near the Sanlam Visitors Centre. Previous productions have included *The Birds* and *Oedipus*. Get there early – before 7am – for a memorable performance.

### Maynardville Open-Air Theatre
*Corner Church & Wolf Streets, Wynberg, Southern Suburbs (021 421 7695/www.artscape.co.za).* **Shows** Jan, Feb. **Credit** AmEx, DC, MC, V.

Quite frankly, there's nothing quite like catching the annual alfresco Shakespeare at Maynardville. With huge trees forming a natural proscenium arch over a stage lit by moonlight, the set designers hardly need to make much effort. And yet they do, and the venue has hosted some of the most innovative versions of the Bard's work seen in South Africa. The drill is easy. Pack a picnic for a pre-show feast on the Maynardville lawns. Take your seat and snuggle up under a blanket for the show. Go home and wait for it to happen all over again next year.

## Theatre companies

### Magnet Theatre/Magnet Theatre Education Trust
*2 Morley Road, Observatory, Southern Suburbs (021 480 7173/www.magnettheatre.co.za).*
Jenny Reznick and Mark Fleischman started Magnet Theatre in 1987, aiming to 'develop the language of physical theatre in South Africa'. Their dynamic creations, many in collaboration with companies like Jazzart, are visual and physical feasts with a firm political backbone. The company also runs workshops throughout the country, mostly working with youth and community groups. Watch the press and website for production details.

### Mothertongue Project
*021 424 7886/www.mothertongue.co.za.*

Mothertongue is a women's collective exploring empowerment, healing and transformation through theatre. Formed in 2000, the company has developed a body of original work that combines story-telling, physical theatre, visual arts, creative writing, ritual and sound. Productions such as *Indawo Yamaphupha – the Space of Dreams* and *Beading My Soul* have received great critical acclaim. The company also holds workshops with young women in schools and women's organisations.

## Circus

### South African National Circus School
*2 Willow Road, Hartleyvale, Observatory, Southern Suburbs (021 692 4287/073 273 3538/ www.ontic.co.za/sacircus).*
Hire your own private circus. Members of the SA National Circus School are available for school performances, birthdays and corporate events. You can catch them at their own aerial premises in Observatory, or they will travel to your function. The trapeze artists also lead teambuilding sessions – ideal for wannabe high flyers.

### Zip Zap Circus School
*Unit 13, Montague Gardens Industrial Park, Montague Drive, Montague Gardens, Northern Suburbs (021 551 9901/www.zip-zap.co.za).*

**Jazzart Dance Theatre.** *See p210.*

Kids who join the Zip Zap Circus School get to do the coolest things – trapeze flying, tumbling, and a lot more in between. The school puts on regular shows around the city, where you get to see just how talented their trainees are. Children from all walks of life have passed through the school's tent flaps, some going on to become professional stunt-people and clowns.

# Dance

While most audiences prefer to watch the popular (but perpetually under-funded) Cape Town City Ballet, it seems that local dancers are moving more and more towards trying their hands (and feet) at ballroom dancing and Latin American salsa classes.

Not many local dance studios are open to just anybody, but there are plenty of local dance clubs and social events where you can let your feet do the talking.

As for performances, Cape Town's dance showpiece is Jazzart's annual fundraiser, **Danscape** (021 410 9848/www.jazzart.co.za), which takes place in early June.

Updated information on events and performances is available from the **Western Province Dance Teachers Association**

(021 979 4974/www.dancedirectory.co.za), and tickets are available through Computicket or Dial-A-Seat (for both, *see p180*).

## Dance companies

### Cape Town City Ballet (CTCB)
*Artscape Theatre Complex, DF Malan Street, Foreshore, City Bowl (021 650 2400/www. capetowncityballet.org.za).* **Tickets** R100-R350. **Credit** AmEx, DC, MC, V. **Map** p275 I3.
Born out of the old UCT Ballet and CAPAB Ballet companies, the 70-year-old CTCB is based at the Artscape Theatre but also performs at Maynardville Open-Air Theatre, the Spier Summer Festival and Muizenberg's Masque Theatre. The company stages classical ballets like *Sleeping Beauty* and the *Nutcracker*, as well as new developments like the rock ballet *Queen at the Ballet*. Its ridiculously cheap matinées sell out fast.

### Dance for All
*Zofin House, 10 Aden Avenue, Athlone (072 170 0924/www.danceforall.co.za).*
Former principal dancer Philip Boyd's DFI project trains youngsters from the city's townships in a signature style that is both neo-classical and Afro-contemporary, presenting original works by local and international choreographers and by company members themselves.

Learn from the experts at **La Rosa**.

### Blush Lounge

*43 Somerset Road, Green Point, Atlantic Seaboard (021 425 0295/www.blushlounge.co.za).* **Fees** R20 per class. **Admission** free Tue-Thur; R30-R50 Sat. **Credit** AmEx, DC, MC, V. **Map** p274 G2.

This cocktail bar/nightclub offers salsa classes (beginners to advanced) every Thursday evening. Everybody's welcome, and you don't need to bring a partner.

### Brigitte Reeve Dance Centre

*Private Studio, UCT Ballet School, Woolsack Drive, Rosebank (021 671 2442).* **Fees** R500 per term. **No credit cards**.

This long-established studio teaches the Horton (strengthening) technique, along with jazz, modern and contemporary dance, encompassing international competitions and tours, biannual shows at the Baxter Theatre, competitions and exam work.

### Cape Academy of Performing Arts

*The Space, Bell Crescent, Westlake Business Park, Tokai (021 701 0599/www.capedancecompany. bizland.com).*

Under the direction of owner and principal dancer Debbie Turner, the 20-year-old Cape Academy of Performing Arts (formerly known as the Academy of Dance) offers tuition by some of South Africa's finest instructors in all aspects of dance and musical theatre.

### Jazzart Dance Theatre

*Artscape Theatre Complex, DF Malan Street, Foreshore, City Bowl (021 410 9848/www. jazzart.co.za).* **Fees** R40 per class.

Jazzart offers training in African dance, improvisation, contemporary, gumboot and mpantsula (gumboot and tap combined), presenting after-hours classes for adults and weekend classes in street dance and creative dance for children. The company is actively involved in the local dance community, collaborating with theatre groups like the Magnet Theatre, and presenting an annual mid-year fundraiser festival called Danscape. **Photo** *p208*.

### La Rosa Spanish Dance Theatre

*Third Floor, Loop Studios, 4 Loop Street, City Bowl (021 421 6437/www.larosa.co.za).* **Classes** 6-7pm Mon, Tue. **Cost** R360 per 10 classes (once a week). **No credit cards**.

This vibrant Spanish dance company performs at cabaret venues across the city, and also offers classes for all ages, taught according to the Spanish dance syllabus and flamenco technique.

### Rhythm Works

*Artscape Theatre Centre, DF Malan Street, City Bowl (082 779 9906/021 434 3752).* **Map** p275 I3.

Choreographer Paul Johnson runs the city's top tap-dancing school, with his protégés hot-stepping their way through a traditional end-of-year show at the Artscape Arena.

### La Salsa Dance School

*Kendridge Primary School, Van Riebeeck Avenue, Kendridge (083 273 5454/www.lasalsa.co.za).* **Fees** free intro class, then R35 per class. **No credit cards**.

La Salsa offers a three-tiered, ten-week programme, which culminates in a vibrant graduation party for new and experienced Salseros.

### ¿Qué Pasa?

*7 Bree Street, City Bowl (083 556 7466/www. quepasa.co.za).* **Admission** R20-R30; R100 for private lesson. **No credit cards**. **Map** p275 H3.

It started out as a Latin dance studio, and soon turned into Cape Town's first dedicated salsa club. There are group classes on Tuesdays, Thursdays and Saturdays.

# Trips Out of Town

ONE OF THE TOP 100 WINERIES IN THE WORLD

ANNO 1916

# BACKSBERG

ESTATE CELLARS

Be sure to visit Backsberg, situated on the slopes of the Simonsberg Mountains.
Enjoy sumptuous lunches in our garden restaurant or indoors at the fireplace.
Sample a wide selection of excellent wines or sip a glass of world-renowned
estate brandy, all created with personal attention and love.

**Wine Tasting**
Open every day
Mon - Fri: 8h00 - 17h00
Sat: 9h30 - 16h30
Sun: 10h30 - 16h30

**Restaurant**
Mon - Sun: 12h00 - 15h30
Tel: +27 21 875 5952

**Weddings, conferences and functions**
Contact Lee-Ann at events@backsberg.co.za

*Making fine wine an every day pleasure*

Tel: +27 21 875 5141  Fax: +27 21 875 5144
info@backsberg.co.za   www.backsberg.co.za

# Winelands

Grape escapes.

It's only an hour's drive from Cape Town (and a very scenic hour at that), but the famous Cape Winelands feel like a different world. There are rolling vineyards, towering mountains, historic wine estates and more than enough wine to keep even the thirstiest old soak satisfied.

Cape wine enjoys an impressive reputation, and the Winelands are home to most of South Africa's premier wine estates. The good news is that nearly every farm and estate in the area offers wine-tasting. The bad news is the legal blood alcohol limit is 0.05g per 100ml (3.5oz). So choose a designated driver or join a tour.

Paarl, Franschhoek and Stellenbosch are the nearest and most famous, but the further you go the more you'll discover. The Winelands, and their rustic, rural gems like Robertson, Montagu and Ceres, offer much, much more than just wine presses and vineyards.

If you need some more assistance in planning your tour of the Winelands, contact the **Wine Desk at the Waterfront** (V&A Waterfront, 021 405 4550/082 822 6127/www.winedesk waterfront.co.za) which can tailor-make a Winelands experience that's slightly off the beaten track. They are also well equipped to assist if you need to send off a shipment of fine reds to a loved one abroad.

## Ceres & Tulbagh

**Ceres** has two claims to fame: fruit juice and snow. Located on yonder side of Michell's Pass, on the R303, the Ceres valley is named after the Roman goddess of fruitfulness, and its Mediterranean climate of 230 days of sun per annum makes it one of South Africa's most important fruit-growing areas.

When the fruits aren't ripening in the valley, the snow is falling on the mountains. Ceres is one of the few places in the Western Cape that experiences regular winter snowfalls. The frosty winter months (usually June and July) see droves of Capetonians donning their thermal underpants and woollen hats and taking the 90-minute drive out to Ceres to build snowmen. The roads tend to be very busy and the area is invariably crowded – so it's a good idea to contact the local tourism bureau (023 316 1287) ahead of time and ask them to recommend the best spots.

Down the road, on 29 September 1969, **Tulbagh** was flattened by an earthquake which measured somewhere between 6.3 and 6.5 on the Richter scale. The old folks still talk about it, and the town is still recovering from it. Most of the buildings on the main road were

**Oom Samie se Winkel**: Stellenbosch's old general store is a national monument. *See p222.*

restored, leaving Church Street with 32 newly declared national monuments.

When the mountains around Tulbagh (which include 2,077m/6,810ft Great Winterhoek) aren't shaking, they're producing a varied terrain for the local winemakers, and giving hikers some interesting hills and valleys to explore.

### GETTING THERE

Ceres is 140km (87 miles) and Tulbagh is 120km (76 miles) from Cape Town. For both, take the N1 northbound and follow the R44 from Paarl to Wellington. For Ceres, take the R303 over Michell's Pass. For Tulbagh, stay on the R44 and look for signs. For organised tours, contact the Cape Town Tourism Office (*see p54*).

### TOURIST INFORMATION

Ceres Tourism Bureau (023 316 1287/www.ceres.org.za).
Tulbagh Tourism Bureau (023 230 1348/www.tourismtulbagh.co.za).

## What to see & do

### Aquila Private Game Reserve

*R46, 10km from Touws Rivier (021 405 4513/ www.aquilasafari.com).* **Cost** R2,865 standard overnight safari with transport. **No credit cards**.
The trouble with some parts of South Africa – especially the Western Cape parts – is that they don't feel very… African. The Aquila reserve and safari lodge, in the southern Karoo highlands, is African.

Very African. Located just outside Touws Rivier near Ceres, the reserve is steeped in Khoi-San and Anglo-Boer War history, with San rock art sites dating back 10,000 years. Aquila's large natural wetland is home to 172 bird species and a wide range of wildlife – including the 'Big Five' (lion, buffalo, rhino, mountain leopard and elephant). Experience the beasts up close on one of the reserve's game drives.

### Groote Vallei Olive Estate

*Off the R46, 4km from Tulbagh (023 230 0660).* **Open** by appointment only for tours and olive tasting. **No credit cards**.
Tulbagh's wine-growing soil and climate also make for fine olive oil – much of which comes from Groote Vallei's 2,000 olive-producing mission trees.

### Klondyke Cherry Farm

*Bo-Swaarmoed Road, 30km from Ceres (023 312 1521).* **Open** Nov-Jan 8am-4.30pm daily.
Klondyke allows visitors to go cherry-picking in its fields during the summer ripening season. The cherries – and the crowds – start in November.

### Matroosberg Private Nature Reserve

*Erfdeel Farm, 35km from Ceres (023 312 2282/ www.matroosberg.com).* **No credit cards**.
Located under Matroosberg Peak (2,247m/7,372ft), this reserve often experiences heavy winter snowfall. There are three ways to tackle the snow: in your own 4x4, on the reserve's private ski slope or on a guided drive aboard the farm's go-anywhere Bedford army truck.

### Tolbos Hiking Trail
*Kleinfontein Farm, Winterhoek (083 235 7832/ 083 453 3448).* **No credit cards**.
This three-hour trail leads up Inkruip Peak, with views over the Witzenberg Plateau, Matroosberg and the Bokkeveld… and, on a clear day, of a very distant Table Mountain. Booking essential.

### Tulbagh Horse Trails
*Vrolikheid Farm, Winterhoek (023 230 0615).* **Cost** R100-R110 per hour. **No credit cards.**
These trails through Witzenberg and Winterhoek vary from hour-long guided strolls through the orchards and vineyards to half-day rides across the Klein Berg River and up into the mountains. Booking essential.

### Tulbagh Wine Route
*Tourist office, 4 Church Street, Tulbagh (023 230 1348/www.tulbaghwineroute.com).* **Open** 9am-5pm Mon-Fri; 10am-4pm Sat; 11am-4pm Sun. **No credit cards**.
The Tulbagh Wine Route hosts some respected wine cellars, from the old Drostdy and Theuniskraal estates to the ultra-modern Saronsberg and innovative Twee Jongen Gezellen.

## Where to eat & drink

### Boulders Bush Pub
*Vindoux Farm, Twee Jonge Gezellen Road, Tulbagh (023 230 0635/www.vindoux.com).* **Open** noon-2pm, 5-10pm Wed-Sat; noon-6pm Sun. **No credit cards**.
Tulbagh's only bush pub offers steaks, salads, seafood, poultry and pasta, along with a spit *braai* and a pizza oven. Live music is also a regular feature on the entertainment menu.

### Paddagang Wine House
*23 Church Street, Tulbagh (023 230 0242).* **Open** 8am-5pm daily. **Credit** AmEx, DC, MC, V.
Paddagang ('froggy way' in Afrikaans in honour of the frogs in its garden) offers traditional Cape cuisine, with dishes such as *bobotie* and *smoorsnoek*.

### Rijk's
*Main Road, Tulbagh (023 230 100/www.rijks.co.za).* **Open** noon-2pm, 7.30-9.30pm daily. **Credit** AmEx, DC, MC, V.
One of the finest restaurants in Tulbagh, Rijk's offers unfussy country cuisine with acclaimed pinotage and semillon from its award-winning cellar.

## Where to stay

### Fairfield Cottages
*Skurweberg Mountains, 6km from Ceres (023 316 6653/082 924 7009/www.fairfieldcottages.co.za).* **Rates** R300-R350. **No credit cards**.
These two cottages – which share an inviting jacuzzi pool – have been restored with a blend of the old (lime-washed furniture and thatched roofs) and the new (art deco lounge suites and chicken wire doors).

### Old Tulbagh Hotel
*22 Van der Stel Street, Tulbagh (023 230 0071/ www.tulbaghhotel.co.za).* **Rates** R425-R625. **Credit** AmEx, DC, MC, V.
Each of the five individually styled bedrooms have king-size beds, which are cooled in summer by overhead fans and warmed in winter by hot water bottles and electric blankets.

## Franschhoek

South Africa's own little 'French Corner' was created by Huguenots – 17th-century Calvinists who fled religious repression in France and came to the Cape, bringing their Bibles and wine recipes with them.

Many of these Huguenots were given land by the Cape's Dutch government in a valley called Olifantshoek (Elephants' Corner) – so called because the area was teeming with wild elephants. The new settlers renamed the valley **Franschhoek** (French Corner), and so began the valley's sense of overplayed Frenchiness.

Today, Franschhoek is faux French to a fault. They celebrate Bastille Day. They wave the *tricolore*, and they give every restaurant, wine farm and corner café a French name.

If it all sounds like a bunch of boules to you, you might at least find yourself in a forgiving mood once you've tasted the local wines and dined at the local restaurants.

The Franschhoek Wine Route – sorry, Les Vignerons de Franschhoek – includes 30 highly regarded wine farms, like Boschendal, La Bri, La Motte, L'Ormarins, Mont Rochelle and Haut Espoir. Franschhoek itself is home to eight of South Africa's top-rated restaurants, along with 29 wine cellars – and, in a rare break from Francophoniness, locals call the town the 'food and wine capital of South Africa'.

**GETTING THERE**
Franschhoek is 78km (50 miles) from Cape Town. Turn right at exit 47 off the N1 and follow the signs. For organised tours, contact the Cape Town Tourism Office (*see p54*).

**TOURIST INFORMATION**
Franschhoek Tourism Bureau (021 876 3603/www.tourismfranschhoek.co.za).

## What to see & do

### Dewdale Trout Farm & Fly Fishery
*Robertsvlei Road (021 876 2755/www. dewdale.com).* **Open** 7.30am-sunset daily. **No credit cards**.
This fly-fishing venue specialises in rainbow, American steelhead and brown trout, and just in case the fish don't bite, picnic baskets and bicycles are also available.

Trips Out of Town

### The Gallery at Grande Provence

*Grande Provence Estate, Main Road (021 876 8600/www.grandeprovence.co.za).* **Open** 10am-6pm daily. **Credit** AmEx, DC, MC, V.

Art consultant Rose Korber stocks the sleek Gallery at Grande Provence. Access to the works of Nina Romm, John Kramer, Colbert Mashile, Deborah Bell and Norman Catherine keeps punters flocking in.

### Huguenot Memorial Museum & Huguenot Museum

*Lambrecht Street (021 876 2532/www.museum. co.za).* **Open** 9am-5pm Mon-Sat; 2-5pm Sun. **Admission** R5; R1 concessions. **Credit** MC, V.

The focal point of the village is its Huguenot Memorial, a statue honouring the French Calvinist settlers' search for freedom of religion. The accompanying museum traces the ancestry of these Huguenots, many of whom helped to establish the Western Cape's wine dynasty.

## Where to eat & drink

### Le Bon Vivant

*22 Dirkie Uys Street (021 876 2717).* **Open** noon-3pm, 7-9.30pm Mon, Tue, Thur-Sun. **Credit** AmEx, MC, V.

This well-kept culinary secret – and that's a rare thing indeed in foodie Franschhoek – offers a five-course tasting menu alongside an à la carte option (try the blesbok fillet).

### Bread & Wine

*Môreson Wine Farm, Happy Valley Road, La Motte (021 876 3692/www.moreson.co.za).* **Open** noon-3pm Wed-Sun. **Credit** AmEx, DC, MC, V.

Resting among Môreson's lemon orchards, Bread & Wine combines delicious focaccia, ciabatta, olive and sourdough breads with the estate's own fine wine – complemented by chef Neil Jewell's sparkling charcuterie selection.

# Best estates

## For wine and romance
**Boschendal**
*Pniel Road, Groot Drakenstein (021 870 4200/www.boschendal.com).* **Open** 8.30am-5pm daily. **Tastings** Individual R15. **Tours** R20. **Credit** AmEx, DC, MC, V.

You'll fall in love with the lime-washed Cape Dutch buildings, the many-splendoured 1685 cellar and the elegant gazebo. And you'll understand why Boschendal is so popular for Valentine's Day picnics.

## For wine and swords
**Haute Cabrière Cellar**
*Pass Road, Franschhoek (021 876 2630/www.cabriere.co.za).* **Open** 9am-4.30pm Mon-Fri; 10.30am-4pm Sat. **Tastings** R25. **Credit** AmEx, DC, MC, V.

During wine-tasting hours (11am-1pm daily) cellarmaster Achim von Arnim, AKA Baron Bubbly, cracks open a bottle of Pierre Jourdan Cap Classique using his antique French cavalry sabre. It's called sabrage. And it shouldn't be attempted at home.

## For wine and empowerment
**Mont Rochelle Vineyards**
*Klein Dassenberg Mountain (021 876 3000/www.montrochelle.co.za).* **Open** 10am-6pm daily. **Credit** AmEx, DC, MC, V.

The estate dates back to 1715. When Miko Rwayitare bought it in 2001, he became the first black man to own a South African wine farm.

## For wine and goats
**Fairview**
*Suid-Agter Paarl Road, Paarl (021 836 2450/ www.fairview.co.za).* **Open** 9am-5pm daily. **Credit** AmEx, DC, MC, V.

Fairview is famous for its spectacular cheeses made using the milk from the 400-strong herd of Swiss Sanaan goats. Wash it down with their robust wines, such as Goats do Roam (get it?).

## For pinotage
**Lanzerac Manor & Winery**
*Lanzerac Road, Stellenbosch (021 886 5641/www.lanzeracwines.co.za).* **Open** 9am-4.30pm Mon-Thur; 9am-4pm Fri; 10am-2pm Sat; 11am-3pm Sun. **Tastings** R16. **Credit** AmEx, DC, MC, V.

Lanzerac is home to Pinotage – a unique Cape blend. It's fruity, it ages well and it tastes like a mature claret.

## For wine and Fabergé eggs
**Hazendal**
*Bottelary Road/M23, Stellenbosch (021 903 5112/www.hazendal.co.za).* **Open** 8.30am-4.30pm Mon-Fri; 10am-3pm Sat, Sun. **Tastings** R10. **Tours** R10 (must be pre-booked). **Credit** AmEx, DC, MC, V.

Hazendal was born in 1699, and reborn 300 years later when new owner Dr Mark Voloshin added the Marvol Museum. The museum features a priceless collection of 20th-century Russian icons, with a private collection of Fabergé eggs and antique vodka bottles.

The **Taal Monument**: a cultural icon. *See p218.*

## Monneaux

*Franschhoek Country House, Main Road (021 876
3386/www.fch.co.za).* **Open** 7am-9.30pm daily.
**Credit** AmEx, DC, MC, V.
The Franschhoek Country House started life in 1890
as a perfume factory, but was converted into a homestead and then into a guesthouse in 1995. The restaurant followed in 1996, and it has since come to be
regarded as one of the finest in the country.

## Le Quartier Français

*16 Huguenot Road (021 876 2151/www.lequartier.
co.za).* **Open** *Bistro* 6.30-10.30am, noon-3.30pm,
6-10pm daily. *Tasting Room* 7am-10pm daily.
**Credit** AmEx, DC, MC, V.
Le Quartier Français features a luxury inn (the Four
Quarters), a fine-dining restaurant (the Tasting
Room) and a casual bistro (iCi). You'll encounter
dishes like lamb burger with marinated tomatoes,
pickled cucumber and avocado cream; orange-glazed
ostrich fillet; lightly smoked warthog loin; and foie
gras parfait with a pickled cherry and radish salad.

## Reuben's

*Oude Stallen Centre, 19 Huguenot Road (021
876 3772).* **Open** noon-3pm, 7-9pm daily.
**Credit** AmEx, DC, MC, V.
Run by chef extraordinaire Reuben Riffel, Reuben's
is regarded as one of South Africa's finest. The menu
doesn't disappoint, offering dishes like salmon fish-
cakes, Szechuan pepper duck pie with rosemary
mash, and chilli salt squid with pickled ginger aïoli.

## Topsi & Co

*Reservoir Street West (021 876 2952).* **Open**
noon-3pm, 7-9.15pm Mon, Wed-Sun. **Credit** AmEx,
DC, MC, V.
Eccentric local chef Topsi Venter serves up interesting dishes like shredded duck served in a crêpe
with nectarines and satay sauce, while her African
grey parrot Dr Arnoldus Pannevis watches from his
cage at the door.

## Where to stay

## Akademie Street Guesthouses

*Akademie Street (021 876 3027/www.aka.co.za).*
**Rates** R600-R2,200. **Credit** AmEx, DC, MC, V.
This trio of five-star guesthouses includes the two-
storey Gelatenheid; Oortuiging, set under a white
stinkwood tree; and Vreugde, with its french doors
which open on to a broad veranda.

## The Franschhoek

*68 Huguenot Street (021 876 4723/www.the
franschhoek.com).* **Rates** R1,200-R2,600. **Credit**
AmEx, DC, MC, V.
This elegantly restored hotel on Huguenot Street
offers six luxurious rooms – each opening out on to
a small shaded garden. The furnishing is excellent,
the rooms are well appointed and, as with all Last
Word Retreats, all local drinks are free.

## Mont Rochelle Hotel & Mountain Vineyards

*Dassenberg Road (021 876 2770/www.mont
rochelle.co.za).* **Rates** R2,500. **Credit** AmEx,
DC, MC, V.
Newly restored after it suffered a devastating fire
in early 2006, La Couronne has relaunched as Mont
Rochelle. It's a boutique hotel with only 16 bedrooms and six suites (make sure to book one with
a splash pool), so individual attention is paramount. Dinner at the Mange Tout restaurant is a
Mediterranean affair.

## Paarl

The gleaming cluster of 50 million-year-old
granite boulders (named Peerlbergh, or 'Pearl
Mountain' by early explorer Abraham
Gabbema) is Paarl's most obvious landmark,
but it's the man-made monument on its slopes
that reveals the most about the town's place

Green as far as the eye can see: **Jonkershoek Nature Reserve.** *See p222.*

in the Cape's history. The towering spire of the **Taal Monument** (follow the signs up Gabbema Doordrift Street, 021 863 2800; **photo** *p217*) celebrates the Afrikaans *taal* (language), and it's this cultural identity that filters through to the town's string of gorgeous churches and historical buildings.

These include the **Paarl Museum** (Oude Pastorie, 303 Main Street, 021 872 2651), housed in the gabled and thatched 1787 Cape Dutch parsonage; **Het Gesticht** (112 Main Street, 021 872 3829), which is the fourth-oldest church in South Africa; and the towering **Toring Kerk** (Corner of Main and Van der Lingen, 021 872 6730), with its 57m (187ft) steeple.

### GETTING THERE
Paarl is 60km (37 miles) from Cape Town. Take the N1 north. After about 60km, turn left on to the R45 into Paarl. For organised tours, contact the Cape Town Tourism Office (*see p54*).

### TOURIST INFORMATION
Paarl Tourism Bureau (021 872 3829/ www.paarlonline.com).

## What to see & do

### Afrikaans Language Museum
*Gideon Malherbe House, 11 Pastorie Avenue (021 872 3441/www.taalmuseum.co.za).* **Open** 9am-5pm Mon-Fri. **Admission** R10; R5 concessions. **No credit cards.**

You don't have to understand all the *assebliefs* and *baie dankies* to appreciate this museum's insights into the Afrikaner language and culture, and its evolution from Dutch, Arabic and Indonesian through its 'Kitchen Dutch' phase to its 'alternative' Afrikaner present.

### Drakenstein Prison
*Wemmershoek Road/R101 (021 864 8095).* **Open** *by appointment only* 9am-2pm Tue-Fri, Sun; 5-9.30pm Sat. **No credit cards.**
The former Victor Verster Prison is where Nelson Mandela spent the last 14 months of his 10,000 days in captivity, and it's these gates that he walked out of as a free man in 1990. While it's still a functional correctional facility, its historical importance makes it a popular roadside stop for photographs.

### Ikhwezi Community Centre
*Jan van Riebeeck Drive (021 868 1707).* **Open** *Craft shop* 8am-5pm Mon-Thur; 8am-4pm Fri; 9am-1pm Sat. **No credit cards.**
This initiative was set up to assist disadvantaged women and children from the Mbekweni township who produce and sell funky arts and crafts.

### KWV Cellars & Wine Emporium
*Kohler Street (021 807 3007/www.kwv-international.com).* **Open** 9am-4.30pm Mon-Sat; 11am-4pm Sun. **Tours** *English* 10am, 10.30am, 2.15pm daily. *German* 10.15am Mon-Sat. **Admission** R22; R10 under-18s. **Credit** AmEx, DC, MC, V.
KWV HQ houses South Africa's largest wine cellar, with the five largest oak vats in the world, along with an emporium of Koöperatiewe Wijnbouwers Vereeniging's famous brandies and fine wines.

## Santé Winelands Hotel & Wellness Centre

*Simonsvlei Road, R45, Paarl-Franschhoek Valley (021 875 8100/www.santewellness.co.za).*
This state-of-the-art spa specialises in vinotherapy treatments (including the cabernet sauvignon wine casket bath) and even has a techno treatment involving soundwaves and colour therapy.

## Where to eat & drink

### De Leuwen Jagt

*Seidelberg Wine Estate, Suid Agter Paarl Road (021 863 5222/www.deleuwenjagt.co.za).* **Open** noon-5pm daily; 6-10pm Sun. **Credit** AmEx, DC, MC, V.
Seidelberg's excellent restaurant offers a gourmet spin on traditional Cape dishes like *bobotie* and *bredie*, with intriguing choices like cold roasted pineapple and peppadew soup, and traditional Cape chicken pie with stewed dried fruit.

### Restaurant at Pontac

*Pontac Manor, 16 Zion Street (021 872 0445/ www.pontac.com).* **Open** noon-3pm, 7-10.30pm daily. **Credit** AmEx, DC, MC, V.
Housed in the estate's renovated storeroom and outbuildings, this restaurant offers fine dining with a New World flair. Signature dishes include springbok served with creamy potato bake and prune sauce.

### Rhebokskloof

*Rhebokskloof Estate, Agter-Paarl (021 869 8386/ www.rhebokskloof.co.za).* **Open** 9am-9pm Mon, Thur-Sun; 9am-5.30pm Tue, Wed. **Credit** AmEx, DC, MC, V.
The two restaurants at this 1692 estate offer a cross-section of South African specialities and exotic dishes, such as braised springbok shanks and marinated ostrich with peanut butter sauce.

## Where to stay

### De Wingerd Wijnland Lodge

*7 Waltham Cross Street (021 863 1994/www. wingerd.co.za).* **Rates** R780. **Credit** MC, V.
Bordering the vineyards on the slopes of Paarl Rock, this lodge offers four luxury rooms and one standard room, all with views over the valley.

### Grande Roche Hotel

*Plantasie Street (021 863 2727/www.grande roche.com).* **Rates** R2,420-R5,200. **Credit** AmEx, DC, MC, V.
Dating back to 1717, this restored Victorian-style national monument offers 29 suites and five standard rooms, plus the excellent Bosman's Restaurant.

### Santé Winelands Hotel & Wellness Centre

*Simonsvlei Road, R45, Paarl-Franschhoek Valley (021 875 8100/www.santewellness. co.za).* **Rates** R3,040 double. **Credit** AmEx, DC, MC, V.

This destination hotel has a spa where visitors can relax in luxurious surroundings. The bedrooms are elegant and the bathtubs are huge.

## Robertson, McGregor & Montagu

**Robertson** is the centre of the Breede River Valley's busy fruit and wine industries and is surrounded by about 30 wine cellars, but you wouldn't think so. There's not too much bustle on the quiet, jacaranda-lined streets, and most of the attractions are located out of town.

**McGregor** is the original one-horse town, populated with artsy characters who live in whitewashed, thatch-roofed houses, and who spend their days pottering and painting.

Unequipped with an explanation for **Montagu**'s hot mineral springs, the area's ancient Quena and Khoikhoi inhabitants called it Xuaka – 'the place where the fiery river meets the burning tongue'. The **Montagu Springs** (Montagu Springs Resort, Uitvlucht Street, 023 614 1050, www.montagusprings.co.za) remain the town's biggest drawcard.

### GETTING THERE

Robertson, McGregor and Montagu are all approx 200km (125 miles) from Cape Town. For Robertson and Montagu, take the Worcester turn off the N1 highway and follow the R60. For McGregor, turn right at the McGregor sign in Robertson. For organised tours, contact the Cape Town Tourism Office (*see p54*).

### TOURIST INFORMATION

McGregor Tourism Bureau (023 625 1954/www.tourismmcgregor.co.za). Montagu Tourism Bureau (023 614 2471/www.tourismmontagu.co.za). Robertson Tourism Bureau (023 626 4437/www.tourismrobertson.co.za).

## What to see & do

### Bird's Paradise

*Johan de Jong Drive, Robertson (023 626 3926).* **Open** 9am-5pm daily. **Entrance** R5-R25. **Credit** MC, V.
This miniature version of Hout Bay's World of Birds houses more than a hundred species, including exotic creatures like macaws, conures and pelicans.

### Dassieshoek & Arangieskop Trails

*Bookings & enquiries at Robertson (023 615 8000).* **Rates** R21-R60. **No credit cards.**
The 38km (23-mile) Dassieshoek and 20km (12-mile) Arangieskop hiking trails venture through Klein Karoo scrub, mountain *fynbos*, steep slopes and wooded ravines, offering a close-up look at the natural treasures of the Robertson Valley.

**Trips Out of Town**

## Montagu Tractor Trips

*Niel Burger's Protea Farm, 30km from Montagu on road to Touws Rivier (023 614 2471).* **Trips** 10am, 2pm Wed (depending on demand); 10am, 2pm Sat. **Cost** R60; R25-R30 children. **No credit cards.**
Farmer Neil Burger's popular three-hour tractor/trailer rides take visitors to the top of the Langeberg mountains for a glass of muscadel, after which he serves up a pot of typical South African *potjiekos* (a kind of stew).

## Robertson Wine Valley

*2 Reitz Street, Robertson (023 626 3167/www.robertsonwinevalley.com).* **Open** 8am-5pm Mon-Fri.
The Robertson wine route represents a total of nearly 45 million vines and 48 wineries of various shapes and sizes within the Ashton-Bonnievale-McGregor-Robertson quadrangle. Cellars include renowned wineries such as Graham Beck, Langverwacht, Rooiberg, Van Loveren, Weltevrede and the Rietvallei Muscadel farm. Although Robertson is less famous than Stellenbosch, it has the advantage of being out of the 'tourist' zone.

## Rock climbing

*De Bos Guest Farm, Montagu (023 614 2532/www.debos.co.za).* **Open** 8am-late daily.
Montagu boasts more than 300 bolted rock climbing routes in its quartzite crags, and the wide variety of edges, cracks and slopes means that you're unlikely to run out of routes to try.

## Where to eat & drink

### Café Maude

*Bon Courage Wine Estate, Robertson (023 626 4178/www.boncourage.co.za).* **Open** 9am-5pm Mon-Fri; 9am-4pm Sat. **Credit** AmEx, MC, V.
Café Maude offers hearty breakfasts and good light lunches under a big pepper tree on the Bon Courage Wine Estate. After your meal, enjoy some wine tasting at the estate's old Cape Dutch Homestead (start with the award-winning Chardonnay Prestige Cuvée).

### Fraai Uitzicht 1798

*Klaasvoogds East Road, between Robertson & Montagu (023 626 6156/www.fraaiuitzicht.com).* **Open** 8.30am-late daily. **Credit** AmEx, DC, MC, V.
The wine cellar at Fraai Uitzicht 1798, the oldest in the Robertson valley, still has the original woodwork and handcrafted beams, creating the perfect environment for its handcrafted merlot. The estate's restaurant boasts the Fine Wine & Dine menu, a seven-course feast with wines for each course.

### Wild Apricot

*Montagu Country Hotel, Bath Street, Montagu (023 614 3125/www.montagucountryhotel.co.za).* **Open** 7.30-10am, 7-9pm daily. **Credit** AmEx, DC, MC, V.
The Montagu Country Hotel's in-house restaurant offers a choice of traditional and continental dishes, while the Dog & Trumpet pub offers pre-dinner drinks and nightcaps for residents.

## Where to stay

### Leo Guesthouse

*8 Church Street, Robertson (023 626 3911).* **Rates** R150-R300. **No credit cards.**
This charming 1860s Victorian/Cape Dutch home offers four well-equipped bedrooms in a wonderful old-world atmosphere.

### Mimosa Guest Lodge

*Church Street, Montagu (023 614 2351/www.mimosa.co.za).* **Rates** R310-R750. **Credit** AmEx, DC, MC, V.
Over the years this luxurious four-star guesthouse has served as a retirement home, a boarding house for teachers and a very basic guesthouse. Newly restored, Mimosa now offers comfortable bedrooms, stylish art deco lounges and a restaurant.

### Robertson Backpackers

*4 Dordrecht Avenue, Robertson (023 626 1280/www.robertsonbackpackers.co.za).* **Rates** R120-R160. **No credit cards.**
As the only backpackers' hostel in the Breede River Valley, Robertson has a lot to live up to. Fortunately it does so admirably, offering accommodation in a spacious old Victorian house with a cosy fireplace and a veranda that seems purpose-built for sipping lazy sundowners.

## Stellenbosch

South Africa's second oldest settlement started life as a frontier town, founded in 1679 by Cape Colonial Governor Simon van der Stel. Since the early 1700s **Stellenbosch** has been the heart of South Africa's wine industry, with well over 300 wine farms and estates included in the vast regional Wine Route.

But it's not just a wine town, it's a university town too, with the University of Stellenbosch – known by its students as Maties (Afrikaans slang for 'buddies') – dating back to 1866. Every morning, students stroll down through the town's mighty oak trees as they move from lecture hall to lecture hall. Those oaks were planted by Van der Stel's early settlers, and they've become such a central part of the town's identity that Stellenbosch is affectionately known as Eikestad: Town of Oaks.

### GETTING THERE

Stellenbosch is 45km (28 miles) from Cape Town. Take the N2 highway past Cape Town International towards Somerset West, take exit 43 and follow the R44 into Stellenbosch. For organised tours, contact the Cape Town Tourism Office (*see p54*).

### TOURIST INFORMATION

Stellenbosch Tourism Bureau (021 883 3584/www.tourismstellenbosch.co.za).

A pause for reflection at the activity-packed **Spier Estate**. *See p222.*

# What to see & do

## Jonkershoek Nature Reserve

*Jonkershoek Valley (021 659 3500/www.capenature.
co.za).* **Open** 8am-4pm daily. **No credit cards.**
**Map** p272 S2.

This large reserve features three rewarding hiking
trails – the shortest and easiest of which is the 6km
(4-mile) Tweede Waterval Trail. **Photo** *p218.*

## Oom Samie se Winkel

*84 Dorp Street (021 887 0797).* **Open** 8.30am-6pm
Mon-Fri; 9am-5.30pm Sat, Sun. **Credit** AmEx,
DC, MC, V. **Map** p272 P3.

Stellenbosch's old *algemeende handelaars* (general
store) is a national monument that dates back almost
200 years. A trading post where Stellenbosch's freed
slaves once sold vegetables, it's still open for business, selling bric-a-brac and souvenirs. **Photo** *p214.*

## Oude Libertas Amphitheatre

*Oude Libertas Farm, Adam Tas Road (021 809
7473/www.oudelibertas.co.za).* **Open** Dec-Mar.
**Credit** MC, V.

This open-air amphitheatre hosts a summer arts
festival, along with Sunday evening picnic concerts.

## Sasol Art Museum

*52 Ryneveld Street (021 808 3693).* **Open** 9am-
4.30pm Tue-Fri; 9am-8pm Wed; 9am-5pm Sat.
**Map** p272 Q2.

While this building houses the university's permanent collection of art, it also displays cutting-edge
contributions from the university's art department.

## Spier Estate

*On the R310 towards Stellenbosch (021 809
1955/www.spier.co.za).* **Credit** AmEx, DC, MC, V.

This one-stop Winelands entertainment site hosts a
summer theatre season in its amphitheatre, and
offers horse riding, a craft market, lakeside picnics,
three dining options and wine tasting. **Photo** *p221.*

## Stellenbosch American Express Wine Route

*36 Market Street (021 886 4310/www.wineroute.
co.za).* **Open** 8.30am-5pm Mon-Fri. **Map** p272 P3.

The Stellenbosch Winelands cover five sub-routes
and more than 300 wine and grape producers.

## Van Ryn Brandy Cellar

*Van Ryn Road, Vlottenburg (021 881 3875).*
**Tours** 10am, 11.30am, 3pm Mon-Fri; 10am, 11.30am
Sat. **Admission** R25. **Credit** AmEx, DC, MC, V.

Van Ryn was the first brandy cellar to open to the
public and offers tours through its historic distillery
(which dates back to 1845) and cellar.

# Where to eat & drink

## De Akker

*90 Dorp Street (021 883 3512).* **Open** 10.30am-late
daily. **Credit** MC, V. **Map** p272 P3 ❶

Dark, smoky and seldom quiet, De Akker is the oldest bar in Stellenbosch, and probably the oldest in
South Africa. And it's still as much of a dive as it's
ever been – a well-loved dive, though.

## Dorp Street Theatre Café

*59 Dorp Street (021 886 6107/www.dorpstraat.
co.za).* **Open** 10am-late Tue-Sat. **Credit** DC, MC, V.
**Map** p272 P3 ❷

This Afrikaans arts institution showcases local theatre, music and poetry readings, with local rock acts
making regular appearances to keep things from
getting too artsy. The café serves light meals, including local favourites like Firecrackers (jalapeños
stuffed with cream cheese and chilli sauce).

## D'Ouwe Werf 1802

*D'Ouwe Werf Country Inn, 30 Church Street (021
887 1608/www.ouwewerf.co.za).* **Open** 7am-9.30pm
daily. **Credit** AmEx, DC, MC, V. **Map** p272 Q3 ❸

South Africa's oldest existing inn – founded in 1802
– serves traditional dishes with Afrikaans and Cape
Malay flavours, along with a comprehensive wine
list and one of the best cheesecakes in town.

## Moyo at Spier

*Spier Estate, Lynedoch Road/R310 (021 809
1100/www.moyo.co.za).* **Open** noon-4pm, 6-11pm
daily. **Credit** AmEx, DC, MC, V.

Moyo's magical feast includes a pan-African buffet
dinner, set in a tented bush camp with tree-house
terraces and romantic tree-top lights. While you eat,
African players and storytellers stroll among the
tables, singing, dancing, drumming and painting
guests' faces in traditional styles.

# Where to stay

## Batavia House

*12 Louw Street (021 887 2914/www.batavia
house.co.za).* **Rates** R400-R1,050. **Credit** AmEx,
DC, MC, V. **Map** p272 Q3 ❶

This five-star boutique hotel is located in a restored
old house on one of the town's handsome oak-lined
streets. Its interiors combine antique furniture and
modern conveniences.

## D'Ouwe Werf

*30 Church Street (021 887 4608/www.ouwewerf.
com).* **Rates** R1,200. **Credit** AmEx, DC, MC, V.
**Map** p272 Q3 ❷

South Africa's oldest existing inn is in the middle of
historic Stellenbosch and, with its 31 individually
styled rooms and excellent restaurant, 1802 (*see
above*), it is a good base from which to explore.

## Victoria House

*21 Van Riebeeck Street (book at tourism office
021 883 3854).* **Rates** R700. **No credit cards.**
**Map** p272 R3 ❸

A rare budget option, Victoria House lets you have
an entire old Victorian home to yourself. That means
high ceilings, timber floors, thick walls, three bedrooms… and just the one bathroom.

# Whale Route

Get up close and personal with the monsters of the deep.

**Cape Agulhas Lighthouse** sits at the southernmost tip of Africa. *See p230.*

## Gansbaai

Forget the 'Big Five', says **Gansbaai**. They're unashamedly marketing the 'Big Two' – and they don't get too much wilder, or bigger, than southern right whales and, more importantly, great white sharks.

What Gansbaai lacks in charm and architectural style, it makes up for with adrenalin-charged thrills – the unassuming little town is internationally known as one of the world's best sites for getting up close and far too personal with these jagged-toothed monsters. Gansbaai is the focal point of what's known as the **Danger Point Peninsula**, a coastal stretch that includes De Kelders, Pearly Beach, Baardskeerdersbos, Kleinbaai and, of course, Danger Point, the infamous site of the sinking of HMS *Birkenhead* in 1852 with the loss of 445 lives, many of those to sharks. The

bravery of the British soldiers on board, who stood fast on deck as the ship foundered so that civilians could board the few lifeboats, has gone down in maritime lore as the Birkenhead Drill: women and children first. You can visit the lighthouse a few kilometres outside Gansbaai, and see the notorious Danger Rock at low tide.

The flipside of Gansbaai's fishy personality is its natural one. Ask the tourism bureau about *fynbos* nature reserves to explore in the area, as well as the amazing rock formations at **De Kelders** ('the caves') – excavations at Klipgat Cave have revealed evidence of Middle Stone Age people about 80,000 years ago, and signs that the Khoisan used these caves about 2,000 years ago.

But if all you want to do is soak up some sun and swim in the sea, head for safe swimming spots at Pearly Beach, Uilenkraalsmond and Stanford Cove (**photo** *p228*).

# Cage diving with sharks

Relive that scene from *Jaws* – only this time it's you dangling over the side of the boat in a metal cage, armed with only a snorkel and mask. Trips are generally between three and five hours long, and are dependent on the weather and visibility – some operators offer a voucher if you don't go out at all. All the operators listed below depart from Kleinbaai except White Shark Adventures, which launches from Gansbaai, meaning a slightly longer boat ride around Danger Point. Rates are R1,000-R1,375 and usually include a meal or snacks plus equipment.

**White Shark Adventures** (028 384 1380).
**White Shark Diving Co** (021 532 0470/ 082 559 6858).
**White Shark Ecoventures** (083 412 3733/ 021 532 0470).
**Shark Lady** (028 312 3287/083 746 8985).
**Marine Dynamics** (028 384 1005/ 082 380 3405).
**Great White Shark Tours** (028 384 1418/ 083 300 2138).
**Shark Diving Unlimited** (028 384 2787/ 082 441 4555).
**White Shark Projects** (021 405 4537/ 028 384 1774).

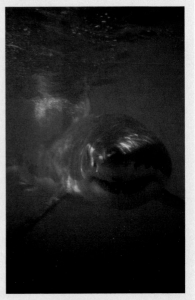

## GETTING THERE

Gansbaai is 175km (110 miles) from Cape Town. Take the Hermanus turn-off from the N2 near Bot River and follow the R43 for 85km (53 miles) through Hermanus, Stanford and  De Kelders into Gansbaai. For organised tours, contact the Cape Town Tourism Office (*see p54*).

## TOURIST INFORMATION

Gansbaai Tourism Bureau (028 384 1439/ www.danger-point-peninsula.co.za/ www.tourismgansbaai.co.za).

## What to see & do

### Danger Point Lighthouse

*Danger Point (028 384 0530).* **Open** *Oct-Mar* 10am-3pm daily; *Apr-Sept* 10am-3pm Sat, Sun. **Admission** *Downstairs* free. *Tower* R13.70 adults; R6.90-R9.20 concessions. **No credit cards.**
Another fascinating landmark along the treacherous eastern Western Cape coastline. History buffs and maritime junkies can either climb the 99 steps to see the 1.7-million candlepower light bulb in the tower, or make do with the example at the bottom, alongside older paraffin and electric bulbs used in days gone by. Hairbrush handles, assorted trinkets,

crockery and cutlery from the wreck of HMS *Birkenhead* are grim reminders of why the lighthouse is so named.

## Where to eat & drink

### Great White House

*5 Geelbek Street, Kleinbaai (028 384 3273).* **Open** 7.30am-6pm Mon-Thur, Sun; 7.30am-late Fri, Sat. **Credit** AmEx, DC, MC, V.
Kleinbaai is a little village just beyond Gansbaai, and the Great White House is a focal point for locals and tourists alike. Aside from heavy breakfasts and light lunches, the friendly hosts also offer a tourist information service on the area, and will organise whale-watching and shark diving tours for you. The signature dish is the melt-in-the-mouth calamari.

### Dyer Island Cruises

*Depart from Kleinbaai (028 384 0406/ 082 801 8014/www.whalewatchsa.com).* **Rates** *Whale-watching cruises* R690 adults; R390 concessions; free under-5s. *Off-season eco cruises* R450 adults; R250 concessions. **Credit** MC, V.
When they're not whale-spotting, Dyer Island Cruises visit the island to see penguins and seabirds and Geyser Rock with its thousands of Cape fur seals. A must for nature lovers.

## Where to stay

### Farm 215

*16km from Gansbaai on the Elim-Baardskeerdersbos gravel road (028 388 0920/www.farm215.co.za).*
**Rates** R550-R850. **Credit** MC, V.

For silence, extremely stylish comfort and endless views from mountains to sea, escape to Farm 215's villa, with a beautiful lap pool, big farmhouse kitchen serving Cape African fusion fare, en suite rooms and king-size beds. Boardwalks connect the villa to garden cottages, with folding doors opening on to wooden decks overlooking plains to the sea. Two lovingly restored self-catering cottages with fireplaces offer even more privacy among the *fynbos*, and are an excellent romantic option. Guided walks and horse trails can be arranged.

### Marine Guest House

*11 Hill Street, Kleinbaai (028 384 0641).*
**Rates** R150-R180. **No credit cards**.

Real value for money right across the road from the sea and a three-minute walk from Kleinbaai harbour where the shark-diving boats launch. Hilané also runs Gansbaai Backpackers (6 Strand Street, rates R90-R130) in Gansbaai.

## Greyton

When upmarket city slickers announce they need a break in the country, they don't really mean a weekend on a muddy farm getting up at dawn to bond with the cows. They mean a place like **Greyton** – packed with country charm but with a civilised dash of sophistication.

This little village corners the market on quaint. Nestling against the Riviersonderend (river without end) Mountains, the town has shady avenues lined with oaks and leiwater streams (irrigation canals), historic thatch-and-whitewash cottages and voluptuous gardens bursting out of their fences. The village was laid out in 1854 on a farm called Weltevreden – 'well satisfied' – and the name fits.

To get the flavour of Greyton in an instant, be there on a Saturday morning for the regular market (9am-noon), where you can mingle with locals and other weekenders, picking up fresh gossip and home-grown country produce such as organic herbs and veggies, breads, cheeses, cakes and bakes, as well as artwork, books, handcrafts and plants. Then wander off for lunch at one of the restaurants under the oaks with the paper.

But while for many visitors the whole point of being in Greyton is to eat a little, shop a little, and nap a lot, there is plenty for the more energetic to do. Pack your walking shoes, because the fresh country air may inspire you to explore the mountains on a variety of marked walks (from an hour to two or three days)

through the *fynbos* – get information on different trails from the tourism office. If that sounds too strenuous, the tourism office also hires out mountain bikes.

Make the time for a day trip (at least) to historic **Genadendal**. Dating back to 1738, it's the oldest mission station on the continent of Africa and, aside from beautiful old architecture, boasts some impressive features, such as South Africa's oldest fire engine and pipe organ, as well as an original Bible printed in Amsterdam in 1694. Not to mention wall-to-wall national monuments – there are 22 around Church Square alone. Actually, almost everything you want to see is on the square, so after a 6km drive from Greyton, park in the shade of the old oaks and take a stroll.

### GETTING THERE

Greyton is 145km (90 miles) from Cape Town. By car, turn off the N2 about 20km (12 miles) past Bot River and follow the R406 to Greyton. For organised tours, contact the Cape Town Tourism Office (*see p54*).

### TOURIST INFORMATION

Genadendal Tourism Bureau (028 251 8291). Greyton Tourism Bureau (028 254 9414/ www.greyton.net).

## Where to eat & drink

### Greyt-on-Main Restaurant

*31 Main Street (028 254 9722).* **Open** 8-11am, 7pm-late Mon, Thur-Sat; noon-3pm Sun. **Credit** AmEx, DC, MC, V.

Greyton is an odd place to find eisbein and sauerkraut, but superb German fare is a major part of the continental mix prepared with passion in this charming old building, once the trading store. Be prepared for bright lighting and service a tad on the slow side at times, but locals know to leave space for chef Greta Richter's delicious chocolate mousse. And what's the rush, anyway? This is one place that will have you going down a notch on your belt.

### Oak & Vigne

*DS Botha Street (028 254 9037).* **Open** 8am-5pm Mon-Thur; 8am-6pm Fri, Sat. **Credit** DC, MC, V.

The buzziest place to go for gourmet breakfasts with the paper or lazy lunches, this is a favourite with both locals and weekenders who gather under the oaks to gossip over deli fare, baked goodies and light lunches of quiches, salads and pasta.

### Pepper Tree

*14 Main Road (028 254 9164).* **Open** 6.30-9.30pm Tue-Sat. **Credit** MC, V.

Locals are raving about the newest restaurant on Greyton's foodie map. A chef lured from the Mantis Collection means you can settle in for a convivial evening of fine food. Fresh fish is delivered daily.

Whale watching at **Hermanus**.

## Where to stay

### Acorns on Oak
*2-4 Oak Street (028 254 9567/www.acorns-on-oak.co.za).* **Rates** R335. **Credit** MC, V.
Set in a beautiful, peaceful garden on the river at the edge of Greyton, Acorns on Oak offers stylish suites with private patios, a heated pool and magnificent views of the surrounding mountains – all a mere ten-minute stroll away from the 'bustle' of Greyton.

### Oewerzicht Luxury Tented River Lodge & Farm Cottages
*9km from Greyton on the Riviersonderend Road (028 254 9831/www.greyton.co.za).* **Rates** R400-R600. **No credit cards**.
For a real city escape, Oewerzicht, a working farm outside town, has six luxury tents set on the banks of the river, each with their own en suite bathroom with hot water shower and flush toilets, and shared kitchen facilities. Borrow the canoe and set off down-river, brave the cable and pulley slide over the water, try out the tractor tubes or simply go fishing. There are also seven self-catering cottages.

## Hermanus

Southern right whales are about 14m long, weigh over 40 tons, and each year from June to November they flock to **Hermanus** to calve and mate, and breach and blow, hurling their vast bodies into the air in one of nature's most spectacular aquabatic displays. All you need is a pair of binoculars to perch on the rocks and watch the show.

Zoom out for the big picture of the whole of **Walker Bay** – recognised by the WWF as one of the world's 12 best whale-viewing sites – by taking a drive up into the mountains on the Rotary Way, where the paragliders take off. (Head out of Hermanus back towards Cape Town for about 2.5km, then turn towards the mountains between two white gateposts.)

The sea immediately in front of the town centre is a boat-free zone during whale season, and the whales frequently frolic just metres from the shore here. Take a walk along the Cliff Path that skirts the rocks for about 12km all the way from the New Harbour to Grotto Beach (it's wheelchair-friendly for the stretch between the Marine and Windsor hotels). If you can't see any whales, listen (and look) out for the town's whale crier. He will be unmistakable, with a kelp horn upon which he blows a kind of morse code to tell you exactly where the whales are (he wears sandwich boards that explain the code). Hermanus is the only town in the world that employs a whale crier.

You'll generally find him near the Old Harbour in front of **Market Square**, the bustling centre of town that's ringed by alleys and lanes of galleries, gift shops and

restaurants, and has a lively crafts market at weekends (every day around Christmas). Across the road is the **Old Harbour Museum** (028 312 1475, open 9am-4.30pm Mon-Sat, 11am-4pm Sun) that tells the history of fishing and the sobering story of whaling, which was once a major industry here. From the 1800s onwards, southern right whales in particular were targeted, as they're rich in oil and accommodating enough to float once they're killed, making them easier to get to shore. They became a protected species in 1935.

### GETTING THERE
Hermanus is 125km (78 miles) from Cape Town. By car, take the Hermanus off-ramp off the N2 near Bot River and follow the R43 for 35km (22 miles) to Hermanus. For organised tours, contact the Cape Town Tourism Office (*see p54*).

### TOURIST INFORMATION
Hermanus Tourism Bureau (028 312 2629/www.tourismhermanus.co.za/www.hermanus.co.za).

## What to see & do

### Fernkloof Nature Reserve
*At the top of Fir Road (028 313 8100/www.fern kloof.com).* **Open** 7am-7pm daily. **Admission** free. Head for the hills when you've had your fill of whales. Over 50km (31 miles) of hiking trails and a

mountain bike trail lead you through fabulous *fynbos* where you can try to spot over 100 bird species. The reserve also has an indigenous nursery.

### Hermanus Whale Cruises
*(028 313 2722/082 369 8931/www.hermanus-whale-cruises.co.za).* **Tours** *June-Dec* 9am, noon, 2pm, 4pm, 6pm daily. *Off season* by arrangement. **Tickets** R400 adults; R150 concessions. **Credit** MC, V.
Hop aboard an authentic fishing boat (Hermanus Whale Cruises) or a twin-hulled motor boat (Southern Right Charters) to get up close to the whales. Trips last around two hours.

### Horse Trail Safaris
*Lakeview Chalets, 17th Avenue (021 703 4396/ www.horsetrailsafaris.co.za for day trails & longer/ 082 729 7776 for hourly rides).* **Rates** R180 1hr ride; R850 full day (incl lunch); R1,800 weekend trail. **No credit cards.**
A gentle canter along the beach from Grotto towards De Kelders will restore your soul, or head into the mountains to lose yourself in nature. Longer trails of up to seven days are also available, and carriage rides along the beach are coming soon.

### Walker Bay Adventures
*(082 739 0159/www.walkerbayadventures.co.za).* **Rates** *Kayaking* R250. *Abseiling* R120 for 2 abseils. *Canoeing* R50-R400. **No credit cards.**
Departing from the Old Harbour, these kayaks are the only boats allowed within the whale sanctuary

Safe swimming and stunning views at **Stanford Cove**. *See p223*.

immediately in front of town – but a gentle two-hour paddle is worthwhile even out of whale season, when you may be lucky enough to see dolphins, seals or penguins. No experience is necessary as the kayaks are stable, and you're accompanied by knowledgeable and qualified guides. If that's not exciting enough, try the abseil from the coastal cliffs. Canoeing on the lagoon is also available.

## Where to eat & drink

### Bientang's Cave
*Below Marine Drive, between Old Harbour & Marine Hotel (028 312 3454).* **Open** 11.30am-4pm Mon-Thur, Sun; 11.30am-4pm, 7-9pm Fri, Sat (weather permitting). **Credit** DC, MC, V.
You have to conquer a flight of stairs, but this is the closest you can get to the whales over a plate of seafood and a glass of wine. Bientang was a Strandloper (a Khoikhoi beachcomber), and this cave in the cliffside was her home. Now it's a restaurant offering fairly standard seafood, but with tables in tiers going right down to the sea – in fact the lower ones get splashed at high tide, and the whales come so close you could swim out to them. The wines (on an award-winning list) are worth a look too – ask to see the cellar, which was Bientang's storeroom.

### Celino's Bistro
*83 Marine Drive (028 313 1224).* **Open** 8am-6pm daily. **Credit** AmEx, DC, MC, V.
In a town filled to bursting with seafood, here's a seafront deli-style eaterie with a delightfully fresh approach. The linefish, for a change, comes with olive tapenade, while the calamari is served with a sweet chilli sauce. Chips are served in tiny buckets, a beef skewer comes with tzatziki and a tortilla, or pick a platter of nuts, feta and pesto, cold smoked meats, and relish with bread and crackers. Outdoor tables look over the cliff path to the sweep of the bay, while inside it's light and trendy.

### Harbour Rock Seagrill & Gecko Bar
*Site 24A, New Harbour (028 312 2920).* **Open** 9am-10pm. **Credit** AmEx, DC, MC, V.
The views are spectacular from this restaurant and bar on a rocky outcrop right above the New Harbour breakwater, looking over bobbing fishing boats and wheeling seagulls towards the Hermanus mountains. The restaurant mixes interesting elements to create feasts from the sea (like calamari steaks stuffed with smoked salmon and nori) along with a range of sushi, while the Gecko Bar next door offers couches for lazing on as you soak up the view and a few drinks.

### Meditterea Seafood Restaurant
*87 Marine Drive (028 313 1685).* **Open** 6-10pm Mon-Sat; noon-2.30pm, 6-10pm Sun. **Credit** DC, MC, V.
A gorgeous position upstairs at a front-row building overlooking the bay, with crete-stoned walls, original art and windows that can be thrown open

to the sea, combined with meticulously prepared, imaginative Mediterranean fare, make this perfect for a special evening. To taste as much as possible, try sharing a range of starters.

## Where to stay

### Auberge Burgundy
*16 Harbour Road (028 313 1201/www.auberge.co.za).* **Rates** R480-R2,695. **Credit** AmEx, DC, MC, V.
This boutique hotel with a French feel is just steps away from Market Square and right across the road from the whales frolicking in the bay.

### Birkenhead House
*Corner 7th Avenue & 11th Street (028 314 8000/www.birkenheadhouse.com).* **Rates** R3,800-R5,950. **Credit** AmEx, DC, MC, V.
If you're after off-the-scale luxury and personal attention in an intimate, beautifully decorated setting, you'll love Birkenhead House, perched right on the rocks above the sea. Friendly hosts provide seamless service and excellent food – and there's pampering to be had in the spa.

### The Marine
*Marine Drive (028 313 1000/www.collection mcgrath.com).* **Rates** R1,800-R5,900. **Credit** AmEx, DC, MC, V.
A landmark on the Hermanus coastline, the five-star Marine has luxury rooms and sea-facing suites fit for a king. Two fine restaurants, a sun terrace for drinks and the Seafood Express Café complete the lush, plush picture.

### Mosselberg on Grotto Beach
*253A 10th Street, Voëlklip (028 314 0055/www.mosselberg.co.za).* **Rates** R1,300-R2,000. **Credit** AmEx, MC, V.
This modern guesthouse, designed by an award-winning architect, has a heated pool, underfloor heating and wooden decks overlooking fynbos and the bay. Each room has its own entrance and a sea-facing balcony, with fantastic fold-away doors that bring the bay right into your room.

# Struisbaai, L'Agulhas & Arniston

When you're fed up with the city, there's not much a walk down **Struisbaai**'s beach can't put into perspective – at 14km of white sand, it's the southern hemisphere's longest beach.

Look out for the original fishermen's houses on either side of the road as you enter Struisbaai – they're all national monuments and much loved by artists. The cottages are known as Hotagterklip – 'left behind the rock' – after a rocky outcrop that caused a sharp detour on the original wagon route. Don't put your camera away, though, you'll want it again soon at Struisbaai's pretty fishing harbour.

**Trips Out of Town**

L'Agulhas is truly the southernmost tip of the African continent, and the place where the mighty Indian and Atlantic oceans collide – rather unremarkably, it must be said. A rock and a plaque mark the precise point about 1km from the lighthouse. The rocky shelf juts out for another 250km, then plummets to a depth of well over 3km (1.8 miles) in the deep southern ocean. Which is probably why the old maps say 'Here be dragons…'

The decidedly Egyptian-looking **Cape Agulhas Lighthouse** (*see below*), the second oldest in South Africa, looks a little out of place here, but its design is an acknowledgement of its historic elder twin: the Pharos of Alexandria lighthouse in Egypt at the far northern end of the continent.

The tiny seaside village of **Arniston** is the perfect antidote for stressed souls. Apart from an abundance of holiday cottages, Arniston has one hotel, one café and one restaurant (aside from the hotel's) – places don't get much slower than here. And that's just the way the locals like it.

You'll hear Arniston called Waen-huiskrans (wagon house cliff), the town's official Afrikaans name, after a huge cave about 2km south of the village. It is said to be large enough to shelter a wagon and its oxen – hence the name. You can visit the cavern at low tide – check with a local for the best time to go. From the hotel, walk along the road away from Kassiesbaai. The last part is over the rocks (take good shoes, the rocks are quite sharp).

The name Arniston arose after the HMS *Arniston* ran aground here in 1815, with the loss of all but six of the 378 people on board. There's a monument to the tragedy opposite the site of the wreck, above the beach.

**De Hoop Nature Reserve & Marine Protected Area** (028 425 5020, www.cape nature.co.za), east of Arniston, is South Africa's most southerly reserve, combining inland fynbos and a freshwater *vlei* (marsh) with coastal dunes, rocky shores and deliciously lonely stretches of beach. There are two circular driving routes, one of which goes to **Koppie Alleen**, a great spot from which to watch whales – this coast has the greatest concentration of southern right whales in the country. There are several walks in the area.

### GETTING THERE

Struisbaai, L'Agulhas and Arniston are approx 230km (143 miles) from Cape Town. For Arniston, take the N2 as far as Caledon and follow the R316 through Napier and Bredasdorp. For Struisbaai and L'Agulhas, take the R319 from Bredasdorp. For organised tours, contact the Cape Town Tourism Office (*see p54*).

### TOURIST INFORMATION

Bredasdorp Tourism (028 424 2584/ www.tourismcapeagulhas.co.za). Cape Agulhas Tourism Bureau (028 435 7185/www.tourismcapeagulhas.co.za).

## What to see & do

### Cape Agulhas Lighthouse & Museum

*Main Road, Cape Agulhas (028 435 6078)*. **Open** 9am-5pm daily. **Rates** R12 adults, R6 concessions. **Credit** AmEx, DC, MC, V.

The museum sheds light on the history of light-houses around the country and the world, not just this one. Be brave: the climb (71 steep steps) to the top of the tower is worth it, both for the view and to see the tiny bulb that packs an astonishing punch – the equivalent of 7.5 million candles. **Photo** *p223.*

### EcoQuad

*Cheers Clubhouse, Struis Crescent, Struisbaai Industrial Area (082 854 5078/www.ecoquad. co.za)*. **Rates** R200 1hr, R300 2hrs, R400 3hrs. **No credit cards**.

This is a scenic quadbike meander that tries to keep environmental damage to a minimum on tracks above L'Agulhas, exploring the *fynbos*, viewing a shipwreck and visiting Zoetendalsvlei, where sea planes landed during World War II. Children over 12 are welcome; bush buggies accommodate younger ones. A picnic option is also available.

## Where to eat & drink

### Lighthouse Restaurant & Curios

*Cape Agulhas Lighthouse (028 435 7580)*. **Open** 8am-10pm daily. **Credit** MC, V.

This is the only chance you'll get in South Africa to eat in a bona fide, working lighthouse. Enjoy tea-room fare – breakfasts, light lunches and afternoon tea – and dinner of steak and seafood.

### Die Waenhuis

*2 Du Preez Street, Arniston (028 445 9797)*. **Open** 6-9pm Mon; noon-2pm Tue-Fri, Sun; noon-2pm, 6-9pm Sat; hours may vary out of season.

This is a casual steak and seafood restaurant behind the local café. The service is sometimes a little slow, but at least you can be sure that the fish is fresh.

## Where to stay

### Arniston Hotel

*Beach Road, Arniston (028 445 9000/www.arniston hotel.com)*. **Rates** R1,100-R1,850. **Credit** MC, V.

The hotel has pride of place right above the bay, with nothing but a lawn and a lane between you and the sea. There's a restaurant, a large and cheerful bar and a terrace. Luxury rooms face either the sea or the pool, and many feature private balconies and fireplaces.

# Garden Route

Leave the city (but not the crowds) behind along this dramatic coastline.

**Plettenberg Bay** is blessed with stunning beaches. *See p237.*

## George

Named after King George III, **George** has evolved from a rural town into a seemingly interminable urban sprawl. The gateway to the **Garden Route**, George is home to a domestic airport terminal, the world famous **Fancourt** golf course (*see below*) and the renowned **Outeniqua Choo-Tjoe** (*see p232*), the steam train that leaves the town daily and follows the dramatic coastline to Knysna.

History buffs will appreciate the **George Museum** (Corner Courtenay & York Streets, 044 873 5343) which houses the extensive collection of Charles Sayer, the ex-editor of the *George & Knysna Herald*. Both the **Dutch Reformed Church** (Courtenay Street) and **St Mark's Cathedral** (Corner Cathedral & York Streets) are worth a visit, though the latter is by appointment only.

Be sure to have your picture taken at the old oak tree on York Street, also known as the slave tree. This famous landmark was planted in 1811 and has an old metal chain and padlock embedded in it.

The **Outeniqua Transport Museum** (Knysna Station, 2 Mission Street, 044 801 8288) is adjacent to the departure point for the Outeniqua Choo-Tjoe. It includes a replica of a station, plus vintage locomotives and vehicles.

### GETTING THERE
George is 440km (273 miles) from Cape Town. Take the N2. For organised tours, contact the Cape Town Tourism Office (*see p54*).

### TOURIST INFORMATION
George Tourism (044 801 9295/ www.tourismgeorge.co.za).

## What to see & do

### Fancourt Hotel & Country Club Golf Estate
*Montagu Street, Blanco (044 804 0000/www. fancourt.co.za).* **Open** 7.30am-2pm daily. **Rates** R170-R1,000. **Credit** AmEx, DC, MC, V.
One of the many reasons George has grown in popularity is because of its proximity to the world-famous and award-winning Fancourt Hotel, Country Club and Golf Course. Host to the President's Cup in

**Knysna**. *See p233.*

2003 and more recently the Women's World Cup of Golf in 2005, this is one stop golf enthusiasts don't want to miss. Set amid stunning scenery, there are no fewer than four top-notch courses to choose from.

### Outeniqua Adventure Tours

*29 Tarentaal Street, Denver Park (044 871 1470).* **Rates** from R50. **No credit cards**.
Almost any excursion is possible with this well-established outdoor adventure company, from bike trips to birdwatching, abseiling, canoeing, scuba diving and canopy tours.

### Outeniqua Choo-Tjoe

*Outeniqua Transport Museum, 2 Mission Street (044 801 8288/www.onlinesources.co.za/chootjoe).* **Rates** R40-R90. **Credit** MC, V.
The romance and adventure of the Outeniqua Choo-Tjoe are iconic. This superbly preserved steam train runs along the Outeniqua Preserved Railway Line between George and Knysna, passing spectacular scenery along the way.

## Where to eat & drink

### Kafe Serefé

*Corner Courtenay & Ironside Streets (044 884 1012).* **Open** 10am-4.30pm Mon; 8.30am-4.30pm, 7-10pm Tue-Sat. **Credit** AmEx, MC, V.
Step into a Turkish wonderland at Kafe Serefé. Jewel-like colours set the scene along with authentically dressed waiting staff and lilting music, while the menu features everything from slow-cooked lamb shanks to hunger-busting shawarmas with all the trimmings.

## Where to stay

### Acorn Guest House

*4 Kerk Street (044 874 0474/www.acornguesthouse. co.za).* **Rates** R385-R660. **Credit** AmEx, DC, MC, V.
This renovated Victorian house is conveniently situated near the best eateries and sights of George. Comfortable bedrooms, a glorious pool deck and wireless internet access make it a popular choice for travellers wanting to stay in touch with home.

### Lands End B&B

*The Point, Beach Road, Victoria Bay (044 889 0123/www.vicbay.com).* **Rates** R350-R650. **Credit** AmEx, MC, V.
Probably the best-known B&B in Victoria Bay, Lands End is spectacularly perched at the end of the bluff and deserves its excellent reputation. Attention to detail, quaint rooms and numerous facilities make this a superb seaside home from home.

## Knysna

It's hard to believe that, just over a decade ago, **Knysna** (pronounced 'nize-na'; **photo** *p232*) was still a sleepy hamlet, much loved by pan pipe-playing hippies. Now it has become a victim of its own popularity, especially over the holiday periods when the main street becomes gridlocked and restaurants overflow with demanding visitors. A visit in the milder winter months cannot be recommended highly enough.

Knysna lies on the shores of a picturesque lagoon that is guarded by two bluffs known as the heads. Only one of them (the eastern one) is accessible by road (follow signs from George Rex Drive near the Engen petrol station to the lookout point), while the other can be reached by catching the Featherbeds Ferry. The town centre reflects Knysna's roots as a forestry station that boomed in the 1800s. Many of the original Victorian buildings still survive and have been sensitively restored, helping to maintain a certain charm despite the town's extraordinary growth.

**Thesen Island** (follow Long Street) is a new, Hamptons-like enclave with an ever-growing number of upmarket clapboard homes and a small and exclusive shopping hub that hosts superb eateries, including Ile de Pain, home of arguably the best sandwich in South Africa. The **Knysna Quays** hum with activity every day and are a good place to browse for gifts and enjoy a waterside meal. Oysters are synonymous with Knysna and people come from far and wide to devour piles of this tasty mollusc at the annual oyster festival in July (044 382 5510/www.oysterfestival.co.za). A popular competition features chefs battling it out to produce the most innovative oyster dish.

Despite its proximity to the ocean, there are no beaches in Knysna. That said, a trip to **Leisure Isle** (follow the signs from George Rex Drive) at high tide affords fabulous swimming in the lagoon. Those intent on the beach can visit Brenton-on-Sea or Noetzie.

Knysna's natural beauty is of course the major drawcard and outdoor enthusiasts come here to satisfy their penchant for lush rainforest hikes and adventure.

### GETTING THERE

Knysna is 500km (310 miles) from Cape Town. Take the N2. For organised tours, contact the Cape Town Tourism Office (*see p54*).

### TOURIST INFORMATION

Tourism Knysna (044 382 5510/ www.tourismknysna.co.za).

## What to see & do

### Eco Afrika Tours

*11 Horne Drive, Leisure Isle (082 925 0716/082 558 9104/www.eco-afrika-tours.co.za).* **Rates** R220. **Credit** MC, V.

**Trips Out of Town**

These cultural excursions to the Knysna Township, co-ordinated by Eco Afrika Tours, are led by a community member who helps to give insight into the lifestyle, customs and traditions of the Xhosa community that lives there. Expect to visit a *shebeen* (tavern), throw the bones at a witch doctor's and meet some of the local children.

### Featherbed Company
*Featherbed Ferry Terminal, Remembrance Drive, off Waterfront Drive (044 382 1693/www.knysna featherbed.com).* **Rates** R70-R395. **Credit** AmEx, DC, MC, V.
The only way to reach the Featherbed Private Reserve, situated on the western Knysna head, is by ferry. On arrival, guests are transported via trailer to the top of the head where they are rewarded with incredible views. The four-hour round trip includes further exploration of the pristine forest, cliffs and caves as well as a generous buffet lunch.

### Knysna Elephant Park
*N2, midway between Knysna & Plettenberg Bay (044 532 7732/www.knysnaelephantpark.co.za).* **Open** 8.30am-4.30pm daily. **Admission** R60-R120. **Walking safaris** R450. **Credit** AmEx, MC, V.
The peaceful pachyderms that live here have mostly been saved from culling operations around the country. Daily tours leave on the half-hour, and visitors will have an opportunity to feed the gentle giants themselves.

### Pezula Resort Hotel & Spa
*East Head, Lagoonview Drive, follow signs from George Rex Drive (044 302 5332/www.pezula.com).* **Rates** *Golf* R125-R785. *Spa* R50-R2,270. **Credit** AmEx, DC, MC, V.
One of the most incredible positions in Knysna, Pezula (the name means 'up there with the Gods') is based right at the top of the eastern Knysna head. Views aside, guests come for the golf, the world-class spa, luxury hotel and excellent restaurant.

### Seal Adventures
*Protea Hotel, Shop 1, Remembrance Drive (044 382 5599/www.sealadventures.co.za).* **Rates** R180-R420. **Credit** MC, V.
Thrill-seekers need look no further. The 'awesome foursome' is their most popular excursion and includes an action-packed half-day of abseiling, quad-biking, canoeing and hiking.

---

# Where to eat & drink

### Firefly
*152A Old Cape Road (044 382 1490).* **Open** 6.30-10pm Tue-Sat. **No credit cards.**
The quirky name refers to a menu that focuses on fiery food from around the world. This tiny restaurant is set in a quaint little cottage and is dressed for the occasion with copious candles and fairy lights galore. Open for dinner only, the *bobotie* spring rolls and mini chicken bunny chows are a must.

### Ile de Pain
*10 The Boatshed, Thesen Harbour Town (044 302 5707).* **Open** 7am-5pm Tue-Fri; 7am-3pm Sat; 9am-1.30pm Sun. Closed Aug. **No credit cards.**
Master baker Markus Farbinger and his chef wife Liezie Mülder are the talented duo behind Ile de Pain, based on Thesen Island. A fifth generation baker, Markus is seriously dedicated to his craft – and the quality of the breads sold and served here is delicious proof. The chalkboard menu is crammed with tempting sophisti-peasant food – from chunky soups (served with the legendary pain de campagne) to heavenly French toast and tangy Welsh rarebit.

### Lush
*29 Thesen Harbour Town (044 382 7196).* **Open** 6.30pm-late daily. **Credit** AmEx, DC, MC, V.
It didn't take long for this sexy new restaurant to become the destination du jour for the town's stylish set. Situated on Thesen Island and overlooking the water, the opulent interior helps to create a sophisticated atmosphere. The menu is refreshing with plenty of innovative choices, including excellent line fish and very tasty Karoo lamb rump.

### 34° South
*Knysna Quays, Waterfront Drive (044 382 7331).* **Open** 9am-10pm daily. **Credit** AmEx, DC, MC, V.
This industrial-chic space hums with seafood-loving punters all day and night, feasting on sushi, oysters and fabulous paella. A great spot to spend a lazy afternoon with an ice-cold beer and a plate of prawns.

### Zachary's
*Pezula Resort Hotel & Spa, Lagoonview Drive (044 302 3333/www.pezula.com).* **Open** 7am-10pm daily. **Credit** AmEx, DC, MC, V.
Based on the luxury Pezula Hotel, this superb restaurant is deserving of its many accolades. Chef Geoffrey Murray's wanderlust shows in his exquisitely crafted fusion dishes that exhibit Asian, Mediterranean and even Creole influences. A knack for marrying local produce with flavours and techniques picked up in far-flung corners of the globe results in a very rewarding dining experience.

---

# Where to stay

### Highfields Backpacker Guesthouse
*2 Graham Street (044 382 6266/www.highfieldsbackpackers.co.za).* **Rates** R80-R300. **No credit cards.**
As far as reasonably priced accommodation goes, this laid-back backpackers' is ideal. The large, renovated house has spacious double rooms as well as dorms. There's also a pool and outdoor deck.

### Lightleys Holiday Houseboats
*Phantom Pass Drive, N2 (044 386 0007/www.houseboats.co.za).* **Rates** R650-R2,200. **Credit** MC, V.
These floating holiday homes guarantee the ultimate in rest and relaxation, and are one of the most

romantic ways to enjoy the Knysna lagoon. Whether you fancy fishing off the boat, exploring the hidden nooks and crannies or taking a midnight skinny dip, this is one of the best ways to get up close and personal with the lagoon.

### Phantom Forest Eco Reserve

*Phantom Pass Road (044 386 0046/www.phantom forest.com).* **Rates** R1,300-R1,700. **Credit** AmEx, DC, MC, V.

You'll be loathe to venture back into civilisation once you've spent a night at the Phantom Forest. On check-in guests leave their vehicles at the bottom of a steep hill from where they are taken up to the lodge in 4x4s. Each treehouse suite is a sophisticated and rustic haven of tranquillity, while facilities like the tree-shaded pool, glass-walled spa and superb restaurant add to the extraordinary experience.

## Mossel Bay

Don't be put off by the flanking industria. With stretches of golden beach lapped by the warm Indian Ocean, **Mossel Bay** (**photo** *p236*) is a town brimming with South African heritage

# Ride on the wild side

Look, the ostrich may be stupid – its brain is only the size of a small stone – but there's no denying that without it, Oudtshoorn would be nothing more than a dusty *dorpie* (small rural town) with a couple of caves thrown in. Thanks to the ostrich boom back in the late 1800s and early 1900s, this town 100km (62 miles) north of George along the N12 is now the commercial heart of the Little Karoo.

When in Oudtshoorn do as the local farmers do – spend your day with the ostriches. First stop: the breeding camp, where a well-informed guide monitors your photo opportunity with Suzy the Stripper and Jack the Ripper – a pair of 27-year-old birds who have been entertaining guests for years. Then stand on ostrich eggs, watch chicks

hatching, and take a lesson in ostrich culinary tastes – which include things like baby's shoes, hairbrushes and stones (delicious if you're an ostrich, apparently).

If this all sounds a bit too placid, take a wild ride on the real live thing. While riding an ostrich is not everyone's idea of a jolly old canter about the paddock, this is something that has to be experienced at least once in a lifetime, and makes a guaranteed tall story for the folks back home.

### Safari Ostrich Show Farm

*Corner Welgeluk & Mosselbay Roads (044 272 7311/www.safariostrich.co.za).* **Open** 7.30am-5pm daily. **Tours** R22-R44. **No credit cards**.

Historic **Mossel Bay** signals the start of the Garden Route. *See p235.*

and a rich maritime history. Plenty of museums, shops and scenic seafood restaurants celebrate the town's colourful past and bright future.

Mossel Bay's most notable attraction is the Dias Museum Complex (1 Market Street, 044 691 1067). Named after the Portuguese explorer Bartholomeu Dias, this development comprises the Maritime Museum and Aquarium, Shell Museum, Old Post Office Tree and Khoi Village. The Maritime Museum boasts a fascinating display of South Africa's early seafaring history, documenting the journeys of the early Dutch, Portuguese and English navigators to whom the origins of several coastal towns at the southern tip of Africa are attributed. Highlights include a life-size replica of Dias's caravel and other Portuguese shipwrecks. The upper level contains a glistening collection of shells. If you're in need of some retail therapy, don't miss the **Craft Art Workshop** (3 Market Street, 044 691 1761) which stocks a variety of products made by local creatives.

Be sure not to skip on a visit to the Post Office Tree. In 1500 a Portuguese sailor left an important letter in a shoe placed underneath a large milkwood tree. Joao da Nova, commander of the third East India fleet, discovered the letter a year later, perhaps unintentionally starting the first post office in the country. It has been declared a national monument.

**GETTING THERE**
Mossel Bay is 400km (250 miles) from Cape Town. Take the N2. For organised tours, contact the Cape Town Tourism Office (*see p54*).

**TOURIST INFORMATION**
Mossel Bay Tourism Bureau (044 691 2202/ www.visitmosselbay.co.za).

## What to see & do
### Cape St Blaize Lighthouse
*Montagu Street (044 690 3015).* **Open** 10am-noon, 12.30-3pm Mon-Fri. **Admission** R7-R14. **No credit cards**.
One of only two manually operated lighthouses in the country, Cape St Blaize was first lit in 1864 and a clockwork system was in use until the late 1970s which required a keeper to wind it up every three hours.

### Face Adrenalin
*Gourits River Bridge (044 697 7001/www.face adrenalin.com).* **Rates** R170-R200. **Credit** MC, V.
A 65m (214ft) jump awaits at the historical Gourits River Bridge, a short drive west of Mossel Bay, offering bungee jumping and upright bridge swinging. For the slightly deranged, Bloukrans Bridge (*see p238*), further north, offers the highest bungee jump in the world, at a monstrous 216m (709ft).

## Where to eat & drink
### Café Gannet
*Protea Hotel Mossel Bay, Corner Market & Church Streets (044 691 1885).* **Open** 6.45am-11pm daily. **Credit** AmEx, DC, MC, V.
With a daily supply of coastal oysters, black mussels and sole from the Mossel Bay harbour, Café Gannet is one of the bay's top seafood establishments. The informal cocktail bar overlooking the bay makes this another idyllic sundowner venue.

### Delfino's Espresso Bar & Pizzeria
*Restaurant 2, Point Village (044 690 5247/www. delfinos.co.za).* **Open** 7am-11.30pm daily. **Credit** AmEx, DC, MC, V.
Order a gourmet pizza or designer sandwich from the modest menu while sipping a glass of wine and soaking up the view. Located on the water's edge, it's also perfect for sundowners and whale watching.

## Where to stay
### Diaz Strand Hotel & Resort
*Beach Boulevard East, Diaz Beach (044 692 8400/ www.diazbeach.co.za).* **Rates** R450-R900. **Credit** AmEx, DC, MC, V.
Perfectly placed at Diaz Beach, this luxurious resort offers breathtaking views of the Indian Ocean and Outeniqua Mountains. Rooms are finished with cherry wood and marble, with sea-facing balconies.

### Santos Express
*Munro Road, Santos Beach (044 691 1995/www. santosexpress.co.za).* **Rates** R170. **Credit** DC, MC, V.
Enjoy the affordable romance of a first-class train carriage permanently stationed next to Santos Beach.

## Plettenberg Bay
Once a sleepy seaside village, in the past decade **Plettenberg Bay** (photo *p231*) has grown into a sprawling mass of holiday homes. Despite its rapid growth and enormous popularity, this former whaling station is still one of the most attractive destinations on the Garden Route and is blessed with stunning beaches.

Plett is relatively quiet out of season, but the Easter weekend and December holidays see it swell to capacity – so much so that shops run out of basic amenities by mid-morning and parking (or the lack of it) becomes a problem.

While in Plett, make sure you pay a visit to the **Robberg Marine and Nature Reserve** (permits available at the entrance gate), around 10km (six miles) from town off Robberg Road. Take a quick half-hour hike or, if you're feeling adventurous, follow the round-trip hike for two hours – either way, you'll be impressed by the jaw-dropping natural beauty of this unspoiled piece of coast.

**Trips Out of Town**

The **Tsitsikamma National Park & Storms River** (042 281 1607/www.sanparks. org/parks/tsitsikamma), 70km (44 miles) from Plettenberg Bay on the N2, is one of the oldest forests in the world and home to a number of hiking trails. This is a nature lover's paradise. Day trippers should purchase a permit to enter the park at the rest stop near the Storms River Bridge and thereafter make their way down to the **Storms River** mouth – a dramatic sight.

### GETTING THERE
Plettenberg Bay is 550km (340 miles) from Cape Town. Take the N2. For organised tours, contact the Cape Town Tourism Office (*see p54*).

### TOURIST INFORMATION
Plettenberg Bay Tourism Centre (044 533 4065/ www.plettenbergbay.co.za).

## What to see & do

### Bungee jumping
*Bloukrans River Bridge (042 281 1458/www.face adrenalin.com)*. **Open** 9am-5pm daily. **Rates** R580. **Credit** AmEx, MC, V.
The world's highest bungee jump is situated just outside Plett on the Bloukrans River Bridge. Adrenalin junkies flock here to conquer this jump, while those who'd rather keep both feet on the ground are well entertained by the screams and dives (some of them more graceful than others). A good measure of whether you're cut out for the jump is if you can endure the hair-raising walk to the bungee station under the bridge.

### Keurbooms River Ferry
*Keurbooms Nature Reserve (044 532 7876/www. ferry.co.za)*. **Cruises** 11am, 2pm & (summer only) 5pm. **Rates** R30-R80. **No credit cards**.
A wonderful way to spend a few hours is to hop on the Keurbooms River Ferry and meander up the river. This company has been taking people on the river for years and their expedition is a wonderful way to explore the beautiful estuary (don't forget your costume for summertime swims). Trips leave three times a day, with charters available for bigger groups and a variety of dining options too.

### Monkeyland
*The Crags, 16km on N2 towards Port Elizabeth (044 534 8906/www.monkeyland.co.za)*. **Open** 8am-5pm daily. **Rates** R50-R100. **Credit** AmEx, DC, MC, V.
Primate lovers and children will no doubt be enamoured by this sanctuary close to Plett. An abundance of different species chatter in the trees above you, inviting closer inspection. A guided tour is recommended to get the most out of the experience. Most of the monkeys here have been rehabilitated from abusive or illegal homes, and some are so tame that they still insist on human contact.

### Ocean Blue Adventures
*1 Hopwood Street, Milkwood Centre, Central Beach (044 533 5083/www.oceanadventures.co.za)*. **Rates** R100-R495. **Credit** DC, MC, V.
Plett is famous for the dolphins that frolic in the bay on an almost daily basis. In the later winter months, visiting whales like to call it a temporary home too, so it's no surprise that there are a number of whale and dolphin spotting tours on offer. The most established company is Ocean Blue Adventures and the daily tours are well worth it for a taste of Plett from an entirely different angle.

## Where to eat & drink

### Blue Bay Café
*Lookout Centre, Main Street (044 533 1390)*. **Open** 8am-10pm daily. **Credit** AmEx, DC, MC, V.
A contemporary café in the centre of town serving up family-friendly food (burgers, gourmet sandwiches and heavily laden salads), this is one place you'll never leave hungry. Friendly staff, consistently tasty fare and a pleasant setting.

### Cornuti al Mare Restaurant & Bar
*1 Perestrella Street (044 533 1277)*. **Open** noon-11pm daily. **Credit** AmEx, DC, MC, V.
This Med-inspired eaterie serves up superb thin-based pizzas and a very good selection of gourmet pastas with light and tasty sauces. As far as position goes, its perch high above Central Beach is ideal – the expanse of big blue can only put you in the holiday mood. The Afro-chic lounge bar is a popular haunt on balmy summer evenings.

## Where to stay

### The Grand
*27 Main Road (044 533 3301/www.thegrand.co.za)*. **Rates** R950-R2,500. **Credit** AmEx, DC, MC, V.
The boutique hotel of choice for hip young things, the Grand has eight achingly luxurious rooms that ooze unassuming style and sex appeal. Described by owner Gail Behr as 'monastery meets bordello', rooms at the Grand feature enormous beds that have to be climbed up on, oversized bathrooms (from Turkish-style baths to showers for two in the centre of the room) and glorious views across Lookout Beach. The Café at the Grand is also a top venue for excellent contemporary cuisine.

### The Plettenberg
*40 Church Street (044 533 2030/www.plettenberg. com)*. **Rates** R2,800-R5,600. **Credit** AmEx, DC, MC, V.
This elegant Georgian-style hotel has one of the most incredible views over Lookout Beach. Not a place for the financially challenged, the Plettenberg is a luxury hotel of the highest degree. But if you can afford it, a stay will remain etched in your memory for years to come.

# West Coast

Stunning scenery, serious surfing and scathing satire.

Plenty of room to swing a beach towel at picture-perfect **Paternoster**. *See p244.*

## Darling

Not that long ago Darling was a remote outpost along the inhospitable West Coast. Today it's less than an hour's drive from Cape Town and boasts two marvellous attractions: the wild flowers that appear each spring and famous South African satirist Tannie (Aunty) Evita Bezuidenhout, who puts in a grand appearance whenever she's got a show on at what used to be the old train station. While the town was originally named after Lieutenant Governor Charles Henry Darling, it's clear that today Tannie Evita is the town's darling.

Actor and activist Pieter-Dirk Uys is the genius behind Tannie Evita and they both occupy a special place in South African history. Drag, satire and scathing political commentary don't begin to do the pair justice. The character of Evita began in a newspaper column in the 1970s during the height of apartheid when she

dished the dirt on politicians who were largely regarded as untouchable. The persona of Tannie Evita grew so strong that she found her way on to the stage in the early 1980s in a series of blistering political plays with brilliant titles such as *Adapt or Dye, A Part Hate A Part Love* and, more recently, *Dekaffirnated*. Things in this country might have shifted, but there's still plenty of grist for Tannie Evita's mill.

When Tannie Evita came to town and painted the tired old station bright pink, Darling's personality also began to shift. Although slap-bang in dairy and wine country, it's now also home to lots of artistic types.

### GETTING THERE

Darling is 72km (44 miles) from Cape Town. Take the R27 north, then turn right on to the R307. At the T-junction turn left to Darling. For organised tours, contact the Cape Town Tourism Office (*see p54*).

Lambert's Bay.

## TOURIST INFORMATION

Darling Tourism Bureau (022 492 3361/
www.darlingtourism.co.za).

## What to see & do

### Darling Wildflower Show

*Darling Sports Club, Darling (022 492 3361/
www.darlingwildflowers.co.za).*

In case you haven't heard, Darling is the flower
power capital of South Africa and September is the
month when the normally arid West Coast does its
Amsterdam impersonation.

### Darling Wine Experience

*Cloof (022 492 2839/www.cloof.co.za).
Groote Post (022 492 2825/www.grootepost.com).
Darling Cellars (022 492 2276/www.darling
cellars.co.za).
Ormonde (022 492 3540).*

Wine farms are producing surprisingly good wines
in unexpected areas and Darling is no exception.
Cloof, Groote Post, Darling Cellars and Ormonde
make up the Darling Wine Experience and you'll
easily be able to pass a morning drifting from one
to the other, comparing what they have to offer and
stocking up on affordable wines to take home.

### Evita se Perron

*Old Darling Railway Station, Arcadia Street, Darling
(022 492 2831/2851/www.evita.co.za).* **Open** 10am-
4pm Tue-Sun, unless there's an evening show.
**Credit** DC, MC, V.

Don't pass up the opportunity to see Evita
Bezuidenhout strut her stuff. She's funny, caustic
and still has that withering kind of humour that can
make cabinet ministers squirm. There's a meal with
the show. If there's no show, you can still pop in for
scones, *koeksisters* (a traditional confection) and coffee at the bar.

## Where to eat & drink

### Hilda's Kitchen at Groote Post

*Groote Post Wine Farm, Darling Hills Road (022
492 2825/www.grootepost.com).* **Open** noon-2.30pm
Wed-Sat. **Credit** AmEx, DC, MC, V.

When you see the sign to Groote Post on your way
up the R27, do make a detour to this historic farm.
Since current owner Peter Pentz (a former dairy
farmer) decided to plant vines, the wines have kept
winning awards. The restaurant, named after the
famous Hildagonda Duckitt, is a lovely place for a
relaxed lunch. Call at least a day ahead if you want
to enjoy a romantic picnic basket under the trees.

## Where to stay

### Darling Lodge
*22 Pastorie Street, Darling (022 492 3062/www. darlinglodge.co.za).* **Rates** R320-R600. **Credit** MC, V.
There are six double ensuite rooms at this stylishly restored old house in the village. It has all the things that make for a comfortable stay – gracious hosts, good beds, nice linen and hearty breakfasts.

### Trinity Guest Lodge & Restaurant
*19 Long Street, Darling (022 492 3430/www.trinity lodge.co.za).* **Rates** R250-R300. **Credit** MC, V.
This restored Victorian guesthouse is one of the nicest places to stay in the village. The rooms are set in a lush garden with a pool. Evening meals are impressive and they regularly hold wine-tasting evenings in conjunction with local winemakers.

## Elandsbaai & Lambert's Bay

**Elandsbaai** is all about the surf, dude, and every water rat knows there's a rocky shelf that helps to form an awesome hollow left-hand wave that will give you the ride of your life. E-Bay's terminally laid-back atmosphere is also what people come for.

It's not just modern-day surfers who have been drawn to this pretty bay. A short walk to **Elandsbaai Cave** reveals a series of handprints left behind by the first people who looked over the sea thousands of years ago. The nearby **Verlorenvlei**, which means 'lost wetland', is a birdwatcher's paradise. It's one of the ten most important wetland areas in the Cape, and is of international importance. Verlorenvlei supports over 200 bird species, including African spoonbills, purple gallinules, goliath herons and white pelicans. One of the best ways to explore this wetland is by canoe and you can hire them from Mike who lives opposite Hotel Eland (yes, that's how he gives directions to find him). Unfortunately, the wetland is under threat as some local farmers, battling the harsh, dry conditions of the West Coast, pump out vast quantities of fresh water to irrigate their thirsty potato crops.

The town of **Lambert's Bay**, 27km (17 miles) north of Elandsbaai, isn't a beauty, but the drive between the two towns is a must and the nearby beaches are unspoilt so you won't have a problem finding a secluded spot. **Bird Island**, the breeding ground of over 11,000

During spring the **West Coast National Park** is carpeted with flowers. *See p243*.

Cape gannets, is just off the harbour and worth a visit. Best time to go is between April and September to watch the gannets' mating dance. Unfortunately Cape fur seals have ear-marked the island as a good takeaway joint, and the bird population is under very serious threat.

### GETTING THERE
Elandsbaai is 220km (136 miles) and Lambert's Bay is 250km (155 miles) from Cape Town. For Elandsbaai, take the R27 north. For Lambert's Bay, follow signs from Elandsbaai. For organised tours, contact the Cape Town Tourism Office (*see p54*).

### TOURIST INFORMATION
Elandsbaai Tourism Bureau (027 432 1000 or call Hotel Eland on 022 972 1640). Lambert's Bay Tourism Bureau (027 432 1000/www.lambertsbay.co.za).

## What to see & do

### Lambert's Bay Boat Charter
*Lambert's Bay Harbour (027 432 1757/082 922 4334)*. **Open** 9am-5pm daily. **No credit cards.**

Head out to sea to watch the dolphins and whales in season. Best time to go is early in the morning before the wind picks up.

### West Coast Safaris & Quads
*10km out of Lambert's Bay (083 306 6684/ www.lambertsbayeco.co.za)*. **No credit cards.**
Scooting around on quad bikes is always fun, especially when you get to play around on the dunes. No experience is needed, and you'll be with an experienced guide at all times. Booking essential.

## Where to eat & drink

### Die Kreefhuis Restaurant
*Strand Street, Lambert's Bay (027 432 2235)*. **Open** 11am-2.30pm, 6pm-late Mon-Sat; 11am-2.30pm Sun. **Credit** AmEx, DC, MC, V.
The seafood platter here is a mountain of crayfish, prawns, calamari, mussels, a choice of two pieces of fish, chips and rice.

### Muisbosskerm
*On the Elandsbaai Road, 5km south of Lambert's Bay (027 432 1017)*. **Open** *Lunch* 1pm. *Dinner* 7pm. **Credit** AmEx, DC, MC, V.

You can't spend time on the West Coast without visiting one of the open-air seafood restaurants, and Muisbosskerm is the real deal. Meals are long and leisurely. Expect *bokkoms* (traditional West Coast dried fish), rollmops, barbecued and baked fish, seafood *bredie* (a type of stew) and crayfish.

## Where to stay

### Hotel Eland
*1 Hunter Street, Elandsbaai (022 972 1640/ www.elandsbay.co.za)*. **Rates** R180-R450. **Credit** AmEx, DC, MC, V.
If you're based at the Eland, which overlooks the beach, you're much sorted. The staff are friendly, well informed and at some point anything newsworthy will be relayed through the bar. The hotel operates on a B&B basis, but the restaurant is well known for great seafood so you won't go hungry.

### Lambert's Bay Hotel
*72 Voortrekker Street, Lambert's Bay (027 432 1126/www.lambertsbayhotel.co.za)*. **Rates** R395-R495. **Credit** AmEx, DC, MC, V.
Five minutes from the beach, the Lambert's Bay Hotel is a safe bet. It has everything you'll need including a swimming pool, restaurant and bar.

## Langebaan

On a clear, still day the **Langebaan Lagoon** is hard to beat. It sparkles like a gem, and seems to be made up of every imaginable shade of blue, green, aqua and turquoise. Given just how beautiful the lagoon is, and its proximity to Cape Town, it's hardly surprising that the town of Langebaan has grown so rapidly and is a favourite holiday destination for anybody who likes messing about in boats.

Each year thousands of birdwatchers also make the trip to this ornithological paradise. For starters there are over 70,000 migratory waders, while some of the other species to look out for include the delicate greenshanks, the busy little stints or the less common bar-tailed godwits. The **West Coast National Park** (*see below*) has a number of strategically placed hides where you can hole up for a morning.

It's in spring, however, when the West Coast National Park really comes into its own and is transformed by the Namaqualand daisies, vygies and other wild flowers that carpet the otherwise sparse veld. You might also be lucky to catch sight of one of the many southern right whales that head up the coast to calve from around June to September. There used to be a whaling station at Donkergat, when sailors kept an eye out for whales for an entirely different reason, but that's been closed for decades and the number of southern right whales has increased steadily over the years.

### GETTING THERE
Langebaan is 124km (77 miles) from Cape Town. Take the R27 north. For organised tours, contact the Cape Town Tourism Office (*see p54*).

### TOURIST INFORMATION
Langebaan Tourism Bureau (022 772 1515/ www.langebaaninfo.com).

## What to see & do

### Cape Sports Centre
*98 Main Road, Langebaan (022 772 1114/www. capesport.co.za)*. **Open** 9am-5pm daily. **Credit** AmEx, DC, MC, V.
The Langebaan Lagoon is every water baby's dream (although the water temperature is often pretty chilly) and you can try your hand at just about every sport under the sun, from kite surfing to kayaking and windsurfing. The Cape Sports Centre, right on the beach, has everything you need if you want to hire gear and they have qualified instructors who can take you through your paces.

### West Coast National Park
*Off the R27, 11km past the Yzerfontein turn-off (022 772 2144/www.sanparks.org)*. **Open** *Apr-Sept* 7am-7.30pm daily. *Oct-Mar* 6am-8pm daily. *Postberg hike* (Aug-Sept flower season) 9am-5pm daily. **No credit cards**.
Grease up your bike or haul out your hiking boots and head for the West Coast National Park which hugs the Langebaan Lagoon. It's an easy drive from Cape Town and the park is a great place to cycle off season, as there are so few cars about. The cherry on the top is the Postberg hike, but it's only open for two months during the flower season and is consequently often booked out. **Photo** *p242*.

## Where to eat & drink

### Froggy's
*29 Main Road, Langebaan (022 772 1869)*. **Open** *Lunch* from noon Wed-Sun. *Dinner* from 6.30pm Tue-Sat. **No credit cards**.
Froggy, the owner of this relaxed restaurant, is an eccentric fellow, who will help you start (and finish) your bottle of wine while he cooks and talks. The food is eclectic as he is. Expect to find caramelised onion-and-brie tart or slow-baked Moroccan lamb shank rich with cinnamon, coriander, ginger and garlic. Froggy's Thai curries are also delicious.

### Geelbek Restaurant
*Langebaan Lagoon, West Coast National Park (022 772 2134)*. **Open** 9am-6pm daily. **Credit** DC, MC, V.
Elmarie Leonard, a descendant of Angela of Bengal (one of the first freed slaves in the Cape), has made it her mission to collect local West Coast recipes as a way of paying homage to the many different nationalities that helped shape the area. She then incorporates these into the dishes she serves at

Geelbek Restaurant, which is housed in a historic old farmstead that was built in 1761. Try the stuffed *harders* (mullet) if it's on the menu, or the *snoekkuite* (roe), also known as West Coast caviar.

## Where to stay

### Farmhouse Hotel
*5 Egret Street, Langebaan (022 772 2062/www. thefarmhouselangebaan.co.za). Rates R500-R990.* **Credit** AmEx, DC, MC, V.
Built around one of the old farmhouses in the area, the Farmhouse Hotel is a Langebaan institution with commanding views over the lagoon and Schaapen Island. The decor is pretty traditional with lots of wood, and the old pictures from the area add a nice touch. The hotel's restaurant has a comprehensive menu if you don't feel like exploring the town, and the bar serves lighter meals such as fish and chips.

### Nirvana Houseboat
*Kraalbaai, Langebaan Lagoon, West Coast National Park (021 689 9718/082 258 0929/www.house boating.co.za). Rates R400-R600.* **No credit cards.**
You could be forgiven for thinking that you have died and gone to heaven when you stay at this luxurious houseboat on the Langebaan Lagoon. The houseboat is moored at sheltered Kraalbaai and you'll be able to swim, fish and boat to your heart's content. The only problem is you might never want to leave. Highly recommended.

## Paternoster

The bays strung out along this headland are stunning. The sea's a sapphire blue and when the spring flowers are in bloom, they carpet the usually sun-baked veld with yellow, white and orange daisies. While Stompneusbaai, Britannia Bay and St Helena all have their own charms, it's usually **Paternoster** (**photo** *p239*) that grabs all the kudos. It's not hard to see why, as the village consists of a cluster of whitewashed cottages, fishing boats and old fishermen with wizened faces that tell a thousand tales.

Paternoster means 'Our Father' and the village was supposedly named after the heartfelt prayers offered up by shipwrecked sailors who found themselves stranded here.

There are still some untouched places that smack of simpler times, and **Cape Columbine Lighthouse** and **Nature Reserve**, just 5km (3 miles) away, is one of them. Built in the 1930s, it is one of the few manned lighthouses left in the country. The houses that form part of the lighthouse complex have been spruced up and offer good self-catering accommodation (021 449 2400/www.npa.co.za to book).

Lying just across the bay from Paternoster is **St Helena Bay**, a bustling harbour bristling with fish factories. It's also a great spot if you're looking for action of the birdwatching, surfing or hiking kind. St Helena is unique in that it's the only place on the West Coast where you can watch the sun rise over the ocean.

### GETTING THERE
Paternoster is 145km (90 miles) from Cape Town. Take the R27 north until you get to the junction with the R45. Turn left and follow the signs to Vredenburg and then on to Paternoster. For organised tours, contact the Cape Town Tourism Office (*see p54*).

### TOURIST INFORMATION
Paternoster & St Helena Tourism Bureau, c/o Vredenburg Tourism (022 715 1142). Velddrif Tourism Bureau (022 783 1821/www.tourismvelddrif.co.za).

## What to see & do

### West Coast Bird Club
*(022 713 3026).*
The West Coast Bird Club always has plenty going on, so join them on the next bird-counting expedition or for a sunset trip on the Berg River. Don't forget your binoculars.

## Where to eat & drink

### Paternoster Hotel
*St Augustin's Road, Paternoster (022 752 2703).* **Open** 7.30am-late Mon-Sat; 8am-4pm Sun. **Credit** AmEx, DC, MC, V.
This a favourite hang-out with holidaymakers and, although the food is unmemorable, the beer is cold and the mood is very relaxed. So you can wander up in your flip-flops and have fish and chips, or the mixed seafood *potjie*, and go home feeling happy. If you really want to splash out, opt for the 'Exotic' on the menu – an enormous seafood platter that will keep you busy for hours.

### Voorstrandt Restaurant
*Strandloper Way, Paternoster (022 752 2038).* **Open** 10am-9pm daily. **Credit** MC, V.
Situated in an old fisherman's cottage right on the beach, this is one of the best restaurants in the area. Try the mild Malay fish curry packed with mussels, fish, prawns and served with rice and *sambals*.

## Where to stay

### Oystercatcher's Haven
*48 Sonkwas Road, Paternoster (022 752 2193/www. oystercatchershaven.com). Rates R425.* **Credit** MC, V.
If you want to spoil yourself, try this elegant three-bedroom B&B. You won't find tacky knick-knacks – just gorgeous, crisp linen and endless views. The pool is a treat and the whole set-up is top notch. They now offer divine dinners as well as breakfast.

# Directory

## Features

# Directory

## Getting Around

### By air

#### Cape Town International Airport

*021 937 1257/086 727 7888/ www.airports.co.za.*
Cape Town International is operated by the Airports Company of South Africa (ACSA). The 22km (15.5-mile) commute between the city centre and the airport on the N2 will take approximately 15-20 minutes if you are lucky enough not to get delayed by peak hour traffic or the roadworks which are common during low season.

Traffic tends to peak between 7am and 9am, and again from 4.30pm to 6pm, so it's advisable to take this into consideration when planning your trip to the airport.

International airlines with direct flights to Cape Town include national carrier South African Airways, Virgin Atlantic, British Airways, Air France, KLM and Lufthansa. Domestic airlines flying between Cape Town and other SA city centres include **SAA** (www.flysaa.co.za), **SA Airlink** (www.saairlink.co.za), **British Airways/Comair** (www.ba.co.za), and **Nationwide** (www.fly nationwide.co.za).

Daily flights to Cape Town are available from all of SA's major centres and you should expect to pay anywhere from R800 to R2,500 for a return ticket depending on season, airline, and if there are any specials on offer.

If you are a budget traveller, the three low-cost carriers

are **Kulula.com** (www.kulula.com), **1 Time** (www.1time.co.za) and **Mango** (www.flymango.com).

Car hire companies at the airport include Avis, Budget and Hertz. Desks are located within both the Domestic and International Arrivals terminal buildings.

As there aren't any train routes to or from Cape Town International, there are various shuttle services to take you to the city and back. **City Hopper** (021 934 4440), **Centurion** (021 934 8281), and **Magic Bus** (021 505 6300) are your best and least expensive mode of transport from the airport to the city centre. You can expect to pay about R150 during the day, but rates tend to be more expensive during the evening. It's advisable to pre-book shuttle services at least two days in advance.

### Airlines

**South African Airways** *reservations, arrival & departure times 021 936 1111/www.flysaa.com.*
**British Airways** *reservations & passenger enquiries 011 921 0222.*
**KLM** *reservations 086 024 7747.*
**Lufthansa** *086 184 2538.*
**Virgin Atlantic** *011 340 3400.*

Public transport in Cape Town is a bit of a gamble and sometimes your best and safest bet is to use a car. If you can't or don't feel like driving, you can hire a car with a driver or use a minibus taxi (*see below*). Minibus taxis are quite

an economical option if you're travelling in a large group.

### Minibus taxis

This is by far the most popular form of public transport in Cape Town. These sometimes unroadworthy minibus taxis transport thousands of commuters in and out of the city daily. Although most of the drivers can be a tad erratic on the roads, minibus taxis are cheap (you can get from one side of the peninsula to the other for a few Rand), generally efficient and punctual. To flag a taxi down, all you need to do is stick out your hand and they'll literally stop anywhere (with a near total disregard for any other road users). Just be sure to find out where the minibus taxi is going and definitely give this mode of transport a miss if you're at all claustrophobic.

### Taxis

Although slightly more expensive, taxis are also a reliable option, charging around R9 per kilometre. Try **Excite** (021 418 4444) or **Unicab** (021 448 1720). Other taxi services can be found in the Yellow Pages or contact the Cape Town Tourism Visitor Information Centre (*see p54*) for a list of recommended companies. For personal tours, try **Legends Tours** (021 674 7055).

A word of advice: make sure you know the fare beforehand. Don't be conned by the few sneaky cabbies who grossly inflate their fares in the hope of duping unsuspecting tourists.

## Rikkis

Rikkis are noisy, overgrown tuk-tuks and are a great form of transport for travelling to the V&A Waterfront and within the city centre. Contact **Rikkis Intercity** (086 174 5547) or hail one on the street.

## Buses

The biggest local bus-service in Cape Town is **Golden Arrow** (0800 656 463/ www.gabs.co.za). They won't take you to some of the more out-of-the-way tourist spots, but they offer a comprehensive assortment of inexpensive routes along most of Cape Town's major routes. Expect to pay between R10 and R15 for a one-way ticket.

The **City Sightseeing Capetown** bus (021 511 6000) is a more tourist-oriented option. The first bus departs from the Two Oceans Aquarium at the V&A

Waterfront at 9.30am (and every 30 mins thereafter until 3.30pm). Tickets are R100 per person and can be bought at the Two Oceans kiosk or on the bus itself, and will take you all over Cape Town and along the Atlantic Seaboard to Camps Bay, letting you jump on and off at will throughout the day.

## Trains

### Cape Town Railway Station (021 449 2991) is

situated in the city centre on Adderley Street and offers routes to all of South Africa's major cities. Tickets can be booked for first- and second-class compartments, but since the difference in fairs is marginal, it's best to fork out the extra few Rands and be assured of a safer ride. Most trains also have dining cars and catering trolleys. Ticket prices and timetables are available from **Shosholoza**

**Meyl** (086 000 8888/ www.spoornet.co.za).

South Africa boasts a recently formed Railway Police division, so travelling by rail is now safer than it used to be.

There are a few luxury options available if you feel like travelling in style. Try the famous **Blue Train** (021 449 2672/www.luxurytrains.co.za) from Cape Town to Pretoria or **Rovos Rail** (021 421 4020/www.rovos.co.za).

## Driving

Cape Town is notorious for having some of the worst driving in the country. As in the UK, motorists drive on the left-hand side of the road. Most locals don't drive like maniacs, but a few seem to neglect some of the basics, like indicating and looking before turning.

Drive defensively on Cape Town roads. Also adhere to speed restrictions, as fines can be severe.

# Time for a detour

New arrivals to Cape Town are ferried from slick international airport to hotel, past the ramshackle shantytowns sprawled on the outskirts of the city. For some, the homes constructed from corrugated iron, plastic, cardboard and wood disappear in a blur, for others the image cements itself, urging investigation.

These squatter camps are in fact where the majority of Capetonians live. The area was originally inhabited by labourers working in the city, but as more and more make-shift houses sprang up and stayed, attempts by the government to demolish them became futile. The installation of running water and electricity has ensured that living conditions have improved.

The endlessly expanding townships are a vibrant place, where you're as likely to find an internet café on the roadside as you are a herd of cows. They are still dangerous places to visit on your own, though, so think twice before you pop by on a whim. Join a township tour led by residents instead.

**Cape Capers** (021 448 3117, www.tour capers.co.za, daily tours start 9am at Burg Street Clock Tower, R280-R460, no credit cards) offer sweeping four-hour tours, which take in three diverse 'non-white' areas – Langa township, Phillipi and Rylands. Visit a community centre, craft market, *shebeen* and township restaurant, as well as new housing developments in the area.

**Andulela** (021 790 2592, 082 695 4695, www.andulela.com, evening tours 4.30-11pm, R350 per person, no credit cards) offer more focused tours, like their unique cooking safari with a visit to Kayamandi Township in Stellenbosch. Mama Shumi will take you on a walk through the township as you stop off to buy ingredients from shops, street vendors and butchers. Enter family homes where you'll chat with the locals over home-made stews and ginger beer.

**Coffee Beans Routes** (021 448 8080, 084 762 4944, www.coffeebeans.co.za, R390) are also a good choice for authentic evening township tours.

## Vehicle hire

Hiring a car in Cape Town is very straightforward. There are several rental agencies such as **Avis** (021 424 1177), **Budget** (021 418 5232) and **Hertz** (021 935 4800). Rates are usually on a per-day basis and according to how many kilometres you've travelled. Shop around before hiring a car, though – some agencies run regular specials where free mileage is part of the deal.

To hire a car, you generally need to be over 25 years old and have a valid international driver's licence.

If you're on a budget, try one of the 'no frills' car rental companies like **Value Car Hire** (021 696 2198/www.valuecarhire.co.za).

## Petrol stations

Petrol (gas) stations can be found throughout Cape Town (particularly along main roads, in the V&A Waterfront and along Buitengracht Street). Most are open 24 hours a day, with a convenience store, but don't tempt fate by driving around remote areas with a near empty tank. At the time of writing petrol cost around R5.40 a litre, though it does tend to fluctuate a lot. Tip your 'petrol jockey' your change up to ten per cent.

## Insurance

Driving on gravel roads can be very dangerous, so go slowly. Establish beforehand whether your hire car insurance covers road damage or not. When you rent a car check your agreement for details of both damage and liability insurance, as levels of cover vary. If you don't have a home policy that covers you for every eventuality, it might be best to pre-book via a multinational company in your home country.

## Parking

In the centre some shopping areas have uniformed attendants to help you park, either for a fee or a tip, during office hours from Monday to Saturday. Some streets have authorised, uniformed parking marshals who can help operate meters and sell parking cards, which are also available from shops and kiosks. Parking marshals are allowed to accept tips but can't solicit them.

There is also an abundance of 'unofficial' car guards (not in uniform), which can make parking a slightly unnerving experience. These car guards, usually in competition with each other, direct you to a vacant parking bay, or ask for money to mind the meter for you. The city authorities are keen to control this practice and recommend that you decline the services of such 'parking attendants'.

Be warned, though, that some do not take rejection well and can become quite abusive, especially when fuelled up by liquor. Keep your windows up, ignore their colourful vocabulary, and instead spend an extra few minutes finding a parking garage or official parking lot. At night, park in a secure, well-lit area.

Vehicles are removed if parked illegally – another reason to avoid the illegal parking spots offered by the 'car guards'. To locate your missing car go to a police station or call the traffic department tow-away section on 021 406 8700. You will have to cough up around R713 if your car has been impounded plus R200-R500 for a parking ticket. You will be charged R29 per day storage fee after the fourth day. When you go along to pick up your car, take along your rental agreement and passport to show officials. Payment is by cash or (local) cheque only.

## Walking

Cape Town is really a driver's town, since it is so spread out. Walking is only a viable means of transport within certain areas once you've got there by car. These include the city centre and the beach-side promenades, which the authorities make a big effort to keep safe and attractive through local initiatives and business partnerships. The areas containing its main attractions are safe and enjoyable to explore on foot, with plenty of street life.

Cape Town is a car town both because of the distances involved but also because you won't feel as vulnerable in a car as strolling the streets. Walking is not safe city-wide, and as a stranger not tuned in to the cues and clues, you should keep your eyes peeled and always take the following precautions:
● Avoid dark, isolated areas.
● Never walk alone.
● If you get lost, a stranger may not be your best source of help. Try to find a police or traffic officer. Or go into the nearest shop.
● You might as well have a huge neon sign above your head that says 'Tourist' if you carry your camera around your neck. Carry it in a shoulder bag.
● Don't carry large sums of money. Keep small change in your wallet or purse and bank notes and credit cards in an inside pocket.
● Never carry your wallet in your back pocket.
● Don't wear any valuable jewellery that you're not prepared to lose.
● Carry your bag close to your body.
● Steer clear of con artists or strangers who offer you the opportunity to get rich quickly.
● If in doubt, call a cab. Always carry the number of a reliable company; see *p246*.

# Resources A-Z

## Age restrictions

The legal age for drinking and buying alcohol is 18. To smoke or purchase tobacco products, you have to be 16. The age of consent is 16.

## Attitude & etiquette

South Africa has an informal atmosphere and people usually introduce themselves by their first names, even in business relationships. Much to the disdain of their harder-working Gauteng cousins, Capetonians are very laidback. Most organised events start punctually, but no Capetonian worth their salt will be less than an hour late for an informal engagement. Blame it on the gorgeous sunsets over the beaches – such influences make it hard to be punctilious.

## Business

Founded in 1804, the Cape Town Regional Chamber of Commerce and Industry is a one-stop shop for business information and advice. Funded by more than 4,500 members, 70 per cent of which are small businesses, the Chamber offers a host of networking opportunities, an interactive website that includes a searchable database, contacts locally and overseas, international trade information and advice. It also provides a comprehensive library, events and exhibition management facilities, specialist advice and links to local, regional and central government. It lists business associations, local financial institutions, property brokers and other services vital to setting up business.

## Business organisations

### Cape Chamber House

*19 Louis Gradner Street, City Bowl (021 402 4300/www.caperegional chamber.co.za).* **Open** 8.30am-4.15pm Mon-Fri. **Map** p275 I3.
The Cape Town Regional Chamber of Commerce and Industry (Cape Regional Chamber) is the leading source for business information and services. Cape Town is a major convention destination as it is regarded as the hub of South African commerce.

### Wesgro

*021 487 8600/www.wesgro.org.za.* Wesgro is the official Trade and Investment Promotion Agency for the Western Cape Province. It is the first point of contact for foreign importers, local exporters and investors wishing to take advantage of Cape investment opportunities.

## Conventions & conferences

### Cape Town International Convention Centre

*Convention Square, 1 Lower Long Street, City Bowl (021 410 5000/ www.capetownconvention.com).* **Map** p275 H3.
The Cape Town International Convention Centre opened in June 2003. The vast array of facilities includes a deluxe hotel, dedicated exhibition space and generous banqueting and meeting facilities.
Other spacious venues include the Good Hope Centre (021 465 4688) and the Civic Centre (021 400 1111), but they are decidedly less glamorous.

## Couriers

Use trusted names such as **DHL Worldwide Express** (086 0345000) or **XPS** (021 380 2400) when you want to courier your parcel without any worries.

## Shipping

**Britannia** (021 556 9448/ www.britannia.co.za) will ship anything from one box to an entire container, or you could try **Island View Shipping** (021 425 2285/ www.ivs.co.za).

## Translators & interpreters

For translation and interpretation services contact **Folio Translation Consultants** (021 426 2727) or **SATI** (South African Translators' Institute) on 021 976 9563.

## Consumer affairs

Call these companies with any consumer-related problems, enquiries and complaints: **Consumer Affairs Office** (021 483 5133); **Consumer Complaint Line** (0800 007 081).

## Customs

There is a huge list of prohibited goods, so if in doubt visit www.sars.gov.za (and go to the Customs link), or call 0860 1212 18.
Personal effects (used, not new) are admitted duty free. Other allowances for visitors to South Africa are as follows (per adult):

- 1 litre of spirits.
- 2 litres of wine.
- 400 cigarettes.
- 50 cigars.
- 50ml perfume.
- 250ml eau de toilette.
- Gifts and souvenirs to the value of R500.

A permit is required for firearms. Available at entry points, it's valid for 180 days, and can be renewed at any South African police station.

## Disabled

Most attractions and hotels are disabled-friendly (for details on the outlying areas, contact the relevant tourism bureaux). Passenger Aid Units (PAU) are on call at all major airports. Larger car rental companies can provide vehicles with hand controls.

The following companies can provide services for disabled travellers:

**Flamingo Tours**
*021 557 4496/www.flamingo tours.co.za.*

**Titch Travel & Tours**
*021 686 5501/www.titchtours.co.za.*

## Drugs

Cannabis (or *dagga*), while freely available, is illegal and its possession a punishable offence. Hard drugs are also available, but once again, illegal and could land you in prison. Among locals, the rave generation favours the likes of ecstasy, but the real problem lies with drugs like mandrax (or buttons), heroin, crack and crystal meth (or *tik*).

## Electricity

The power supply is 220/230 volts AC. The standard plug in South Africa is the 15-amp round-pin, three-prong plug. The European-type two-pin plug can be used with an adaptor plug (which can be bought at most supermarkets). Remember to bring transformers along for larger appliances where necessary. Most hotels have 110-volt outlets for electric shavers.

## Embassies & consulates

**Belgium Consulate General**
*19th Floor, LG Building, Thibault Square (021 419 4690).*
**British Consulate**
*Southern Life Centre, 8 Riebeeck Street, City Bowl (021 405 2400).* **Map** p275 H3.
**Canadian High Commission**
*19th Floor, Reserve Bank Building, 60 St George's Mall, City Bowl (021 423 5240).* **Map** p275 H4.
**French Consulate**
*78 Queen Victoria Street, City Bowl (021 423 1575).* **Map** p274 G4.
**German Consulate General & Embassy**
*19th Floor, Safmarine House, 22 Riebeeck Street, City Bowl (021 405 3000).* **Map** p275 H3.

**New Zealand Hon Consulate General**
*345 Landsdowne Road, Landsdowne (021 696 8561).*
**Royal Netherlands Embassy**
*100 Strand Street, Corner Buitengracht Street, City Bowl (021 421 5660).* **Map** p275 H3.
**US Consulate**
*2 Reddam Avenue, West Lake, Tokai (021 702 7300).*

## Emergencies

**Ambulance** 10177.
**Police** 10111.
**Fire** 021 480 7700.
**Mountain Rescue Service** 021 948 9900.
**Poison Crisis Centre** 021 689 5227
**Red Cross Children's Hospital** 021 658 5111.
**National Sea Rescue Institute** 021 449 3500.

## Gay & lesbian

For further information on Gay & Lesbian Cape Town, see *p175* **Gay & Lesbian**.

**Gay, Lesbian & Bisexual Helpline** *021 4222 500.*
**Open** 1-9pm Mon-Sun.

# Slanguage

You would think that in a city where everyone speaks English you'd find your way around easily. But with 11 official languages that all feed off one another, you might just get some friendly local telling you 'check you at the braai, it's gonna be a jol' or 'it's good weather to catch a tan, we're leaving now now'. So, to avoid any confusion, here's a helpful guide to the most common South African slang words.
**Braai** A barbecue, an extremely popular South African past-time, where you're likely to eat things off the grill, accompanied by lots of beer and maybe bread and salads.
**Bru/boykie/bra/china** A friend, buddy, mate, used for men and, strangely, sometimes women.
**Catch a tan** To suntan, mostly carried out on the Clifton beaches when you should be at work.
**Dankie** Not so much slang, it's Afrikaans for 'thank you'.
**Dop** An alcoholic drink.
**Eish!** Expression of disbelief.

**Howzit/Hoesit** Very nifty, a greeting and 'how are you' combined.
**Izzit** An expression of disbelief, as in 'Is it?'. Add it to the end of sentences to mean 'You're kidding'.
**Jol** A very good time, anything from a party to a good shopping spree.
**Just now/now now** This can mean anything from 'in a little while' to 'when I get around to it' to 'the next day'.
**Lekker** Cool, nice, sounds good (the opposite is vrot, kak or sif).
**Lank** Very. As in 'it's lank cool'.
**Sweet/kiff** Same as lekker *(see above)*.
**Robot** Don't be alarmed, this is a traffic light.
**Slap chips** French fries. 'Slap' means floppy, even though they're just as rigid as anywhere else in the world.
**Moerse** An over-used swear word, used liberally as an adjective, implying a lot or huge, or even great. As in 'A moerse party' ('the mother of all parties'), 'A moerse hangover'('a mother of a hangover').
**Kak** Afrikaans for 'shit'. Used often.

**Out in Africa Gay & Lesbian Film Festival** *021 461 4027/ www.oia.co.za.*
**Triangle Project Health** *021 465 9289.* Information, counselling and support.
**ATIC** *021 797 3327.* Aids information and counselling centre.
**Wolanani HIV/Aids Service Agency** *021 447 2091 www.wolalani.co.za.*

## Health

As a visitor you'll want to be treated in a private hospital where there's less red tape to deal with and more staff to go around. The city's private hospitals are world-class. In fact, many tourists come here to receive specialised care. Your travel insurance (a must for all overseas tourists) should help to cover most, if not all, of the cost. Speak to your travel agent to get the best advice on what medical insurance package to go for. Should you require emergency medical assistance, again Cape Town has some of the world's finest paramedics on hand to assist you.

## AIDS

Southern Africa has some of the world's highest HIV and AIDS statistics, which have resulted in AIDS research and education programmes that are on a par with First World nations. If you suspect that you may have contracted an infection, you can call the **National AIDS Helpline** (0800 012 322) for immediate assistance on where to go to get anti-retroviral (ARV) treatment.

## Contraception & abortion

All mother-and-child health services – including family planning, contraception and abortions – are free to South Africans and tourists at

government institutions. Condoms are also issued free of charge at these locations. Pregnancy tests can be purchased for between R10 and R80 and the 'morning after' pill can be purchased over the counter for around R50 at most pharmacies.

### Cape Town Station Reproductive Health Clinic
*Cape Town Railway Station, City Bowl (021 425 2004).* **Open** 7am-3.45pm Mon-Fri. **Map** p275 H4.

### Chapel Street Clinic
*Corner Chapel & Balfour Streets, Woodstock, Southern Suburbs (021 465 2793).* **Open** 7.30am-3pm Mon-Fri.

### Marie Stopes Clinic
*91 Bree Street, City Bowl (021 422 4660).* **Open** 8.30am-4.30pm Mon-Fri, 8.30am-12.30pm Sat. **Map** p274 G4.

## Doctors/dentists

Call Directory Enquiries (1023) or consult the Yellow Pages (10118/www.yellowpages.co.za) for a list of registered medical/dental practitioners in your area. As a tourist you may have to make a booking for an appointment beforehand and be required to settle your account up-front and in cash.

### SAA-Netcare Travel Clinic
*58 Strand Street, City Bowl (021 419 3172/www.travelclinic.co.za).* **Credit** AmEx, DC, MC, V. **Map** p275 H4.
This facility offers tourists medical advice on any vaccinations required and diseases endemic to the region you're visiting, and can also supply handy first-aid travel kits.

## Helplines

The following helplines all operate 24 hours daily.

**Alcoholics Anonymous** *021 510 2288.*
**Childline** *08000 55 555/021 762 819/www.childline.org.za.*
**Gender Violence Helpline** *0800 150 150/www.stopwomen abusehelpline.org.za.*

**Lifeline** *0861 322 322/ www.lifeline.org.za.*
**Narcotics Anonymous** *0881 30 03 27/www.na.org.za.*
**National Aids Helpline** *0800 012 322/www.aidshelpline.org.za.*
**Rape Crisis Centre** *021 447 9762/www.rapecrisis.org.za.*

## Pharmacies

The following pharmacies are open late:

### Clicks Glengariff Pharmacy
*2 Main Road, Sea Point, Atlantic Seaboard (021 434 8622).* **Open** 7am-11pm Mon-Sat; 9am-9pm Sun. **Credit** AmEx, DC, MC, V. **Map** p273 C2.

### Lite-Kem
*24 Darling Street, City Bowl (021 461 8040).* **Open** 8am-11pm Mon-Fri; 9am-11pm Sat, Sun. **Credit** AmEx, DC, MC, V. **Map** p275 H4.

### M-Kem Medicine City
*Corner Durban & Raglan Roads, Bellville, Northern Suburbs (021 948 5706).* **Open** 24hrs daily. **Credit** AmEx, DC, MC, V.

## ID

You have to be 18 or over to get into a club, but bouncers won't ask to see your ID unless they think you still look like a teenager. Leave your passport in a safe at your hotel if you're just sightseeing for the day.

## Internet

Most of the top hotels in Cape Town now offer Wi-Fi. On the off chance that the hotel doesn't have internet access, they should be able to direct you to a nearby internet café.

There are plenty of cyber cafés, like the **Internet Cyber Café** (Main Road, Sea Point, 021 434 6624, open 10am-4pm daily). Most coffee shops now also offer Wi-Fi services.

If you're staying in South Africa for a lengthy period of time, it may be worth opening an account with a local service provider. Try **iAfrica** (www.iafrica.com, 021 689 9925), **Polka.co.za**

**Directory**

(www.polka.co.za, 0860 00 4455) or **M-Web** (www.mweb.co.za, 0860 032 000).

## Language

South Africa has no fewer than 11 official languages: Afrikaans, English, Ndebele, Xhosa, Zulu, Sepedi, Sesotho, Setswana, siSwati, Venda and Tsonga. In the Western Cape, English, Afrikaans and Xhosa are the most commonly spoken. Staff at some establishments and attractions speak German (there is a large German community in Cape Town), French or Italian.

## Left luggage

Left Luggage is a company that will hold your baggage when you cannot. Contact them on 021 936 2884 at Cape Town Airport's domestic terminal and on 021 936 2494 for the office at the International terminal.

## Legal help

### Law Society of the Cape of Good Hope
*29th & 20th Floors, ABSA Centre, 2 Riebeeck Street, City Bowl (021 443 6700).* **Map** p275 H3.

### Legalwise Leza Legal Insurance
*Shop 4, Fountain Place, 1 Heerengracht, Adderley Street, City Bowl (021 419 6905).* **Map** p275 H3.

### Legal Resources Centre
*54 Shortmarket Street, City Bowl (021 423 8285).* **Map** p274 G3.

## Libraries

Visitors may register as temporary members at any Cape Town City Library branch (see the telephone directory under Municipality of Cape Town). City Library Head Office 021 467 1500 can also help.

## Lost property

The lost-and-found division at Cape Town International can be contacted on 021 937 1263. If you've lost something while on your travels in the city, report the loss at a police station, leaving your contact number and address. Alternatively, you can try posting an ad in the classifieds of one of the local papers.

## Media

### Magazines

The market is oversaturated with local magazines and imports tend to be grossly overpriced. *Cosmopolitan, Elle, Marie Claire, InStyle* and *Glamour* all have local versions. If you're after a bit of sleaze and celebrity, look out for *Tvplus, People* and *Heat.*

### Newspapers

Local newspapers focus on local content, exposing the latest wheelings and dealings of corrupt politicians and controversial sportspeople. There are also community weekly newspapers such as the *Atlantic Sun,* which informs on a very local level. *Mail & Guardian* comes out every Thursday and has an excellent entertainment section.

**Morning**: *Cape Times & Business Day* (English), *Die Burger* (Afrikaans).
**Afternoon**: *Cape Argus* (English).
**Sunday**: *Sunday Cape Argus* (English), *Sunday Times* (English), *Rapport* (Afrikaans).

### Radio

Cape Talk (567AM) gives detailed weather information by area, news, traffic reports, arts and entertainment updates and is a great source of info for any tourist. Other local, largely music-oriented FM

radio stations such as 5FM (89.9FM), KFM (94.5FM), Heart (104.9FM) and Good Hope FM (94-97FM) pepper their line-ups with South African music and include information on live performances. Fine Music Radio (101.3FM) has a more classical line-up.

### TV

SABC (South African Broadcasting Commission) owns SABC 1, 2 and 3. SABC 1 caters almost exclusively to the black market and has local shows and news, plus older dubbed programmes in the main local languages and soaps. SABC 2 also has multi-lingual programmes, including Afrikaans. SABC 3 is in English and tries to cater for a higher income bracket with much US and some British programming. e.tv is a privately owned station that tries to push the limits in its line-up: some not so great local shows along with big US series. Unfortunately, Eat is renowned for its constant reruns of films and series, which can be a bit irritating. M-net is a subscriber channel, big on sport, series and movies. Dust is South Africa's own digital satellite TV provider and offers local, American, British and European channels.

## Money

### Banks

**ABSA Bank LTD**
*136 Adderley Street, City Bowl (021 480 1911).* **Map** p275 H4.

**First National Bank**
*82 Adderley Street, City Bowl (021 487 6000).* **Map** p275 H4.

**Nedbank**
*85 St George's Mall, City Bowl (021 469 9500).* **Map** p275 H4.

**Standard Bank**
*10th Floor, Standard Bank Towers, Standard Bank Building,*

*Heerengracht, City Bowl (021 406 2611).* **Map** p275 I3.

## Bureaux de change

Foreign exchange facilities can be found at larger commercial banks, along with the Cape Town Tourism Visitor Information centres (*see p255*), the airport and bureaux de change such as Rennies Travel and American Express.

**American Express** *V&A Waterfront, Atlantic Seaboard (021 419 3917); Thibault House, Thibault Square, City Bowl (021 425 7991).* **Map** p275 H1.
**Rennies Travel** *22 Riebeeck Street, City Bowl (021 410 3600/www. renniestravel.co.za).* **Map** p275 H3.

## Credit cards & ATMs

South Africa has a modern and sophisticated banking system, and most shops and hotels accept credit cards, including international cards such as AmEx, Diners Club, Visa, MasterCard and their affiliates. In country areas the use of cards might be restricted. Standard credit cards cannot be used to pay for petrol (gas) as this is illegal; only special 'garage cards' or cash are accepted. Automatic Teller Machines (ATMs) are widespread and accept most international cards. Most ATMs also offer the option to top up mobile phone credit.

### Lost or stolen cards
**American Express** *0800 991021 traveller's cheques/ 011 710 4747 cards.*
**Diners Club** *011 358 8406.*
**MasterCard** *0800 990 418.*
**Visa** *0800 990 475.*

## Currency

The local currency is the South African Rand. The Rand tends to be weak on international currency markets, making Cape Town a great destination for bargain hunters. (At press time there were R7 to the dollar and R13.9 to the pound.)

● R1 = 100 South African cents.
● Coins in circulation: 5c, 10c, 20c, 50c, R1, R2, R5.
● Banknotes in circulation: R10, R20, R50, R100, R200.

## Tax

South Africa has adopted a Value Added Tax system of 14 per cent on purchases and services. If you are a foreign visitor, you can reclaim VAT on purchases you're taking out of the country if their prices total more than R250. You cannot reclaim on services.

Go to the VAT office at the airport, in the international departure hall, leaving yourself plenty of time before your plane departs. You'll need your original tax invoiced receipts and your passport, along with the purchased goods. Once you've filled in a form and had your application accepted, you can pick up a refund in your home currency from one of the banks in the departure lounge. You can also do the paperwork at the VAT Refund Offices at the Tourism Visitor Information centres (*see p255*).

## Natural hazards

South African tap water is safe to drink, unless a specific notice states otherwise.

The sun in South Africa is much stronger than in Europe and it is essential for visitors to use a good sunscreen for protection. Factor 30+ and up is highly recommended. Skin cancer has become a very serious concern in sun-worshipping Cape Town.

Venomous snakes and spiders might occasionally be encountered. If you are bitten, try to get a good look at the animal so that you can identify it and then call the poison helpline (021 689 5227) for assistance.

## Opening hours

Most of the shops in the city centre and suburbs are open between 9am and 5-5.30pm weekdays and on Saturdays till 1pm. Major malls may open at 9am and close at 6pm (or even 9pm, Sundays and most public holidays included, sometimes with a 10am start).

Government agencies keep to traditional weekday-only hours. Most banks open at 9am and close at 3.30pm on weekdays, and open from 9am to 11am on Saturday mornings.

Muslim-owned businesses close between noon and 2pm on Fridays.

# Travel advice

For current information on travel to a specific country – including the latest news on health issues, safety and security, local laws and customs – contact your home country's government department of foreign affairs. Most have websites with useful advice for would-be travellers.

**Australia**
www.smartraveller.gov.au

**Canada**
www.voyage.gc.ca

**New Zealand**
www.safetravel.govt.nz

**Republic of Ireland**
foreignaffairs.gov.ie

**UK**
www.fco.gov.uk/travel

**USA**
http://travel.state.gov

**Directory**

## Police stations

If you have been a victim of crime, you can contact the police nationwide on 10111. Be sure to give them your contact details and tell them what area and town you are phoning from. To report a crime, you can call in at your closest police station (a list can be found in the back of the Yellow Pages, in the blue section of the telephone directory, or by calling Directory Enquiries on 1023).

**Cape Town Charge Office**
021 467 8000.
**Cape Town International Airport Police Station** 021 934 0707.
**Cape Town Railway Station Charge Office** 021 443 4334.

## Postal services

The South African Post Office (0860 111 502/www.sapo.co.za) is one of the cheapest ways to keep in touch, though they can't always guarantee safe and timely delivery if you're sending a letter via standard mail. For a few more Rands, registered mail is a far safer bet and you can also get a tracking number for your parcel. Sending an overseas postcard costs from R3.80, while letters in standard envelopes cost from around R4.40, depending on how they are sent. The post office also offers a 24-hour door-to-door delivery service between major centres.

Most post offices are open from 8.30am to 4.30pm on weekdays and from 8am to noon on Saturdays. Some of the smaller offices vary their hours on certain days. Postal stamps are easily available from post offices, newsagents and selected retail outlets.

It's inadvisable to send money or important documents via ordinary post. Instead send them by registered post or make use of a courier and

shipping company like **FedEx** (0 8000 33339/ www.fedex.com/za), **UPS** (021 555 2745/www.ups. co.za) or **TNT** (0860 12 2441/ www.tnt.com).

## Religion

### St George's Cathedral (Anglican)
*Corner of Queen Victoria & Wale Streets, City Bowl (021 424 7360/www.stgeorgescathedral.com).* **Map** p274 G4.

### Buddhist Information
*6 Morgenrood Road, Kenilworth, Southern Suburbs (021 761 2978/ www.kagyu.org.za).*

### Central Methodist Mission
*Corner Longmarket & Burg Streets, Greenmarket Square, City Bowl (021 422 2744).* **Map** p275 H4.

### Dutch Reformed Church
*Groote Kerk, 39 Adderley Street, City Bowl (021 422 0569).* **Map** p275 H4.

### Greek Orthodox Church
*75 Mountain Road, Woodstock, Southern Suburbs (021 447 4147).*

### Hindu Temple Siva Aalayam
*41 Ruth Street, Rylands, Southern Suburbs (083 794 2542/021 638 2542).*

### Jewish Cape Town Hebrew Congregation
*88 Hatfield Street, City Bowl (021 465 1405).* **Map** p274 G5.

### The Nurul Islam Mosque
*134 Buitengracht Street, City Bowl (021 432 4202/ www.nurulislam mosque.org.za).* **Map** p274 G4.

### Salvation Army
*Corner Vrede & Plein Streets, City Bowl (021 423 4613).* **Map** p274 G5.

### St Mary's Roman Catholic Cathedral
*Roeland Street, opposite Parliament, City Bowl (021 461 1167).* **Map** p274 G4.

### Uniting Presbyterian Church
*St Stephens Road, opposite Pinelands Police Station, Southern Suburbs (021 531 8408).*

## Safety & security

Regretfully, South Africa has a terrible reputation where crime is concerned. The good news is that, with preparations for the 2010 World Cup well under way, crime is an issue that is being tackled very hard.

Cape Town is one of the safer cities in the country and boasts a number of effective crime deterrents such as CCTV cameras in the CBD and regular police and security patrols; but, as in any other city, you should still be on guard. Petty crime, vandalism, pickpocketing and muggings are unfortunately still common occurrences and tourists can be viewed as easy pickings. This can be avoided to some extent by applying some common sense.

Don't be an obvious tourist with a camera around your neck, be careful with your belongings, and try to park in well-lit areas at night and with a car guard in attendance. Credit cards are accepted just about everywhere so try not to keep too much cash on you, and be even more careful when withdrawing money from ATMs or converting traveller's cheques.

Lately, Cape Town has been plagued by tourist muggings in the Table Mountain National Park. You're strongly advised that, if you feel like stretching your legs on the lovely mountain, you do so in a group and tell people where you're going and when to expect you back. If you do see any suspicious activity, leave immediately and report it to the Park authorities. There are regular patrols within the Park and a good idea is to take a whistle and a can of pepper spray with you on your walk.

## Smoking

Smoking is prohibited in all public places. Some restaurants and bars provide specially demarcated smoking sections.

## Study

You can learn a local language, or a foreign one, at one of the many language schools dotted around town. Call Cape Town International School of Languages on 021 674 4117.

## Telephones

### Making a call

The international code for SA is 27, followed by the local regional code. An area code has to be dialled when making a phone call to a number in your local area. Cape Town is (0)21, Jo'burg is (0)11, Pretoria is (0)12 and Durban is (0)31. If you're experiencing difficulties getting through to a particular number, contact Directory Enquiries (1023), or consult a phone directory for further assistance (there is a list of useful numbers at the front).

### Public phones

Distinctive green and blue public telephone booths can be found all over Cape Town and the Peninsula, in shopping malls, hotels, post offices, cafés and most tourist locations. Public phones are either coin- or card-operated. Phone cards can be bought at post offices, grocery stores, newsagents and Telkom offices.

### Mobile phones

If you have a mobile phone that can operate on SA's GSM network, you could consider purchasing a sim

card from one of the three national networks:
**Cell C** www.cellc.co.za
**Vodacom** www.vodacom.co.za
**MTN** www.mtn.co.za

Sim cards are available from the service providers' outlets (in most shopping centres) or you can purchase them at almost all newsagents and grocery stores such as Checkers, Pick 'n' Pay, Spar and Woolworths.

## Time

South Africa is two hours ahead of GMT, seven ahead of Eastern Standard Winter Time and ten ahead of Pacific Standard Time. South Africa does not have daylight saving time in summer.

## Tipping

Tips and gratuities, especially in restaurants, are usually expected and the general guideline is 15% of your total bill. Feel free, however, to tip more or less depending on the quality of the service you receive but make sure that, when eating out, the gratuity hasn't already been included in your bill. Some restaurants automatically include a service charge for tables over a certain number or if your bill exceeds a certain amount.

Taxi drivers are usually given 10% of the total fare, porters up to R5 a bag and petrol pump attendants R2–R5 for washing your windows, pumping your tyres, filling up your car, and sympathising with you every time you bemoan the rising cost of petrol.

Car guards, especially in the city, can be a different breed altogether (*see p28* **Mind your motor**). Usually they'll settle for between R2 and R5 depending on how long they've guarded your car. If there's a festival on, it's tourist season or they think they scored a nice

parking spot for you (and helped you into it), they won't be shy about asking for more. Remember, it is acceptable to tip according to the quality of the service you received.

## Toilets

Most public toilets in shopping malls and restaurants are clean and should be used rather than the public facilities in the city centre and surrounds, which are not always clean.

## Tourist information

The **Cape Town Tourism Visitor Centre** (021 426 4260/www.cape-town.org) is on the corner of Castle and Burg Streets in the city centre. If you're having trouble making up your mind what to include in your itinerary, they'll be more than willing to make a few suggestions. They have maps, brochures, tour outings and all the information on the latest happenings in the Mother City. You can also make bookings and reservations at the helpdesks.

The V&A Waterfront also has a smaller visitor centre, the Cape Town Tourism Office (021 405 4500), which is located at the Waterfront Clock Tower.

## Visas & immigration

### Visa requirements

Citizens of the UK, the Republic of Ireland, Germany, Italy and Australia do not need visas, as long as they have a passport valid for 30 days beyond the length of their trip, a return ticket, proof of accommodation and, if travelling for business, a letter from the inviting organisation.

**Directory**

If they stay for longer than 90 days (up to a year is allowed without a visa), they also need a letter from a chartered accountant offering proof of funds.

The requirements for trips of up to 90 days are the same for US travellers, but for longer trips a visa is required.

For more information, consult www.southafrica house.com/Consulate.htm (UK citizens), www.sa embassy.org (US citizens) or http://home-affairs.pwv. gov.za (South Africa's home affairs department).

Entry requirements can change at any time, so check carefully on the above sites and with your airline/travel agent well in advance of your planned departure date.

## Weights & measures

South Africa uses the metric system. Useful conversions are given below.

1 kilometre = 0.62 miles
1 metre = 1.094 yards
1 centimetre = 0.39 inches
1 kilogram = 2.2 pounds
1 gram = 0.035 ounces
1 litre = 1.75 pints
0°C = 32°F

## When to go

Cape Town's climate is in general Mediterranean, with warm, dry summers and mild, moist winters. On the coast during summer (November to February) the temperature ranges from 15°C (59°F) up to 27°C (81°F). Inland it increases by 3-5°C (37-41°F). During winter (May to August) it ranges between 7°C (45°F) and 18°C (65°F). Inland the mornings are 5°C (41°F) and midday around 22°C (72°F).

Cape Town's long, balmy summer nights are invariably filled with some kind of festival, fun run, concert or carnival. The weeks around Christmas and New Year are especially hectic. Slather on the factor 30 sunscreen, though, because the summer sun is no joke, and it's quite easy to forget when you're splashing about on the beach. Also watch out for the 'Cape Doctor' that appears as if from nowhere in summer. This south-easterly wind helps to clear the air, and drapes Table Mountain with a snow-white tablecloth of clouds.

The season starts getting slightly chillier around April. The lovely autumn

colours draw people out of town to forests in Newlands and Constantia, as well as the Winelands.

Wintertime is synonymous with rain. Occasional storms wreak havoc on telephone poles and townships are often flooded.

The vagaries of Cape Town's weather, however, mean that winter storms can be followed by mild, sunny days, and Christmas (summer) can be cool and rainy.

### Public holidays

New Year's Day (1 Jan); Human Rights Day (21 Mar); Good Friday; Family Day (Easter Monday); Freedom Day (27 Apr); Workers Day (1 May); Youth Day (16 June); National Women's Day (9 Aug); Heritage Day (24 Sept) Day of Reconciliation (16 Dec); Christmas Day (25 Dec); Day of Goodwill (26 Dec).

## Working

Find information from your nearest Department of Home Affairs office if you're in South Africa. If you're abroad, do so on the websites given under the Visa section (see above).

**Department of Home Affairs Subdirectorate** Temporary Residence, Private Bag X114, Pretoria 0001, South Africa (012 810 6126).

# Weather averages

| | Average daily max (°C/°F) temperature | Average daily min (°C/°F) temperature | Monthly rainfall (mm/in) |
|---|---|---|---|
| January | 26/79 | 16/61 | 15/0.6 |
| February | 27/81 | 16/61 | 17/0.7 |
| March | 25/77 | 14/57 | 20/0.8 |
| April | 23/73 | 12/54 | 41/1.6 |
| May | 20/68 | 9/48 | 68/2.7 |
| June | 18/64 | 8/46 | 93/3.7 |
| July | 18/64 | 7/45 | 82/3.2 |
| August | 18/64 | 8/46 | 77/3.0 |
| September | 19/66 | 9/48 | 40/1.6 |
| October | 21/70 | 11/52 | 30/1.2 |
| November | 24/75 | 13/55 | 14/0.5 |
| December | 25/77 | 15/59 | 17/0.7 |

Directory

# Further Reference

## Books

### Fiction & literature

**Boyd, William** *A Good Man in Africa*
Entertaining farce of a lowly British diplomat grappling with colonial arrogance, local corruption and sexual frustration in a fictitious African state.
**Brink, André** *Rumours of Rain, A Dry White Season, Praying Mantis*
Intriguing politicised novels written in a haunting voice.
**Brown, Andrew** *Coldsleep Lullaby*
Winner of the *Sunday Times* Fiction Award in 2006, this compelling novel combines the genre of the crime thriller with historical drama.
**Coetzee, JM** *Disgrace, Waiting for the Barbarians, The Life and Times of Michael K* and *Dusklands*
Winner of the Nobel Prize for literature in 2003, this remarkable writer's novels go to the very heart of the South African psyche and question the political and social landscape of the country.
**Duiker, K Sello** *The Quiet Violence of Dreams* and *Thirteen Cents*
Duiker convincingly depicted the harsh realities of Cape Town's underbelly, exploring issues such as homelessness, mental illness, drug abuse, prostitution and the overwhelming sense of isolation to be found in any city. He sadly committed suicide in 2005.
**Eaton, Tom** *The De Villiers Code*
A ruthless parody of Dan Brown's commercial phenomenon, *The Da Vinci Code*, in an authentic South African setting.
**Fugard, Athol** *Blood Knot, Boesman and Lena, A Lesson from Aloes, 'Master Harold'... and the Boys, The Road to Mecca, My Children! My Africa!, Playland*
Works by one of South Africa's most esteemed playwrights, most famous as a campaigning dramatist, tackling issues of apartheid.
**Galgut, Damon** *The Good Doctor*
Shortlisted for the 2003 Man Booker prize, Galgut's novel explores post-apartheid South Africa, where deep-rooted social and political tensions threaten shared dreams for the future.
**Gordimer, Nadine** *July's People, Burger's Daughter, Sport of Nature*
Nobel prize-winning novelist dealing with the tensions of her racially divided country.

**Jooste, Pamela** *Frieda and Min, Dance with a Poor Man's Daughter, People Like Ourselves*
Contemporary fiction focusing on the realities ordinary people face in the new South Africa.
**Matthee, Dalene** *Circles in a Forest, Fiela's Child*
Beautiful historical novels with the lush Knysna Forest as a backdrop.
**Mda, Jakes** *Heart of Redness, Ways of Dying*
Magic realism gets a contemporary African twist.
**Michener, James** *The Covenant*
Epic tale of empire building and the creation of a country full of turmoil.
**Paton, Alan** *Cry the Beloved Country*
A South African classic about families, racism and ultimate reconciliation.
**Schreiner, Olive** *The Story of an African Farm*
Written in the late 19th century, Schreiner's novel applies a Dickensian cast to radical ideals about women and society. A book that is widely acclaimed as an early South African classic.
**Schonstein, Patricia** *A Time of Angels, Skyline*
New on the scene with magical realism touches to create a sense of timelessness in Cape Town.
**Sharpe, Tom** *Indecent Exposure, Riotous Assembly*
A blazing satire of apartheid, written with typical best-selling aplomb.
**Sleigh, Dan** *Islands*
The first years of the settlement of the Dutch colony in the Cape are documented through the accounts of seven historically based characters.
**Van Niekerk, Marlene** *Triomf*
Novel of post-apartheid South Africa seen through the eyes of a poor white Afrikaans family.

### Non-fiction

**Bosman, Herman Charles** *My Life and Opinions*
A collection of autobiographical writings by one of South Africa's most loved humourists.
**Breytenbach, Breyten** *The True Confessions of an Albino Terrorist*
Memoir of his seven-year imprisonment in South Africa.
**Cameron, Edwin** *A Witness to AIDS*
In his memoir, Supreme Court of Appeal Justice Edwin Cameron gives an extremely personal and frank account of contracting and living with HIV/AIDS.

**Dommisse, Ebbe** *Anton Rupert: A Biography*
The incredible life story of one of the richest businessmen in the world, whose group of Rembrandt companies owns brands such as Cartier, Mont Blanc and Dunhill.
**Du Preez, Max** *Pale Native*
Roving, liberal reporter writes of his times in troubled SA.
**Elion, Barbara & Strieman, Mercia** *Clued up on Culture*
An excellent source of info on local customs and political correctness.
**Gilliomee, Herman** *The Afrikaners*
Traces the history of the Afrikaner from Dutch settler to apartheid's master. Where does the Afrikaner stand in the 21st century?
**Harlan, Judith** *Mamphela Ramphele: Challenging Apartheid in South Africa*
A biography of Mamphela Ramphele, a woman who, as a doctor, teacher and advisor to the Mandela government, challenged racial and gender inequities in South Africa.
**Kanfer, Stefan** *The Last Empire: De Beers, Diamonds and the World*
History of the De Beers diamond empire. A story of cutthroat capitalism, and the economic and racial development of South Africa.
**Krog, Antjie** *Country of My Skull, A Change of Tongue, Down to My Last Skin*
Krog analyses the country and its people in an erudite and contemporary manner.
**Malan, Rian** *My Traitor's Heart*
Malan, a writer from a well-known Afrikaner family, explores the brutalities of apartheid.
**Mandela, Nelson** *Long Walk to Freedom*
Autobiographical account of his life. It should be next to everyone's bed.
**Nicol, Mike** *Mandela: The Authorised Biography*
Authorised by close friends and relatives, this comprehensive biography includes 60 interviews with world leaders and friends, as well as previously unpublished photos and letters.
**Mutwa, Credo** *Indaba, My Children*
Be enchanted by myths and legends from all over Africa.
**Pakenham, Thomas** *The Boer War, The Scramble for Africa*
Quintessential Brit-based history.
**Tutu, Desmond** *No Future Without Forgiveness*
Essential reading to gain a sense of empathy.

**Directory**

**Welsh, Frank** *History of South Africa*
This single volume covers it all.

## Food & wine

**Cheifitz, Phillippa** *Lazy Days*
West Coast cuisine, perfect for those languid, hot summer holidays.
**Engelbrecht, Stan & De Beer, Tamsen** *African Salad: A Portrait of South Africans at Home*
Acclaimed photographer Stan Engelbrecht documents 120 authentic South African families and their favourite recipes.
**Platter, John** *SA Wine Guide*
A new version comes out every year to stay up to date on all the quaffing possibilities in SA.
**Platter, John and Erica** *Africa Uncorked*
The Platters go in search of weird wine around the continent. Fun romp through unexpected wine country.
**Williams, Faldela** *The Cape Malay Cookbook*
Practise your new favourite flavours.

## Film

**Amandla!** (Lee Hirsch 2002)
Stunning documentary telling the story of protest music in South Africa, which was inextricably linked to the struggle against apartheid.
**Country of My Skull** (John Boorman 2003)
Adapted from Antjie Krog's book on the TRC, this follows a foreign journalist tracking the TRC.
**Cry, The Beloved Country** (Zoltan Korda 1951 and Darrell James Roodt 1995)
Famous film adaptation of novel of the same name by Alan Paton.
**Cry Freedom** (Richard Attenborough 1987)
True story of an inspiring friendship in an impossible time.
**Gandhi** (Richard Attenborough 1982)
Insight into Gandhi's experiences as a young lawyer in South Africa.
**Mapantsula** (Oliver Schmitz 1988)
A stirring film set in shanty towns and a white middle-class shopping centre in Johannesburg.
**Promised Land** (Jason Xenopulos 2002)
Adapted from the Afrikaans novel by Karel Schoeman, this is a story about hidden truths and near impossible quests.
**Road to Mecca** (Athol Fugard, Peter Goldsmid 1992)
A moving story of Helen Martin's Owl House.
**Sarafina!** (Darrell James Roodt 1992)
Adapted from Mbongeni Ngema's stage musical. Whoopi Goldberg

plays an idealistic teacher who helps an impressionable teenage girl to throw off the shackles of apartheid.
**Shot Down** (Andrew Worsdale 1987)
Worsdale describes this film as 'the only record of young white leftie anxiety amid the turmoil of the 1980s'.
**Tsotsi** (Gavin Hood 2005)
A ruthless gang leader undergoes an existential crisis after finding a baby on the back seat of a car that he has hijacked.
**U-Carmen eKhayelitsha** (Dimpho Di Kopan 2005)
George Bizet's 1875 opera, *Carmen*, is dramatically transformed in this Xhosa film adaptation set in the densely populated township of Khayelitsha.

## Music

**Abdullah Ibrahim** *Knysna Blue* (1994)
Story of this jazz pianist's return to Cape Town.
**Bayete** *Mbombela* (1987), *Hareyeng Haye* (1991), *Mmalo-We* (1993), *Africa Unite* (1997), *What About Tomorrow* (1999)
Despite band members coming and going, frontman Jabu Khanyile has been the golden thread that's run through Bayete since the early 1980s, and he's still entertaining fans today with the same fusion of West and South African jazz.
**Brenda Fassie** *Memeza* (2001), *Mina Nawe* (2002)
Cape Town's queen of pop.
**Freshly Ground** *Jika Jika* (2003), *Nomvula* (2004)
Winner of the MTV Europe award for Best African Act 2006.
**Johnny Clegg** *Third World Child* (1987), *Shadowman* (1988), *Cruel, Crazy Beautiful World* (1990), *Heat, Dust and Dreams* (1993)
Clegg is also known as the 'White Zulu', and if you see him dance, you'll know why. He has been performing with the groups Juluka and Suvuka since the apartheid years, combining Zulu and English lyrics with Celtic influences.
**Ladysmith Black Mambazo** *The Ultimate Collection* (2001)
A band that embodies the musical traditions suppressed in old SA.
**Lucky Dube** *Soul Taker* (2001)
South Africa's greatest reggae star.
**Lungiswa** *Ekhaya* (2000)
Fresh talent from Cape Town's Langa township.
**Mafikizolo** *Sibongile* (2002), *Kwela* (2003), *Van Toeka Af* (2004) and *Six Mabone* (2006)
Award-winning *kwaito*-pop with retro Sophiatown influences.

**Mzwakhe Mbuli** *Born Free but Always in Chains* (2000)
The pro-democracy 'people's poet' now imprisoned for a crime he claims he didn't commit.
**Rebecca Malope** *Free at Last: South African Gospel* (1997)
Nelson Mandela's favourite gospel singer.
**Soweto String Quartet** *Zebra Crossing* (1994), *Renaissance* (1996), *Millenia* (1998), *Four* (2001), *Our World* (2003)
An alleged favourite in Nelson Mandela's office, SSQ (as they're known by fans) incorporate the rhythms of *kwela* and jazz into their feel-good music.
**Winston Mankunku Ngozi** *Abantwana Be Afrika* (2004), *Molo Africa* (2000)
A leading jazz saxophonist from Cape Town.
**Yvonne Chaka Chaka** *The Best of Yvonne Chaka Chaka Vol.1* (2001), *Bombani* (1999)
A leading figure in South African popular music.
**Zola** *Undiwembe* (2001), *Khokuvula* (2002)
The undisputed king of *kwaito*.

## Websites

**Cape for Kids**
*www.capeforkids.com*
Plenty of ideas for family fun.
**Cape Town Magazine**
*www.capetownmagazine.co.za*
Keep abreast of all the exciting goings-on.
**Cape Town Today**
*www.capetowntoday.co.za*
Lively entertainment guide.
**Cape Town Tourism**
*www.cape-town.org*
All the information you need about the city's resources – from golf courses to plastic surgeons.
**Hike Cape Town**
*www.hikecapetown.co.za*
Hike your way around the Cape Town Peninsula.
**Lets Go Cape Town**
*www.letsgocapetown.co.za*
Explore the endless entertainment and outdoor activities of the city.
**South African Weather Service**
*www.weathersa.co.za*
Check out the forecast.
**Western Cape Tourism**
*www.capetourism.org*
Official tourist board site, with plenty of practical detail.
**Wine Tasting Uncovered**
*www.uncoverthecape.co.za/wine-farms.htm*
List of wine regions and estates.
**Yellow Pages Online**
*www.yellowpages.co.za*
Comprehensive business directory.

Directory

# Index

Note: page numbers in
bold indicate section(s)
giving key information on
topic; *italics* indicate
illustrations.

Index

# Advertisers' Index

| Place of interest and/or entertainment | ...... |
| Railway stations | ......................... |
| Parks | ........................................... |
| Hospitals | ...................................... |
| Area name | .......................... CLIFTON |
| Hotel | ........................................... ❶ |
| Restaurants & Cafés | ........................... ❶ |
| Pubs & Bars | ................................... ❶ |

# Maps

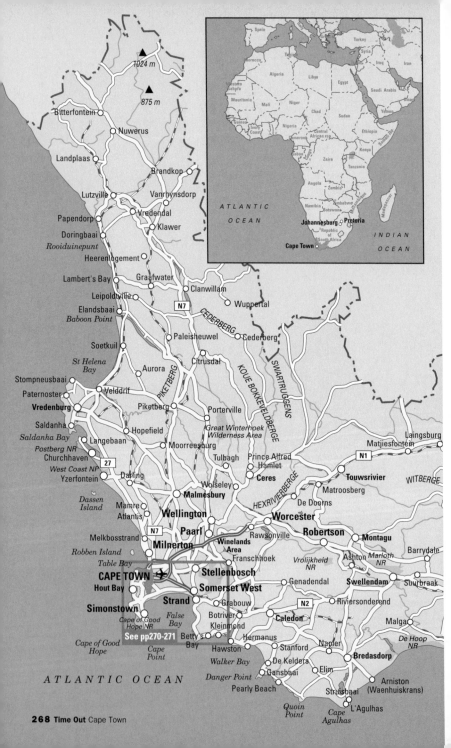

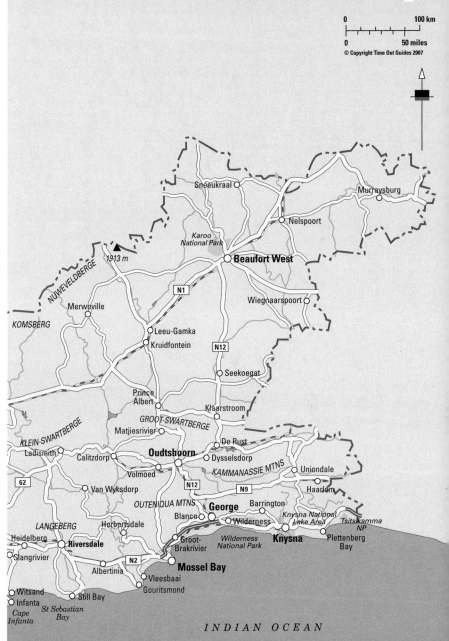

# The Western Cape

0           100 km

0         50 miles

© Copyright Time Out Guides 2007

Sneeukraal

Murraysburg

Nelspoort

Karoo
National Park

▲
1913 m

**Beaufort West**

NUWEVELDBERGE

Merweville

KOMSBERG

N1

Wiegnaarspoort

Leeu-Gamka
Kruidfontein

N12

Seekoegat

Prince
Albert

Klaarstroom

GROOT-SWARTBERGE

Matjiesrivier

KLEIN-SWARTBERGE

De Rust

Ladismith

Calitzdorp

**Oudtshoorn**

Dysselsdorp

KAMMANASSIE MTNS

Uniondale

Volmoed

62

Van Wyksdorp

N12

N9

Haarlem

OUTENIQUA MTNS

**George**

Barrington

Blance

Knysna National
Lake Area

Tsitsikamma
NP

LANGEBERG

Herbertsdale

Wilderness

Heidelberg

**Riversdale**

Groot-
Brakrivier

Wilderness
National Park

**Knysna**

Plettenberg
Bay

Slangrivier

N2

Albertinia

**Mossel Bay**

Witsand

Vleesbaai

Infanta

Still Bay

Gouritsmond

Cape
Infanta

St Sebastian
Bay

*INDIAN OCEAN*

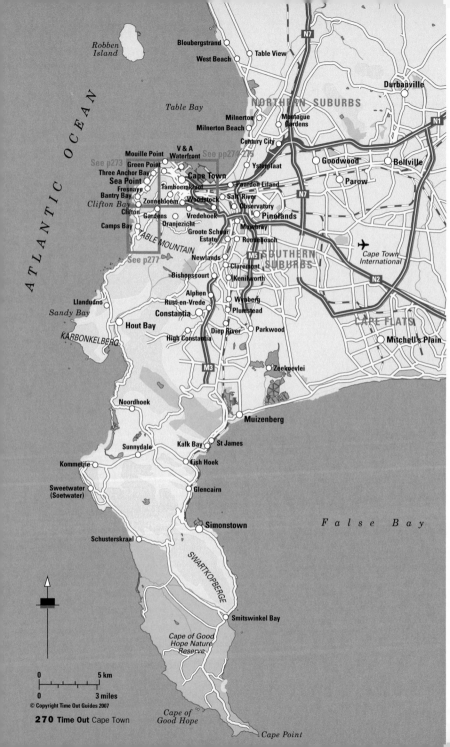

Robben
Island

*Table Bay*

**NORTHERN SUBURBS**

Bl"ubergstrand

West Beach

Table View

Durbanville

N7

N1

Milnerton

Montague
Gardens

Milnerton Beach

Century City

Goodwood

Bellville

*A T L A N T I C   O C E A N*

Mouille Point

V & A
Waterfront

See pp274/275

Ysterplaat

Parow

Three Anchor Bay

Green Point

Cape Town

Vaarden Eiland

N7

Sea Point

Fresnaye

Tamboerskloof

Salt River

Bantry Bay

Zonnebloem

Woodstock

Observatory

*Clifton Bay*

Clifton

Gardens

Vredehoek

Pinelands

See p273

Oranjezicht

Muysbray

Camps Bay

Groote Schuur
Estate

Rondebosch

**SOUTHERN
SUBURBS**

Cape Town
International

*TABLE MOUNTAIN*

Newlands

Claremont

N2

See p277

Bishopscourt

Kenilworth

M5

Llandudno

Alphen

Wynberg

*CAPE FLATS*

*Sandy Bay*

Rust-en-Vrede

Plumstead

Constantia

Mitchell's Plain

*KARBONKELBERG*

Hout Bay

Diep River

Parkwood

High Constantia

M3

Zeekoevlei

Noordhoek

Muizenberg

Sunnydale

Kalk Bay

St James

Kommetjie

Fish Hoek

*F a l s e   B a y*

Sweetwater
(Soetwater)

Glencairn

Simonstown

Schusterskraal

*SWARTKOPBERGE*

Smitswinkel Bay

N

0        5 km

*Cape of Good
Hope Nature
Reserve*

0        3 miles

© Copyright Time Out Guides 2007

*Cape of
Good Hope*

**270 Time Out** Cape Town

*Cape Point*

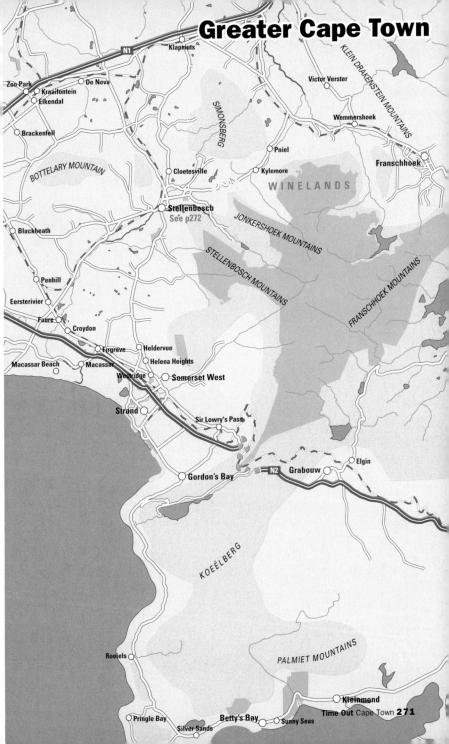

# Greater Cape Town

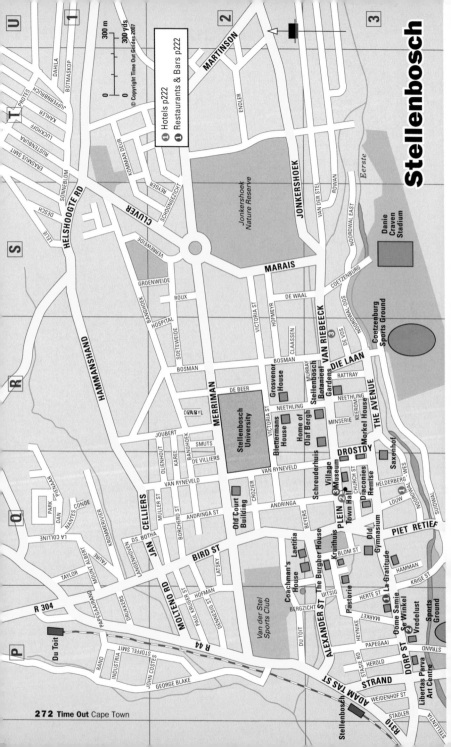

# Stellenbosch

Hotels p222
Restaurants & Bars p222

© Copyright Time Out Guides 2007

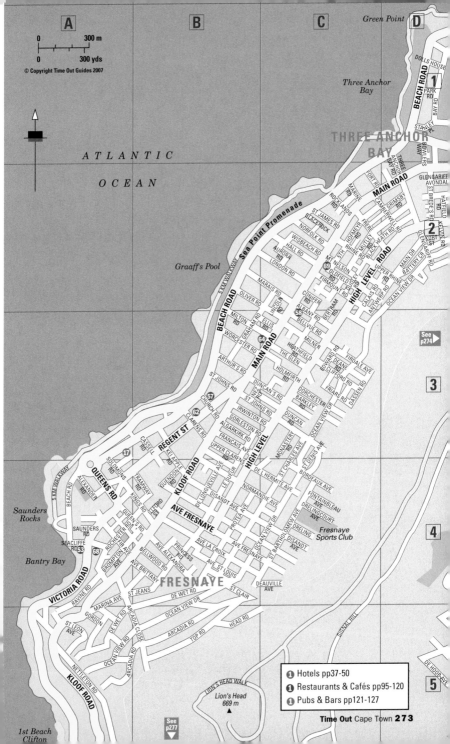

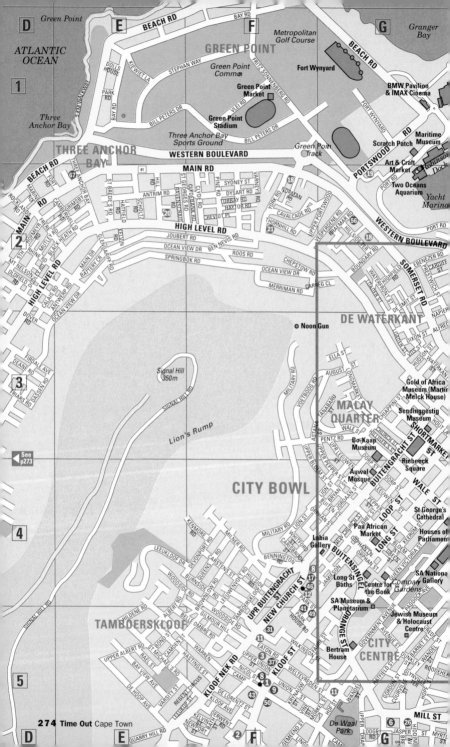

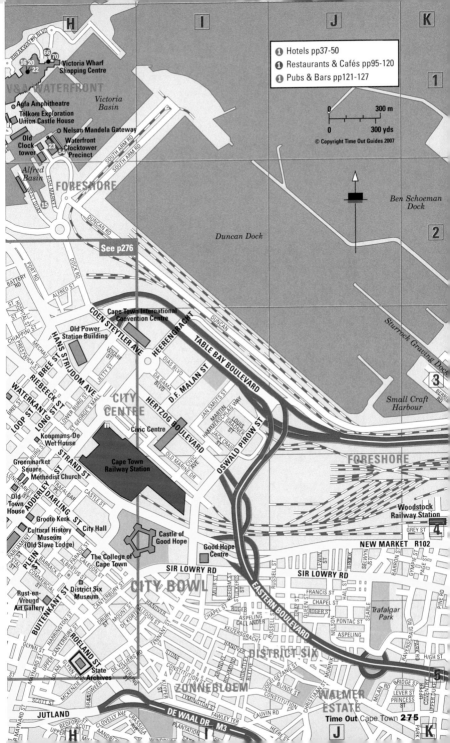

**1** Hotels pp37-50
**1** Restaurants & Cafés pp95-120
**1** Pubs & Bars pp121-127

0    300 m
0    300 yds
© Copyright Time Out Guides 2007

1

Ben Schoeman
Dock

2

Duncan Dock

Sturrock Graving Dock

Small Craft
Harbour

3

BREAKWATER BLVD
16 20
22
66 70
Victoria Wharf
Shopping Centre

V&A WATERFRONT

Victoria
Basin

Agfa Amphitheatre
Telkom Exploration
Union Castle House

Nelson Mandela Gateway
Old
Clock
tower
23
Waterfront
Clocktower
Precinct

Alfred
Basin
FISH MARKET
15

WEST WAY

SOUTH ARM RD
SOUTH ARM RD

FORESHORE

DUNCAN RD

See p276

BATTERY RD
PORT RD
DOCK RD
ALFRED ST

HOSPITAL ST
CHIAPPINI ST
PRESTWICH ST

COEN STEYTLER AVE

Cape Town International
Convention Centre
Old Power
Station Building

HANS STRIJDOM AVE
BREE ST
MECHAU ST

RIEBEECK ST

WATERKANT ST

BREE ST

HEERENGRACHT

WHARF ST
JETTY ST

DIAS ST
DA GAMA
BLVD

TABLE BAY BOULEVARD

DUNCAN

D.F. MALAN ST

LOOP ST
LONG ST

CITY
CENTRE

HERTZOG BOULEVARD

LOWER BURG ST
ST GEORGE'S MALL

Koopmans-De
Wet House

Civic Centre

JAN SMUTS ST
MARTIN
HAMMERSCHLAG WAY
LOUIS
GRADNER ST
JACK CRAIG
OLD MARINE DR
CIVIC
AVE

OSWALD PIROW ST

FORESHORE

STRAND ST

Greenmarket
Square
Methodist Church

CASTLE ST

TRAFALGAR ST
DARLING

ADDERLEY

Old
Town
House

Groote Kerk
Cultural History
Museum
(Old Slave Lodge)

PARLIAMENT ST

City Hall

PLEIN
ST

BARRACK ST

The College of
Cape Town

ALBERTUS ST

CALEDON ST

Castle of
Good Hope

SIR LOWRY RD

Good Hope
Centre

Woodstock
Railway Station
GREY ST
4

NEW MARKET   R102

LIEVIN
ST

BERWYN
SELWYN ST

SIR LOWRY RD

BARRON ST
GYMPIE ST
PAGE ST

PINE RD

Cape Town
Railway Station

Rust-en-
Vreugd
Art Gallery

COMMERCIAL ST

CANTERBURY ST

District Six
Museum

CITY BOWL

BUITENKANT ST

HARRINGTON ST

ROELAND ST

GLYNN ST
MAYNARD ST

STATE
Archives

DE VILLIERS ST
MCKENZIE ST

State
Archives

CONSTITUTION ST
STONE ST
COMMERCIAL ST

HANOVER ST
ROGER ST
ASPELING
CALLANDER ST
KEIZERSGRACHT

CHAPEL ST

MUIR ST
BEDFORD ST
STUCKERIS ST
RUSSELL ST

EASTERN BOULEVARD

FRANCIS ST
CHAPEL ST
ROGER ST
PONTAC ST
ASPELING
NELSON ST

Trafalgar
Park

SEARLE ST

HALL ST
RUSSELL ST

RAVENSCRAIG RD

HIGH ST

DISTRICT SIX

MUNNIK

VIDGE GEZANG ST
CHRISTIAAN ST
BLINDE ST
CONSTITUTION

WALMER
ESTATE

RIDGE ST
LEVER ST
PRINCESS
ST
MILAN RD

CAUVIN RD

UPPER MILL ST
UPPER
CLIFF
PARK

5

ZONNEBLOEM

LYMINGTON ST
FAWLEY TER

HERES ST

JUTLAND

DE WAAL DR   M3

CLOVELLY AVE
CRASSULA

PLANTATION

H    I    J    K

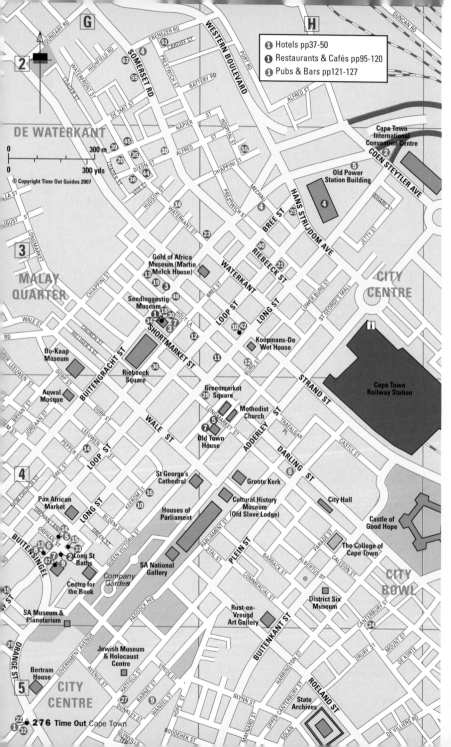

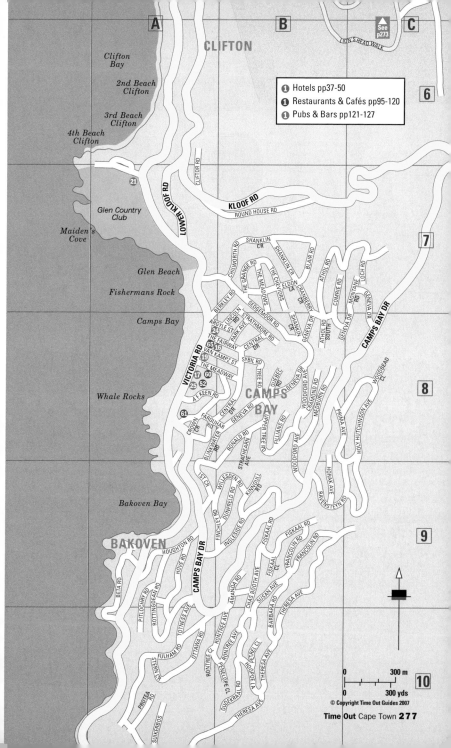

# DISCOVER MORE CITIES

## Tell us what you think and you could win £100-worth of City Guides

Your opinions are important to us and we'd like to know what you like and what you don't like about the Time Out City Guides

For your chance to win, simply fill in our short survey at timeout.com/guidesfeedback

Every month a reader will win £100 to spend on the Time Out City Guides of their choice – a great start to discovering new cities and you'll have extra cash to enjoy your trip!